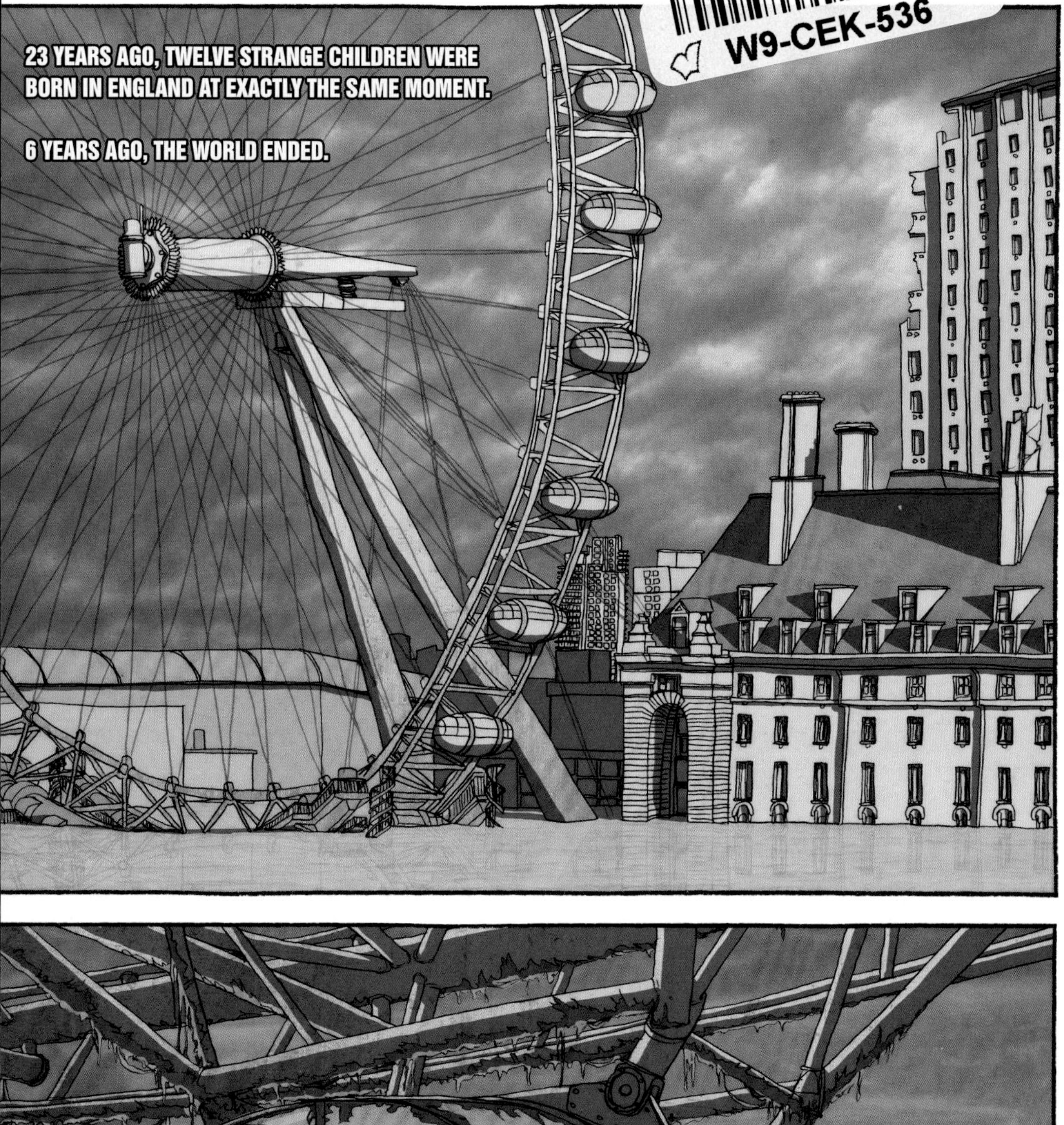
23 YEARS AGO, TWELVE STRANGE CHILDREN WERE BORN IN ENGLAND AT EXACTLY THE SAME MOMENT.
6 YEARS AGO, THE WORLD ENDED.

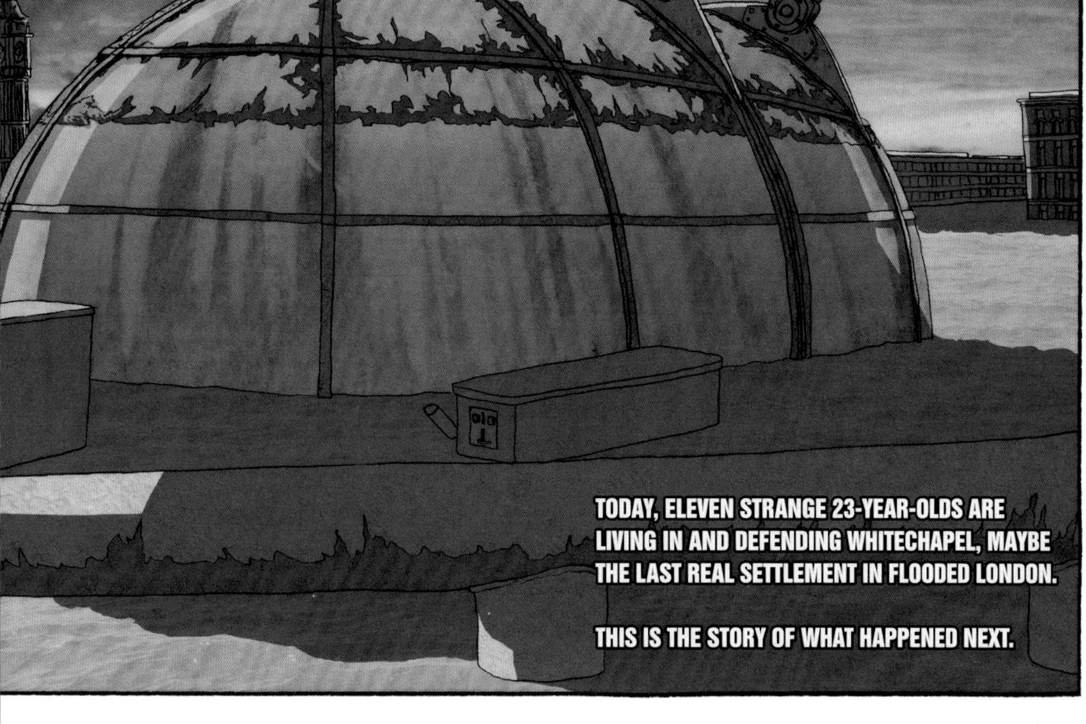
TODAY, ELEVEN STRANGE 23-YEAR-OLDS ARE LIVING IN AND DEFENDING WHITECHAPEL, MAYBE THE LAST REAL SETTLEMENT IN FLOODED LONDON.
THIS IS THE STORY OF WHAT HAPPENED NEXT.

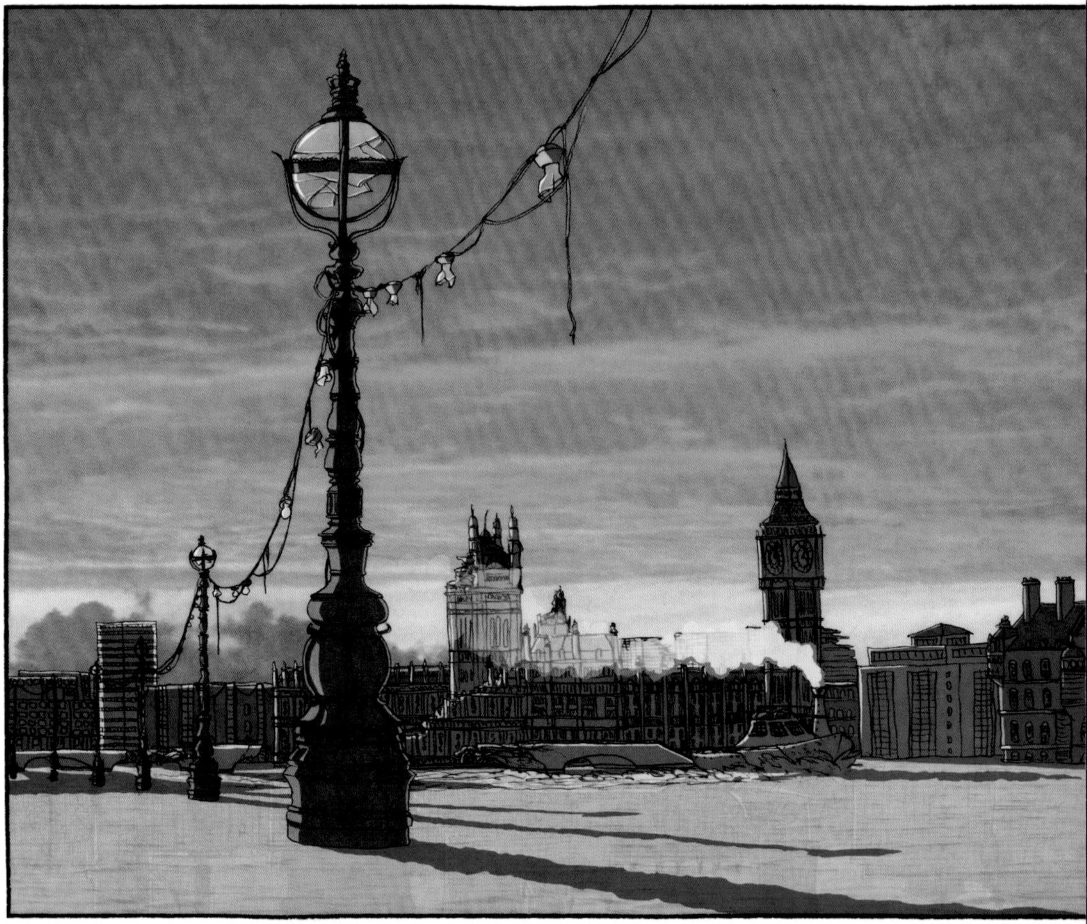

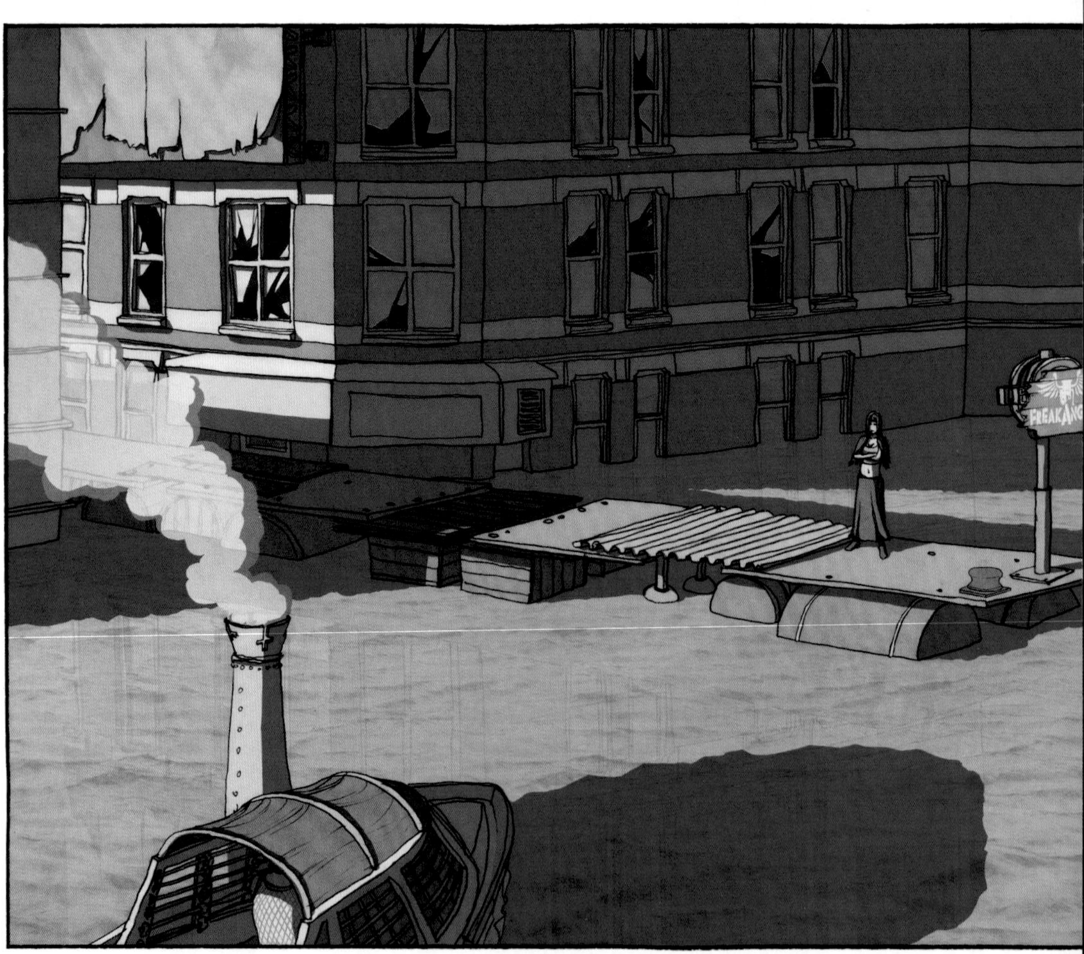

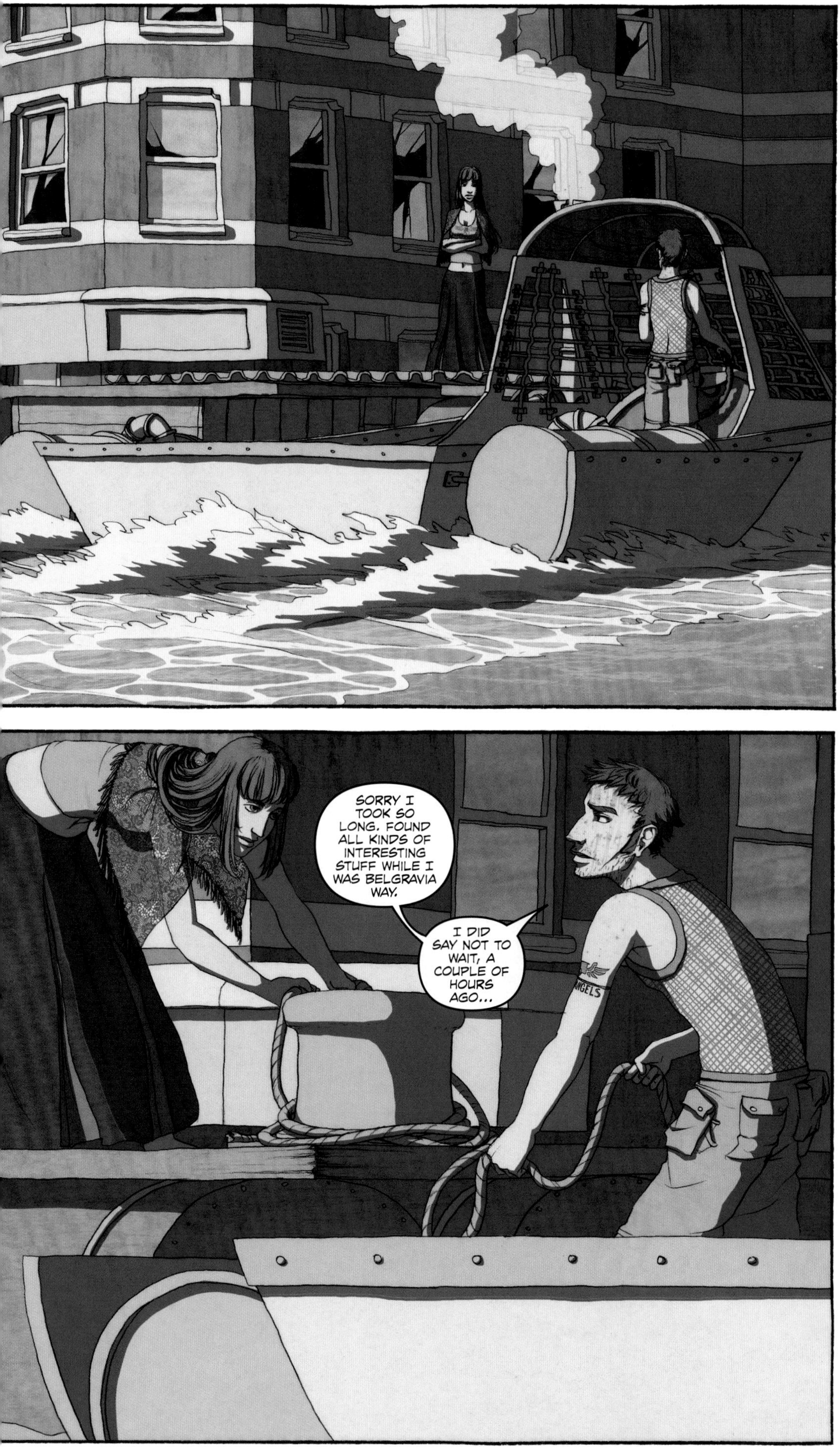
SORRY I TOOK SO LONG. FOUND ALL KINDS OF INTERESTING STUFF WHILE I WAS BELGRAVIA WAY.
I DID SAY NOT TO WAIT, A COUPLE OF HOURS AGO...

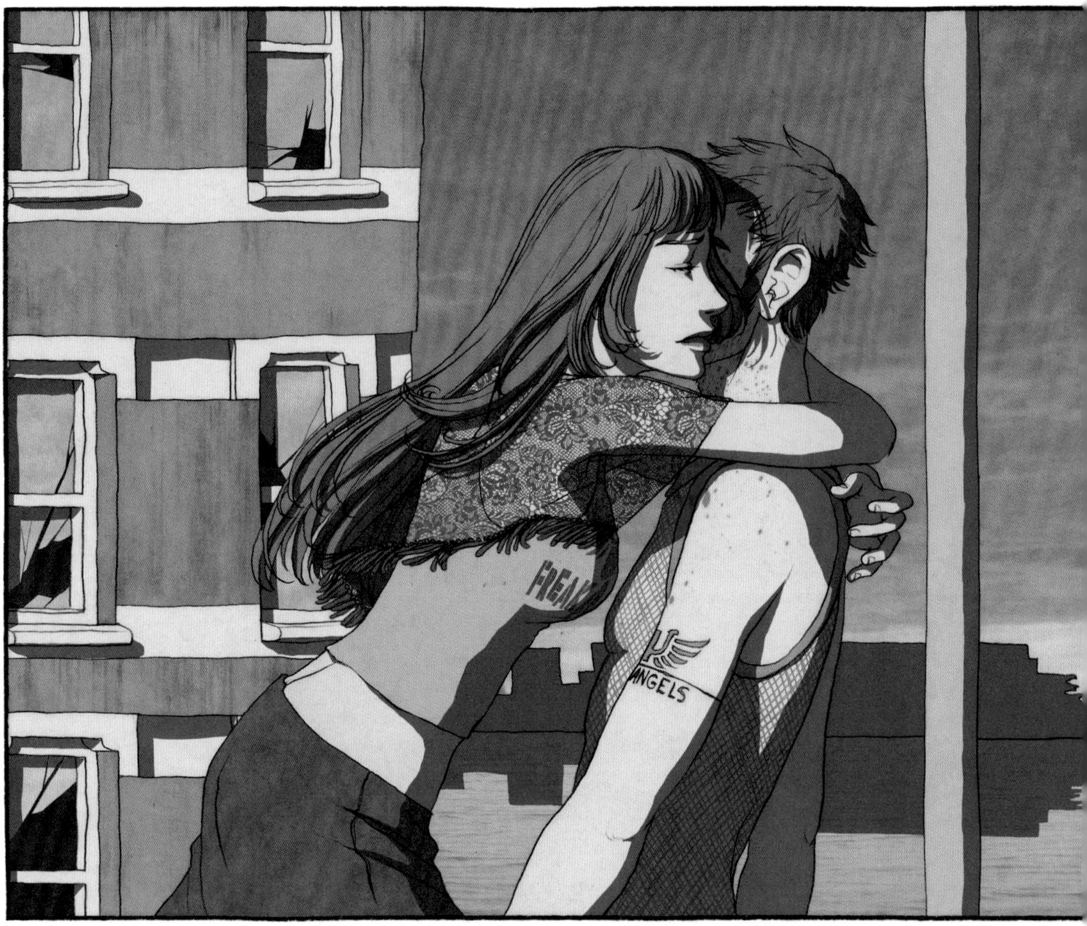
FREAK
ANGELS

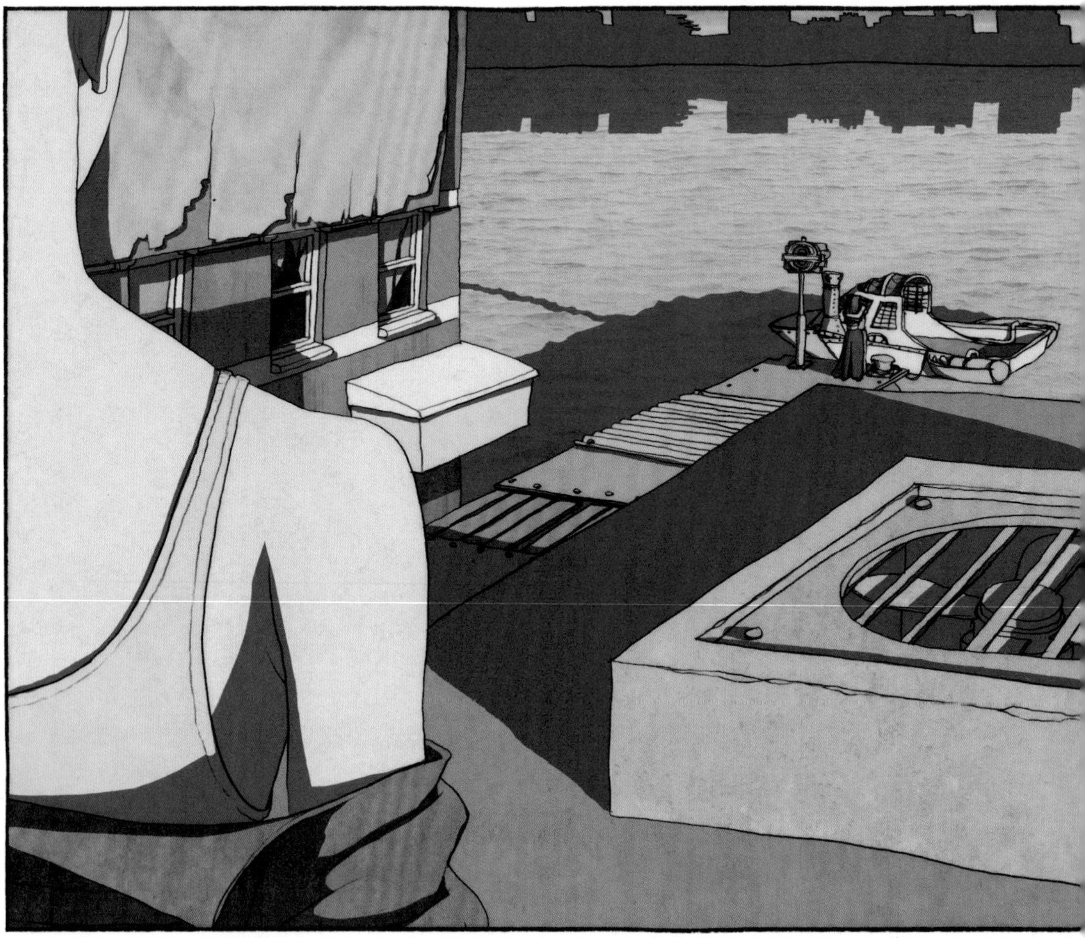

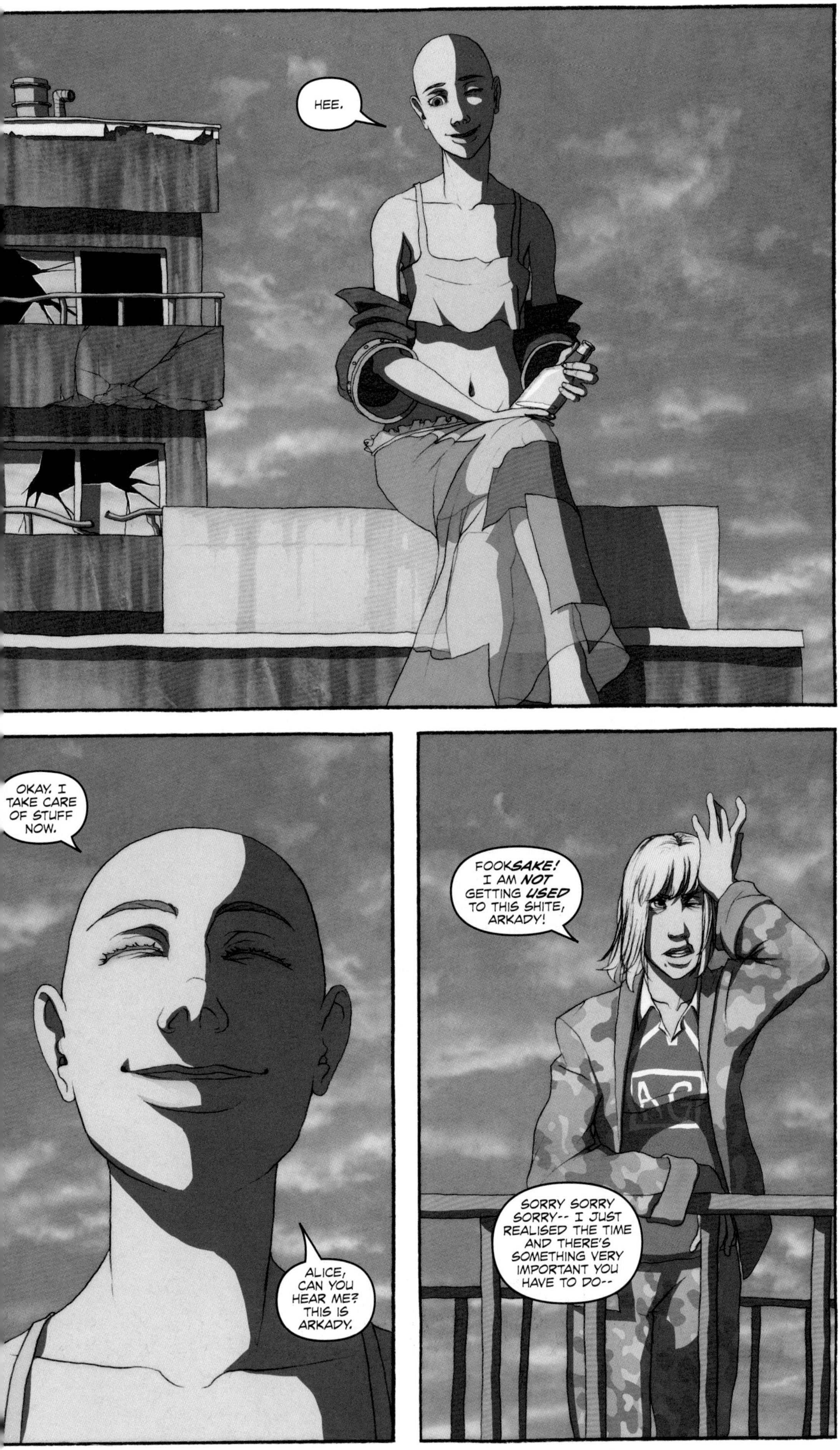
HEE.
OKAY. I TAKE CARE OF STUFF NOW.
ALICE, CAN YOU HEAR ME? THIS IS ARKADY.
FOOK*SAKE!* I AM *NOT* GETTING *USED* TO THIS SHITE, ARKADY!
SORRY SORRY SORRY-- I JUST REALISED THE TIME AND THERE'S SOMETHING VERY IMPORTANT YOU HAVE TO DO--

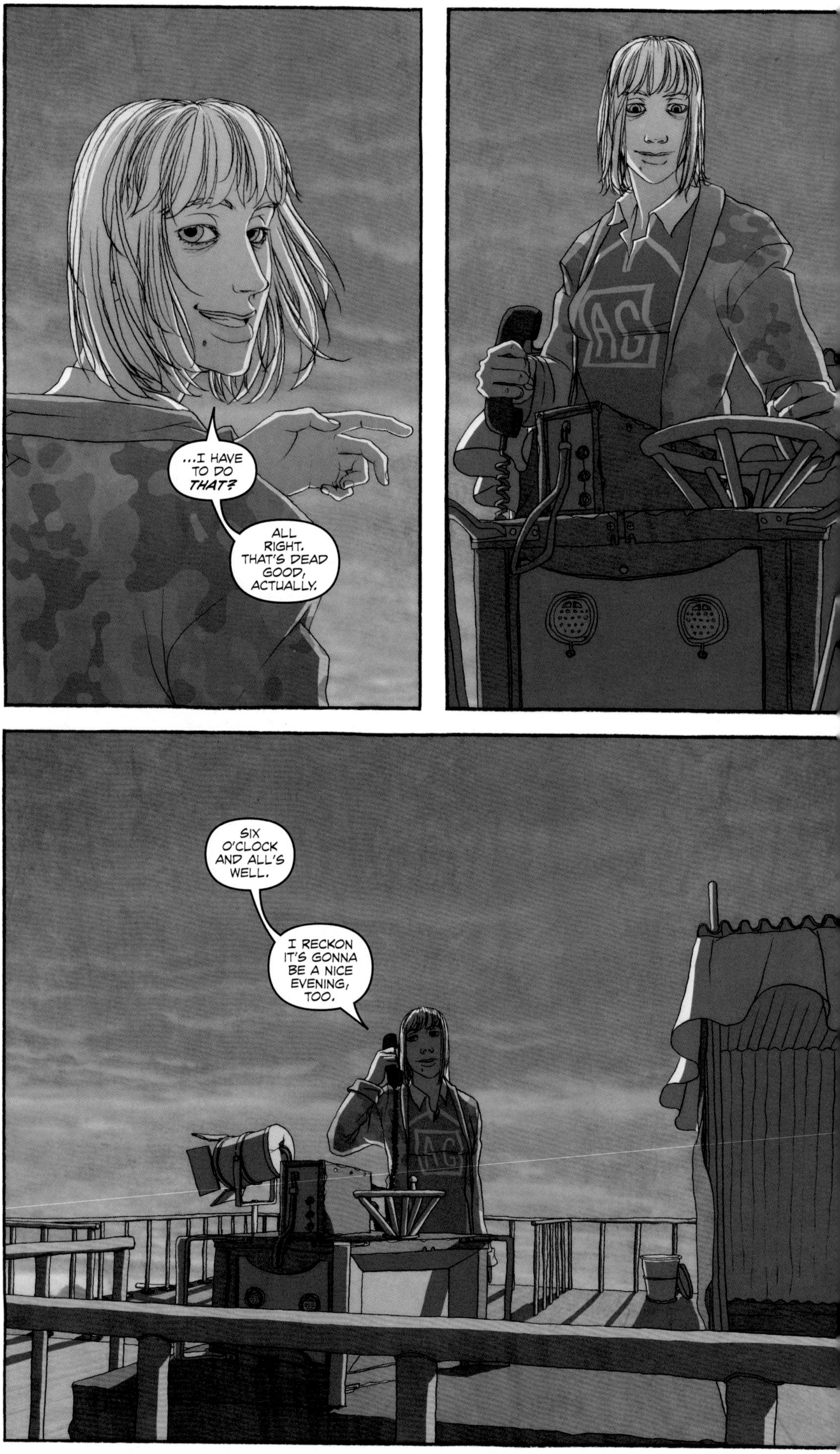
...I HAVE TO DO *THAT?*
ALL RIGHT. THAT'S DEAD GOOD, ACTUALLY.
SIX O'CLOCK AND ALL'S WELL.
I RECKON IT'S GONNA BE A NICE EVENING, TOO.

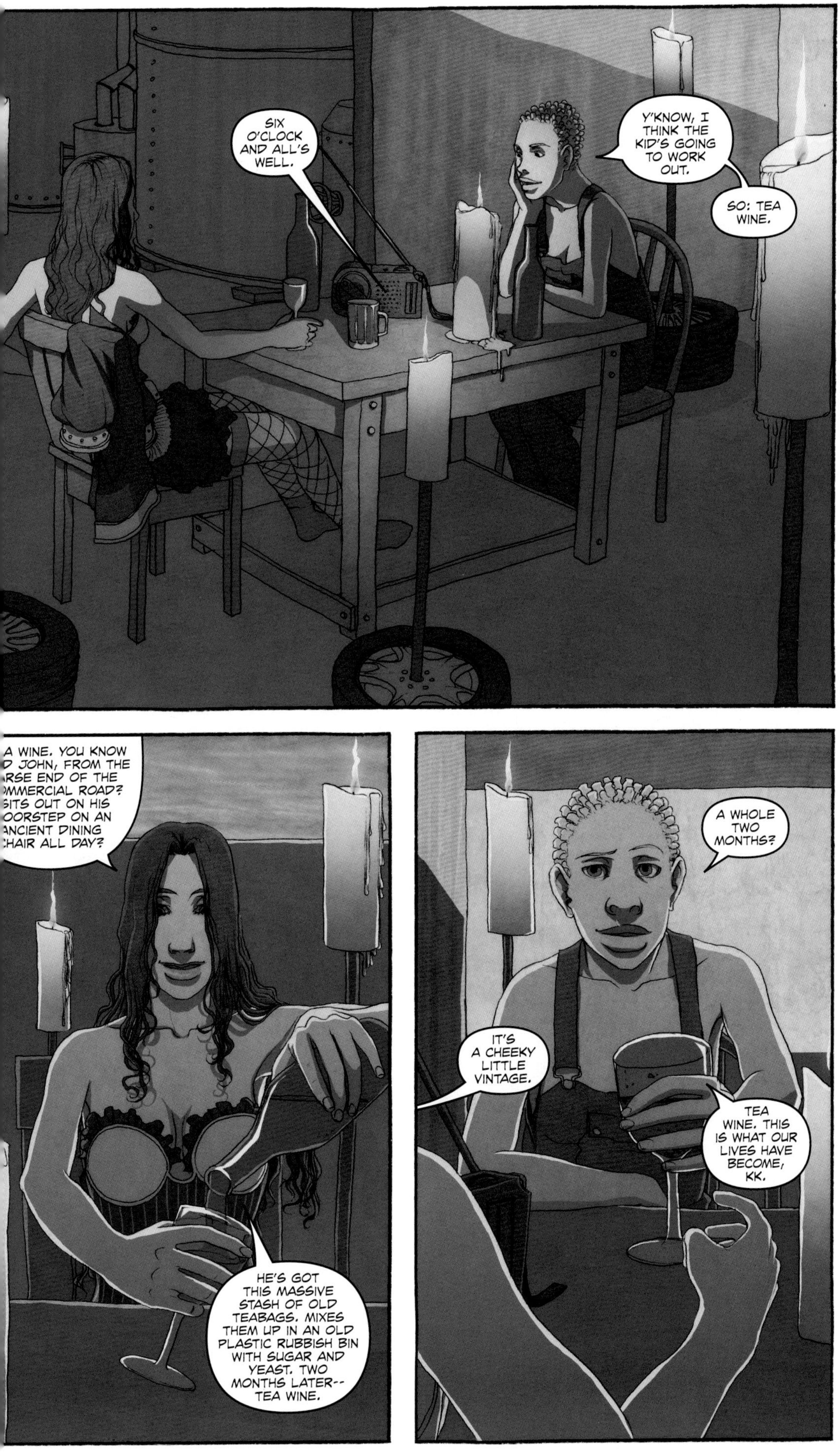
SIX O'CLOCK AND ALL'S WELL.
Y'KNOW, I THINK THE KID'S GOING TO WORK OUT.
SO: TEA WINE.
A WINE. YOU KNOW D JOHN, FROM THE RSE END OF THE OMMERCIAL ROAD? SITS OUT ON HIS OORSTEP ON AN ANCIENT DINING CHAIR ALL DAY?
HE'S GOT THIS MASSIVE STASH OF OLD TEABAGS. MIXES THEM UP IN AN OLD PLASTIC RUBBISH BIN WITH SUGAR AND YEAST. TWO MONTHS LATER-- TEA WINE.
A WHOLE TWO MONTHS?
IT'S A CHEEKY LITTLE VINTAGE.
TEA WINE. THIS IS WHAT OUR LIVES HAVE BECOME, KK.

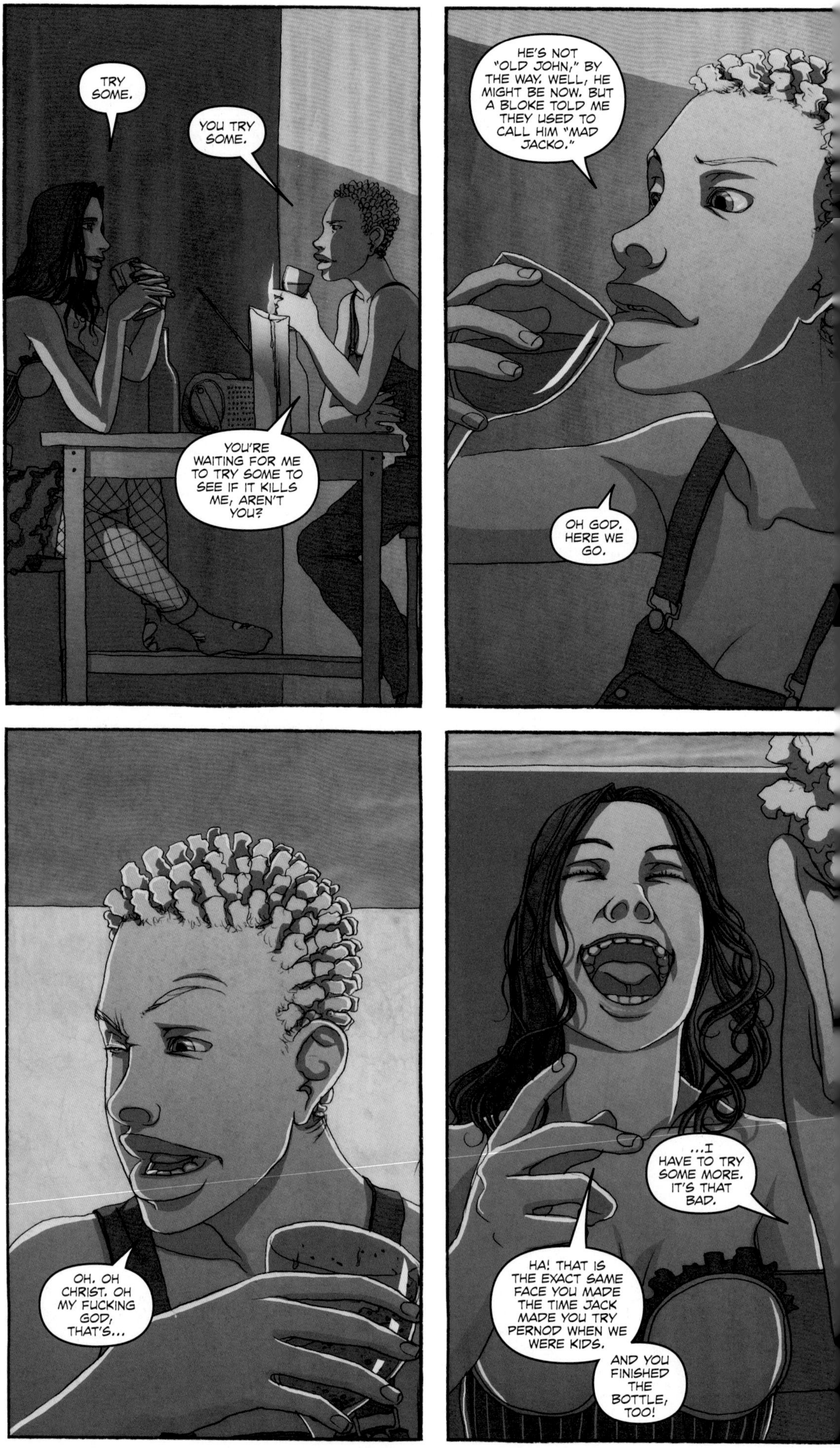
TRY SOME.
YOU TRY SOME.
YOU'RE WAITING FOR ME TO TRY SOME TO SEE IF IT KILLS ME, AREN'T YOU?
HE'S NOT "OLD JOHN," BY THE WAY. WELL, HE MIGHT BE NOW. BUT A BLOKE TOLD ME THEY USED TO CALL HIM "MAD JACKO."
OH GOD. HERE WE GO.
OH. OH CHRIST. OH MY FUCKING GOD, THAT'S...
...I HAVE TO TRY SOME MORE. IT'S THAT BAD.
HA! THAT IS THE EXACT SAME FACE YOU MADE THE TIME JACK MADE YOU TRY PERNOD WHEN WE WERE KIDS.
AND YOU FINISHED THE BOTTLE, TOO!

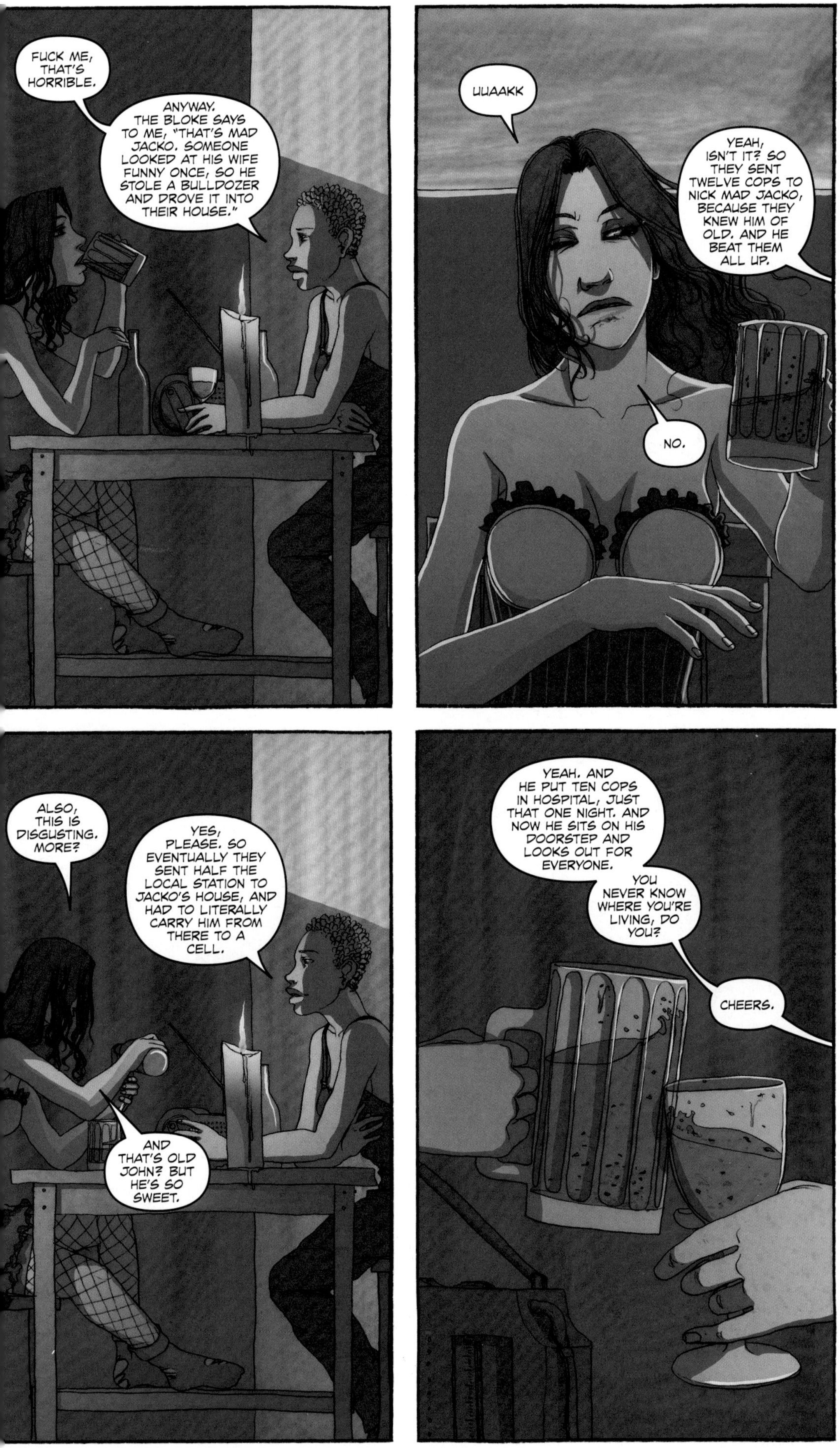
FUCK ME, THAT'S HORRIBLE.
ANYWAY. THE BLOKE SAYS TO ME, "THAT'S MAD JACKO. SOMEONE LOOKED AT HIS WIFE FUNNY ONCE, SO HE STOLE A BULLDOZER AND DROVE IT INTO THEIR HOUSE."
UUAAKK
YEAH, ISN'T IT? SO THEY SENT TWELVE COPS TO NICK MAD JACKO, BECAUSE THEY KNEW HIM OF OLD. AND HE BEAT THEM ALL UP.
NO.
ALSO, THIS IS DISGUSTING. MORE?
YES, PLEASE. SO EVENTUALLY THEY SENT HALF THE LOCAL STATION TO JACKO'S HOUSE, AND HAD TO LITERALLY CARRY HIM FROM THERE TO A CELL.
AND THAT'S OLD JOHN? BUT HE'S SO SWEET.
YEAH. AND HE PUT TEN COPS IN HOSPITAL, JUST THAT ONE NIGHT. AND NOW HE SITS ON HIS DOORSTEP AND LOOKS OUT FOR EVERYONE.
YOU NEVER KNOW WHERE YOU'RE LIVING, DO YOU?
CHEERS.

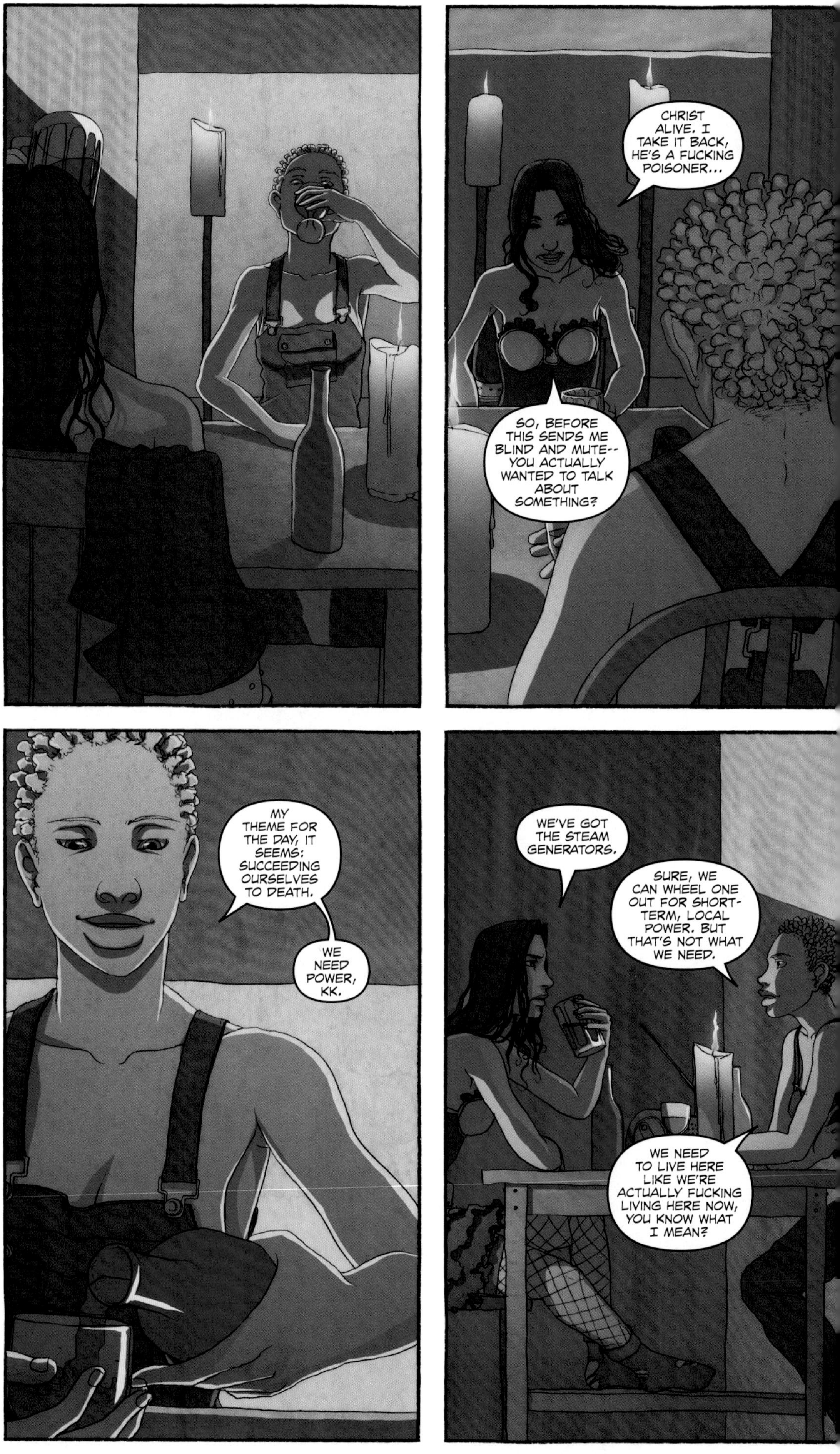
CHRIST ALIVE. I TAKE IT BACK, HE'S A FUCKING POISONER...
SO, BEFORE THIS SENDS ME BLIND AND MUTE-- YOU ACTUALLY WANTED TO TALK ABOUT SOMETHING?
MY THEME FOR THE DAY, IT SEEMS: SUCCEEDING OURSELVES TO DEATH.
WE NEED POWER, KK.
WE'VE GOT THE STEAM GENERATORS.
SURE, WE CAN WHEEL ONE OUT FOR SHORT-TERM, LOCAL POWER. BUT THAT'S NOT WHAT WE NEED.
WE NEED TO LIVE HERE LIKE WE'RE ACTUALLY FUCKING LIVING HERE NOW, YOU KNOW WHAT I MEAN?

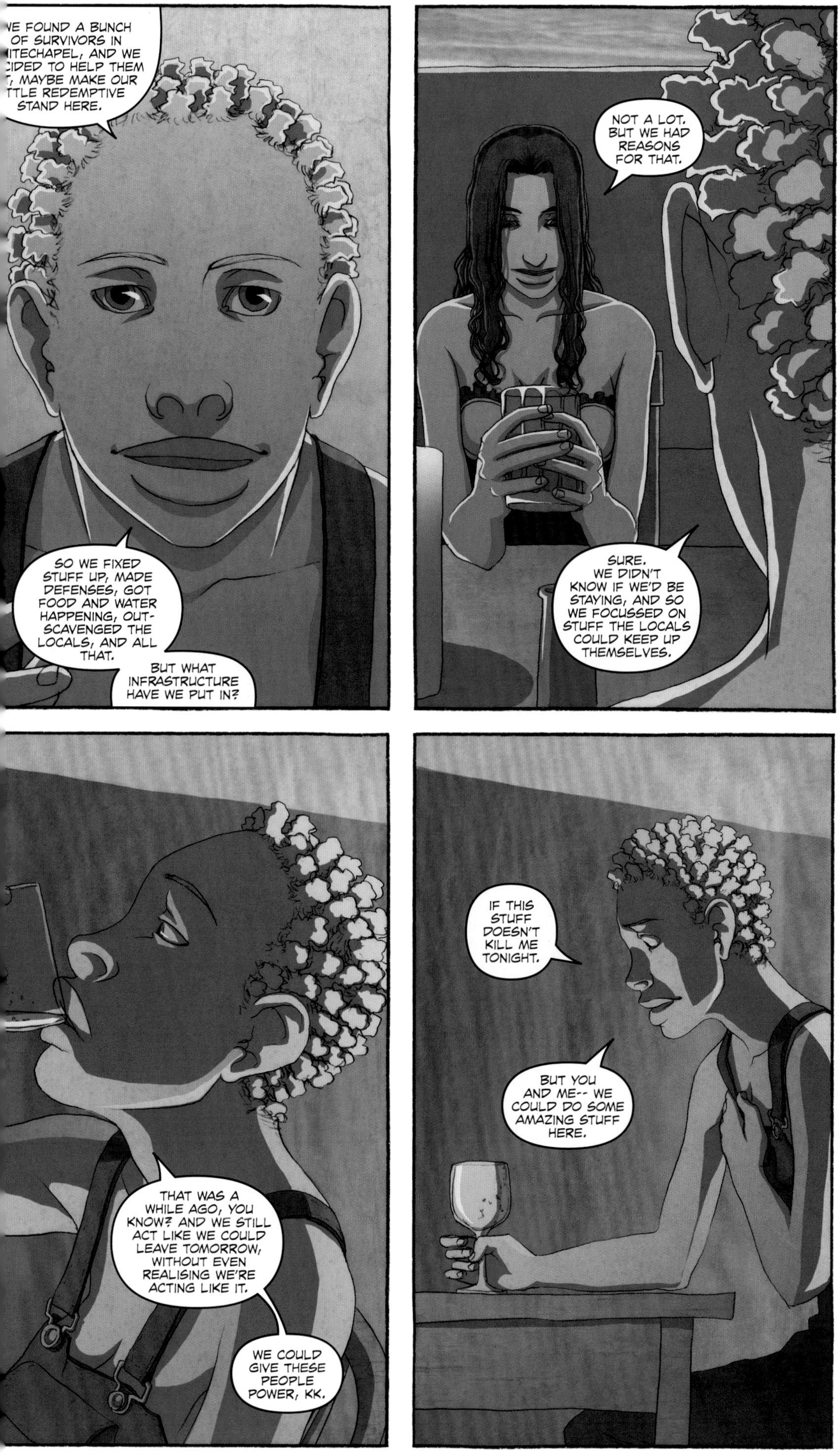

VE FOUND A BUNCH OF SURVIVORS IN ITECHAPEL, AND WE CIDED TO HELP THEM T, MAYBE MAKE OUR TTLE REDEMPTIVE STAND HERE.
SO WE FIXED STUFF UP, MADE DEFENSES, GOT FOOD AND WATER HAPPENING, OUT-SCAVENGED THE LOCALS, AND ALL THAT.
BUT WHAT INFRASTRUCTURE HAVE WE PUT IN?
NOT A LOT. BUT WE HAD REASONS FOR THAT.
SURE. WE DIDN'T KNOW IF WE'D BE STAYING, AND SO WE FOCUSSED ON STUFF THE LOCALS COULD KEEP UP THEMSELVES.
THAT WAS A WHILE AGO, YOU KNOW? AND WE STILL ACT LIKE WE COULD LEAVE TOMORROW, WITHOUT EVEN REALISING WE'RE ACTING LIKE IT.
WE COULD GIVE THESE PEOPLE POWER, KK.
IF THIS STUFF DOESN'T KILL ME TONIGHT.
BUT YOU AND ME-- WE COULD DO SOME AMAZING STUFF HERE.

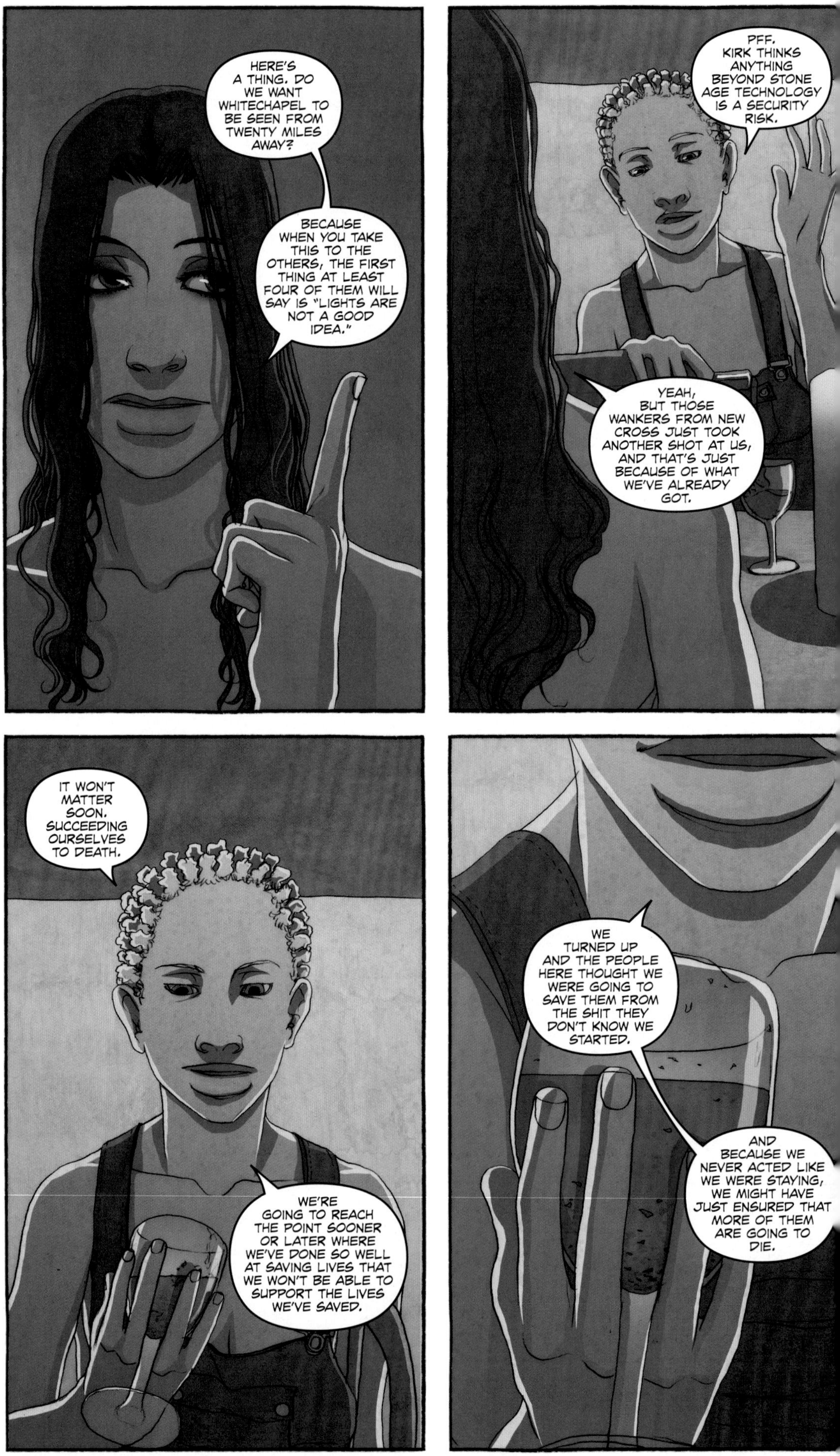
HERE'S A THING. DO WE WANT WHITECHAPEL TO BE SEEN FROM TWENTY MILES AWAY?
BECAUSE WHEN YOU TAKE THIS TO THE OTHERS, THE FIRST THING AT LEAST FOUR OF THEM WILL SAY IS "LIGHTS ARE NOT A GOOD IDEA."
PFF. KIRK THINKS ANYTHING BEYOND STONE AGE TECHNOLOGY IS A SECURITY RISK.
YEAH, BUT THOSE WANKERS FROM NEW CROSS JUST TOOK ANOTHER SHOT AT US, AND THAT'S JUST BECAUSE OF WHAT WE'VE ALREADY GOT.
IT WON'T MATTER SOON. SUCCEEDING OURSELVES TO DEATH.
WE'RE GOING TO REACH THE POINT SOONER OR LATER WHERE WE'VE DONE SO WELL AT SAVING LIVES THAT WE WON'T BE ABLE TO SUPPORT THE LIVES WE'VE SAVED.
WE TURNED UP AND THE PEOPLE HERE THOUGHT WE WERE GOING TO SAVE THEM FROM THE SHIT THEY DON'T KNOW WE STARTED.
AND BECAUSE WE NEVER ACTED LIKE WE WERE STAYING, WE MIGHT HAVE JUST ENSURED THAT MORE OF THEM ARE GOING TO DIE.

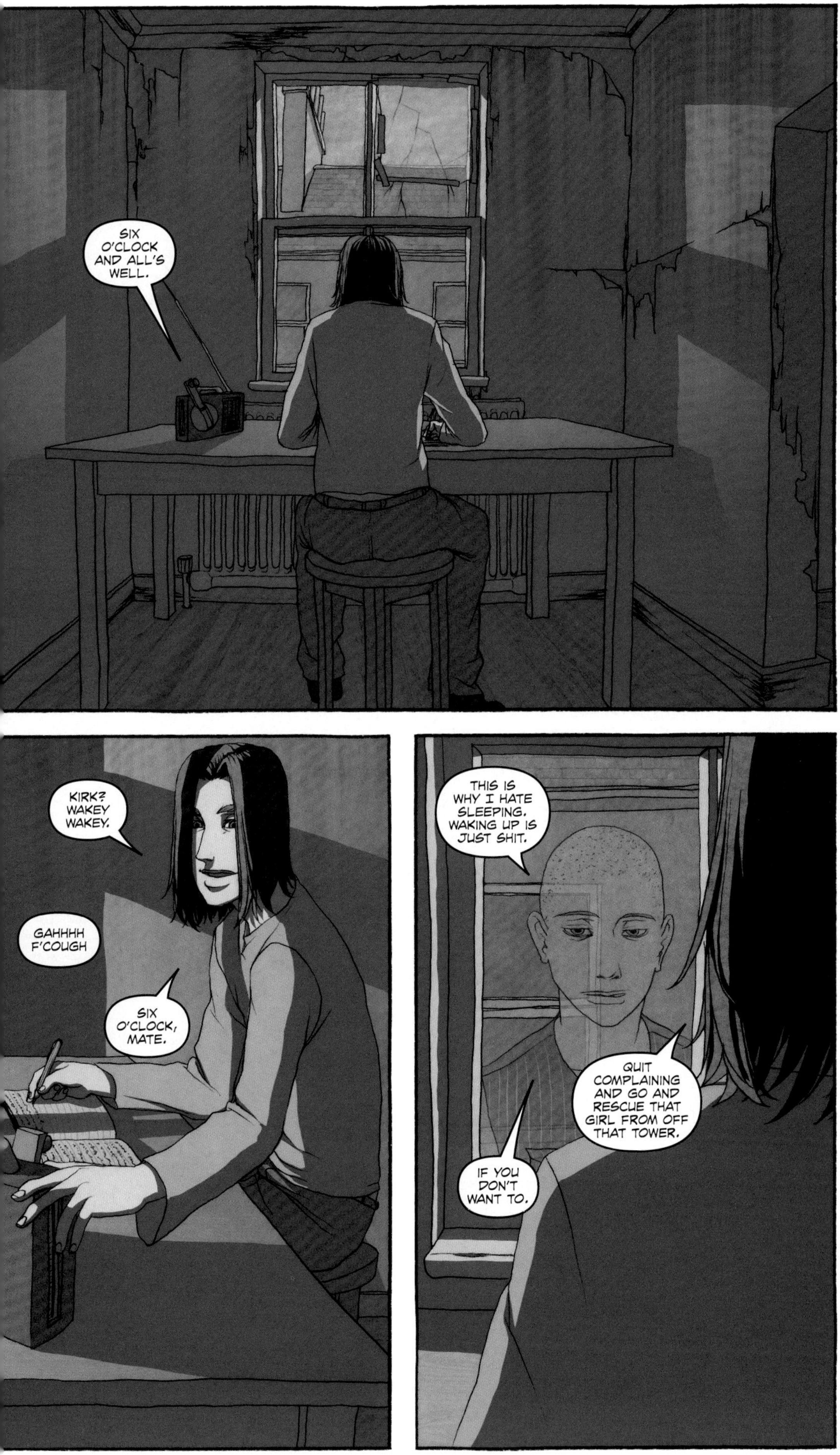
SIX O'CLOCK AND ALL'S WELL.
KIRK? WAKEY WAKEY.
GAHHHH F'COUGH
SIX O'CLOCK, MATE.
THIS IS WHY I HATE SLEEPING. WAKING UP IS JUST SHIT.
QUIT COMPLAINING AND GO AND RESCUE THAT GIRL FROM OFF THAT TOWER.
IF YOU DON'T WANT TO.

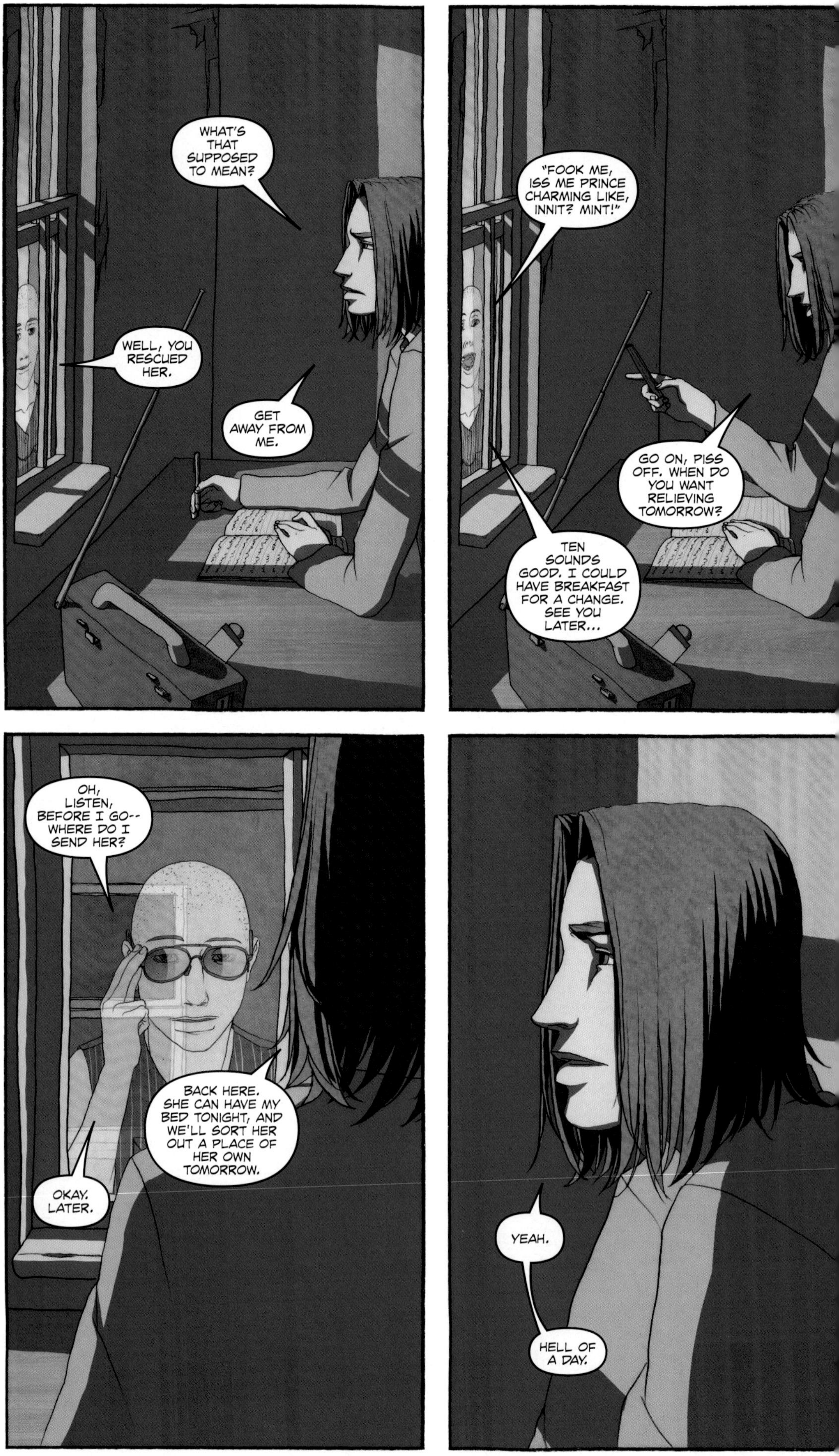
WHAT'S THAT SUPPOSED TO MEAN?
WELL, YOU RESCUED HER.
GET AWAY FROM ME.
"FOOK ME, ISS ME PRINCE CHARMING LIKE, INNIT? MINT!"
GO ON, PISS OFF. WHEN DO YOU WANT RELIEVING TOMORROW?
TEN SOUNDS GOOD. I COULD HAVE BREAKFAST FOR A CHANGE. SEE YOU LATER...
OH, LISTEN, BEFORE I GO-- WHERE DO I SEND HER?
BACK HERE. SHE CAN HAVE MY BED TONIGHT, AND WE'LL SORT HER OUT A PLACE OF HER OWN TOMORROW.
OKAY. LATER.
YEAH.
HELL OF A DAY.

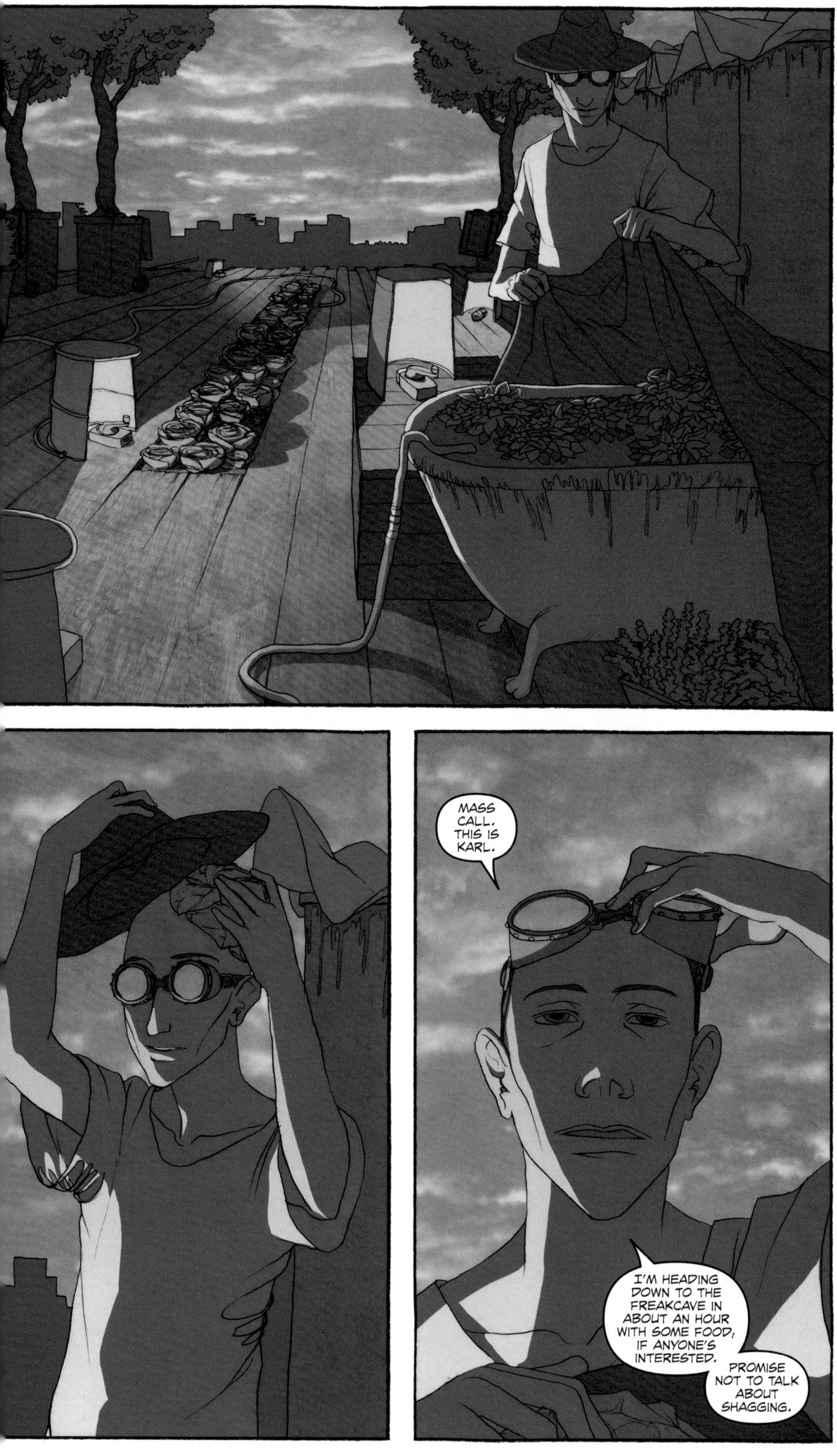
MASS CALL. THIS IS KARL.
I'M HEADING DOWN TO THE FREAKCAVE IN ABOUT AN HOUR WITH SOME FOOD, IF ANYONE'S INTERESTED.
PROMISE NOT TO TALK ABOUT SHAGGING.

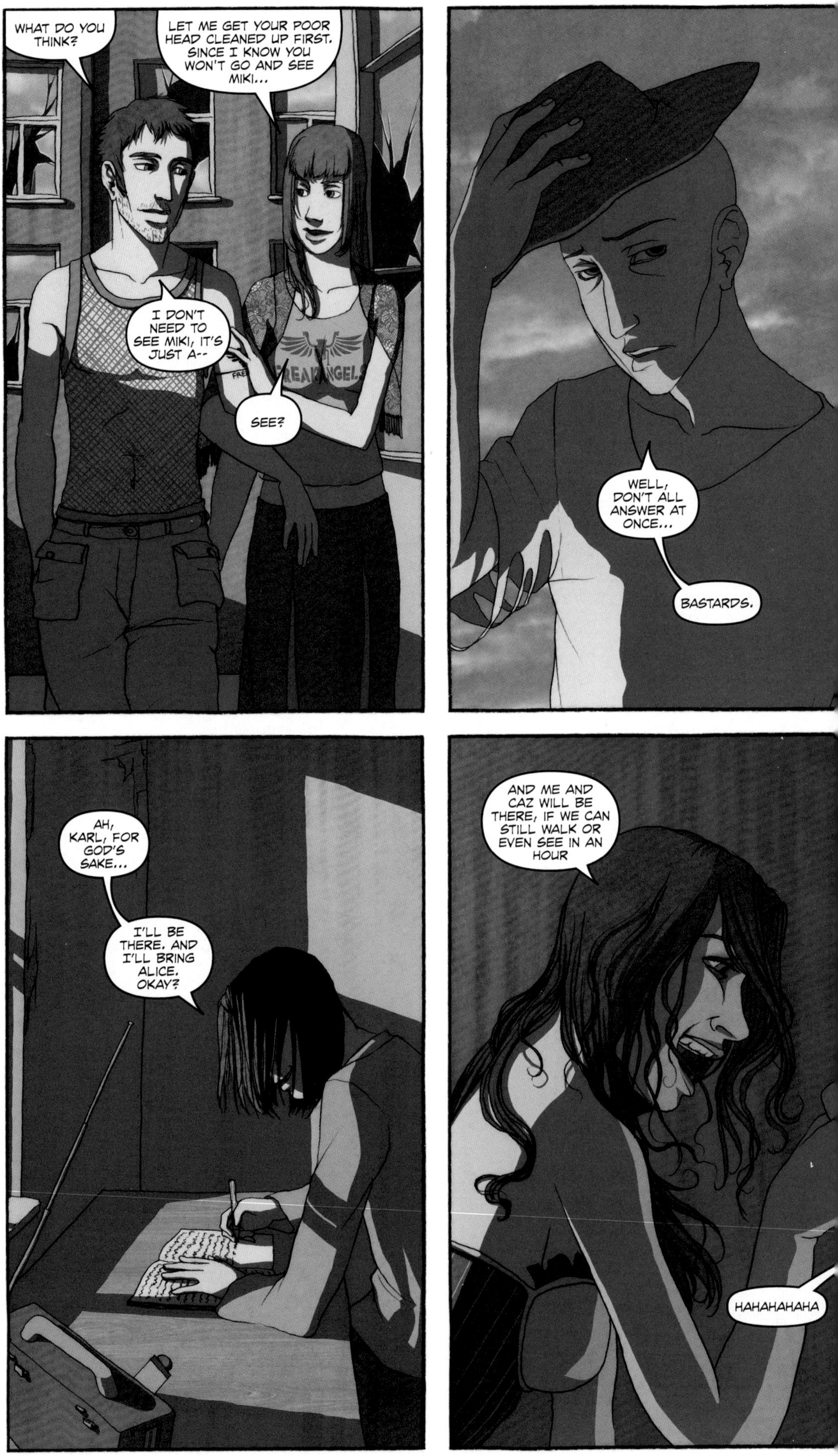
WHAT DO YOU THINK?
LET ME GET YOUR POOR HEAD CLEANED UP FIRST. SINCE I KNOW YOU WON'T GO AND SEE MIKI...
I DON'T NEED TO SEE MIKI, IT'S JUST A--
SEE?
WELL, DON'T ALL ANSWER AT ONCE...
BASTARDS.
AH, KARL, FOR GOD'S SAKE...
I'LL BE THERE. AND I'LL BRING ALICE. OKAY?
AND ME AND CAZ WILL BE THERE, IF WE CAN STILL WALK OR EVEN SEE IN AN HOUR
HAHAHAHAHA

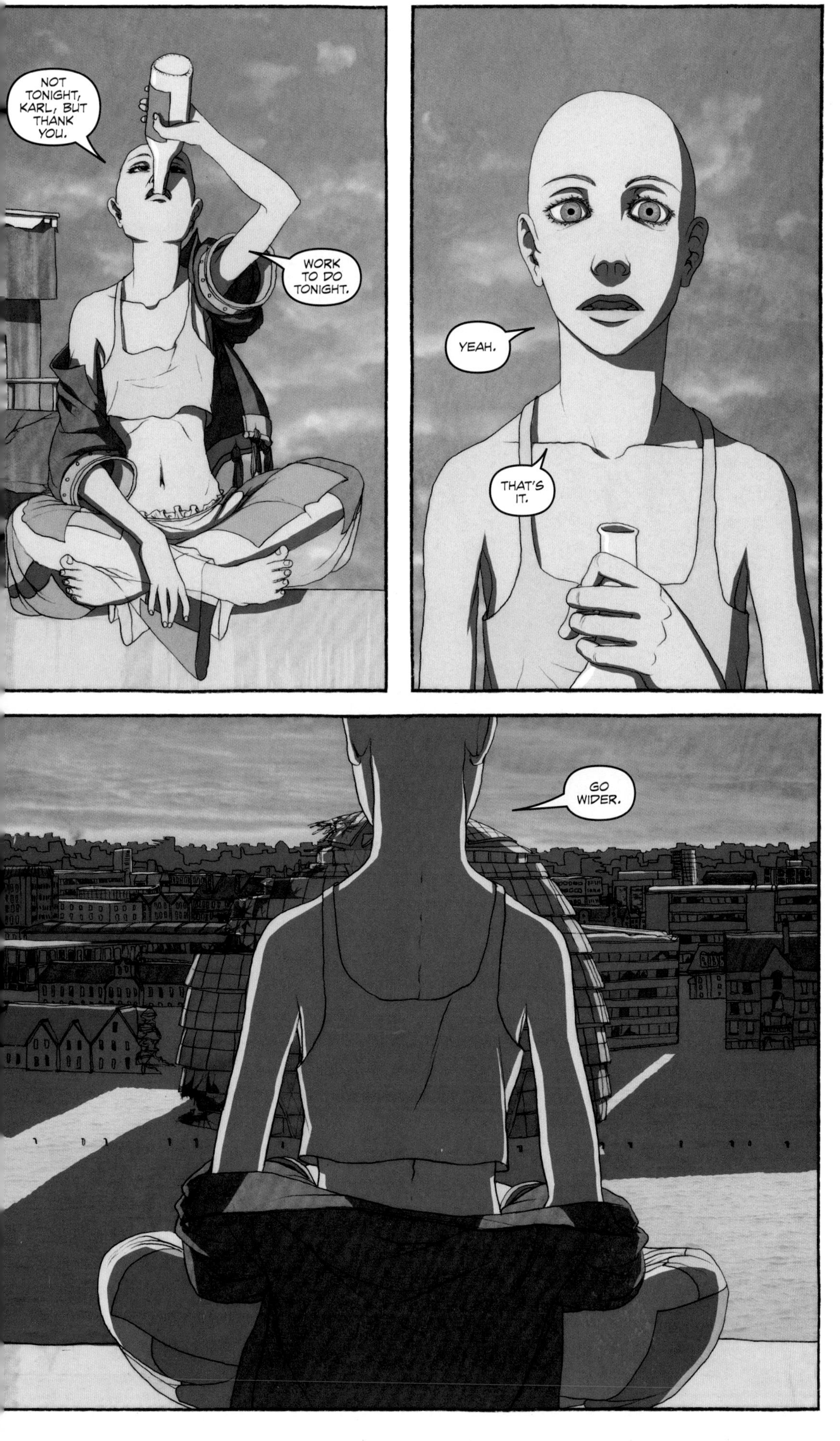
NOT TONIGHT, KARL, BUT THANK YOU.
WORK TO DO TONIGHT.
YEAH.
THAT'S IT.
GO WIDER.

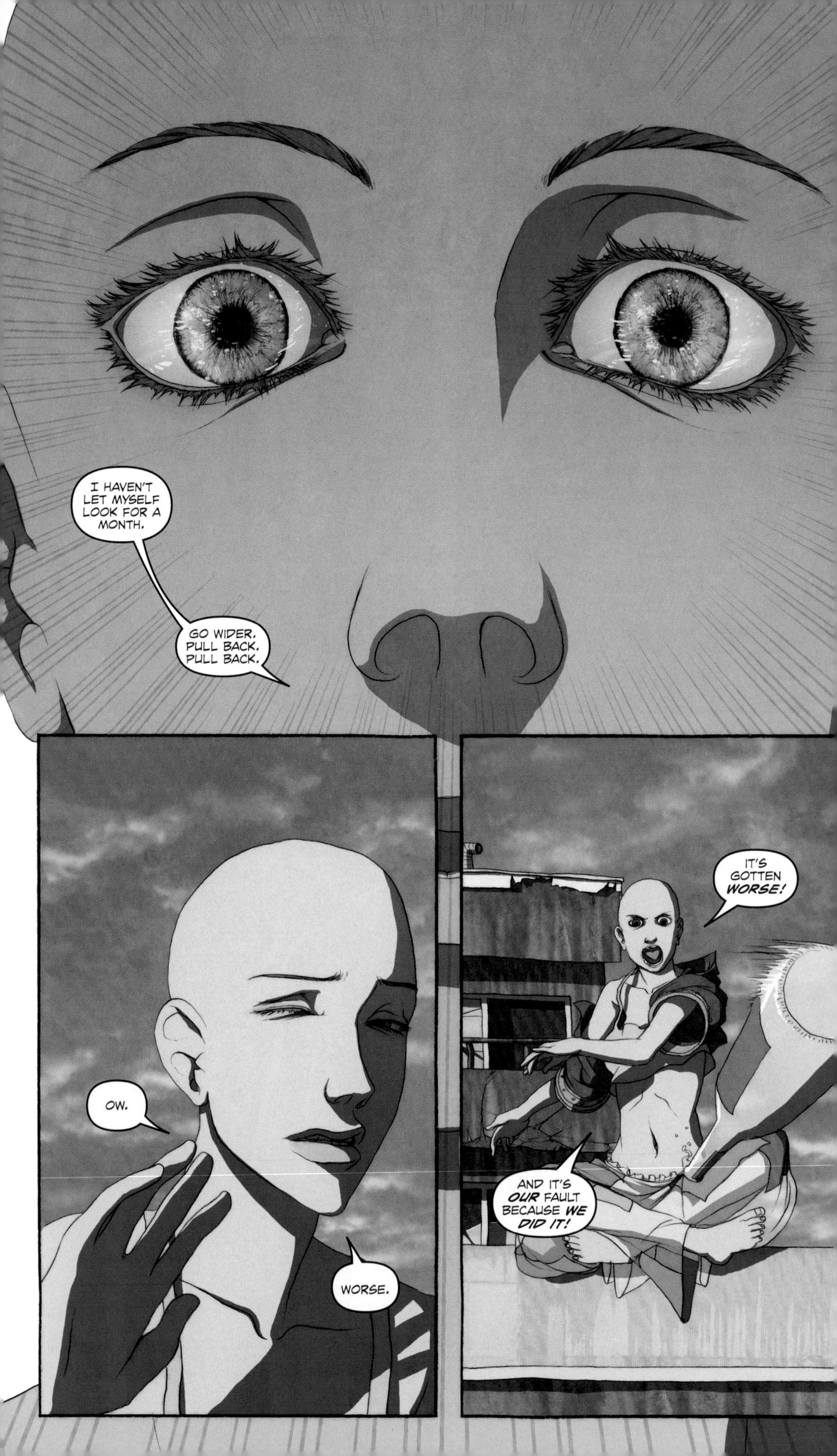
I HAVEN'T LET MYSELF LOOK FOR A MONTH.
GO WIDER. PULL BACK. PULL BACK.
OW.
WORSE.
IT'S GOTTEN *WORSE!*
AND IT'S *OUR* FAULT BECAUSE *WE DID IT!*

THERE.

KARL, IT'S MIKI. I COULD USE SOMETHING TO EAT.

AND IT'S ALL QUIET IN HERE FOR A CHANGE.

SINCE THE REST OF YOU DECIDED TO LEAVE NO WOUNDED THIS AFTERNOON...

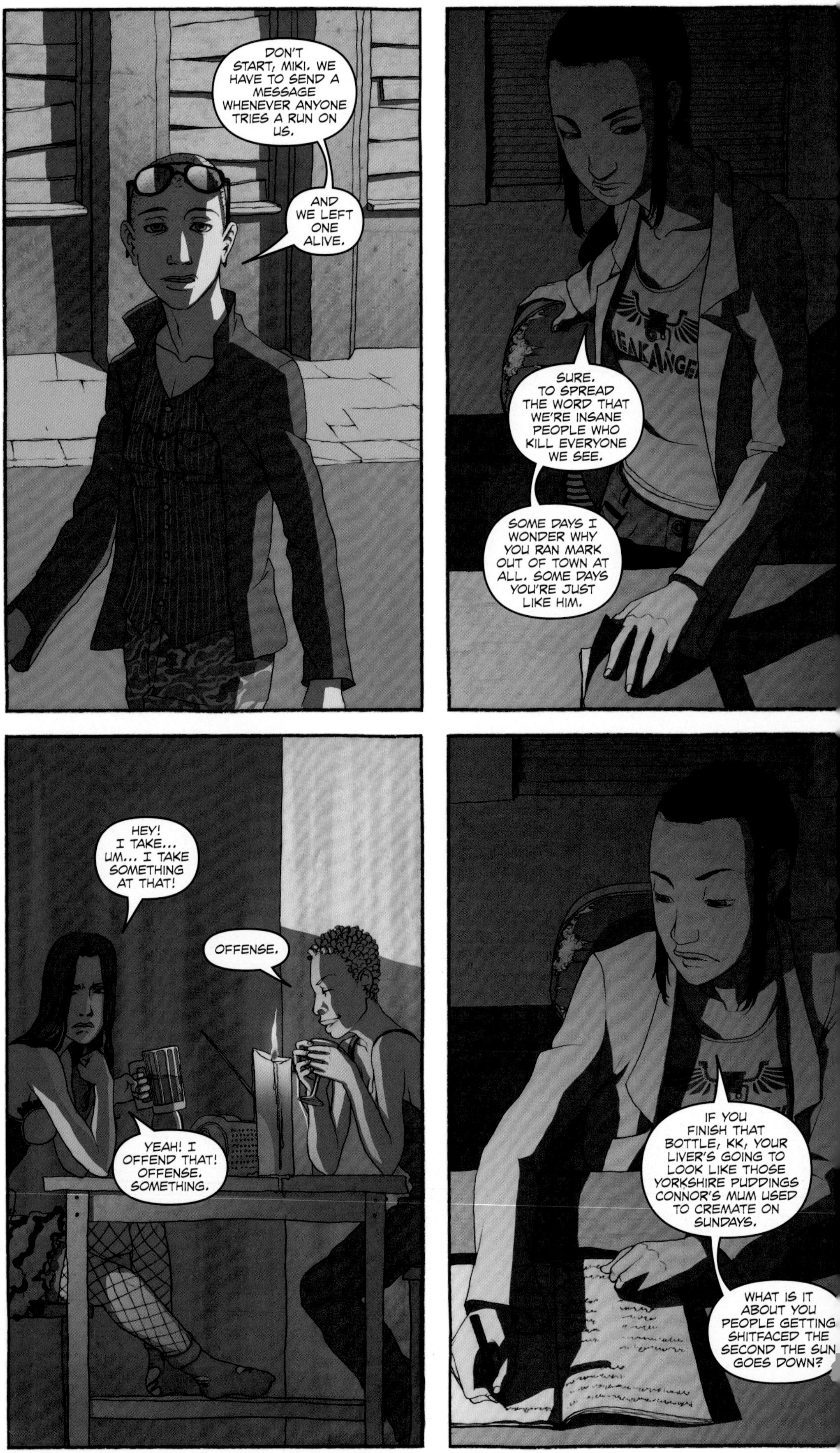

DON'T START, MIKI. WE HAVE TO SEND A MESSAGE WHENEVER ANYONE TRIES A RUN ON US.
AND WE LEFT ONE ALIVE.
SURE. TO SPREAD THE WORD THAT WE'RE INSANE PEOPLE WHO KILL EVERYONE WE SEE.
SOME DAYS I WONDER WHY YOU RAN MARK OUT OF TOWN AT ALL. SOME DAYS YOU'RE JUST LIKE HIM.
HEY! I TAKE... UM... I TAKE SOMETHING AT THAT!
OFFENSE.
YEAH! I OFFEND THAT! OFFENSE. SOMETHING.
IF YOU FINISH THAT BOTTLE, KK, YOUR LIVER'S GOING TO LOOK LIKE THOSE YORKSHIRE PUDDINGS CONNOR'S MUM USED TO CREMATE ON SUNDAYS.
WHAT IS IT ABOUT YOU PEOPLE GETTING SHITFACED THE SECOND THE SUN GOES DOWN?

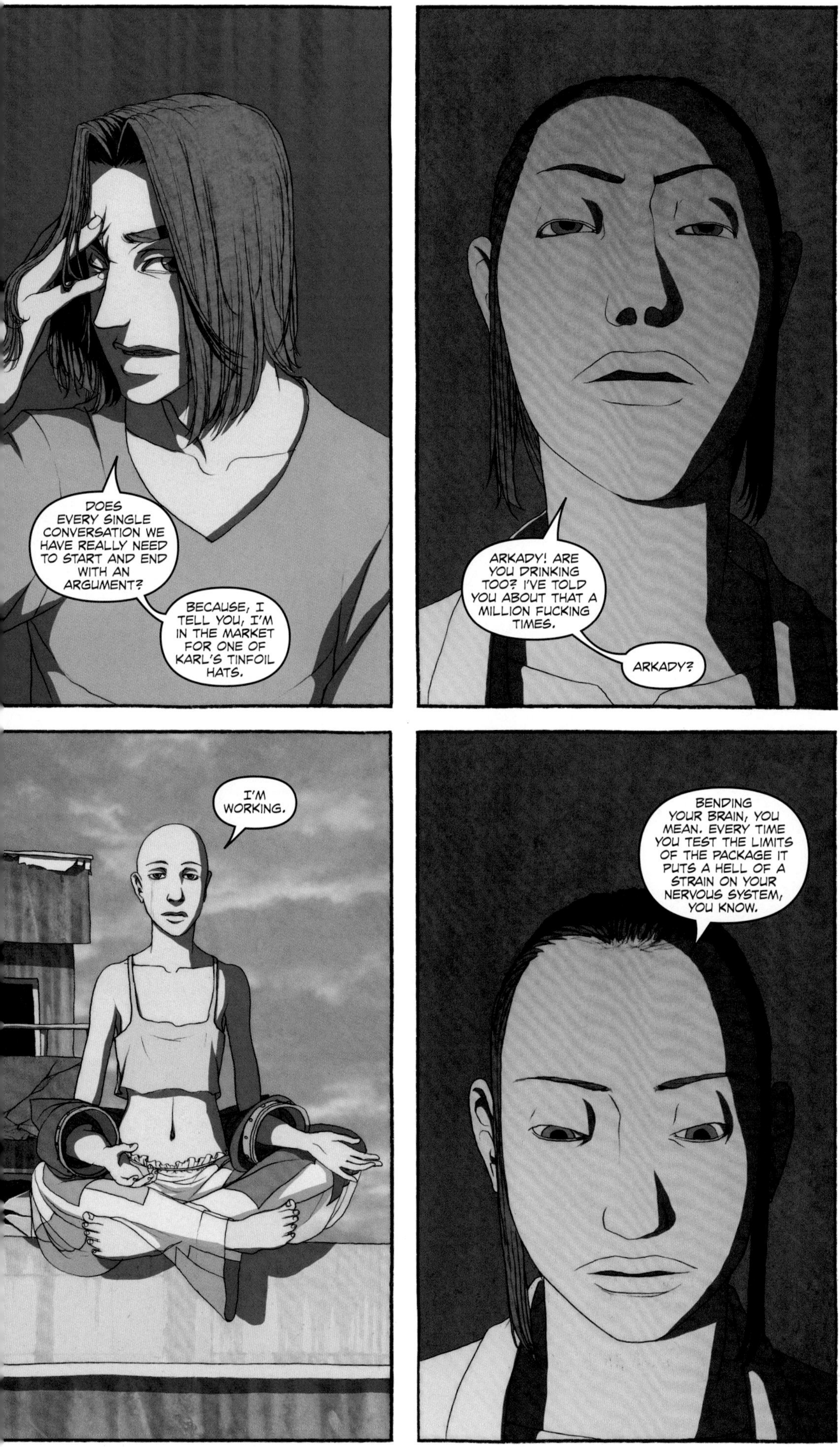
DOES EVERY SINGLE CONVERSATION WE HAVE REALLY NEED TO START AND END WITH AN ARGUMENT?
BECAUSE, I TELL YOU, I'M IN THE MARKET FOR ONE OF KARL'S TINFOIL HATS.
ARKADY! ARE YOU DRINKING TOO? I'VE TOLD YOU ABOUT THAT A MILLION FUCKING TIMES.
ARKADY?
I'M WORKING.
BENDING YOUR BRAIN, YOU MEAN. EVERY TIME YOU TEST THE LIMITS OF THE PACKAGE IT PUTS A HELL OF A STRAIN ON YOUR NERVOUS SYSTEM, YOU KNOW.

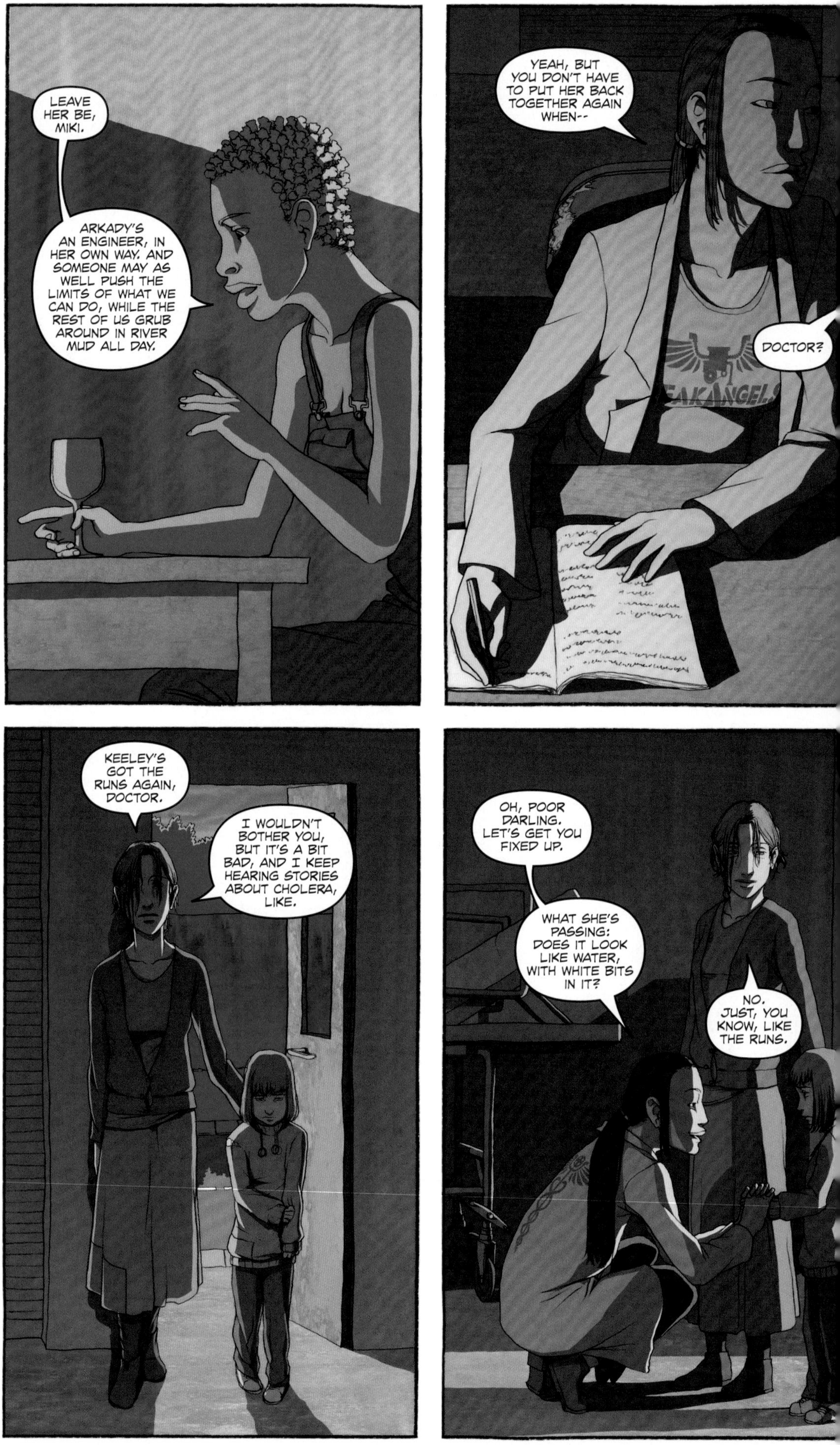
LEAVE HER BE, MIKI.
ARKADY'S AN ENGINEER, IN HER OWN WAY. AND SOMEONE MAY AS WELL PUSH THE LIMITS OF WHAT WE CAN DO, WHILE THE REST OF US GRUB AROUND IN RIVER MUD ALL DAY.
YEAH, BUT YOU DON'T HAVE TO PUT HER BACK TOGETHER AGAIN WHEN--
DOCTOR?
KEELEY'S GOT THE RUNS AGAIN, DOCTOR.
I WOULDN'T BOTHER YOU, BUT IT'S A BIT BAD, AND I KEEP HEARING STORIES ABOUT CHOLERA, LIKE.
OH, POOR DARLING. LET'S GET YOU FIXED UP.
WHAT SHE'S PASSING: DOES IT LOOK LIKE WATER, WITH WHITE BITS IN IT?
NO. JUST, YOU KNOW, LIKE THE RUNS.

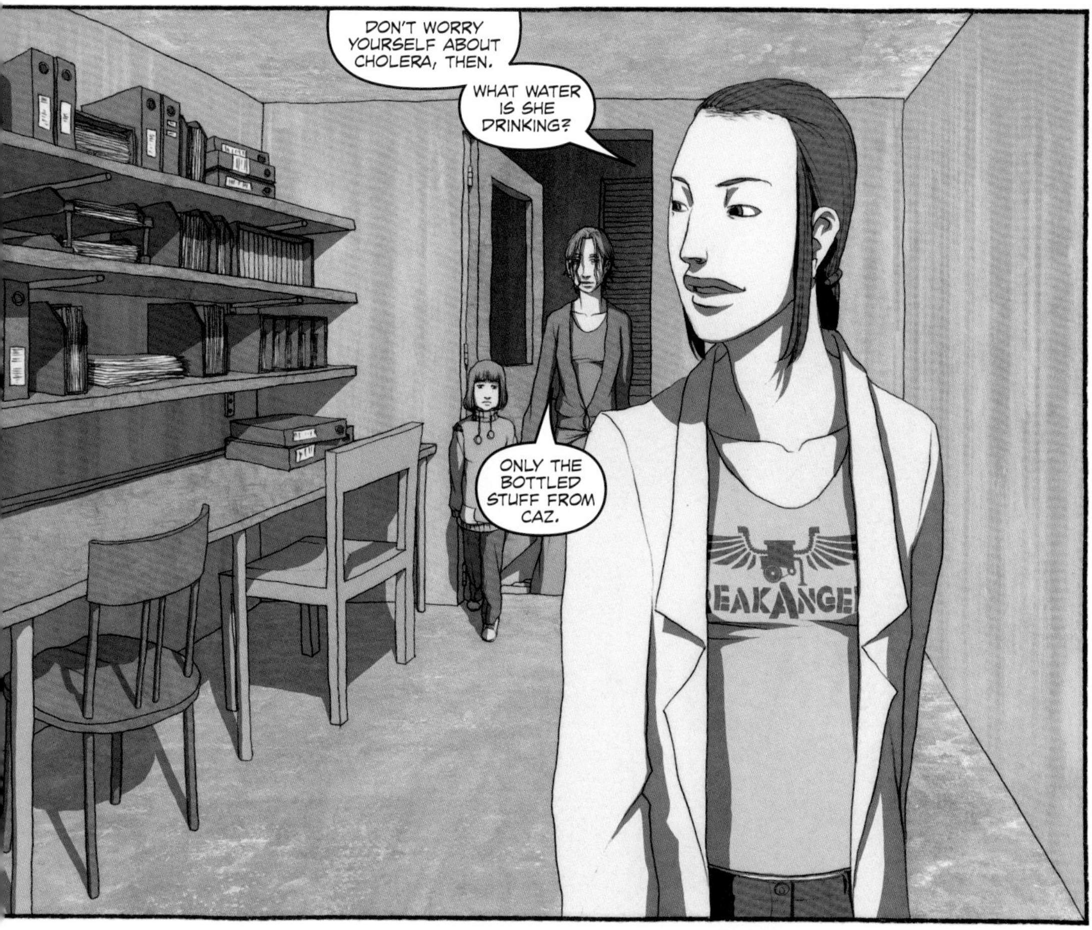
DON'T WORRY YOURSELF ABOUT CHOLERA, THEN.
WHAT WATER IS SHE DRINKING?
ONLY THE BOTTLED STUFF FROM CAZ.
REAKANGE

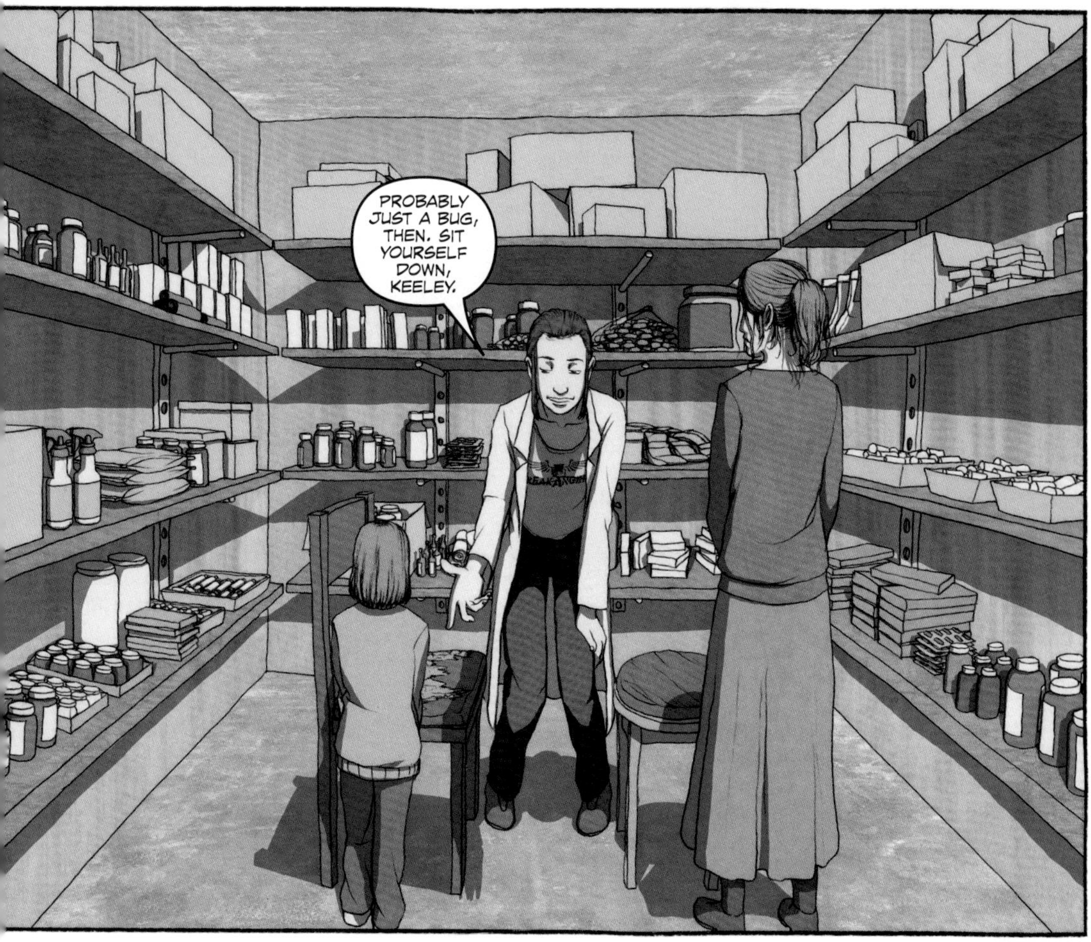
PROBABLY JUST A BUG, THEN. SIT YOURSELF DOWN, KEELEY.

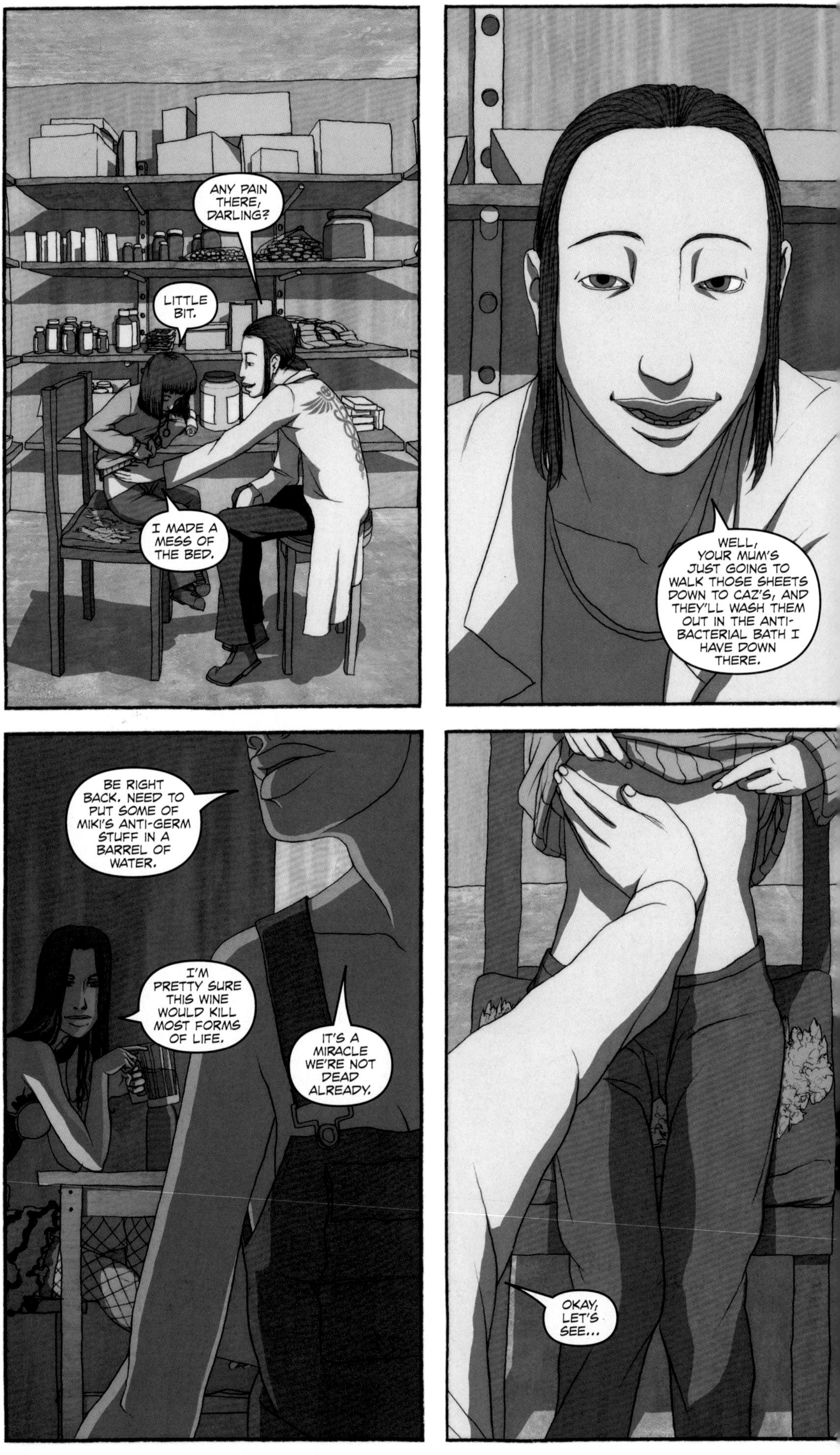
ANY PAIN THERE, DARLING?
LITTLE BIT.
I MADE A MESS OF THE BED.
WELL, YOUR MUM'S JUST GOING TO WALK THOSE SHEETS DOWN TO CAZ'S, AND THEY'LL WASH THEM OUT IN THE ANTI-BACTERIAL BATH I HAVE DOWN THERE.
BE RIGHT BACK. NEED TO PUT SOME OF MIKI'S ANTI-GERM STUFF IN A BARREL OF WATER.
I'M PRETTY SURE THIS WINE WOULD KILL MOST FORMS OF LIFE.
IT'S A MIRACLE WE'RE NOT DEAD ALREADY.
OKAY, LET'S SEE...

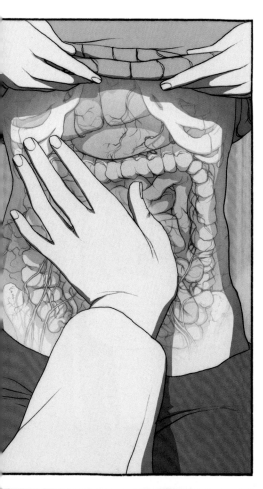

JUST A BIT OF SENSITIVITY. WE CAN FIX THAT RIGHT UP.

LIGHT MEALS FOR THE NEXT DAY, OKAY? AND MOSTLY PLANTS.

I'M GOING TO GIVE YOU SOMETHING CALLED PULSATILLA. YOU JUST CRUNCH THEM UP IN YOUR MOUTH AND SWALLOW.

YOU'RE GOING TO TAKE ONE NOW, AND NOT DRINK ANYTHING FOR FIFTEEN MINUTES. AFTER THAT, START DRINKING WATER.

THEN TAKE ONE BEFORE BED, AND THEN ONE IN THE MORNING. AFTER THAT, ONE A DAY UNTIL THEY RUN OUT.

AND THAT'LL BE THAT. COME AND SEE ME AGAIN IF YOU LIKE, TO MAKE SURE.

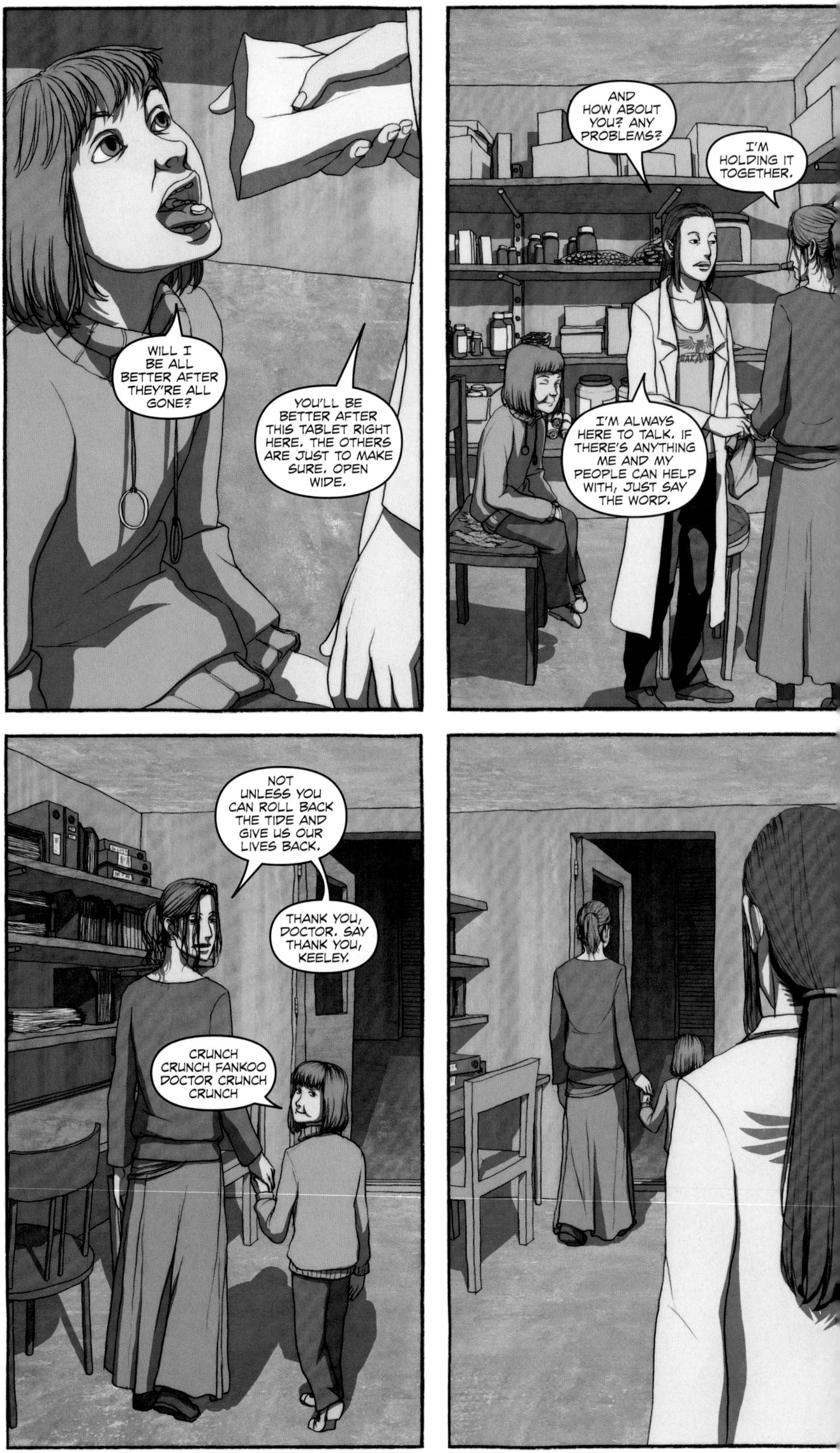
WILL I BE ALL BETTER AFTER THEY'RE ALL GONE?
YOU'LL BE BETTER AFTER THIS TABLET RIGHT HERE. THE OTHERS ARE JUST TO MAKE SURE. OPEN WIDE.
AND HOW ABOUT YOU? ANY PROBLEMS?
I'M HOLDING IT TOGETHER.
I'M ALWAYS HERE TO TALK. IF THERE'S ANYTHING ME AND MY PEOPLE CAN HELP WITH, JUST SAY THE WORD.
NOT UNLESS YOU CAN ROLL BACK THE TIDE AND GIVE US OUR LIVES BACK.
THANK YOU, DOCTOR. SAY THANK YOU, KEELEY.
CRUNCH CRUNCH FANKOO DOCTOR CRUNCH CRUNCH

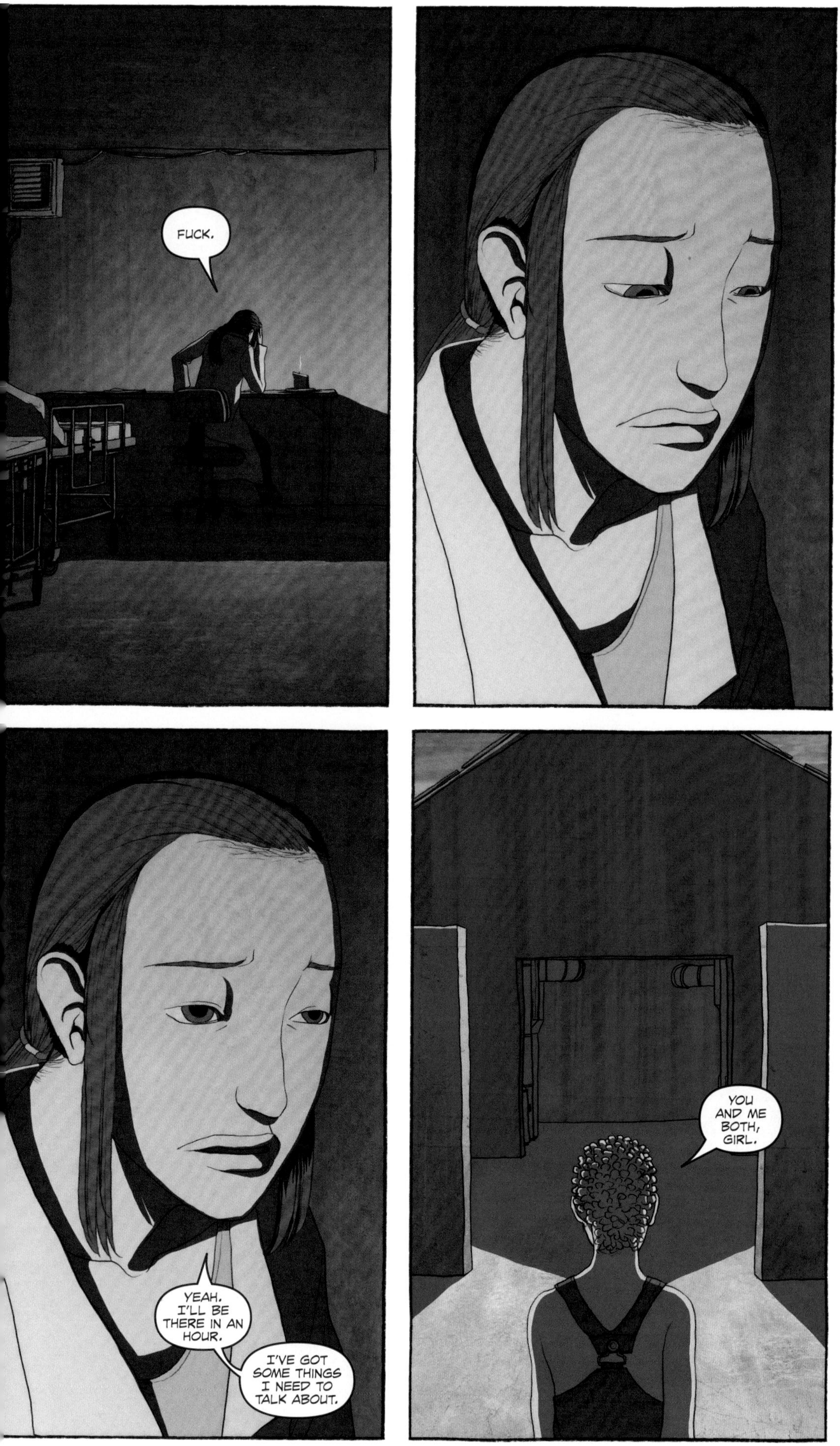
FUCK.
YEAH. I'LL BE THERE IN AN HOUR.
I'VE GOT SOME THINGS I NEED TO TALK ABOUT.
YOU AND ME BOTH, GIRL.

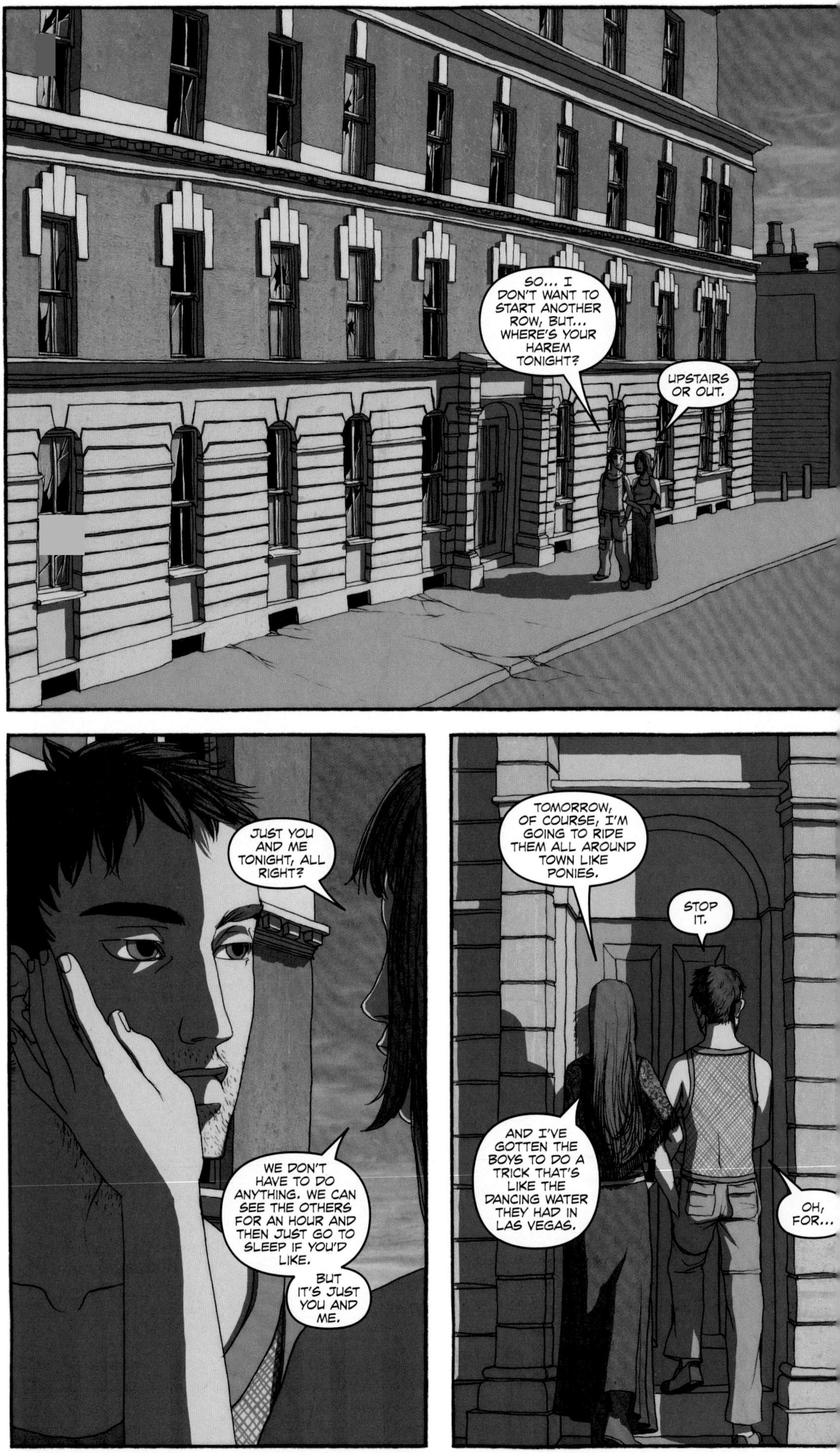
SO... I DON'T WANT TO START ANOTHER ROW, BUT... WHERE'S YOUR HAREM TONIGHT?
UPSTAIRS OR OUT.
JUST YOU AND ME TONIGHT, ALL RIGHT?
WE DON'T HAVE TO DO ANYTHING. WE CAN SEE THE OTHERS FOR AN HOUR AND THEN JUST GO TO SLEEP IF YOU'D LIKE.
BUT IT'S JUST YOU AND ME.
TOMORROW, OF COURSE, I'M GOING TO RIDE THEM ALL AROUND TOWN LIKE PONIES.
STOP IT.
AND I'VE GOTTEN THE BOYS TO DO A TRICK THAT'S LIKE THE DANCING WATER THEY HAD IN LAS VEGAS.
OH, FOR...

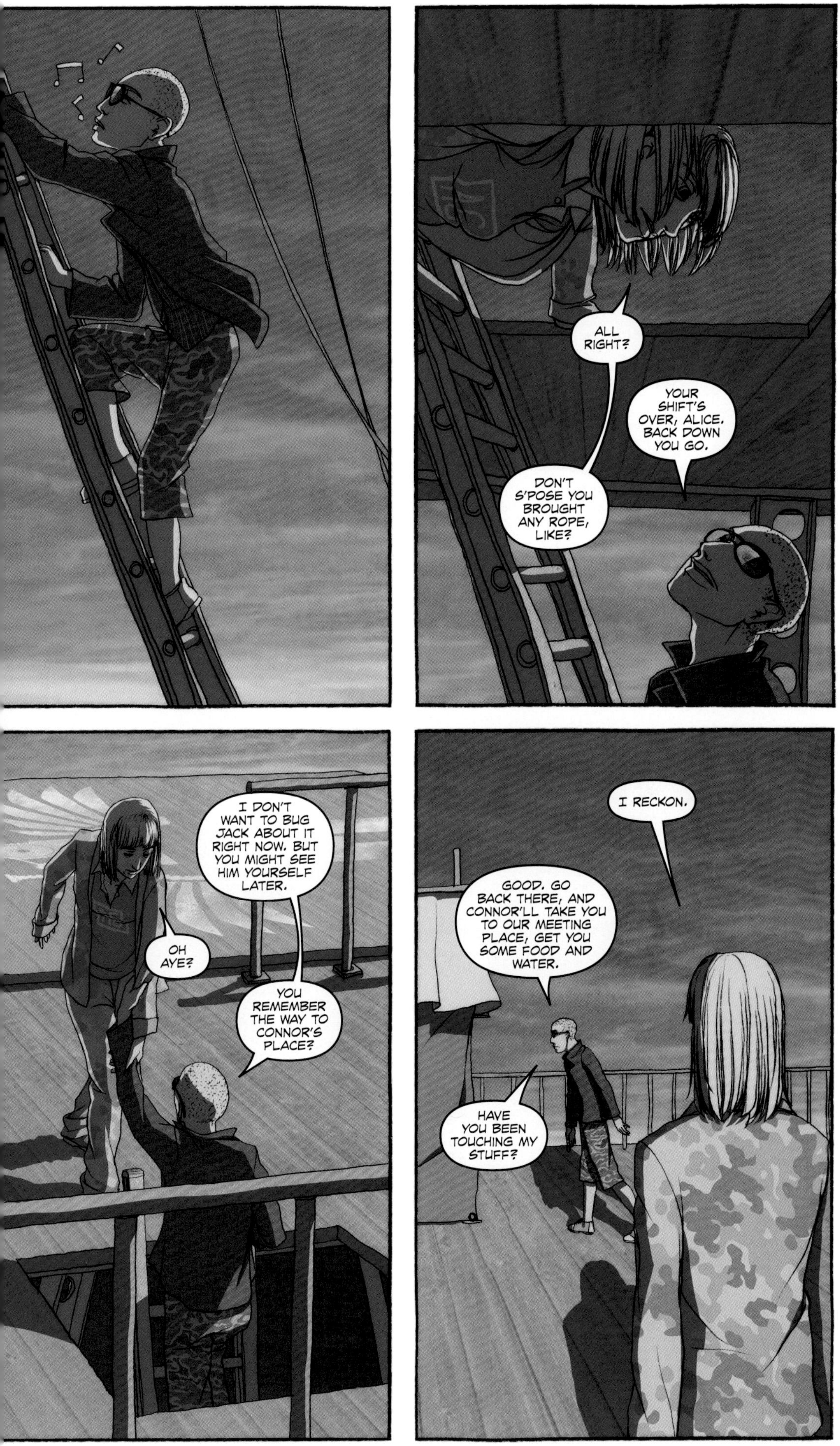
ALL RIGHT?
YOUR SHIFT'S OVER, ALICE. BACK DOWN YOU GO.
DON'T S'POSE YOU BROUGHT ANY ROPE, LIKE?
I DON'T WANT TO BUG JACK ABOUT IT RIGHT NOW. BUT YOU MIGHT SEE HIM YOURSELF LATER.
OH AYE?
YOU REMEMBER THE WAY TO CONNOR'S PLACE?
I RECKON.
GOOD. GO BACK THERE, AND CONNOR'LL TAKE YOU TO OUR MEETING PLACE, GET YOU SOME FOOD AND WATER.
HAVE YOU BEEN TOUCHING MY STUFF?

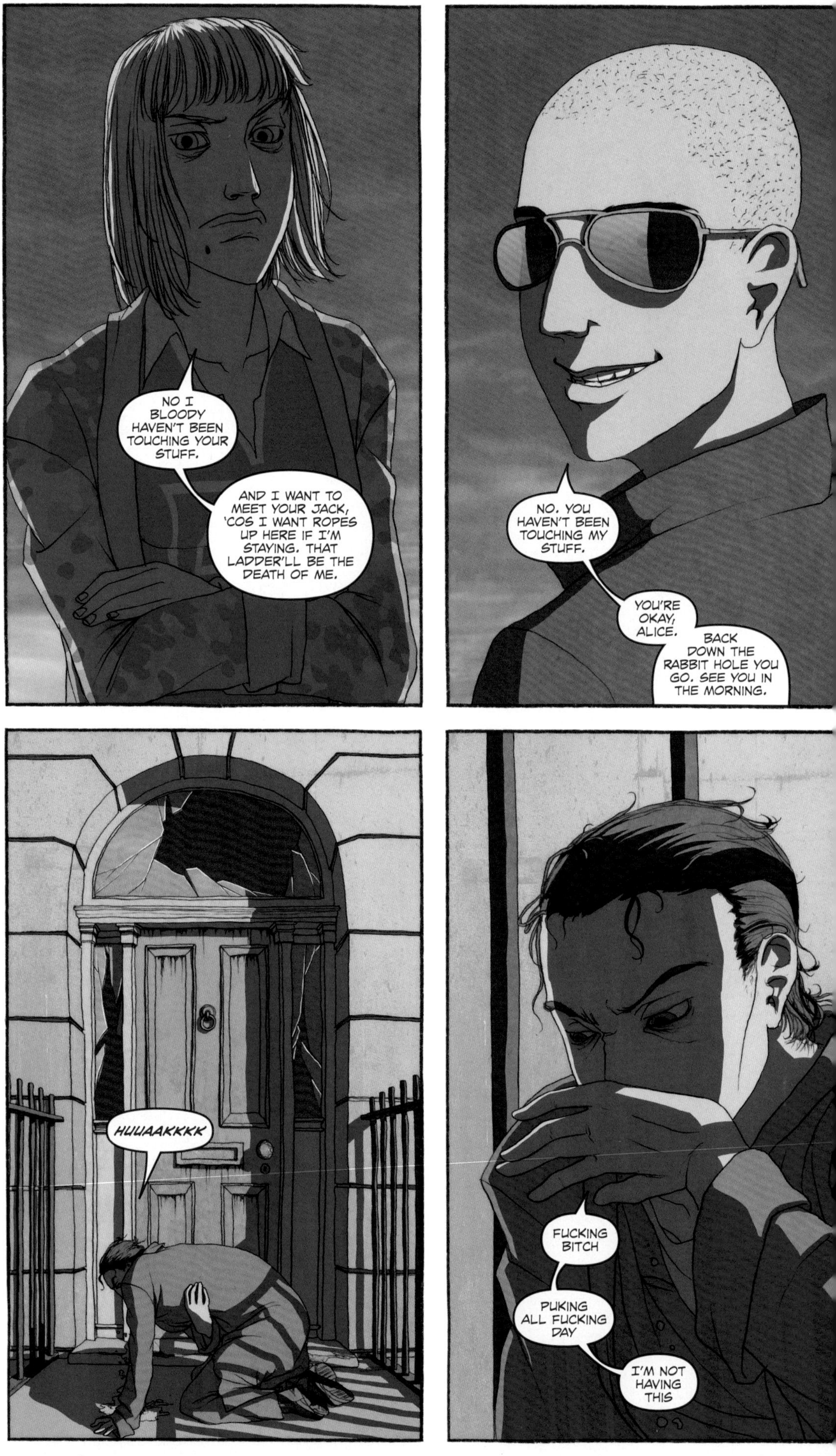
NO I BLOODY HAVEN'T BEEN TOUCHING YOUR STUFF.
AND I WANT TO MEET YOUR JACK, 'COS I WANT ROPES UP HERE IF I'M STAYING. THAT LADDER'LL BE THE DEATH OF ME.
NO. YOU HAVEN'T BEEN TOUCHING MY STUFF.
YOU'RE OKAY, ALICE.
BACK DOWN THE RABBIT HOLE YOU GO. SEE YOU IN THE MORNING.
HUUAAKKKK
FUCKING BITCH
PUKING ALL FUCKING DAY
I'M NOT HAVING THIS

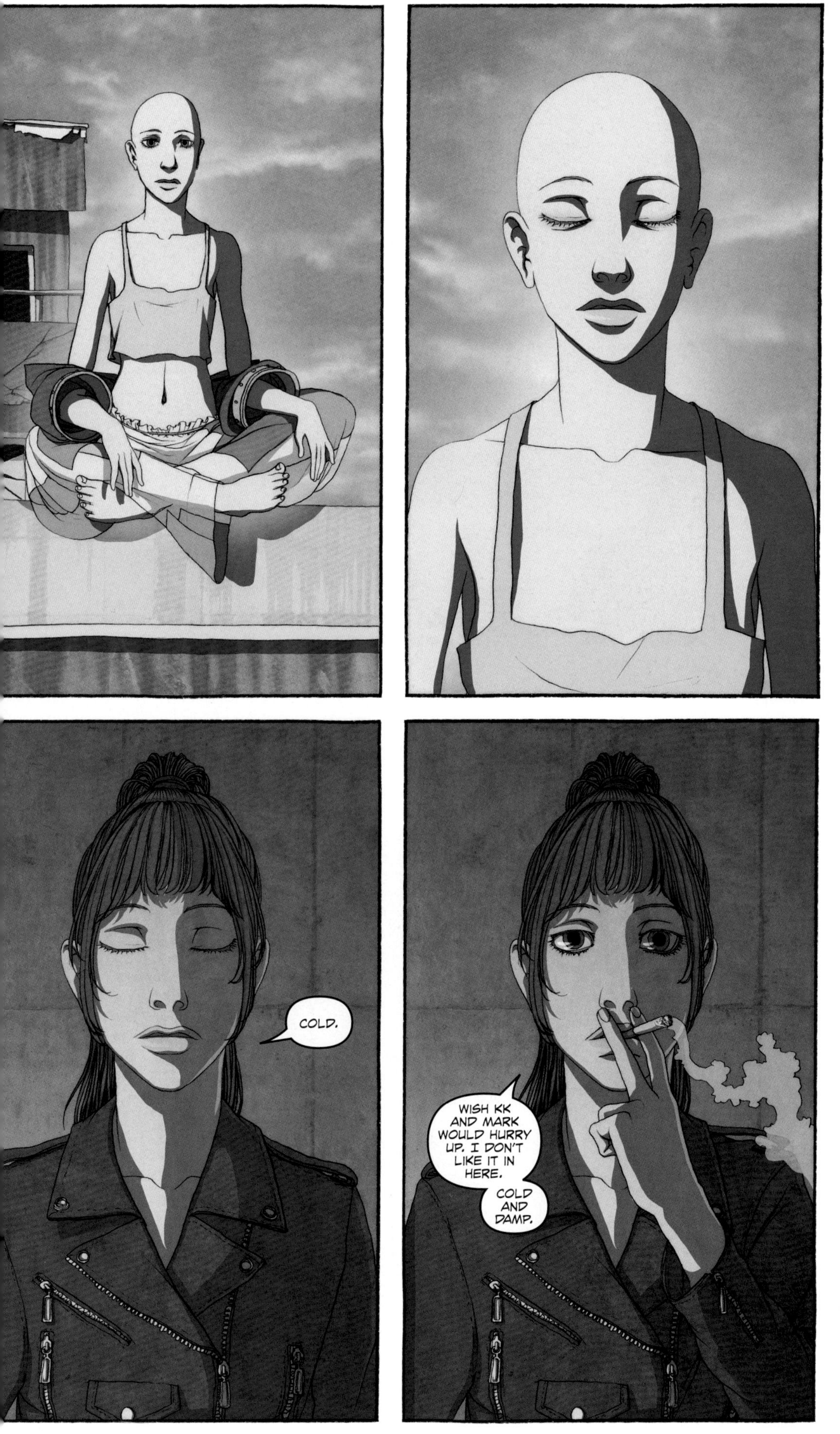
COLD.
WISH KK AND MARK WOULD HURRY UP. I DON'T LIKE IT IN HERE.
COLD AND DAMP.

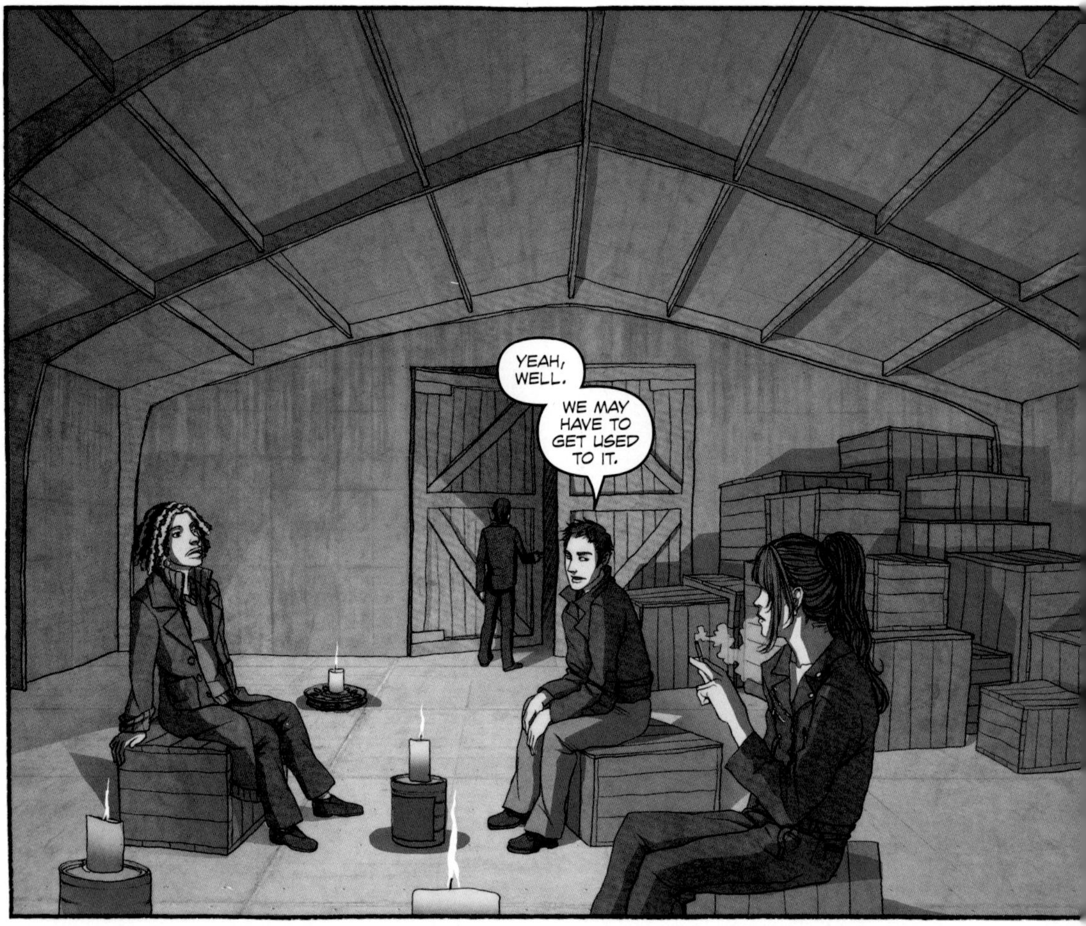
YEAH, WELL.
WE MAY HAVE TO GET USED TO IT.

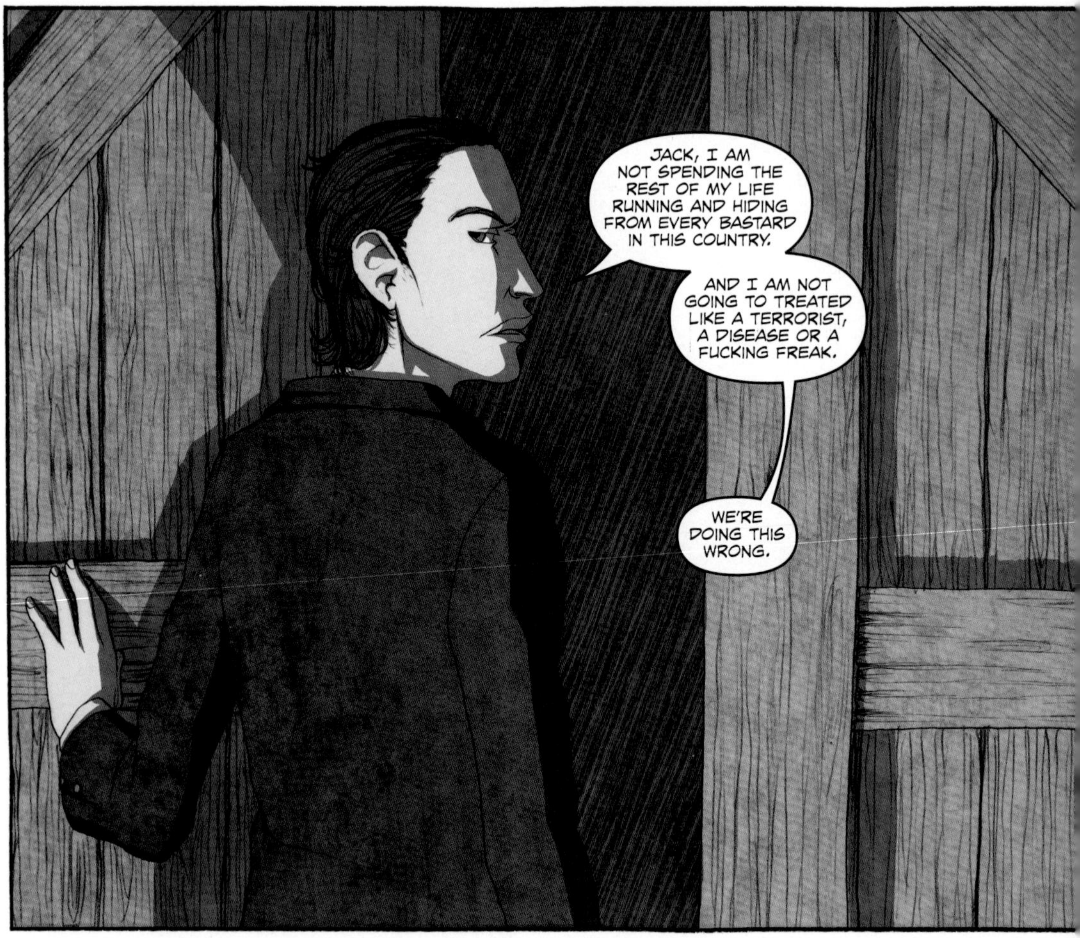
JACK, I AM NOT SPENDING THE REST OF MY LIFE RUNNING AND HIDING FROM EVERY BASTARD IN THIS COUNTRY.
AND I AM NOT GOING TO TREATED LIKE A TERRORIST, A DISEASE OR A FUCKING FREAK.
WE'RE DOING THIS WRONG.

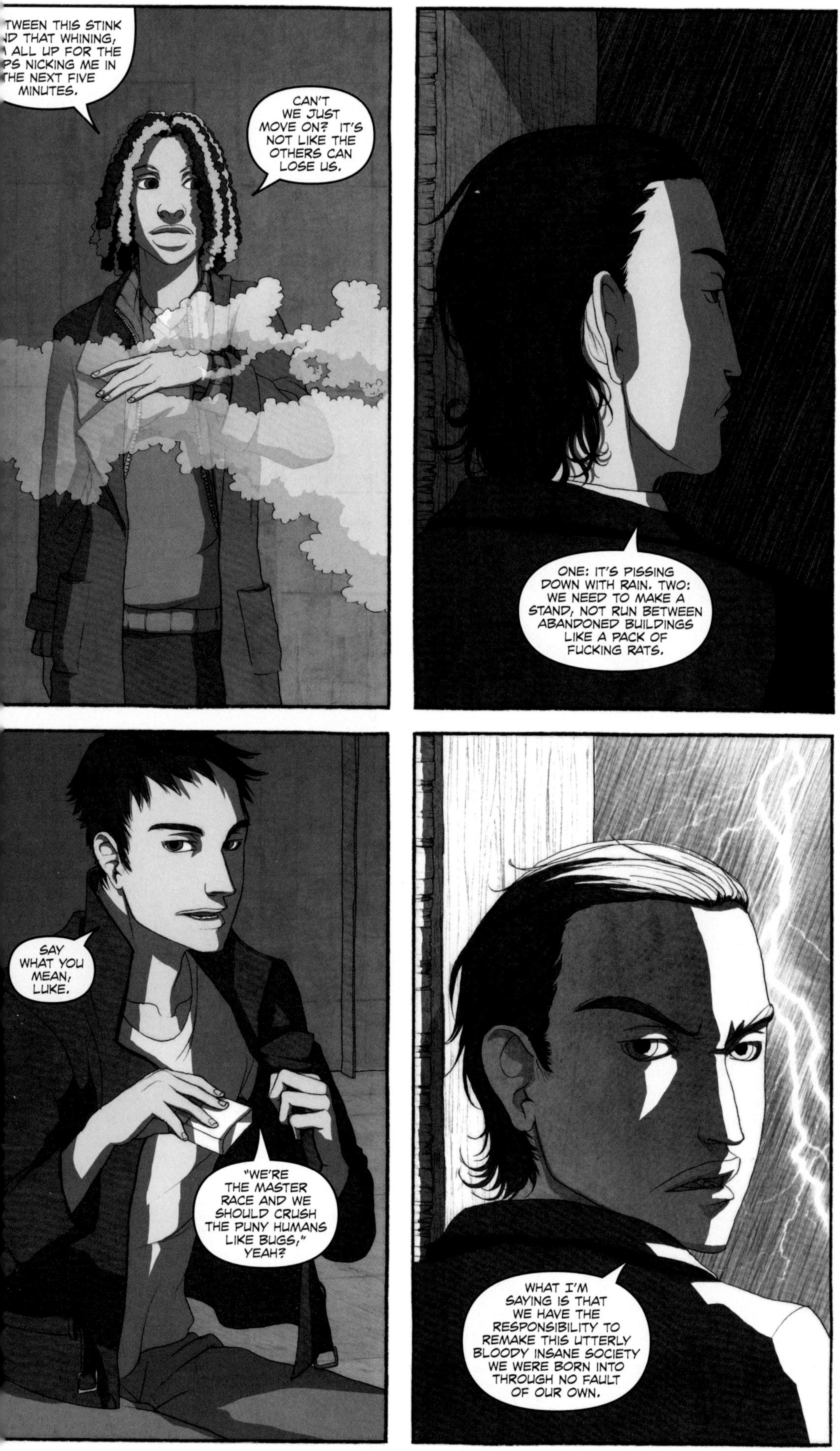
TWEEN THIS STINK ND THAT WHINING, ALL UP FOR THE PS NICKING ME IN THE NEXT FIVE MINUTES.
CAN'T WE JUST MOVE ON? IT'S NOT LIKE THE OTHERS CAN LOSE US.
ONE: IT'S PISSING DOWN WITH RAIN. TWO: WE NEED TO MAKE A STAND, NOT RUN BETWEEN ABANDONED BUILDINGS LIKE A PACK OF FUCKING RATS.
SAY WHAT YOU MEAN, LUKE.
"WE'RE THE MASTER RACE AND WE SHOULD CRUSH THE PUNY HUMANS LIKE BUGS," YEAH?
WHAT I'M SAYING IS THAT WE HAVE THE RESPONSIBILITY TO REMAKE THIS UTTERLY BLOODY INSANE SOCIETY WE WERE BORN INTO THROUGH NO FAULT OF OUR OWN.

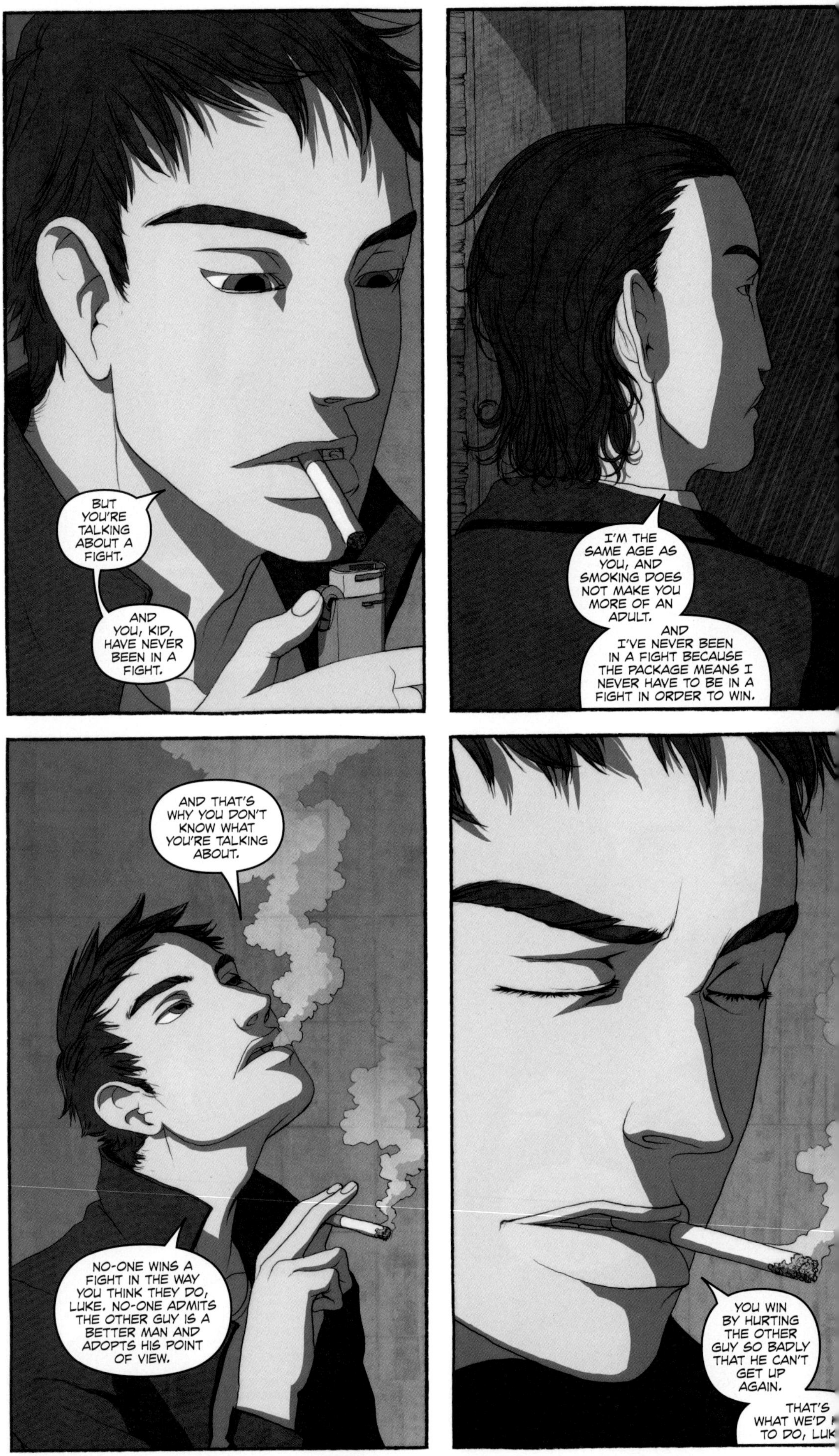
BUT YOU'RE TALKING ABOUT A FIGHT.
AND YOU, KID, HAVE NEVER BEEN IN A FIGHT.
I'M THE SAME AGE AS YOU, AND SMOKING DOES NOT MAKE YOU MORE OF AN ADULT.
AND I'VE NEVER BEEN IN A FIGHT BECAUSE THE PACKAGE MEANS I NEVER HAVE TO BE IN A FIGHT IN ORDER TO WIN.
AND THAT'S WHY YOU DON'T KNOW WHAT YOU'RE TALKING ABOUT.
NO-ONE WINS A FIGHT IN THE WAY YOU THINK THEY DO, LUKE. NO-ONE ADMITS THE OTHER GUY IS A BETTER MAN AND ADOPTS HIS POINT OF VIEW.
YOU WIN BY HURTING THE OTHER GUY SO BADLY THAT HE CAN'T GET UP AGAIN.
THAT'S WHAT WE'D
TO DO, LUK

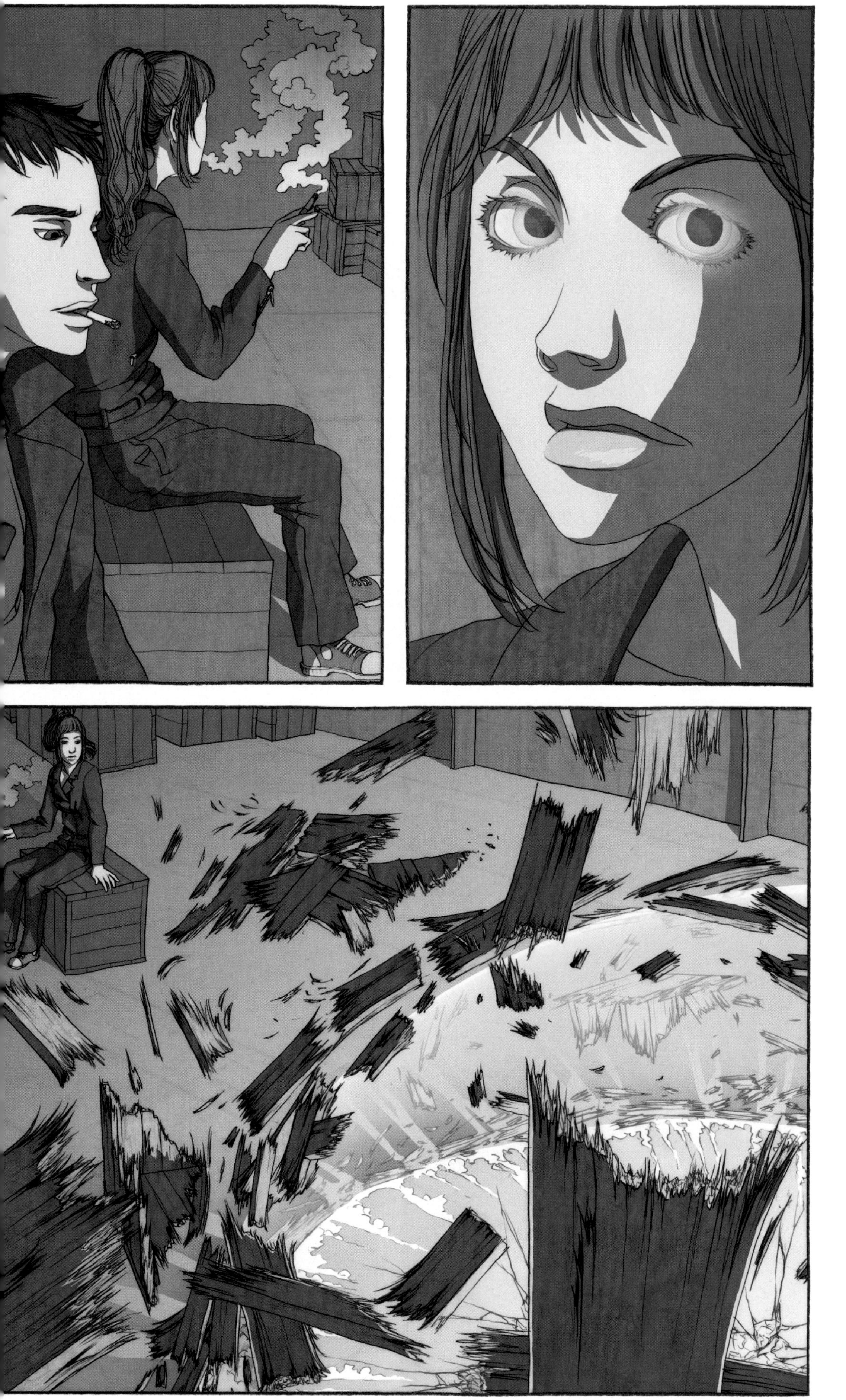

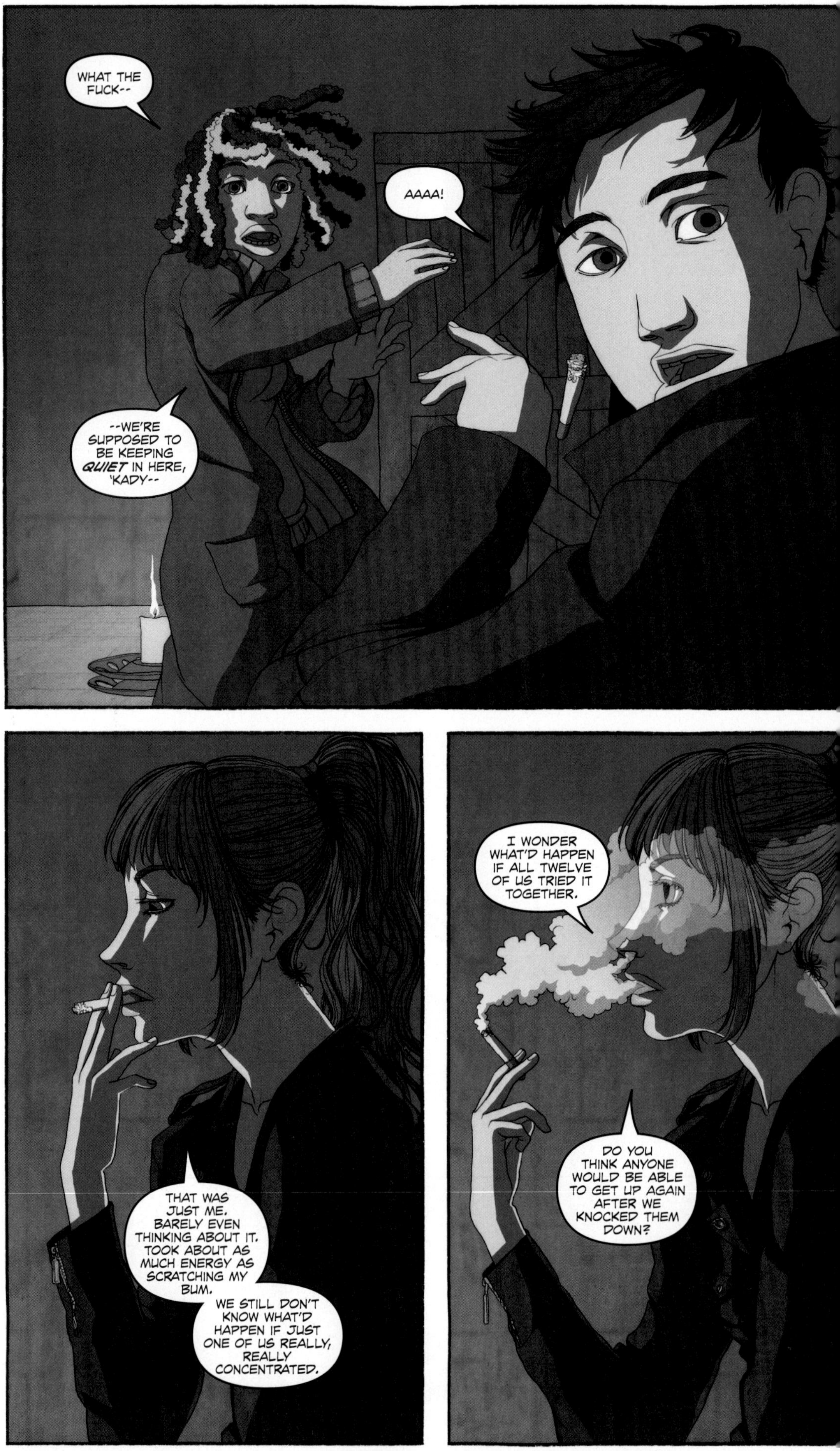
WHAT THE FUCK--
AAAA!
--WE'RE SUPPOSED TO BE KEEPING *QUIET* IN HERE, 'KADY--
THAT WAS JUST ME. BARELY EVEN THINKING ABOUT IT. TOOK ABOUT AS MUCH ENERGY AS SCRATCHING MY BUM.
WE STILL DON'T KNOW WHAT'D HAPPEN IF JUST ONE OF US REALLY, REALLY CONCENTRATED.
I WONDER WHAT'D HAPPEN IF ALL TWELVE OF US TRIED IT TOGETHER.
DO YOU THINK ANYONE WOULD BE ABLE TO GET UP AGAIN AFTER WE KNOCKED THEM DOWN?

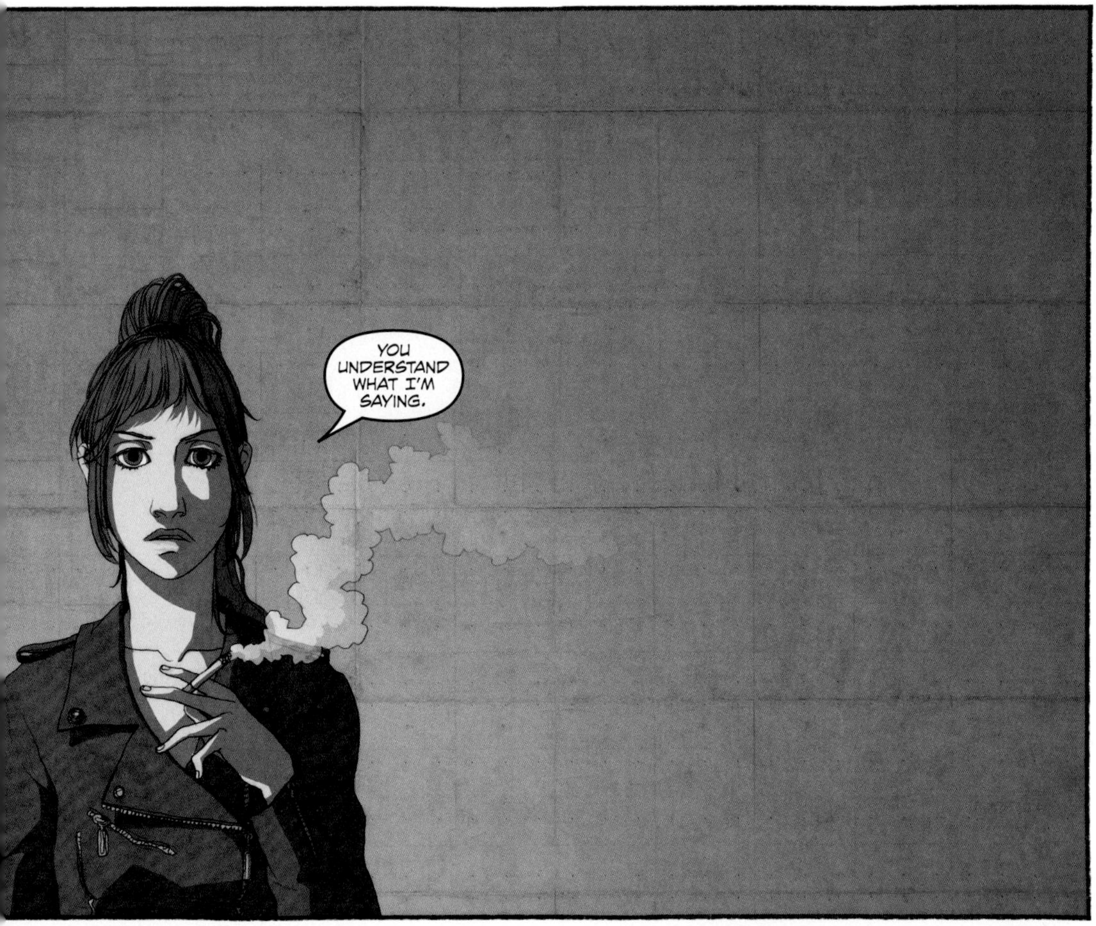
YOU UNDERSTAND WHAT I'M SAYING.

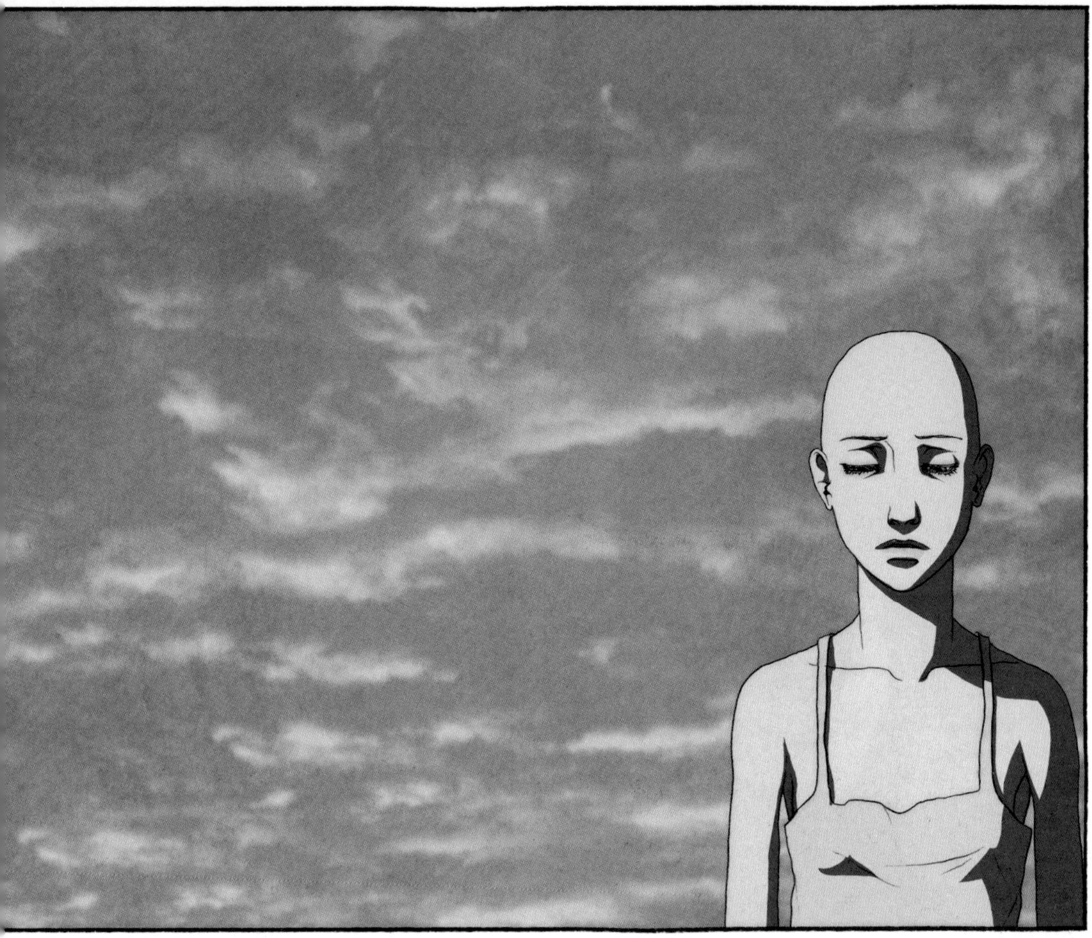

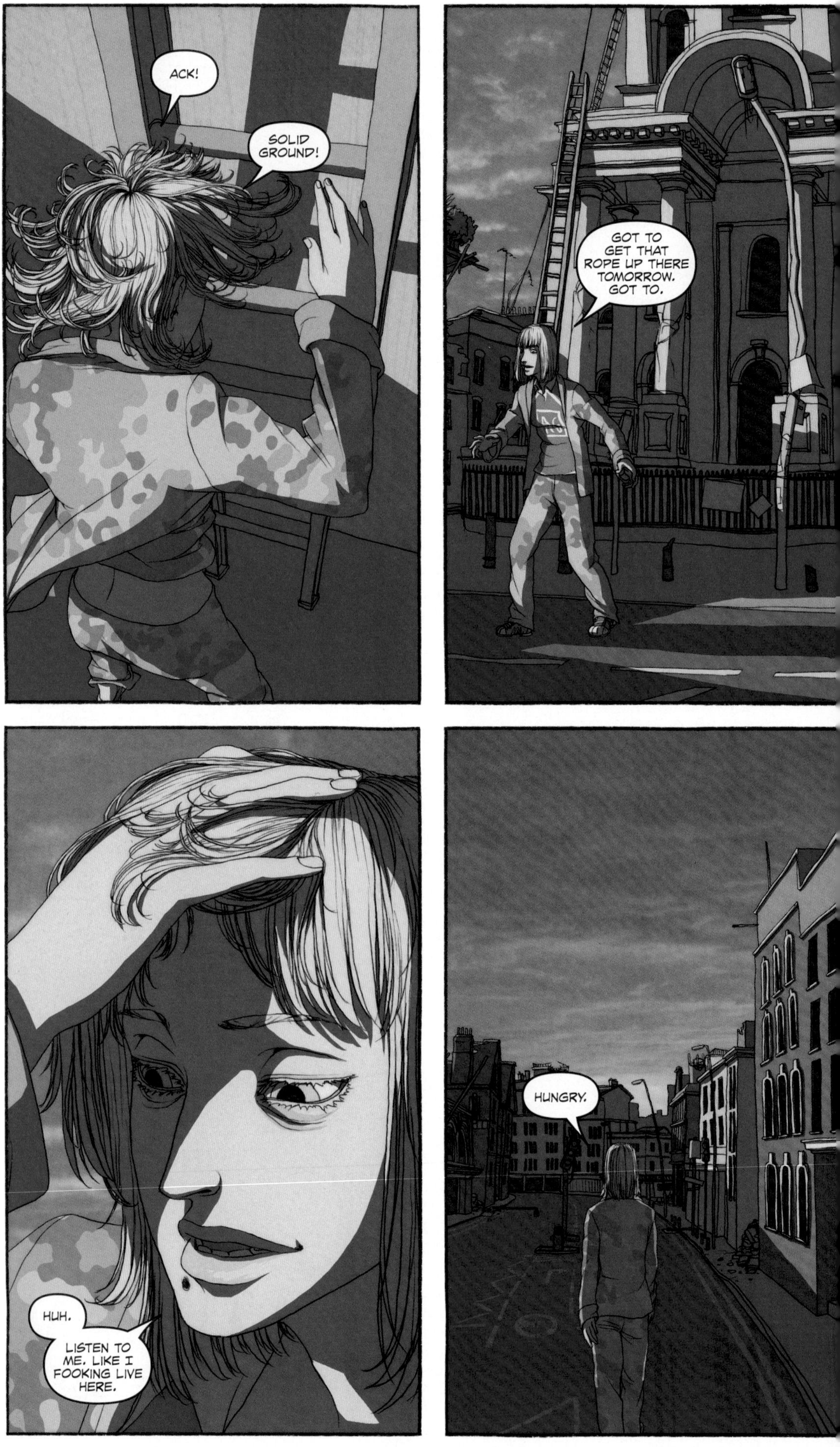
ACK!
SOLID GROUND!
GOT TO GET THAT ROPE UP THERE TOMORROW. GOT TO.
HUH.
LISTEN TO ME. LIKE I FOOKING LIVE HERE.
HUNGRY.

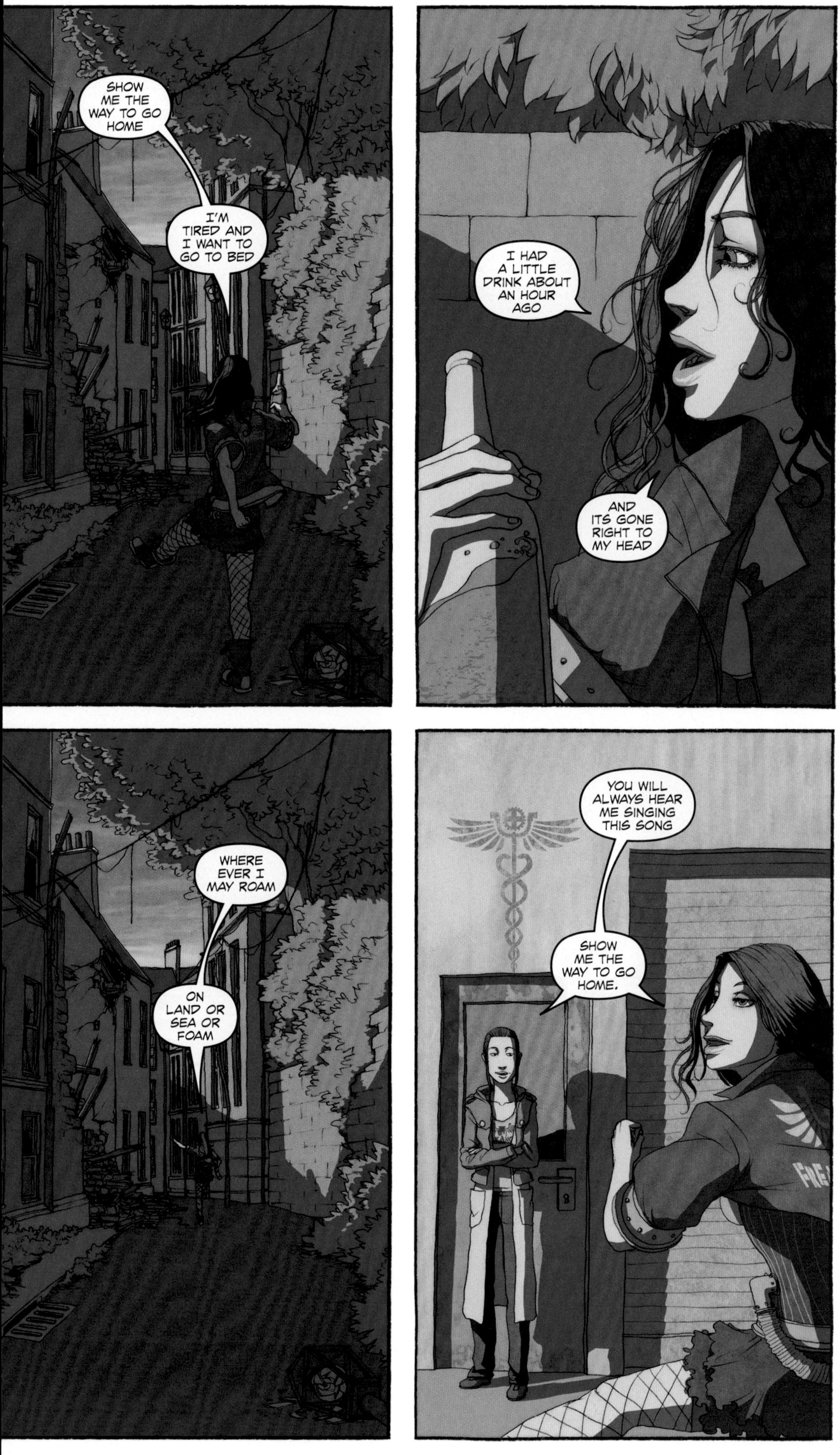
SHOW ME THE WAY TO GO HOME
I'M TIRED AND I WANT TO GO TO BED
I HAD A LITTLE DRINK ABOUT AN HOUR AGO
AND ITS GONE RIGHT TO MY HEAD
WHERE EVER I MAY ROAM
ON LAND OR SEA OR FOAM
YOU WILL ALWAYS HEAR ME SINGING THIS SONG
SHOW ME THE WAY TO GO HOME.

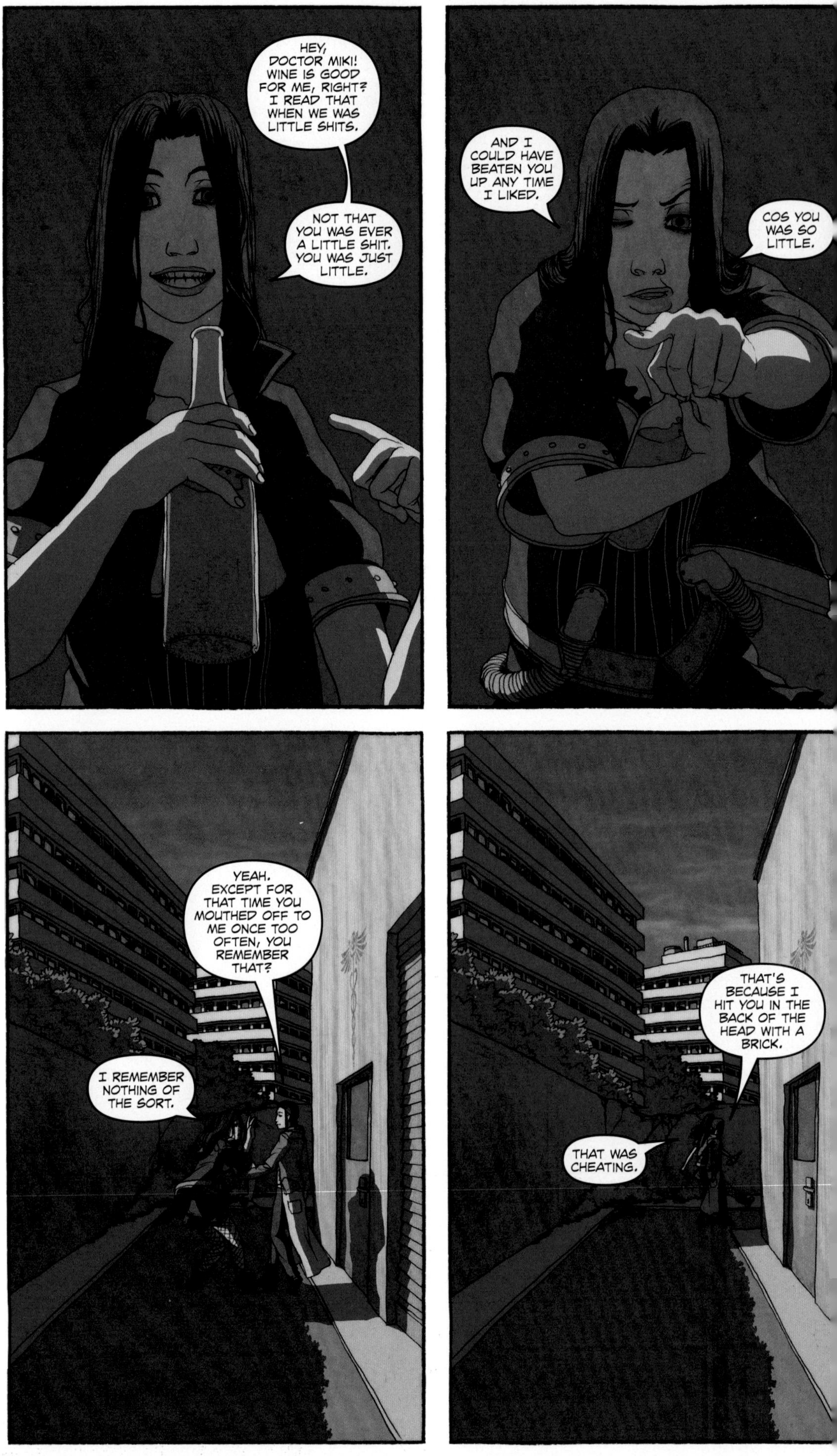
HEY, DOCTOR MIKI! WINE IS GOOD FOR ME, RIGHT? I READ THAT WHEN WE WAS LITTLE SHITS.
NOT THAT YOU WAS EVER A LITTLE SHIT. YOU WAS JUST LITTLE.
AND I COULD HAVE BEATEN YOU UP ANY TIME I LIKED.
COS YOU WAS SO LITTLE.
YEAH. EXCEPT FOR THAT TIME YOU MOUTHED OFF TO ME ONCE TOO OFTEN, YOU REMEMBER THAT?
I REMEMBER NOTHING OF THE SORT.
THAT'S BECAUSE I HIT YOU IN THE BACK OF THE HEAD WITH A BRICK.
THAT WAS CHEATING.

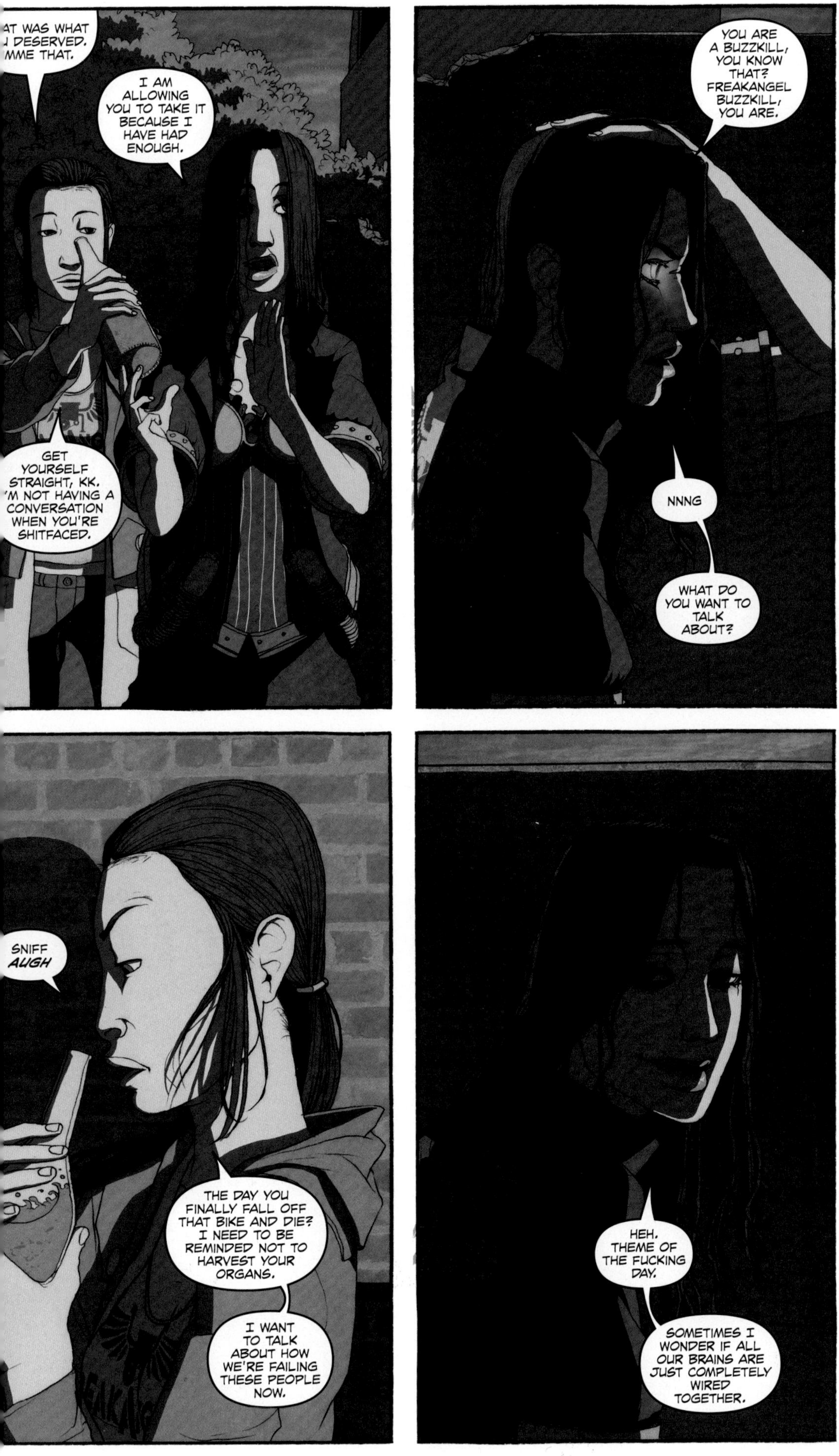
AT WAS WHAT
U DESERVED.
MME THAT.
I AM ALLOWING YOU TO TAKE IT BECAUSE I HAVE HAD ENOUGH.
GET YOURSELF STRAIGHT, KK. 'M NOT HAVING A CONVERSATION WHEN YOU'RE SHITFACED.
YOU ARE A BUZZKILL, YOU KNOW THAT? FREAKANGEL BUZZKILL, YOU ARE.
NNNG
WHAT DO YOU WANT TO TALK ABOUT?
SNIFF AUGH
THE DAY YOU FINALLY FALL OFF THAT BIKE AND DIE? I NEED TO BE REMINDED NOT TO HARVEST YOUR ORGANS.
I WANT TO TALK ABOUT HOW WE'RE FAILING THESE PEOPLE NOW.
HEH. THEME OF THE FUCKING DAY.
SOMETIMES I WONDER IF ALL OUR BRAINS ARE JUST COMPLETELY WIRED TOGETHER.

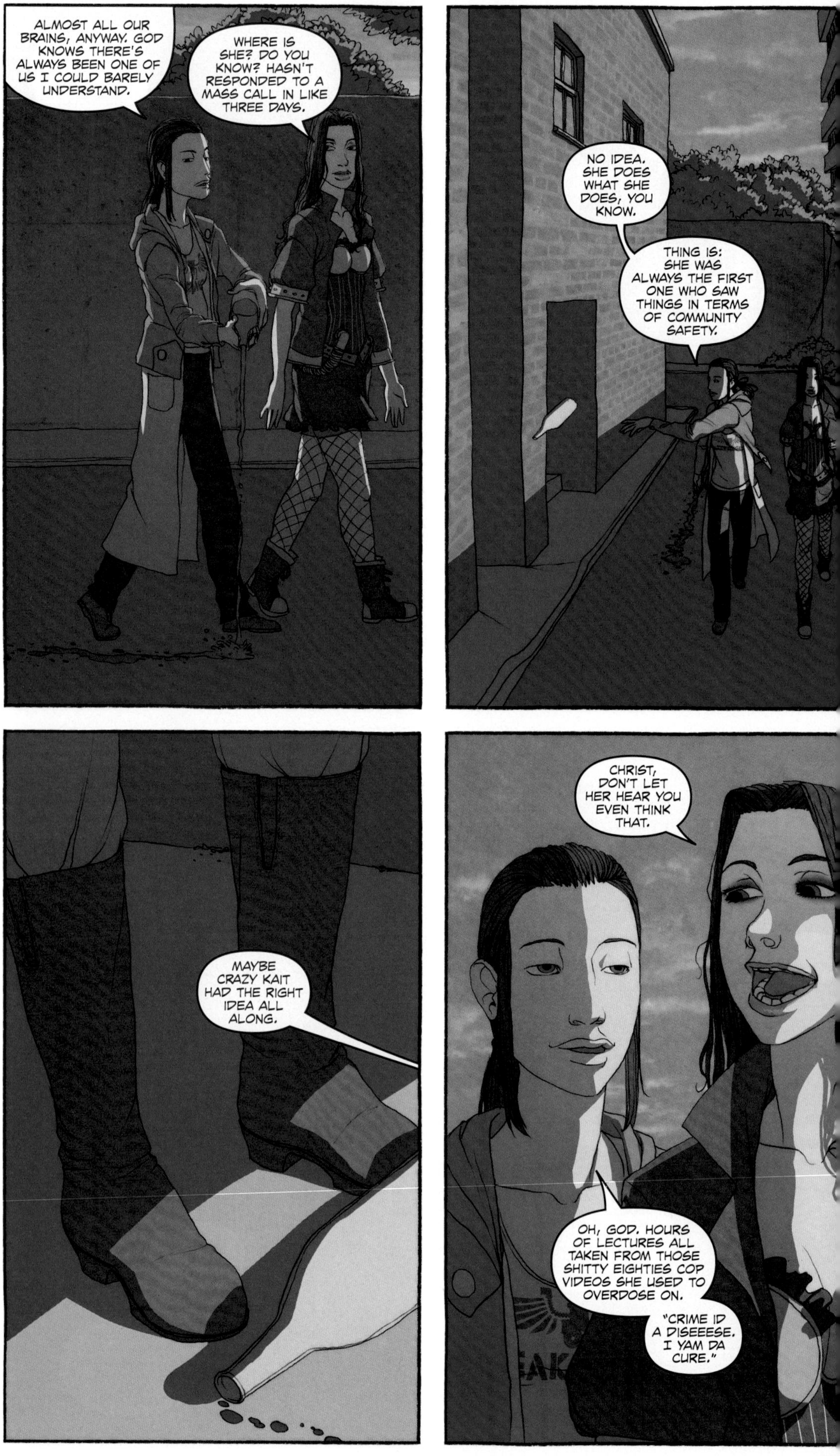
ALMOST ALL OUR BRAINS, ANYWAY. GOD KNOWS THERE'S ALWAYS BEEN ONE OF US I COULD BARELY UNDERSTAND.
WHERE IS SHE? DO YOU KNOW? HASN'T RESPONDED TO A MASS CALL IN LIKE THREE DAYS.
NO IDEA. SHE DOES WHAT SHE DOES, YOU KNOW.
THING IS: SHE WAS ALWAYS THE FIRST ONE WHO SAW THINGS IN TERMS OF COMMUNITY SAFETY.
MAYBE CRAZY KAIT HAD THE RIGHT IDEA ALL ALONG.
CHRIST, DON'T LET HER HEAR YOU EVEN THINK THAT.
OH, GOD. HOURS OF LECTURES ALL TAKEN FROM THOSE SHITTY EIGHTIES COP VIDEOS SHE USED TO OVERDOSE ON.
"CRIME ID A DISEEESE. I YAM DA CURE."

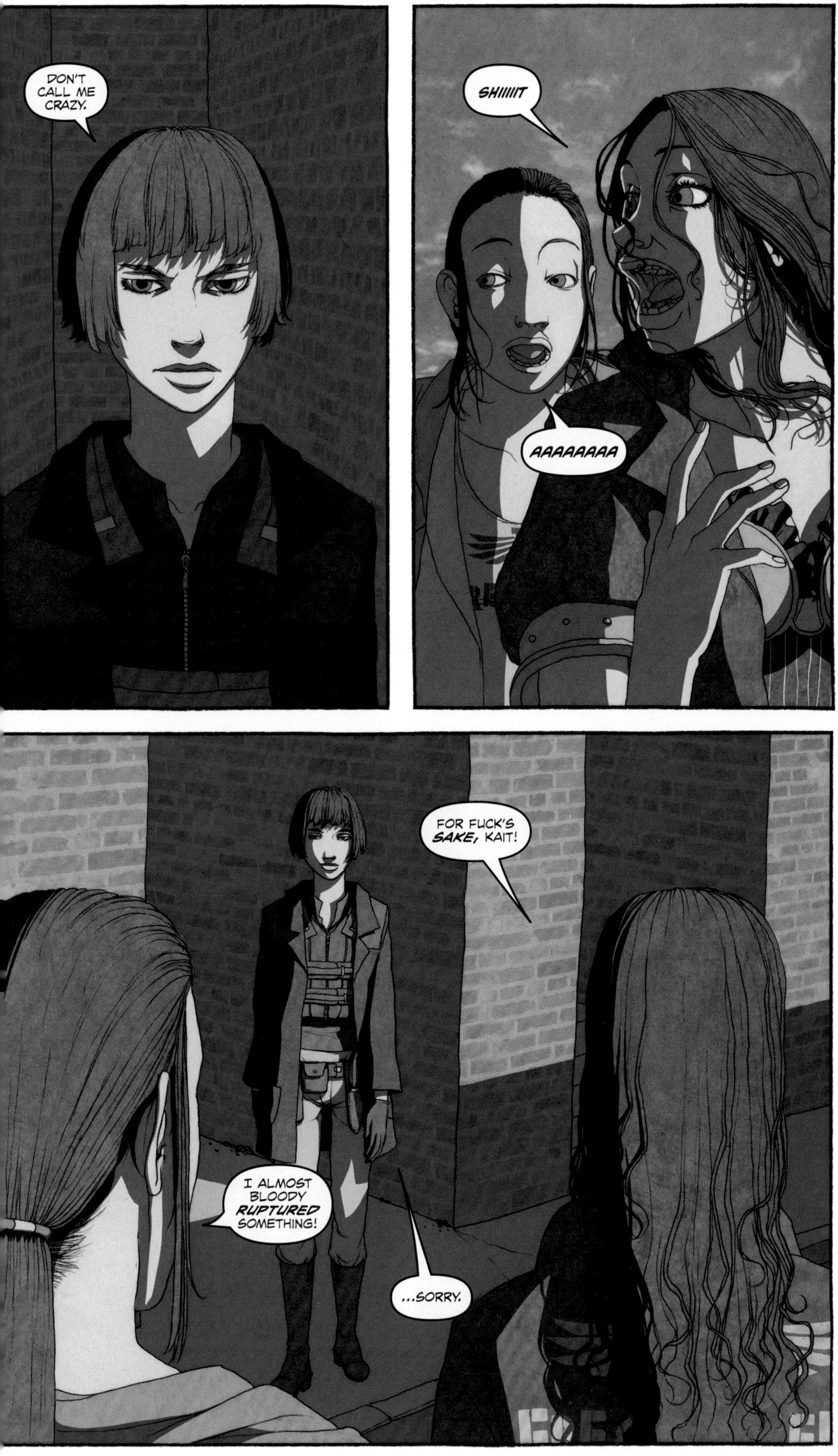
DON'T CALL ME CRAZY.
SHIIIIIT
AAAAAAAA
FOR FUCK'S SAKE, KAIT!
I ALMOST BLOODY RUPTURED SOMETHING!
...SORRY.

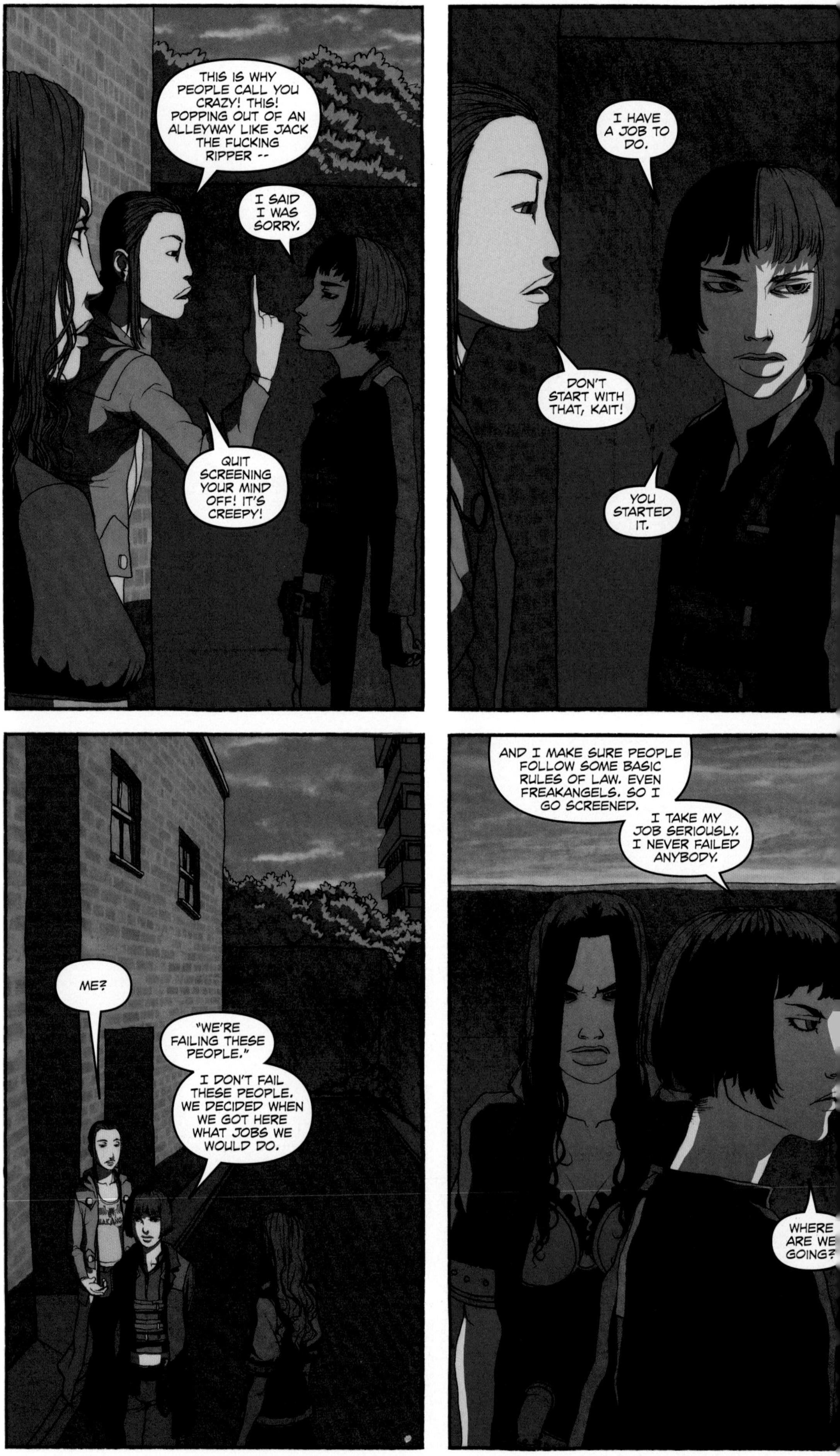
THIS IS WHY PEOPLE CALL YOU CRAZY! THIS! POPPING OUT OF AN ALLEYWAY LIKE JACK THE FUCKING RIPPER --
I SAID I WAS SORRY.
QUIT SCREENING YOUR MIND OFF! IT'S CREEPY!
I HAVE A JOB TO DO.
DON'T START WITH THAT, KAIT!
YOU STARTED IT.
ME?
"WE'RE FAILING THESE PEOPLE."
I DON'T FAIL THESE PEOPLE. WE DECIDED WHEN WE GOT HERE WHAT JOBS WE WOULD DO.
AND I MAKE SURE PEOPLE FOLLOW SOME BASIC RULES OF LAW. EVEN FREAKANGELS. SO I GO SCREENED.
I TAKE MY JOB SERIOUSLY. I NEVER FAILED ANYBODY.
WHERE ARE WE GOING?

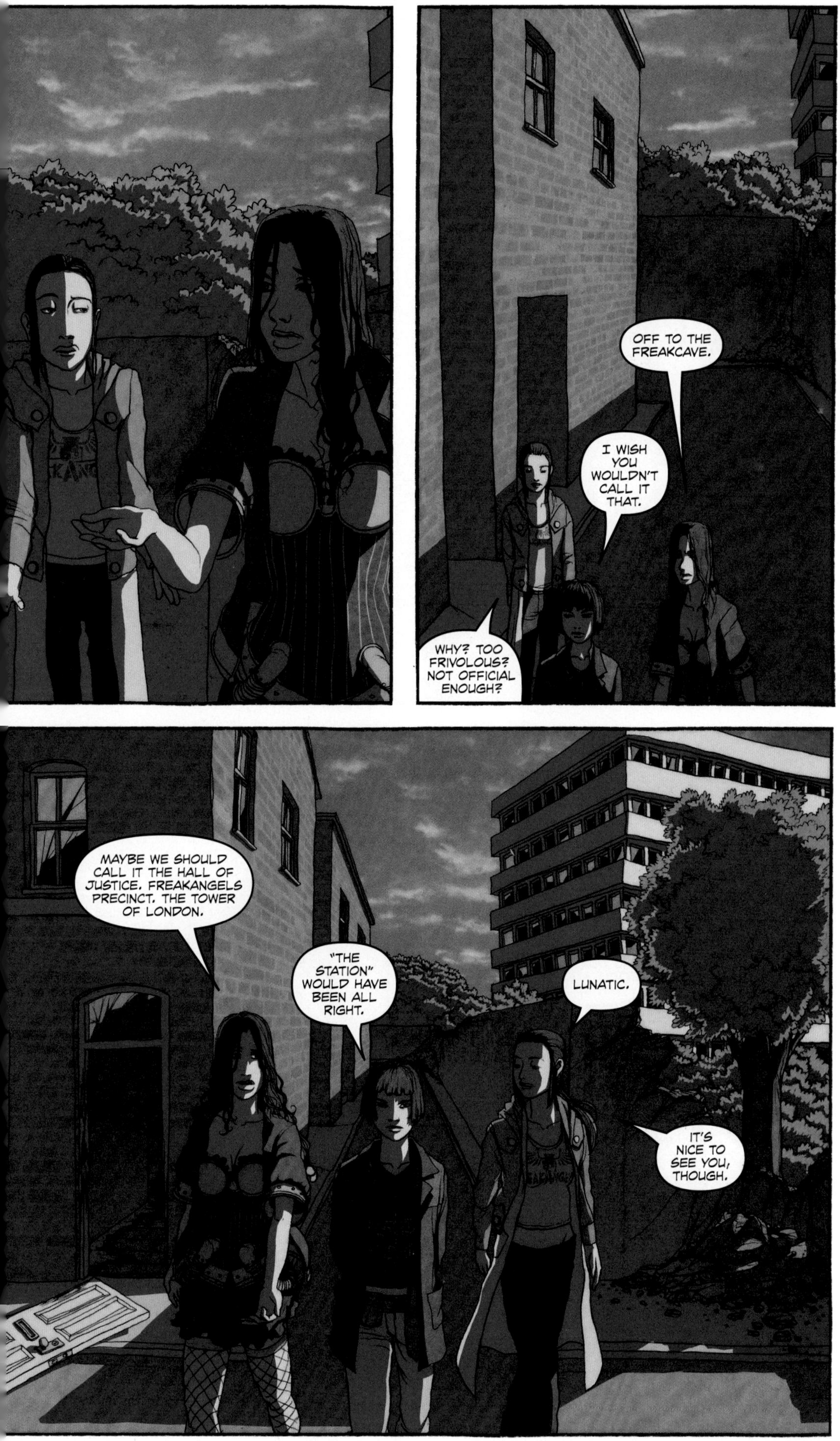
OFF TO THE FREAKCAVE.
I WISH YOU WOULDN'T CALL IT THAT.
WHY? TOO FRIVOLOUS? NOT OFFICIAL ENOUGH?
MAYBE WE SHOULD CALL IT THE HALL OF JUSTICE. FREAKANGELS PRECINCT. THE TOWER OF LONDON.
"THE STATION" WOULD HAVE BEEN ALL RIGHT.
LUNATIC.
IT'S NICE TO SEE YOU, THOUGH.

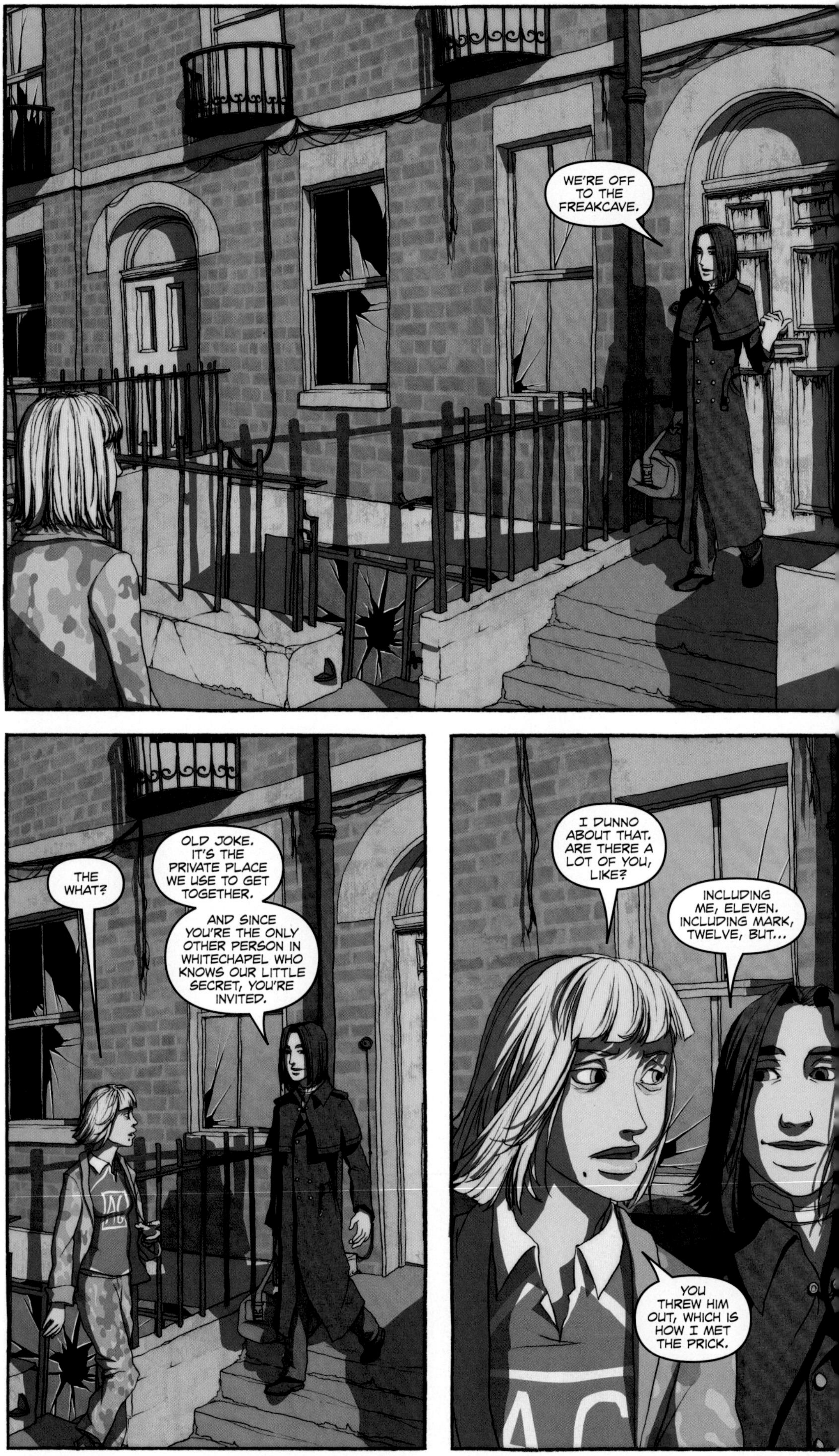
WE'RE OFF TO THE FREAKCAVE.
THE WHAT?
OLD JOKE. IT'S THE PRIVATE PLACE WE USE TO GET TOGETHER.
AND SINCE YOU'RE THE ONLY OTHER PERSON IN WHITECHAPEL WHO KNOWS OUR LITTLE SECRET, YOU'RE INVITED.
I DUNNO ABOUT THAT. ARE THERE A LOT OF YOU, LIKE?
INCLUDING ME, ELEVEN. INCLUDING MARK, TWELVE, BUT...
YOU THREW HIM OUT, WHICH IS HOW I MET THE PRICK.

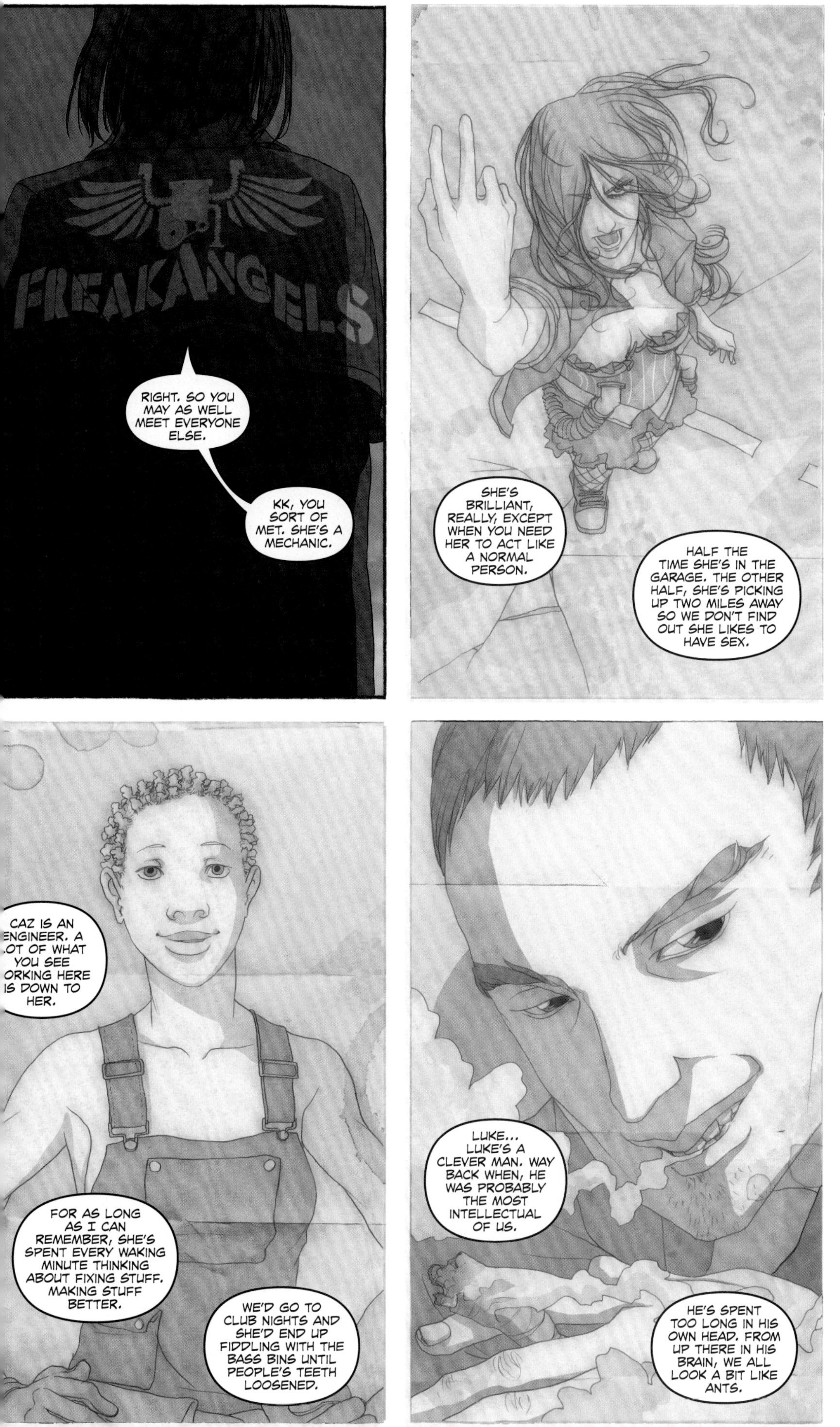
FREAKANGELS
RIGHT. SO YOU MAY AS WELL MEET EVERYONE ELSE.
KK, YOU SORT OF MET. SHE'S A MECHANIC.
SHE'S BRILLIANT, REALLY, EXCEPT WHEN YOU NEED HER TO ACT LIKE A NORMAL PERSON.
HALF THE TIME SHE'S IN THE GARAGE. THE OTHER HALF, SHE'S PICKING UP TWO MILES AWAY SO WE DON'T FIND OUT SHE LIKES TO HAVE SEX.
CAZ IS AN ENGINEER. A OT OF WHAT YOU SEE ORKING HERE IS DOWN TO HER.
FOR AS LONG AS I CAN REMEMBER, SHE'S SPENT EVERY WAKING MINUTE THINKING ABOUT FIXING STUFF. MAKING STUFF BETTER.
WE'D GO TO CLUB NIGHTS AND SHE'D END UP FIDDLING WITH THE BASS BINS UNTIL PEOPLE'S TEETH LOOSENED.
LUKE... LUKE'S A CLEVER MAN. WAY BACK WHEN, HE WAS PROBABLY THE MOST INTELLECTUAL OF US.
HE'S SPENT TOO LONG IN HIS OWN HEAD. FROM UP THERE IN HIS BRAIN, WE ALL LOOK A BIT LIKE ANTS.

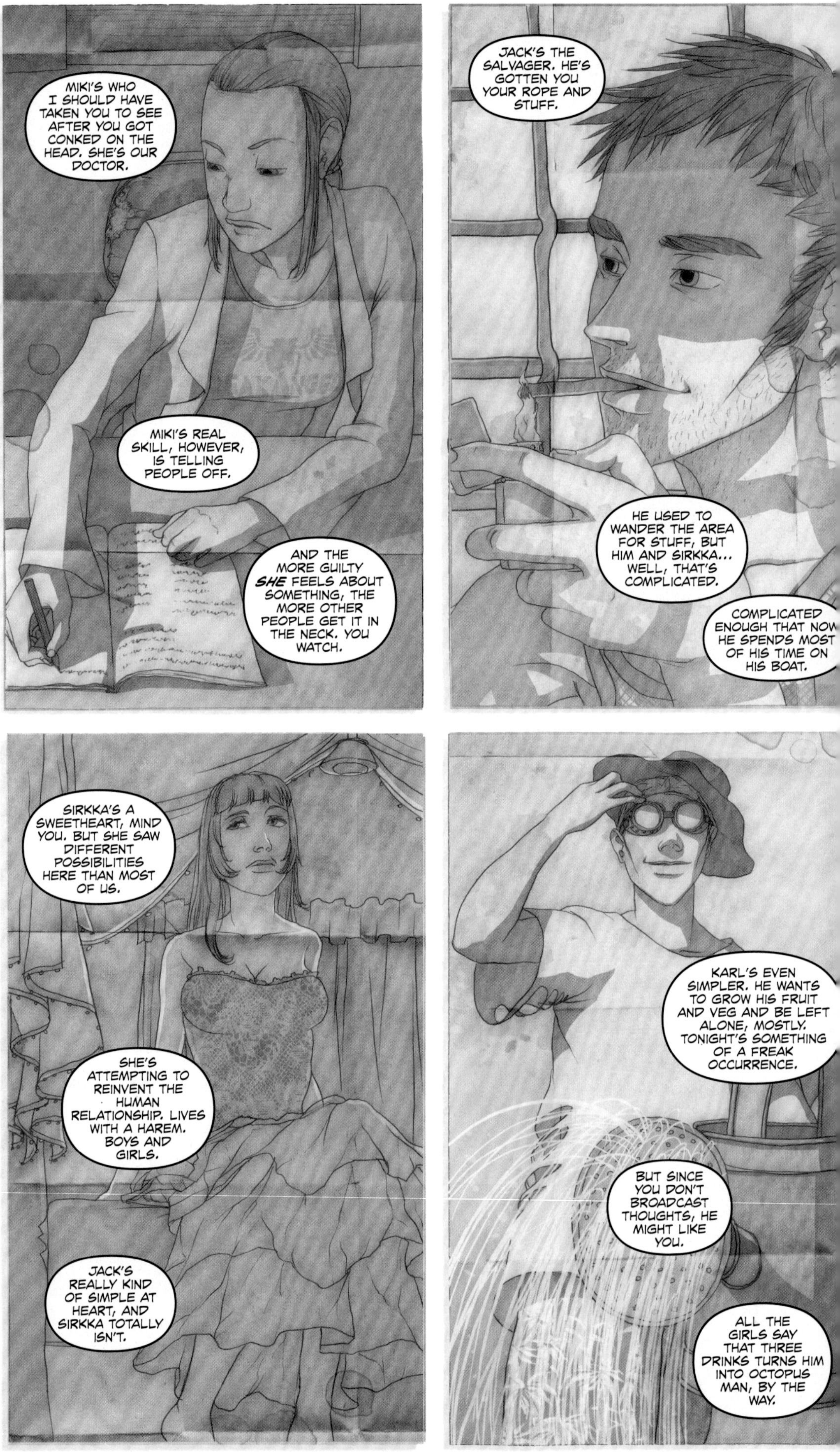
MIKI'S WHO I SHOULD HAVE TAKEN YOU TO SEE AFTER YOU GOT CONKED ON THE HEAD. SHE'S OUR DOCTOR.
MIKI'S REAL SKILL, HOWEVER, IS TELLING PEOPLE OFF.
AND THE MORE GUILTY *SHE* FEELS ABOUT SOMETHING, THE MORE OTHER PEOPLE GET IT IN THE NECK. YOU WATCH.
JACK'S THE SALVAGER. HE'S GOTTEN YOU YOUR ROPE AND STUFF.
HE USED TO WANDER THE AREA FOR STUFF, BUT HIM AND SIRKKA... WELL, THAT'S COMPLICATED.
COMPLICATED ENOUGH THAT NOW HE SPENDS MOST OF HIS TIME ON HIS BOAT.
SIRKKA'S A SWEETHEART, MIND YOU. BUT SHE SAW DIFFERENT POSSIBILITIES HERE THAN MOST OF US.
SHE'S ATTEMPTING TO REINVENT THE HUMAN RELATIONSHIP. LIVES WITH A HAREM. BOYS AND GIRLS.
JACK'S REALLY KIND OF SIMPLE AT HEART, AND SIRKKA TOTALLY ISN'T.
KARL'S EVEN SIMPLER. HE WANTS TO GROW HIS FRUIT AND VEG AND BE LEFT ALONE, MOSTLY. TONIGHT'S SOMETHING OF A FREAK OCCURRENCE.
BUT SINCE YOU DON'T BROADCAST THOUGHTS, HE MIGHT LIKE YOU.
ALL THE GIRLS SAY THAT THREE DRINKS TURNS HIM INTO OCTOPUS MAN, BY THE WAY.

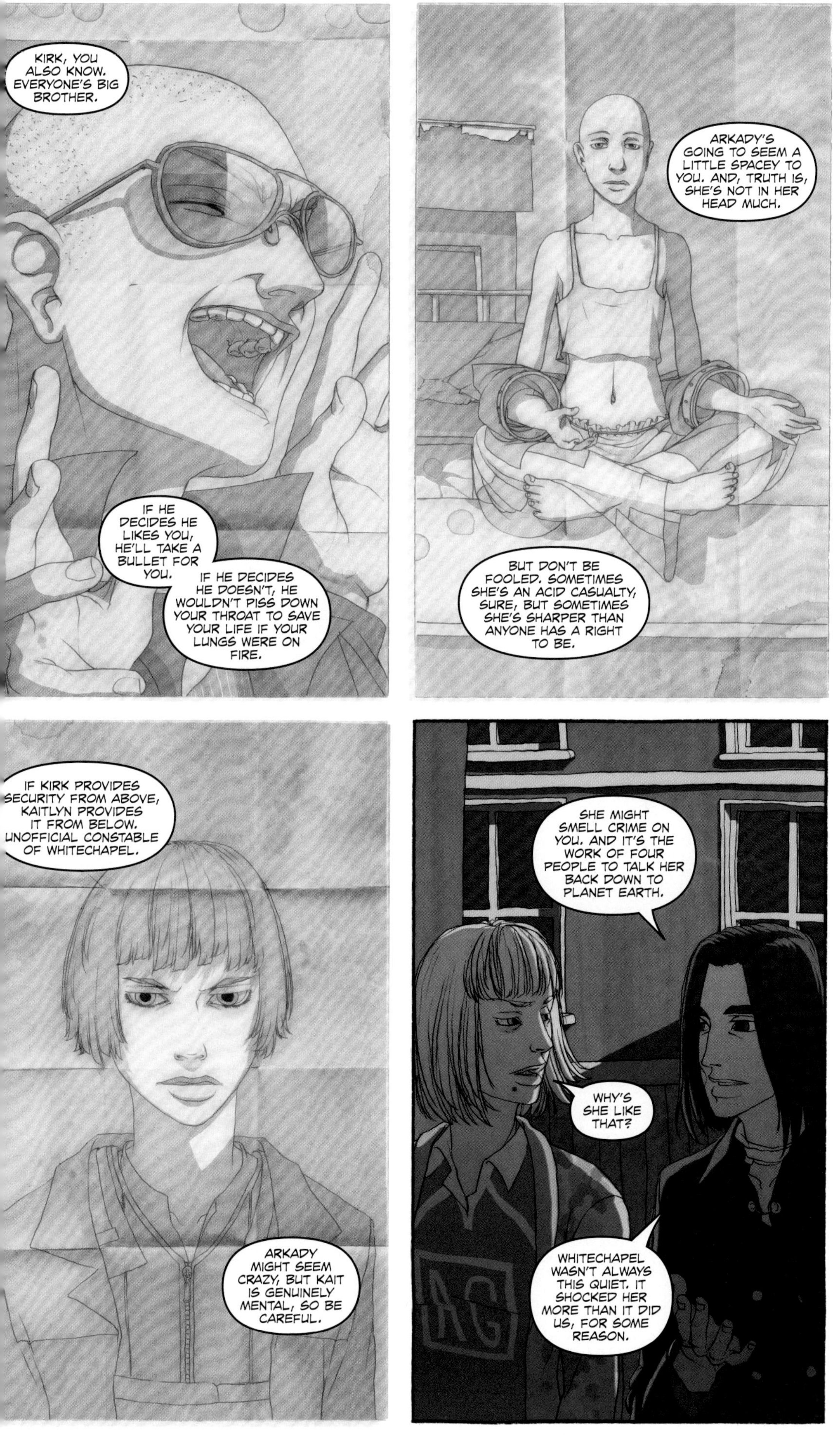
KIRK, YOU ALSO KNOW. EVERYONE'S BIG BROTHER.
IF HE DECIDES HE LIKES YOU, HE'LL TAKE A BULLET FOR YOU.
IF HE DECIDES HE DOESN'T, HE WOULDN'T PISS DOWN YOUR THROAT TO SAVE YOUR LIFE IF YOUR LUNGS WERE ON FIRE.
ARKADY'S GOING TO SEEM A LITTLE SPACEY TO YOU. AND, TRUTH IS, SHE'S NOT IN HER HEAD MUCH.
BUT DON'T BE FOOLED. SOMETIMES SHE'S AN ACID CASUALTY, SURE, BUT SOMETIMES SHE'S SHARPER THAN ANYONE HAS A RIGHT TO BE.
IF KIRK PROVIDES SECURITY FROM ABOVE, KAITLYN PROVIDES IT FROM BELOW. UNOFFICIAL CONSTABLE OF WHITECHAPEL.
ARKADY MIGHT SEEM CRAZY, BUT KAIT IS GENUINELY MENTAL, SO BE CAREFUL.
SHE MIGHT SMELL CRIME ON YOU. AND IT'S THE WORK OF FOUR PEOPLE TO TALK HER BACK DOWN TO PLANET EARTH.
WHY'S SHE LIKE THAT?
WHITECHAPEL WASN'T ALWAYS THIS QUIET. IT SHOCKED HER MORE THAN IT DID US, FOR SOME REASON.

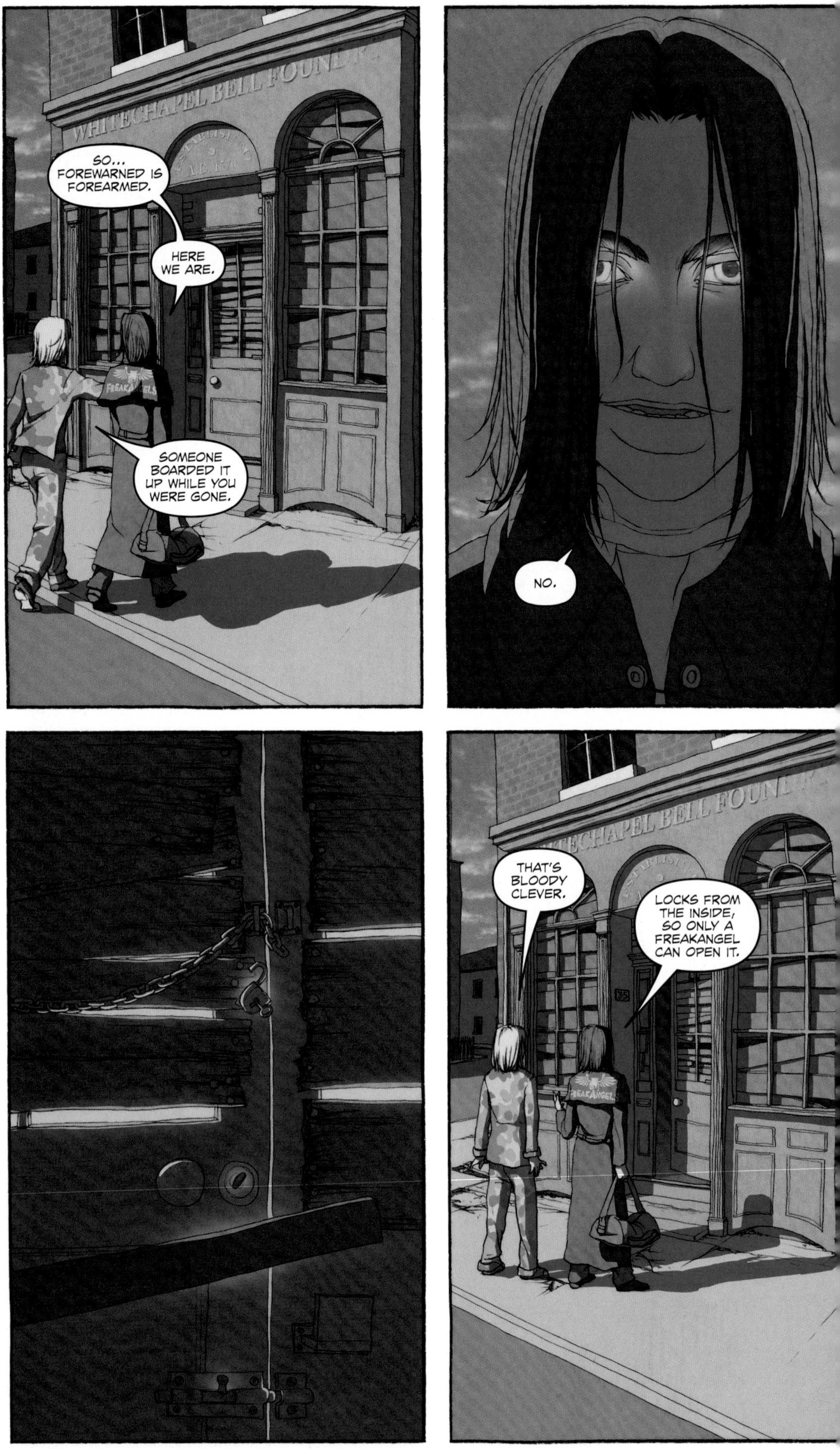
SO... FOREWARNED IS FOREARMED.
HERE WE ARE.
SOMEONE BOARDED IT UP WHILE YOU WERE GONE.
NO.
THAT'S BLOODY CLEVER.
LOCKS FROM THE INSIDE, SO ONLY A FREAKANGEL CAN OPEN IT.

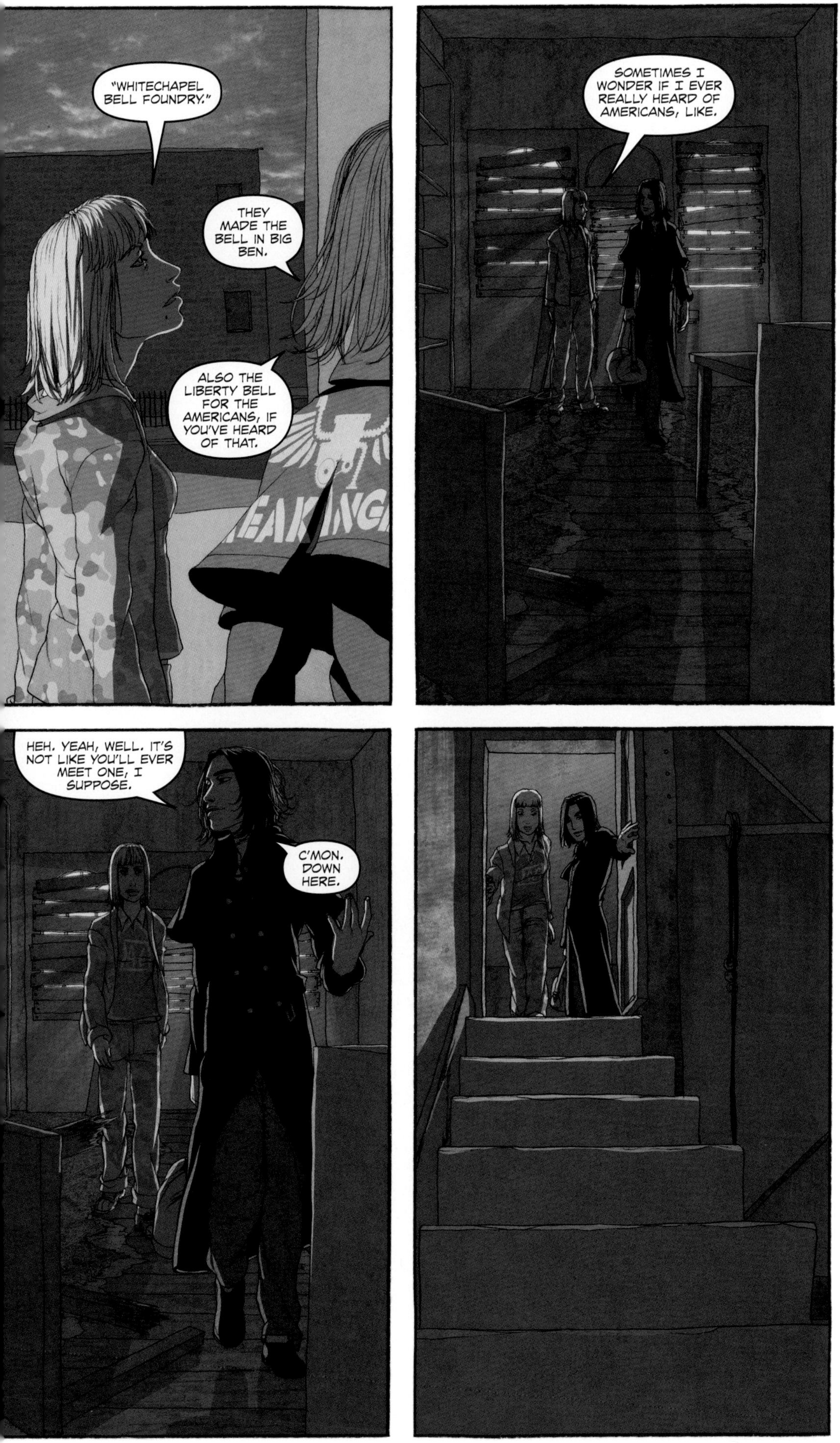
"WHITECHAPEL BELL FOUNDRY."
THEY MADE THE BELL IN BIG BEN.
ALSO THE LIBERTY BELL FOR THE AMERICANS, IF YOU'VE HEARD OF THAT.
SOMETIMES I WONDER IF I EVER REALLY HEARD OF AMERICANS, LIKE.
HEH. YEAH, WELL. IT'S NOT LIKE YOU'LL EVER MEET ONE, I SUPPOSE.
C'MON. DOWN HERE.

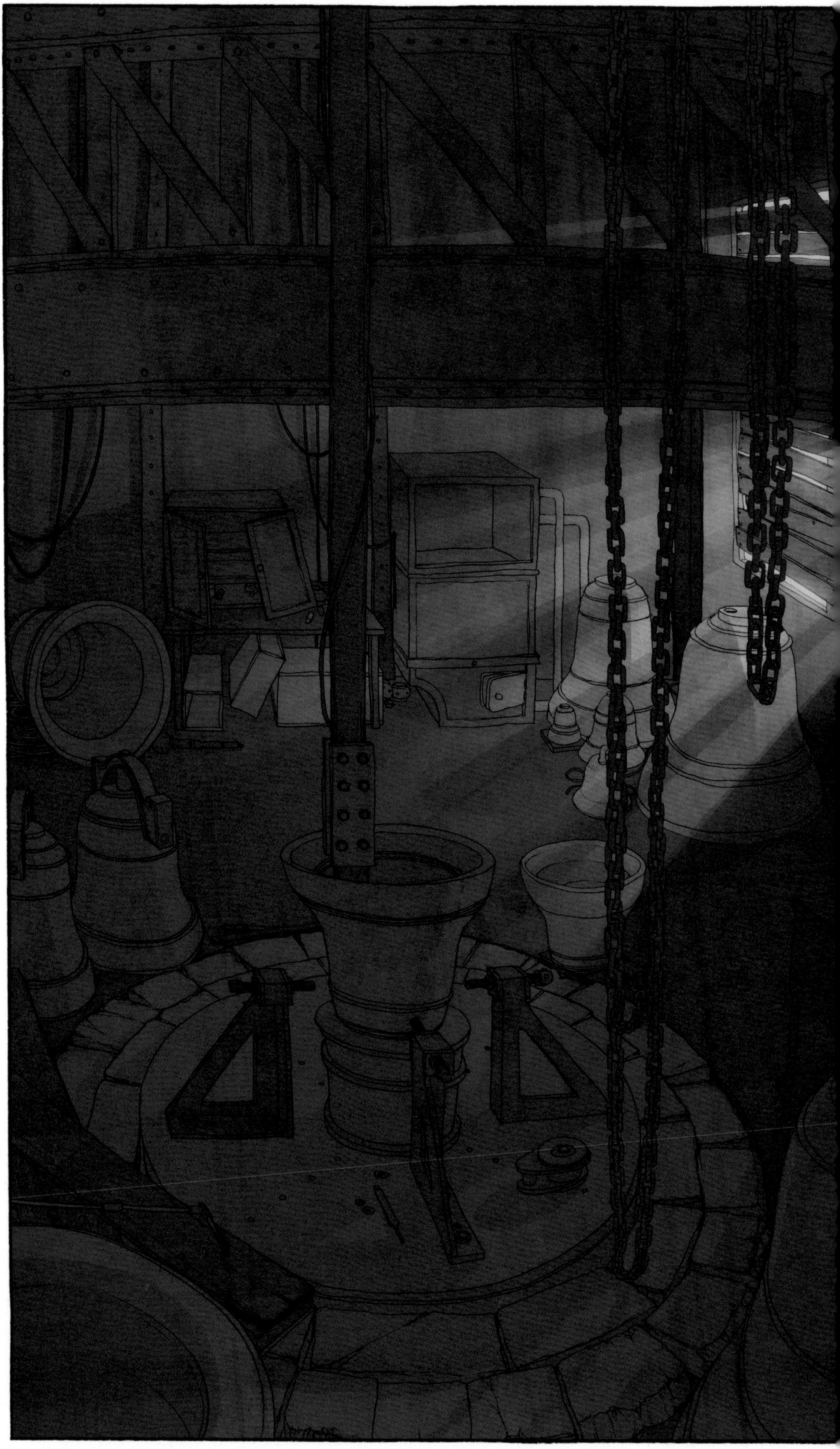

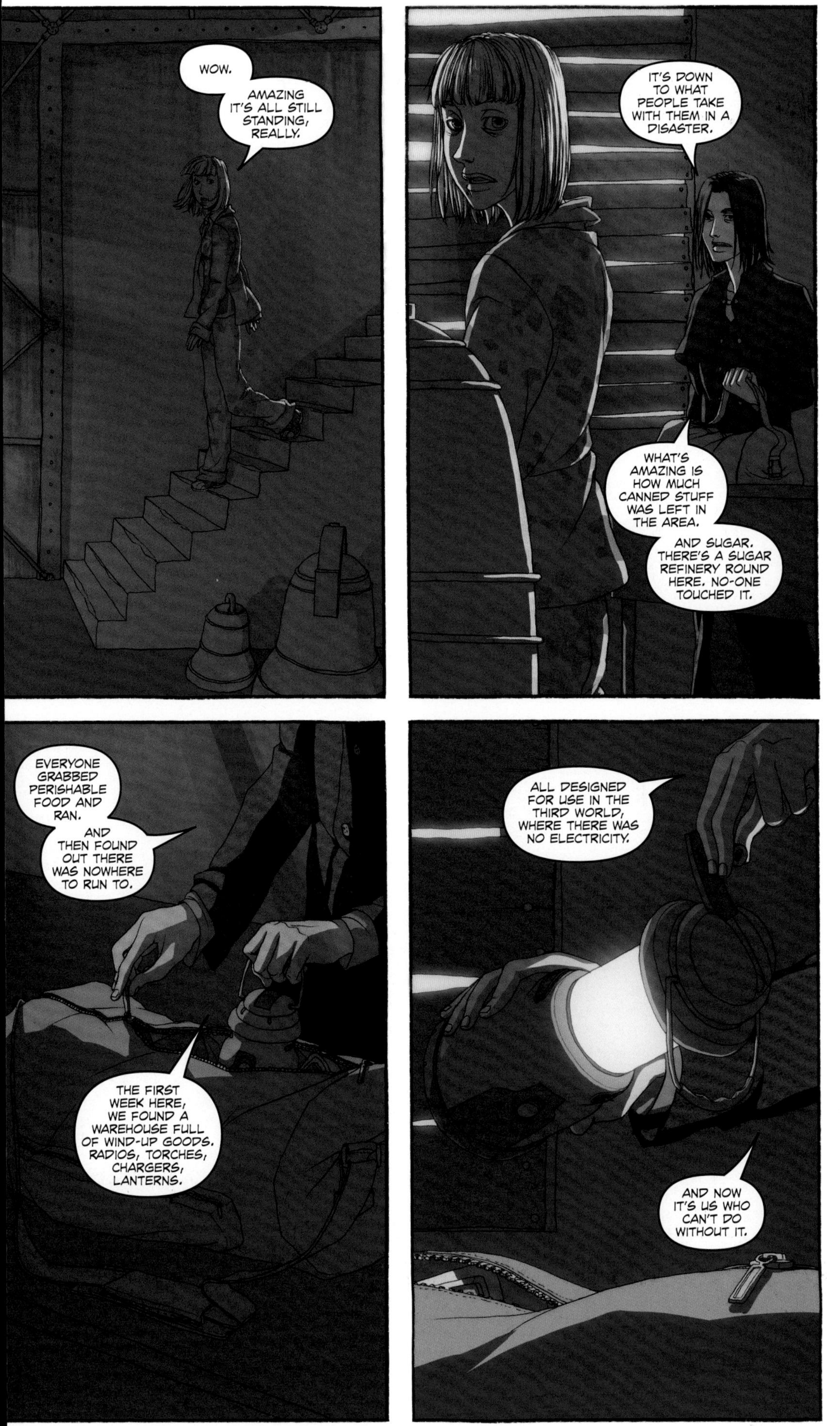
WOW.
AMAZING IT'S ALL STILL STANDING, REALLY.
IT'S DOWN TO WHAT PEOPLE TAKE WITH THEM IN A DISASTER.
WHAT'S AMAZING IS HOW MUCH CANNED STUFF WAS LEFT IN THE AREA.
AND SUGAR. THERE'S A SUGAR REFINERY ROUND HERE. NO-ONE TOUCHED IT.
EVERYONE GRABBED PERISHABLE FOOD AND RAN.
AND THEN FOUND OUT THERE WAS NOWHERE TO RUN TO.
THE FIRST WEEK HERE, WE FOUND A WAREHOUSE FULL OF WIND-UP GOODS. RADIOS, TORCHES, CHARGERS, LANTERNS.
ALL DESIGNED FOR USE IN THE THIRD WORLD, WHERE THERE WAS NO ELECTRICITY.
AND NOW IT'S US WHO CAN'T DO WITHOUT IT.

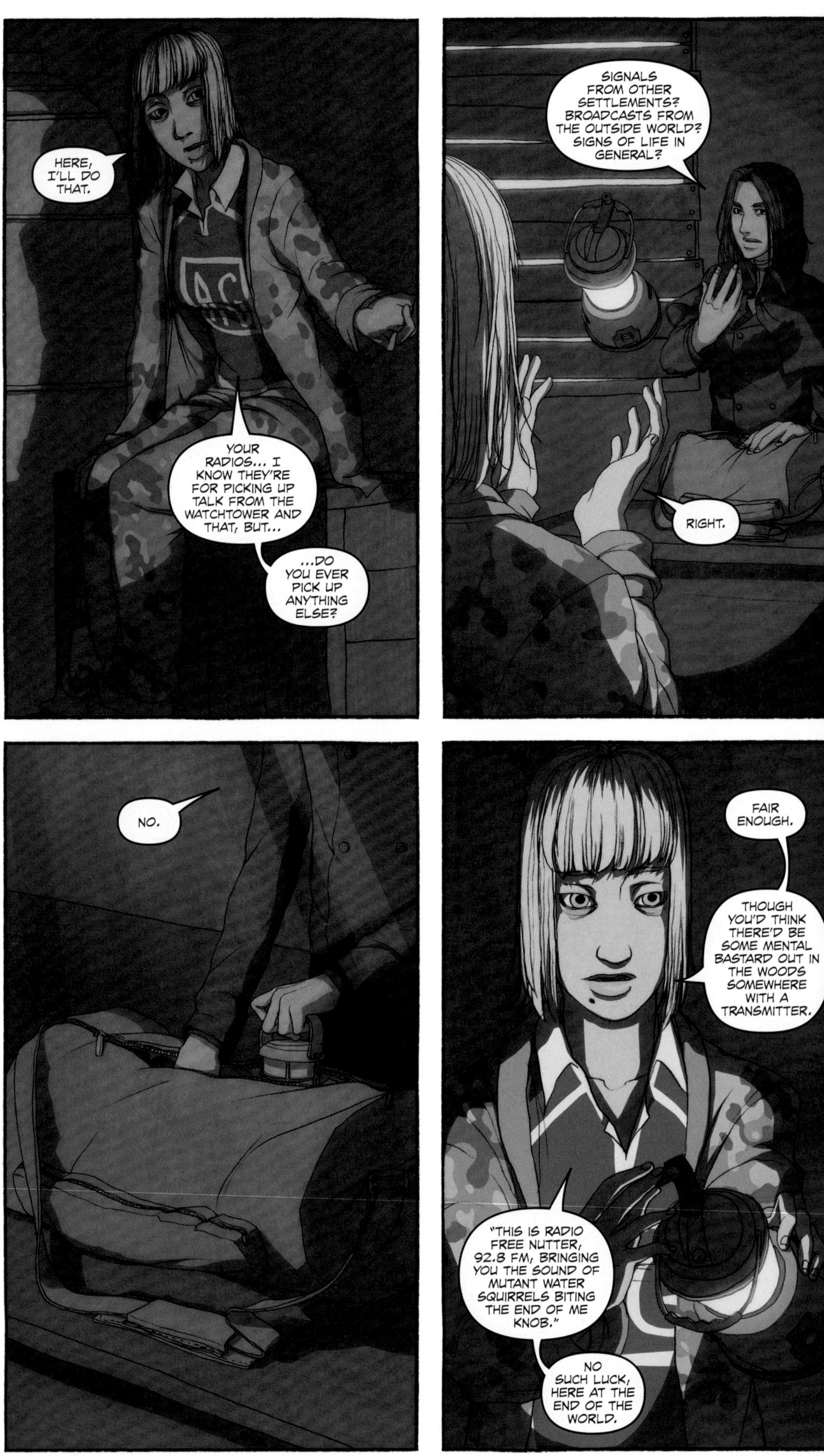

HERE, I'LL DO THAT.
YOUR RADIOS... I KNOW THEY'RE FOR PICKING UP TALK FROM THE WATCHTOWER AND THAT, BUT...
...DO YOU EVER PICK UP ANYTHING ELSE?
SIGNALS FROM OTHER SETTLEMENTS? BROADCASTS FROM THE OUTSIDE WORLD? SIGNS OF LIFE IN GENERAL?
RIGHT.
NO.
FAIR ENOUGH.
THOUGH YOU'D THINK THERE'D BE SOME MENTAL BASTARD OUT IN THE WOODS SOMEWHERE WITH A TRANSMITTER.
"THIS IS RADIO FREE NUTTER, 92.8 FM, BRINGING YOU THE SOUND OF MUTANT WATER SQUIRRELS BITING THE END OF ME KNOB."
NO SUCH LUCK, HERE AT THE END OF THE WORLD.

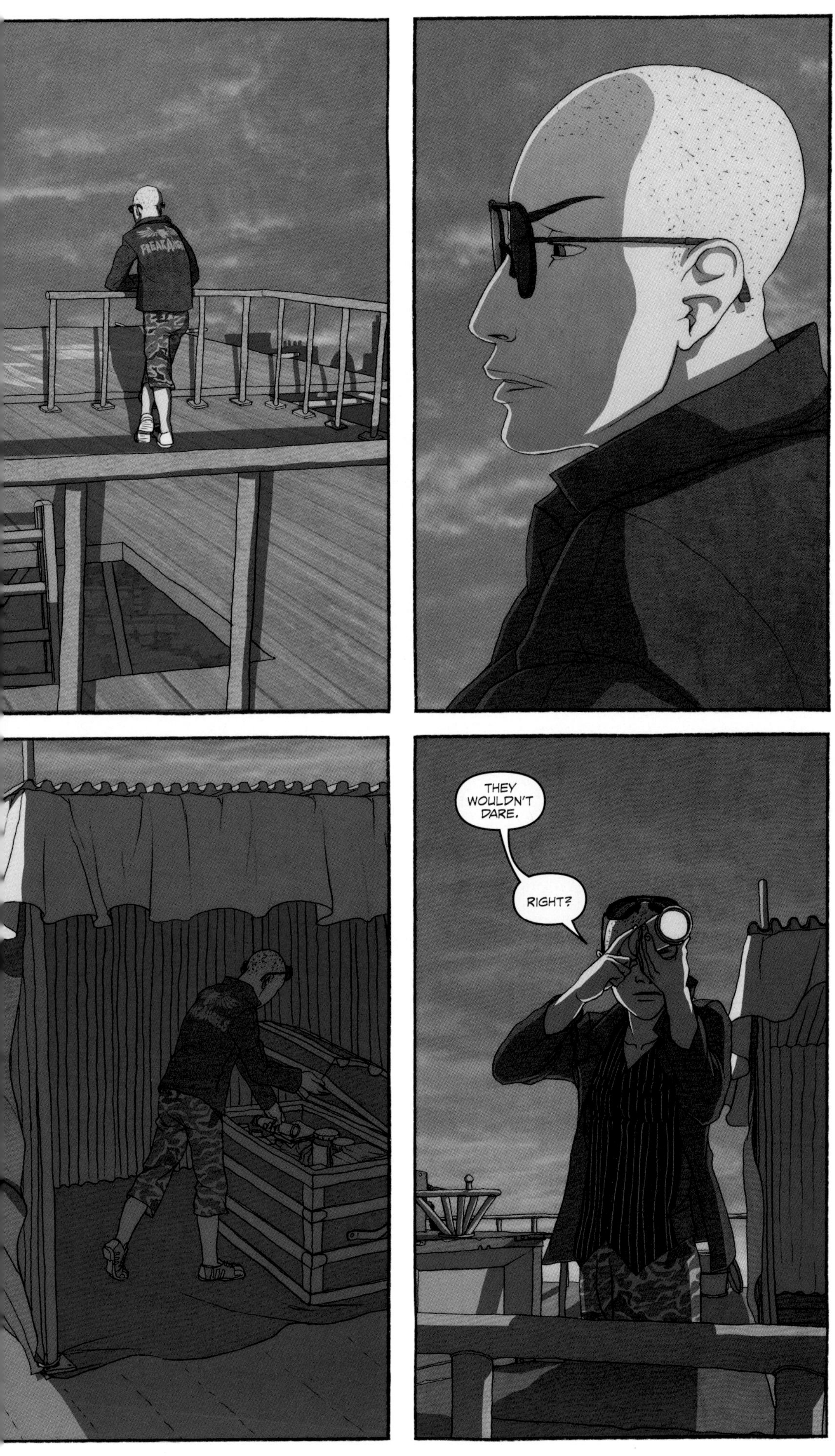
THEY WOULDN'T DARE.
RIGHT?

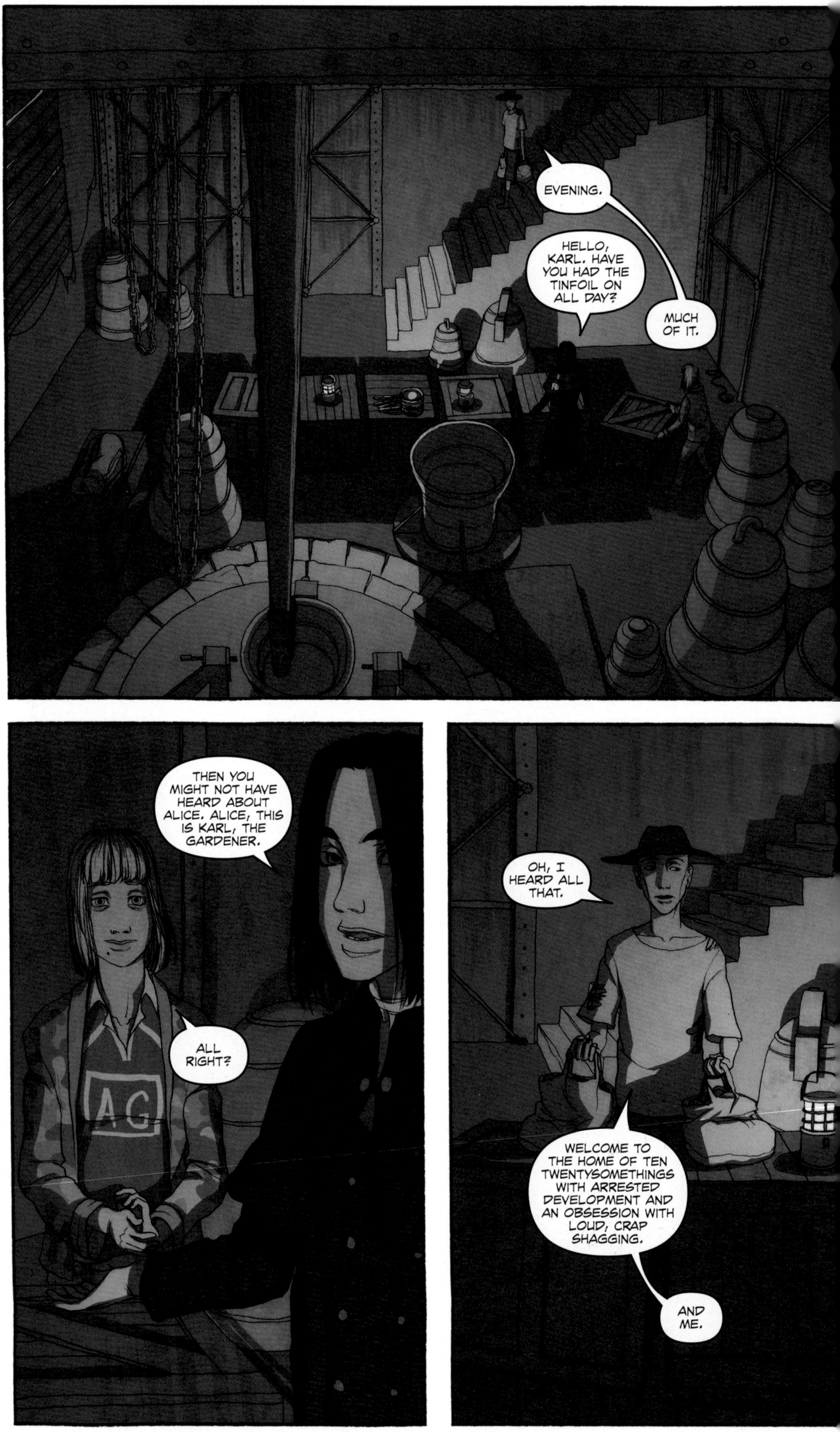
EVENING.
HELLO, KARL. HAVE YOU HAD THE TINFOIL ON ALL DAY?
MUCH OF IT.
THEN YOU MIGHT NOT HAVE HEARD ABOUT ALICE. ALICE, THIS IS KARL, THE GARDENER.
ALL RIGHT?
AG
OH, I HEARD ALL THAT.
WELCOME TO THE HOME OF TEN TWENTYSOMETHINGS WITH ARRESTED DEVELOPMENT AND AN OBSESSION WITH LOUD, CRAP SHAGGING.
AND ME.

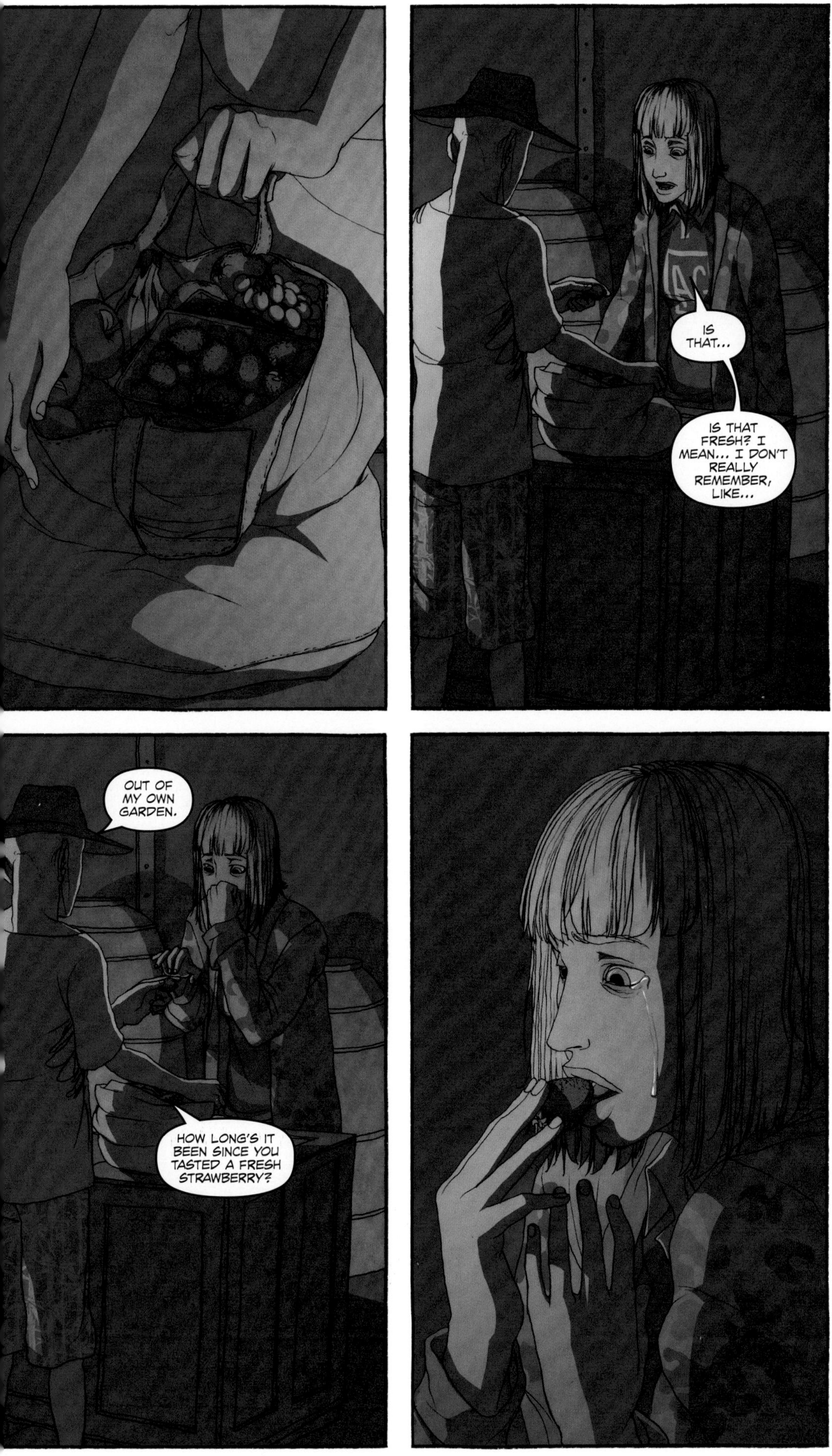
IS THAT...
IS THAT FRESH? I MEAN... I DON'T REALLY REMEMBER, LIKE...
OUT OF MY OWN GARDEN.
HOW LONG'S IT BEEN SINCE YOU TASTED A FRESH STRAWBERRY?

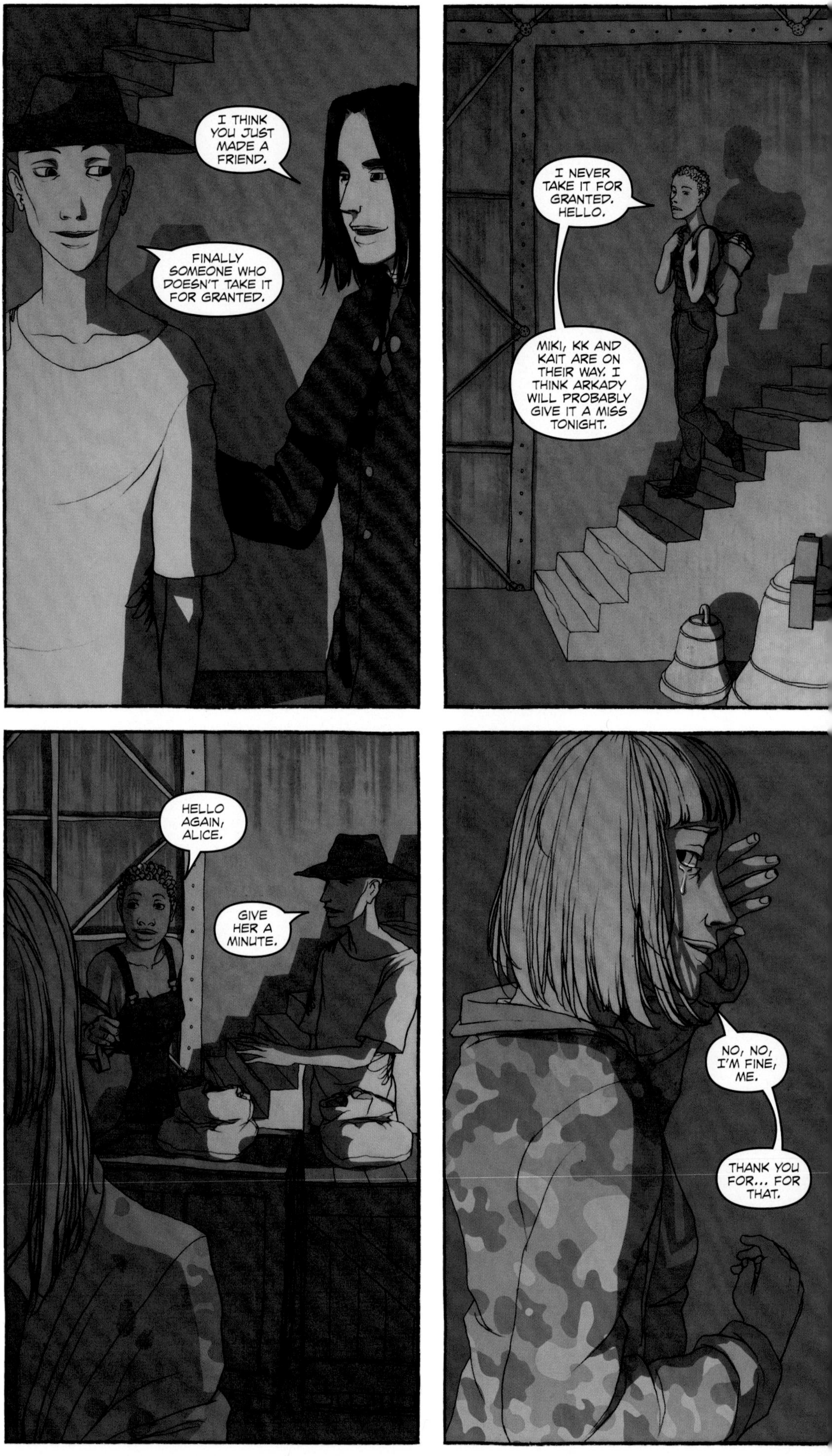
I THINK YOU JUST MADE A FRIEND.
FINALLY SOMEONE WHO DOESN'T TAKE IT FOR GRANTED.
I NEVER TAKE IT FOR GRANTED. HELLO.
MIKI, KK AND KAIT ARE ON THEIR WAY. I THINK ARKADY WILL PROBABLY GIVE IT A MISS TONIGHT.
HELLO AGAIN, ALICE.
GIVE HER A MINUTE.
NO, NO, I'M FINE, ME.
THANK YOU FOR... FOR THAT.

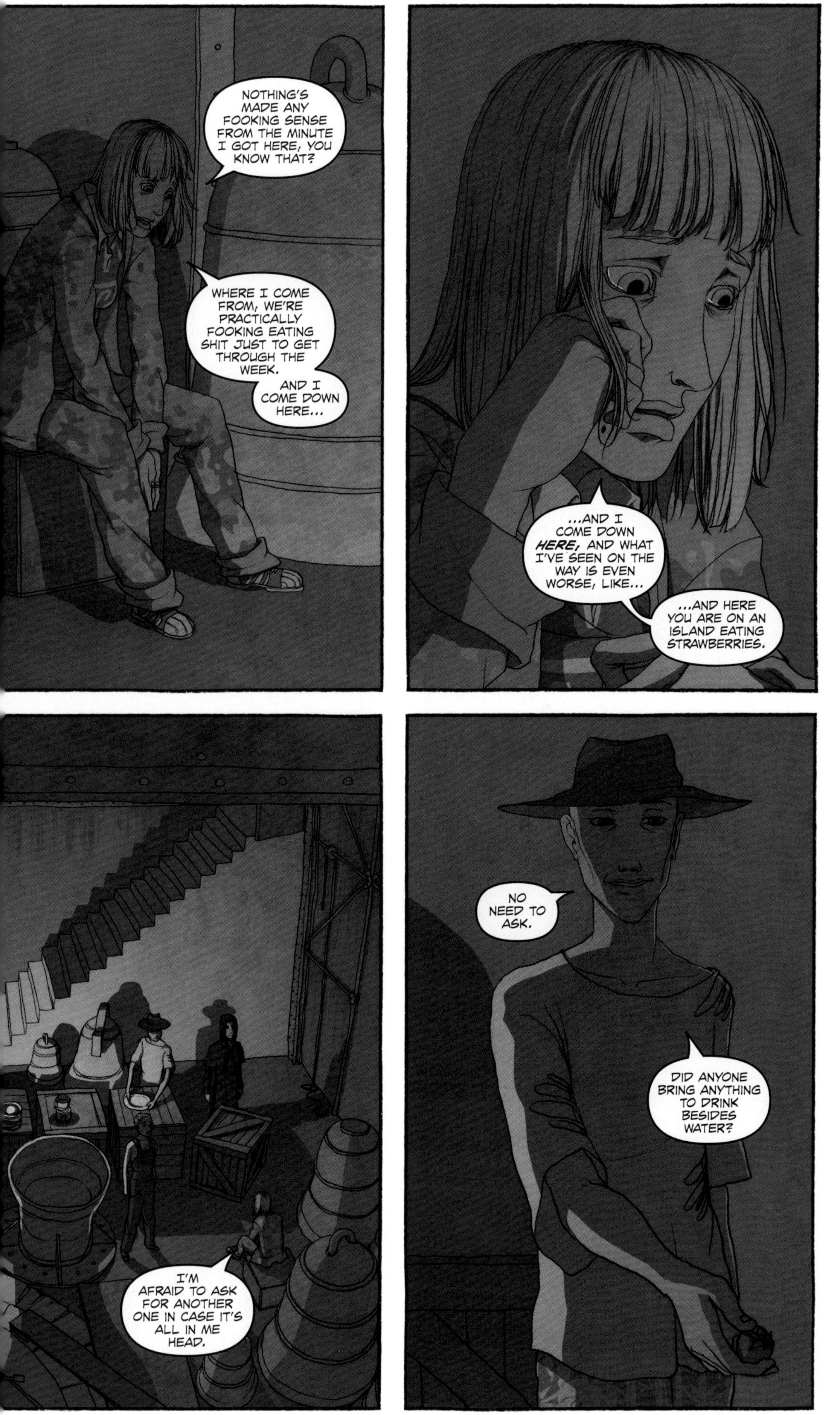
NOTHING'S MADE ANY FOOKING SENSE FROM THE MINUTE I GOT HERE, YOU KNOW THAT?
WHERE I COME FROM, WE'RE PRACTICALLY FOOKING EATING SHIT JUST TO GET THROUGH THE WEEK.
AND I COME DOWN HERE...
...AND I COME DOWN *HERE,* AND WHAT I'VE SEEN ON THE WAY IS EVEN WORSE, LIKE...
...AND HERE YOU ARE ON AN ISLAND EATING STRAWBERRIES.
I'M AFRAID TO ASK FOR ANOTHER ONE IN CASE IT'S ALL IN ME HEAD.
NO NEED TO ASK.
DID ANYONE BRING ANYTHING TO DRINK BESIDES WATER?

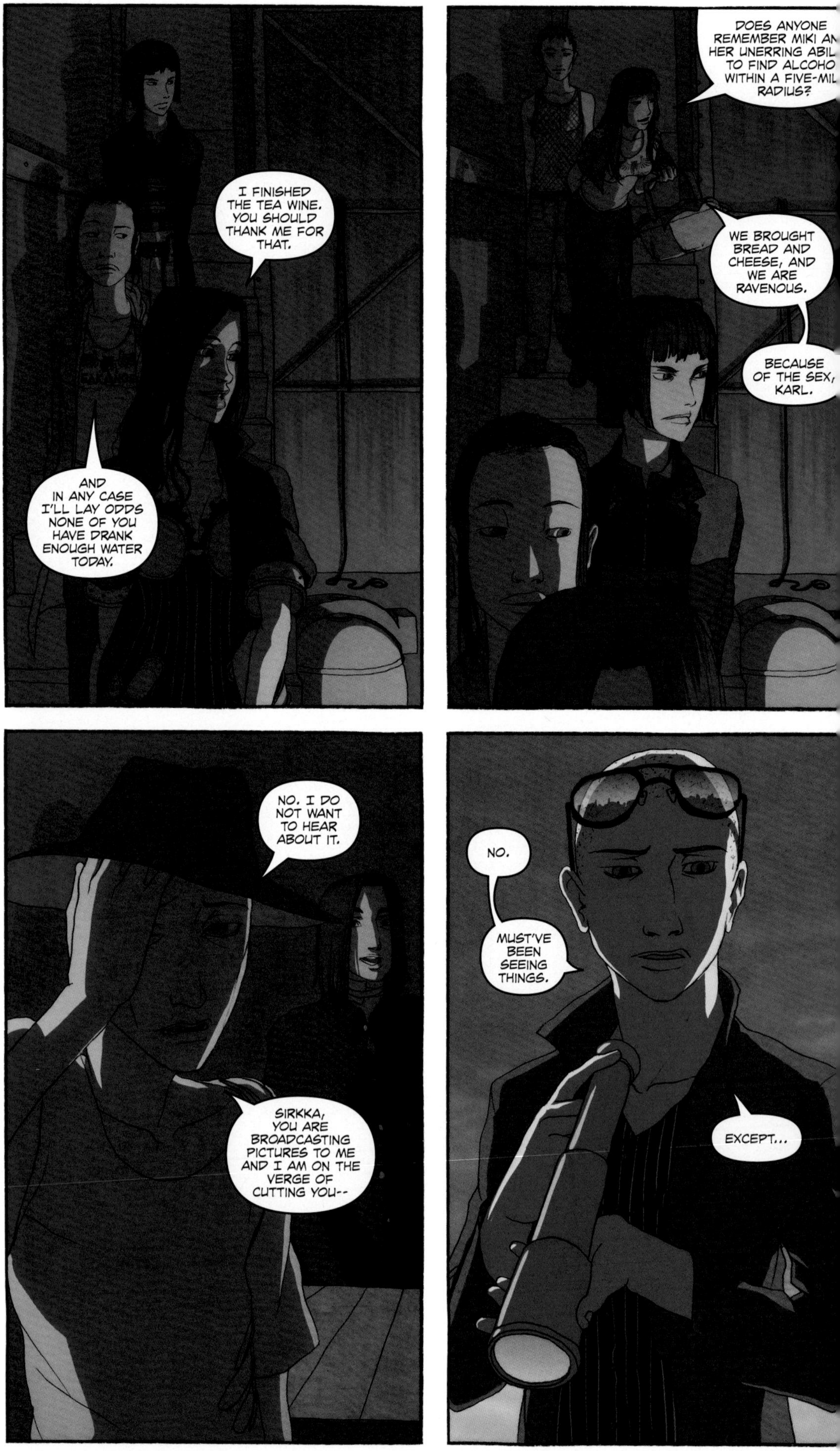
I FINISHED THE TEA WINE. YOU SHOULD THANK ME FOR THAT.
AND IN ANY CASE I'LL LAY ODDS NONE OF YOU HAVE DRANK ENOUGH WATER TODAY.
DOES ANYONE REMEMBER MIKI AN HER UNERRING ABIL TO FIND ALCOHO WITHIN A FIVE-MIL RADIUS?
WE BROUGHT BREAD AND CHEESE, AND WE ARE RAVENOUS.
BECAUSE OF THE SEX, KARL.
NO. I DO NOT WANT TO HEAR ABOUT IT.
SIRKKA, YOU ARE BROADCASTING PICTURES TO ME AND I AM ON THE VERGE OF CUTTING YOU--
NO.
MUST'VE BEEN SEEING THINGS.
EXCEPT...

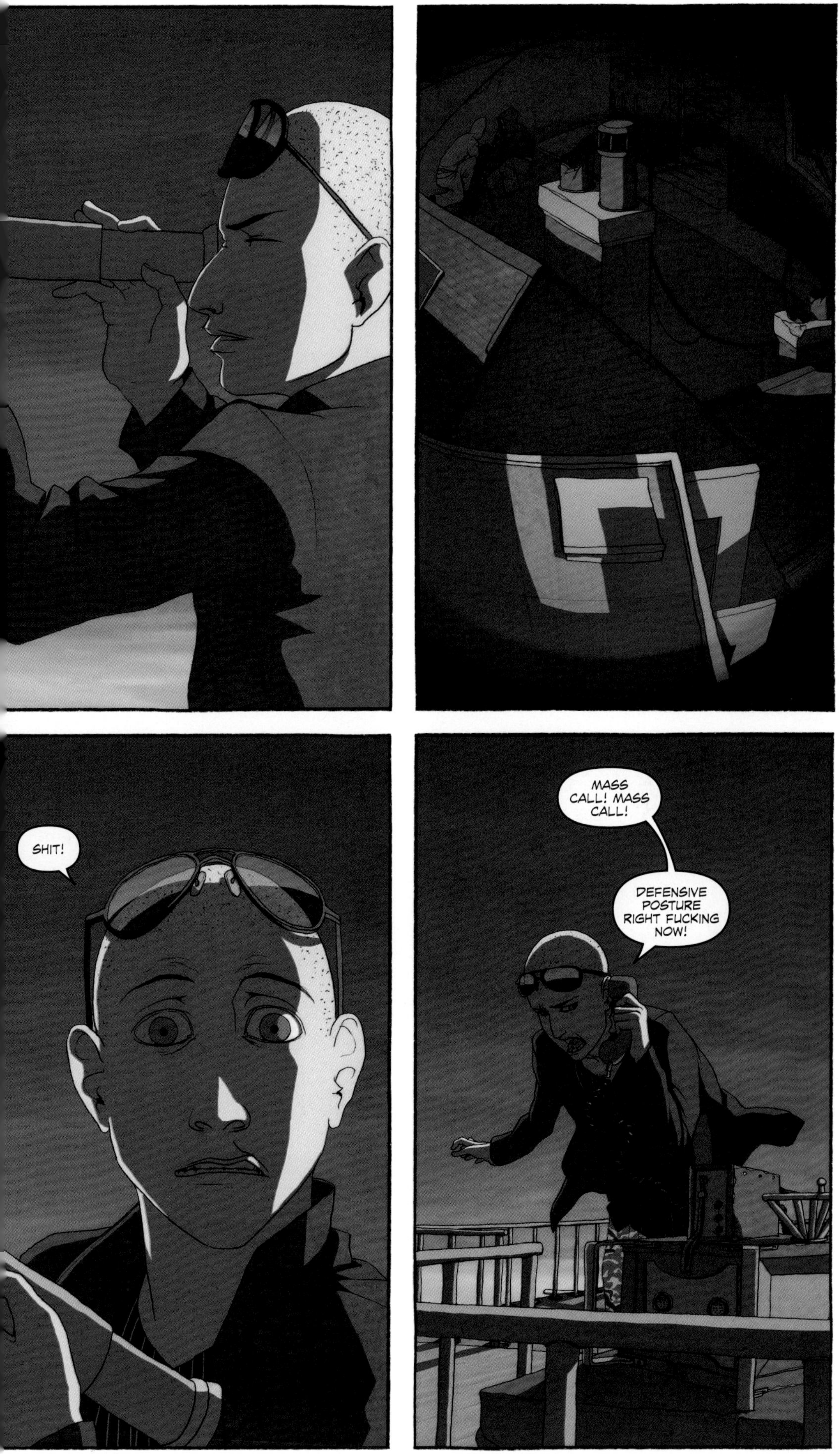
SHIT!
MASS CALL! MASS CALL!
DEFENSIVE POSTURE RIGHT FUCKING NOW!

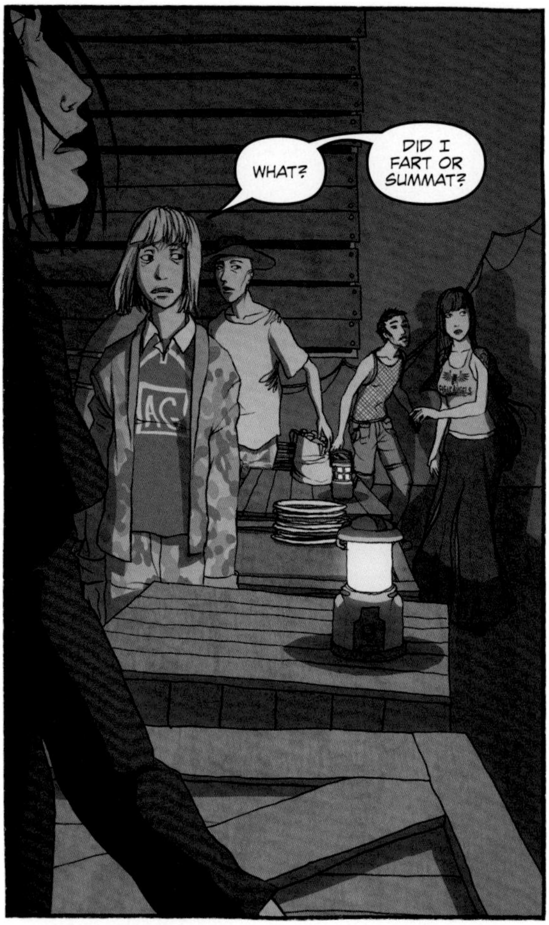
WHAT?
DID I FART OR SUMMAT?

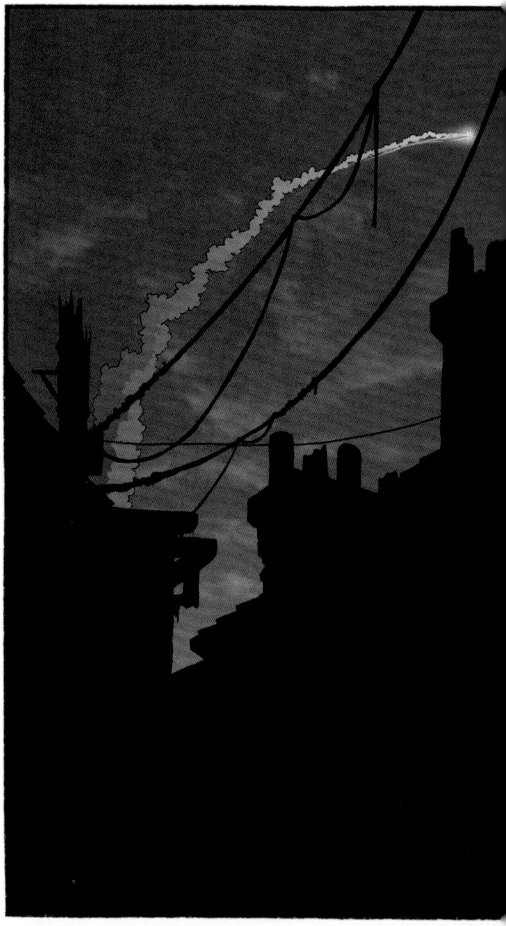

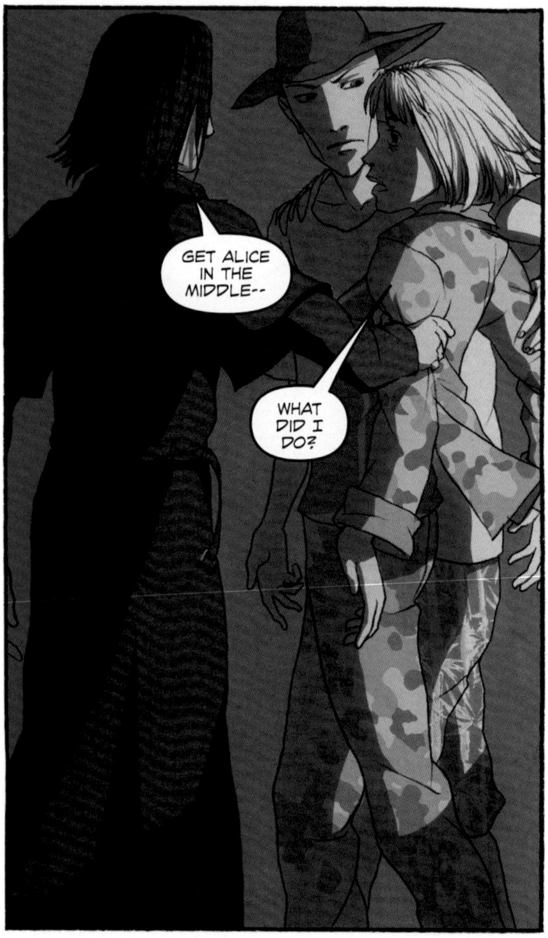
GET ALICE IN THE MIDDLE--
WHAT DID I DO?

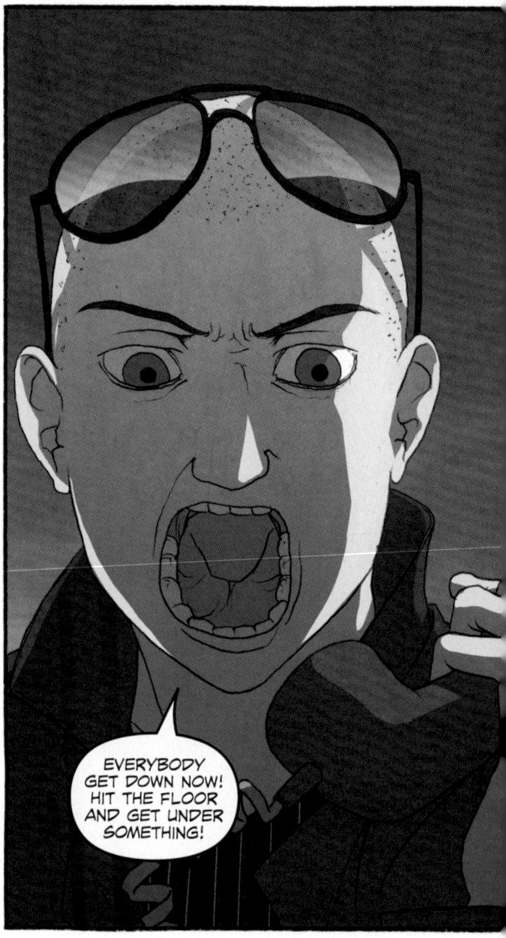
EVERYBODY GET DOWN NOW! HIT THE FLOOR AND GET UNDER SOMETHING!

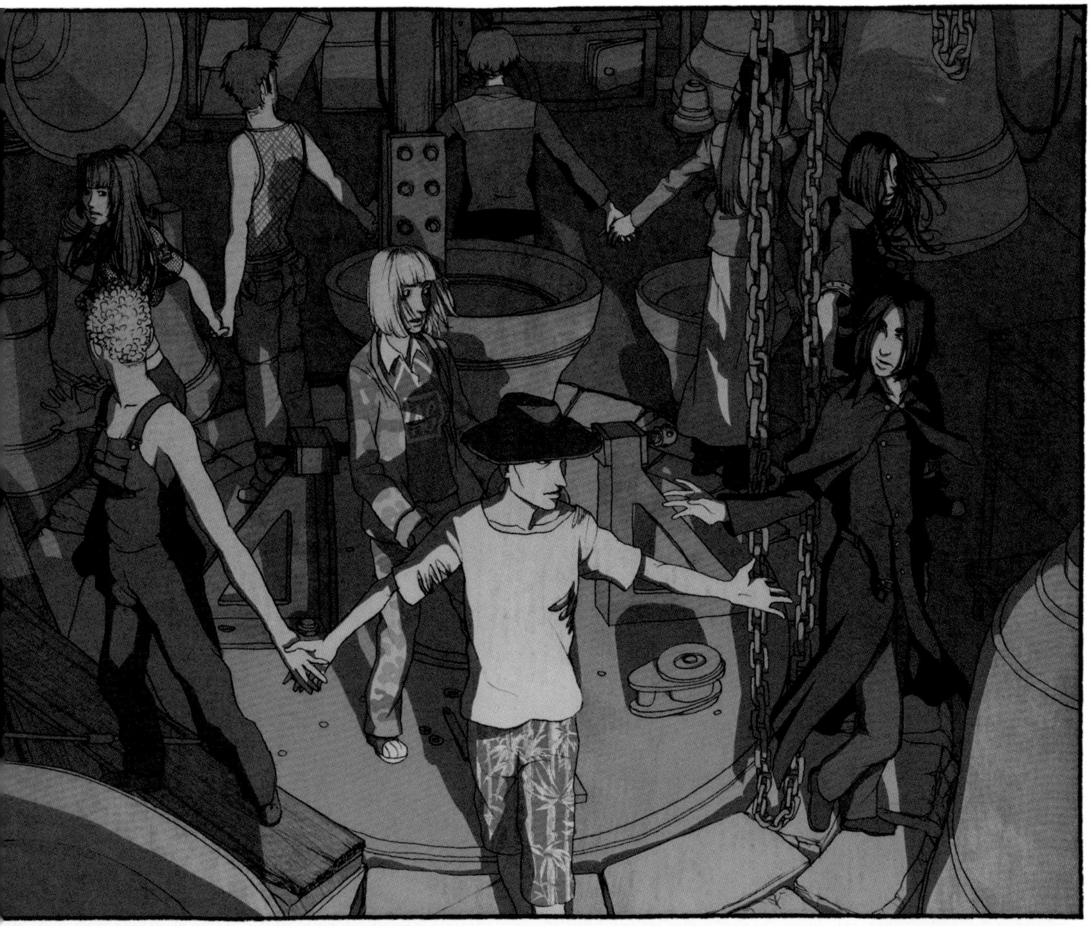
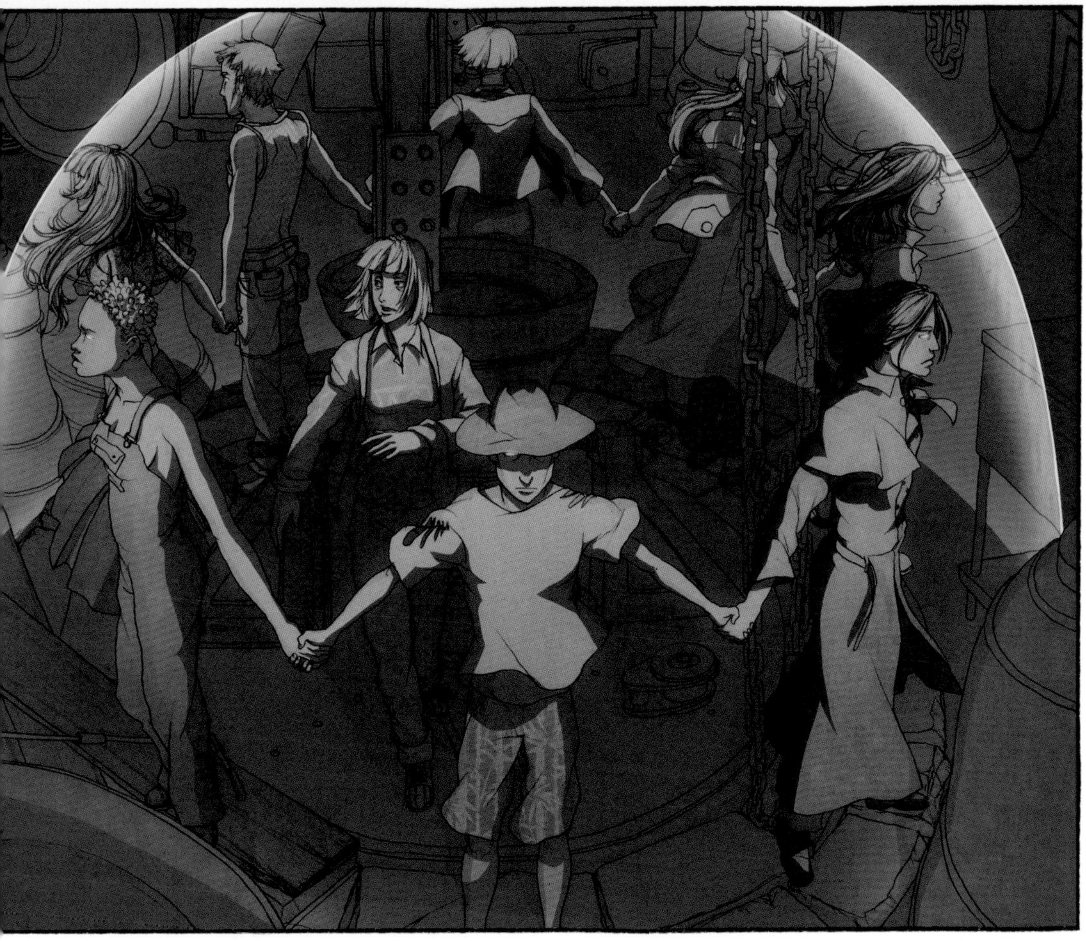

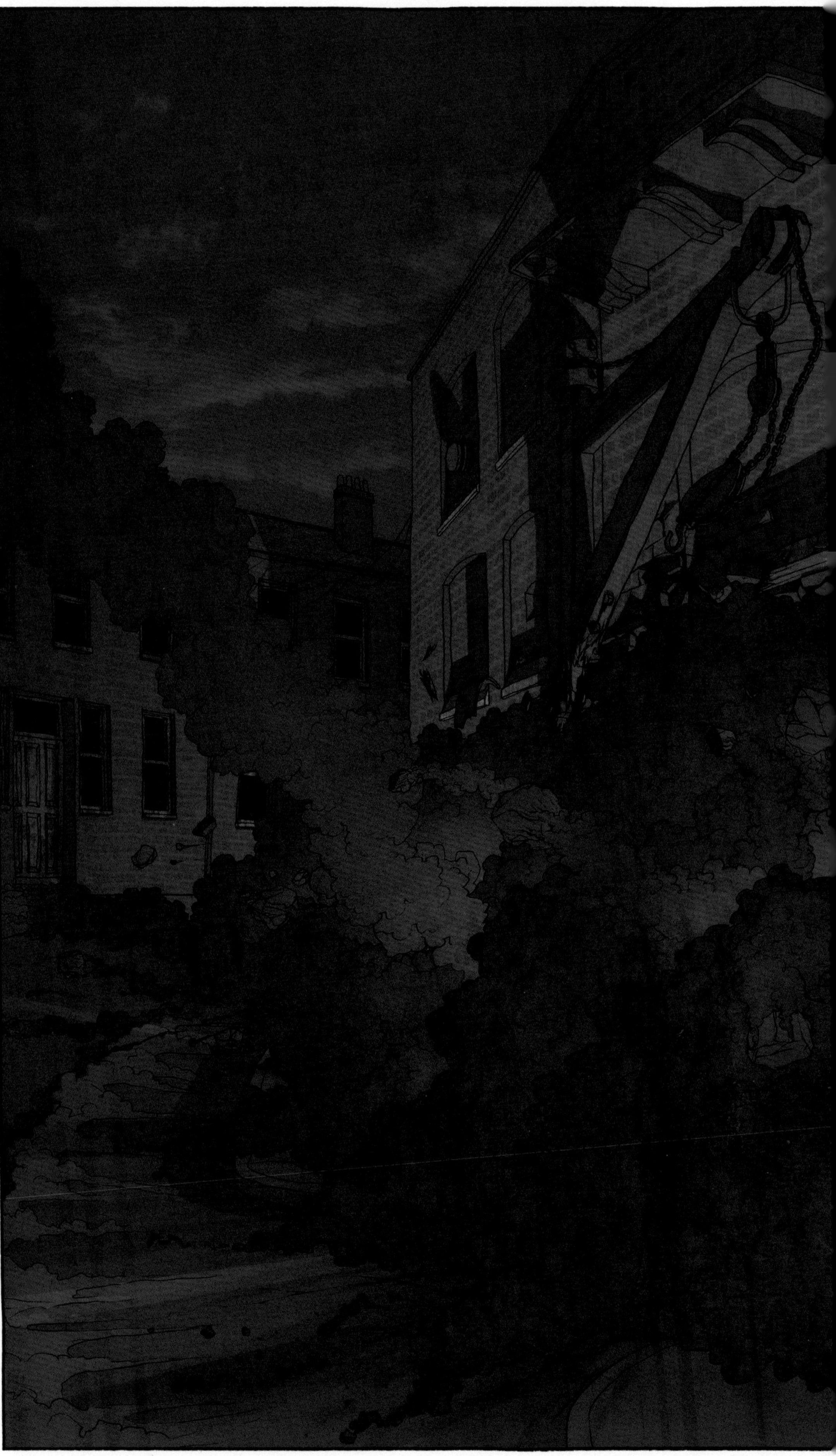

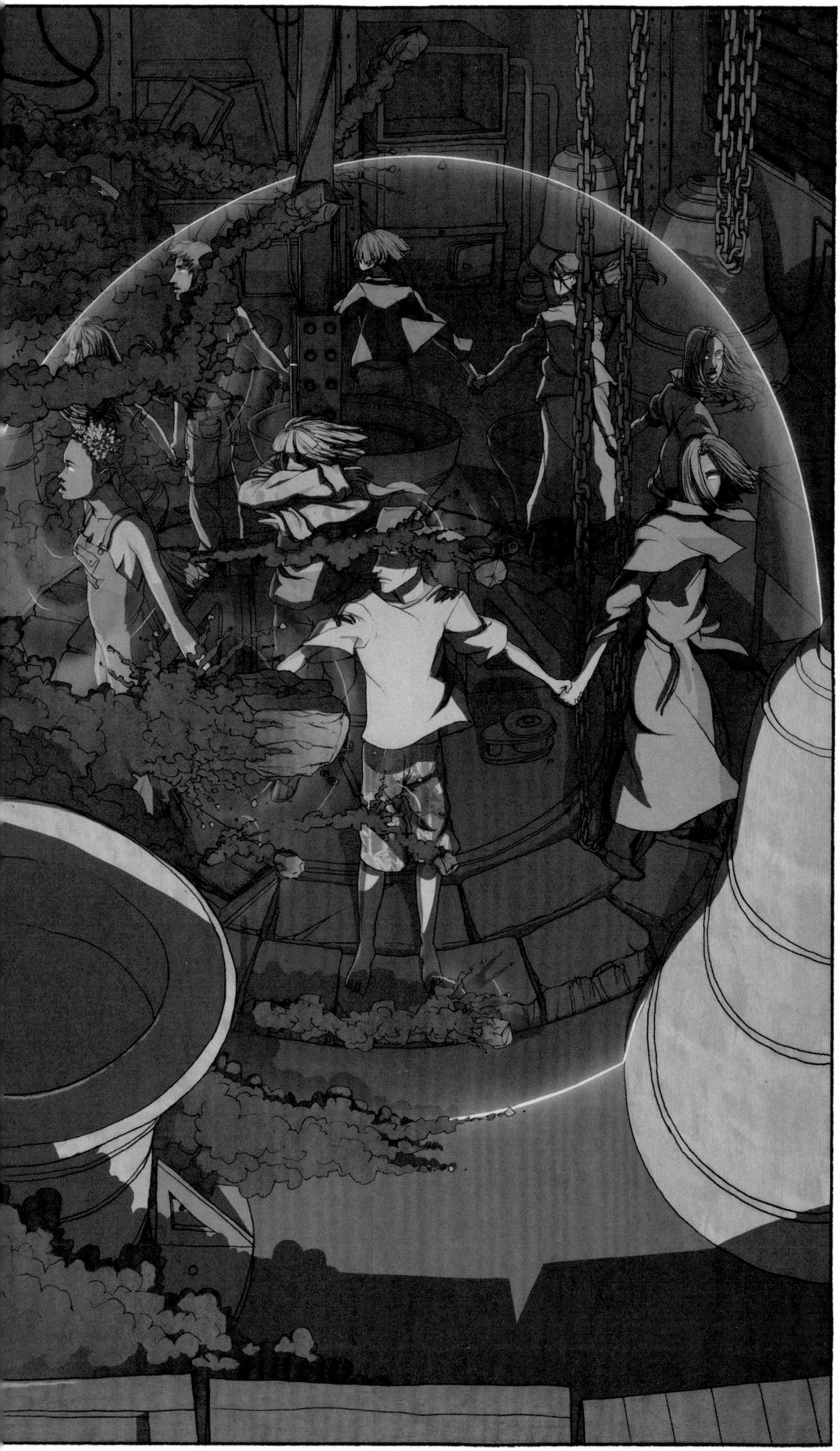

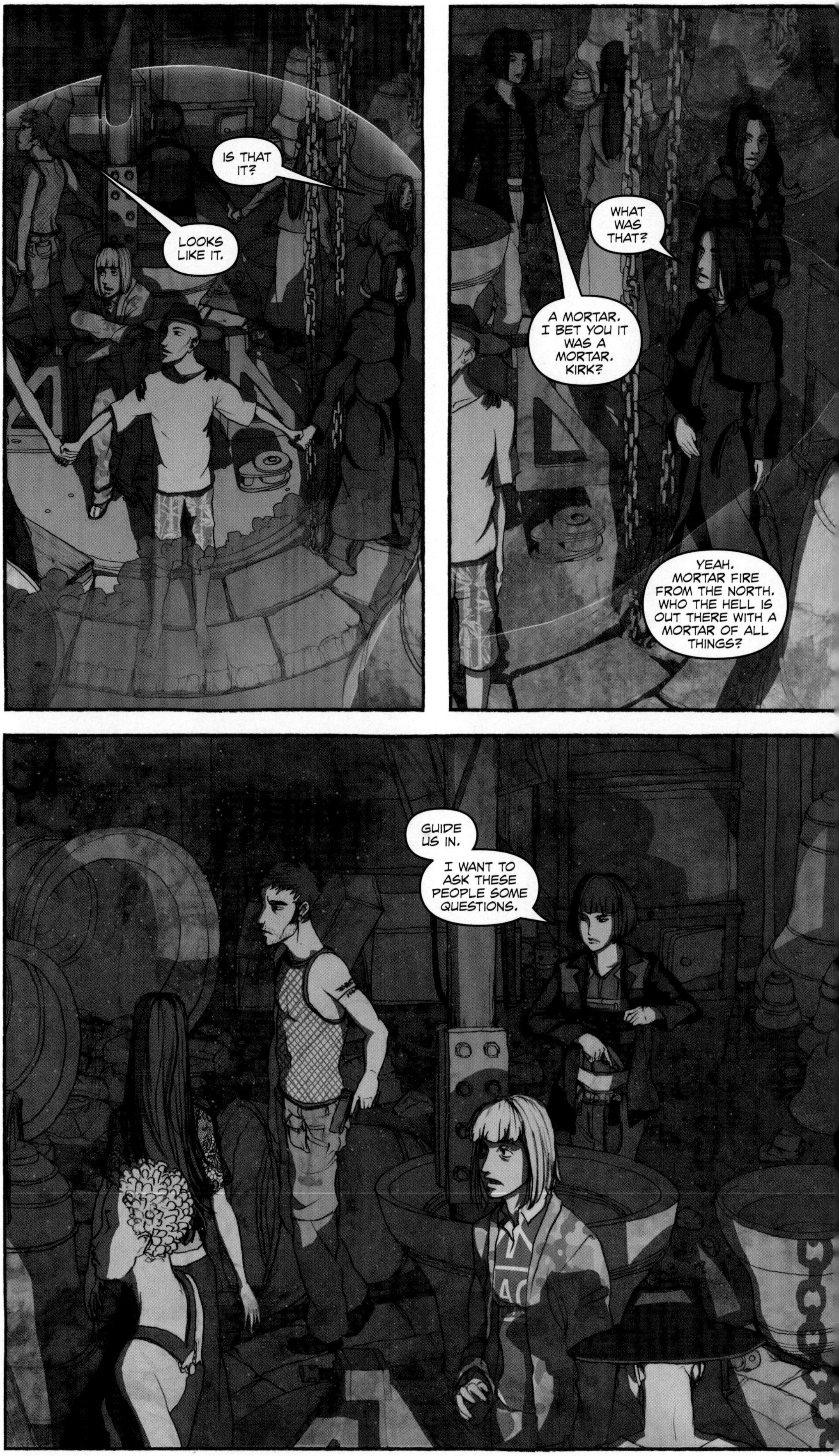
IS THAT IT?
LOOKS LIKE IT.
WHAT WAS THAT?
A MORTAR. I BET YOU IT WAS A MORTAR. KIRK?
YEAH. MORTAR FIRE FROM THE NORTH. WHO THE HELL IS OUT THERE WITH A MORTAR OF ALL THINGS?
GUIDE US IN.
I WANT TO ASK THESE PEOPLE SOME QUESTIONS.

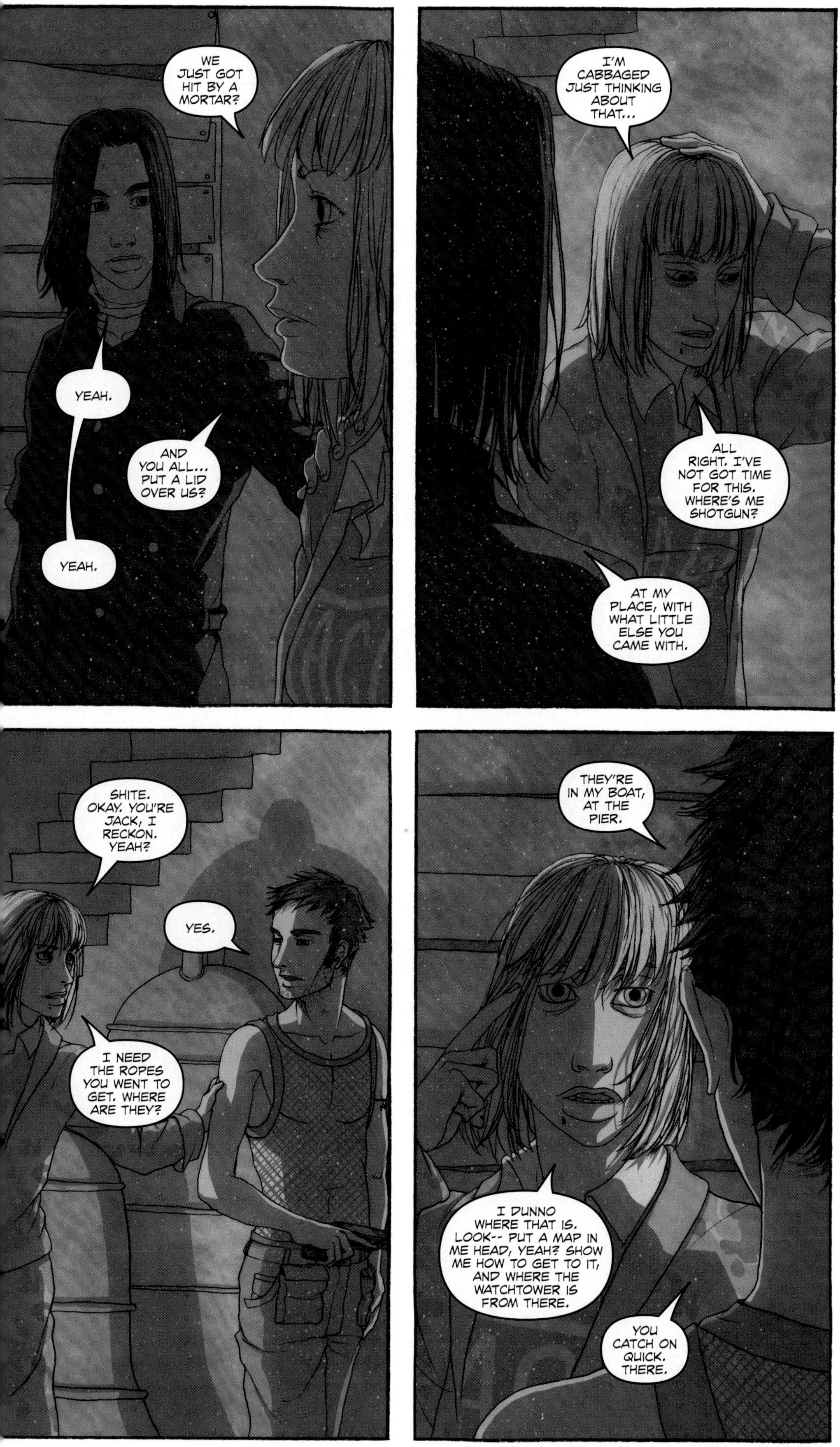
WE JUST GOT HIT BY A MORTAR?
YEAH.
AND YOU ALL... PUT A LID OVER US?
YEAH.
I'M CABBAGED JUST THINKING ABOUT THAT...
ALL RIGHT. I'VE NOT GOT TIME FOR THIS. WHERE'S ME SHOTGUN?
AT MY PLACE, WITH WHAT LITTLE ELSE YOU CAME WITH.
SHITE. OKAY. YOU'RE JACK, I RECKON. YEAH?
YES.
I NEED THE ROPES YOU WENT TO GET. WHERE ARE THEY?
THEY'RE IN MY BOAT, AT THE PIER.
I DUNNO WHERE THAT IS. LOOK-- PUT A MAP IN ME HEAD, YEAH? SHOW ME HOW TO GET TO IT, AND WHERE THE WATCHTOWER IS FROM THERE.
YOU CATCH ON QUICK. THERE.

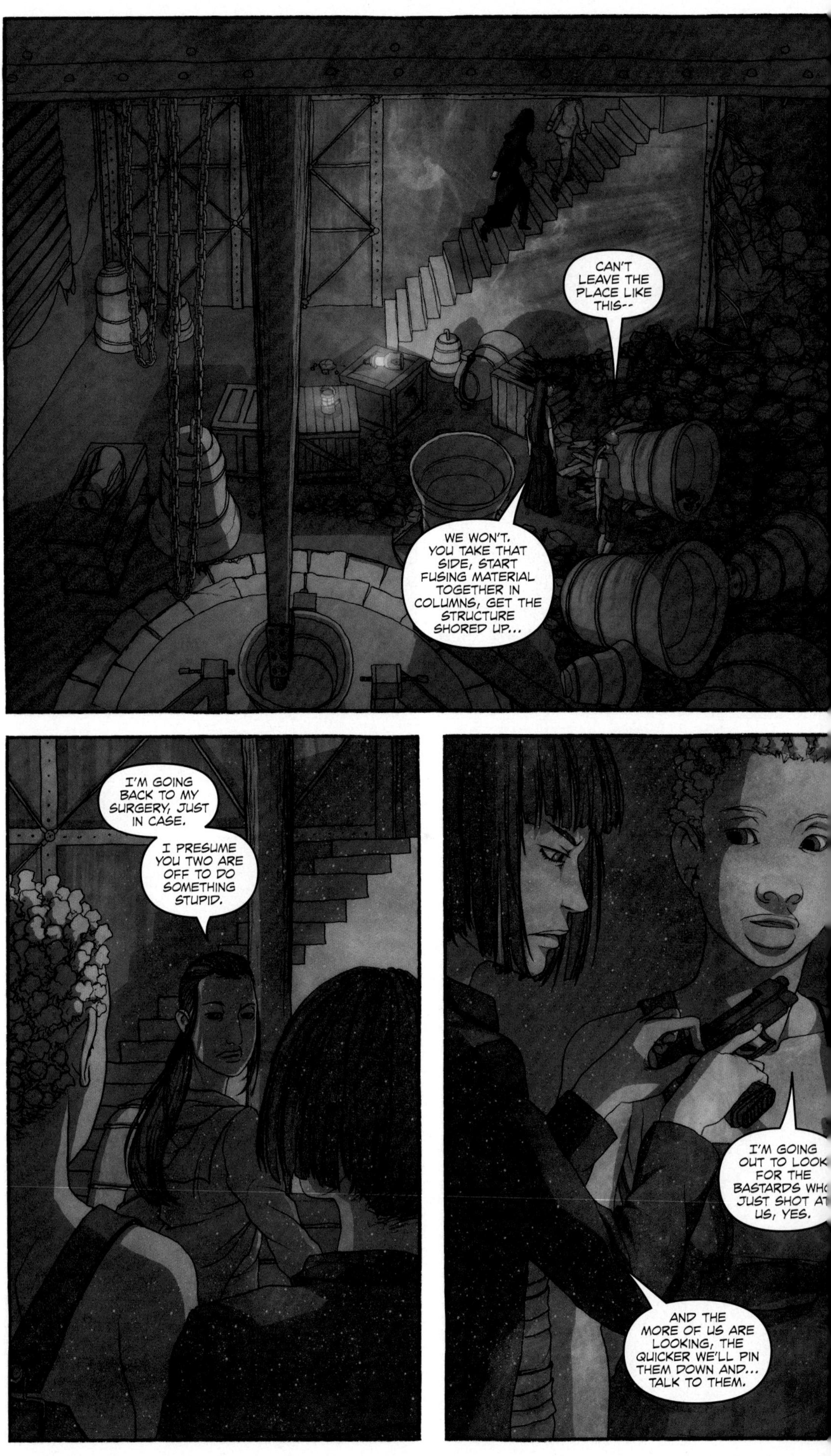
CAN'T LEAVE THE PLACE LIKE THIS--
WE WON'T. YOU TAKE THAT SIDE, START FUSING MATERIAL TOGETHER IN COLUMNS, GET THE STRUCTURE SHORED UP...
I'M GOING BACK TO MY SURGERY, JUST IN CASE.
I PRESUME YOU TWO ARE OFF TO DO SOMETHING STUPID.
I'M GOING OUT TO LOOK FOR THE BASTARDS WH JUST SHOT AT US, YES.
AND THE MORE OF US ARE LOOKING, THE QUICKER WE'LL PIN THEM DOWN AND... TALK TO THEM.

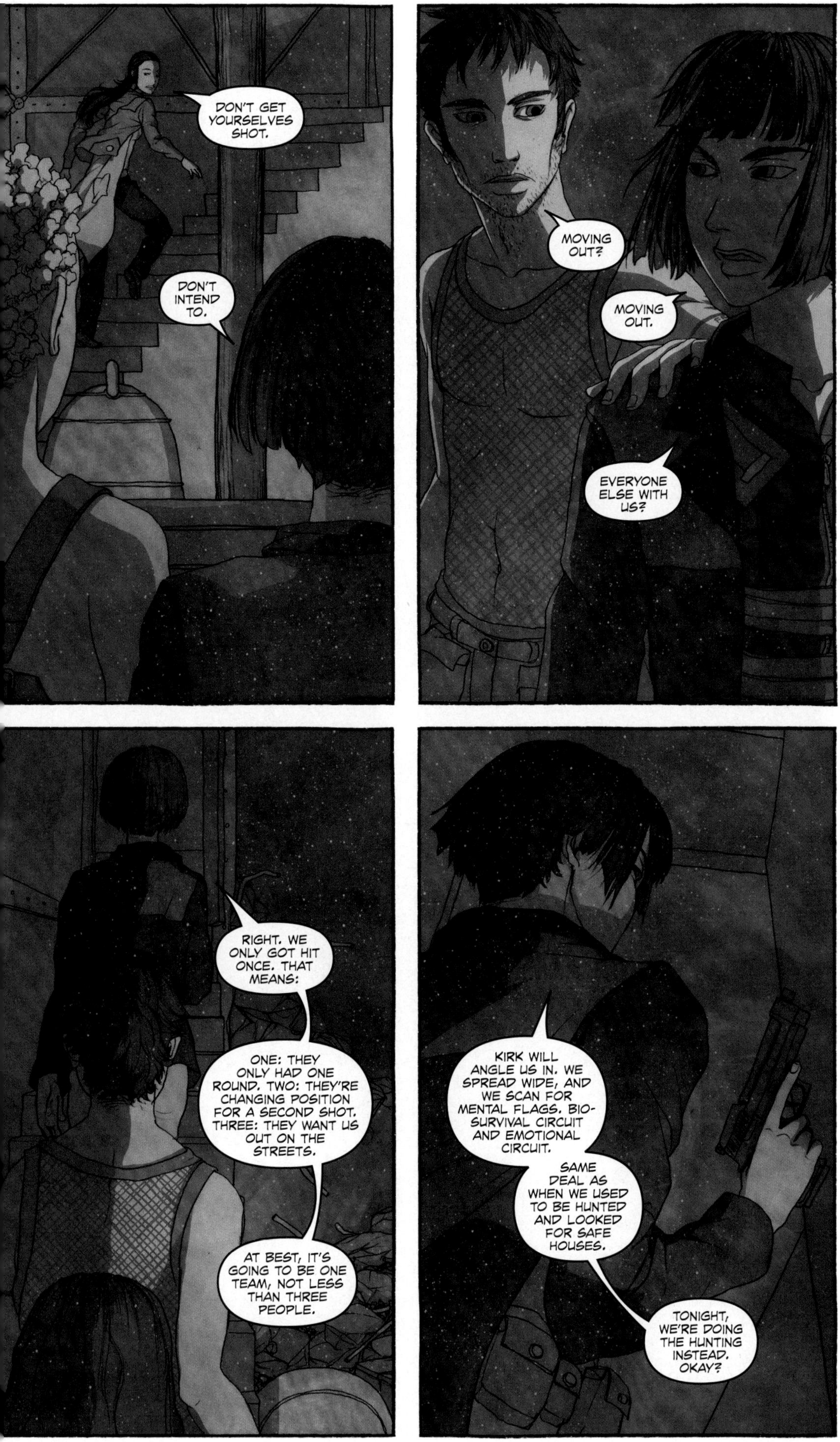
DON'T GET YOURSELVES SHOT.
DON'T INTEND TO.
MOVING OUT?
MOVING OUT.
EVERYONE ELSE WITH US?
RIGHT. WE ONLY GOT HIT ONCE. THAT MEANS:
ONE: THEY ONLY HAD ONE ROUND. TWO: THEY'RE CHANGING POSITION FOR A SECOND SHOT. THREE: THEY WANT US OUT ON THE STREETS.
AT BEST, IT'S GOING TO BE ONE TEAM, NOT LESS THAN THREE PEOPLE.
KIRK WILL ANGLE US IN. WE SPREAD WIDE, AND WE SCAN FOR MENTAL FLAGS. BIO-SURVIVAL CIRCUIT AND EMOTIONAL CIRCUIT.
SAME DEAL AS WHEN WE USED TO BE HUNTED AND LOOKED FOR SAFE HOUSES.
TONIGHT, WE'RE DOING THE HUNTING INSTEAD. OKAY?

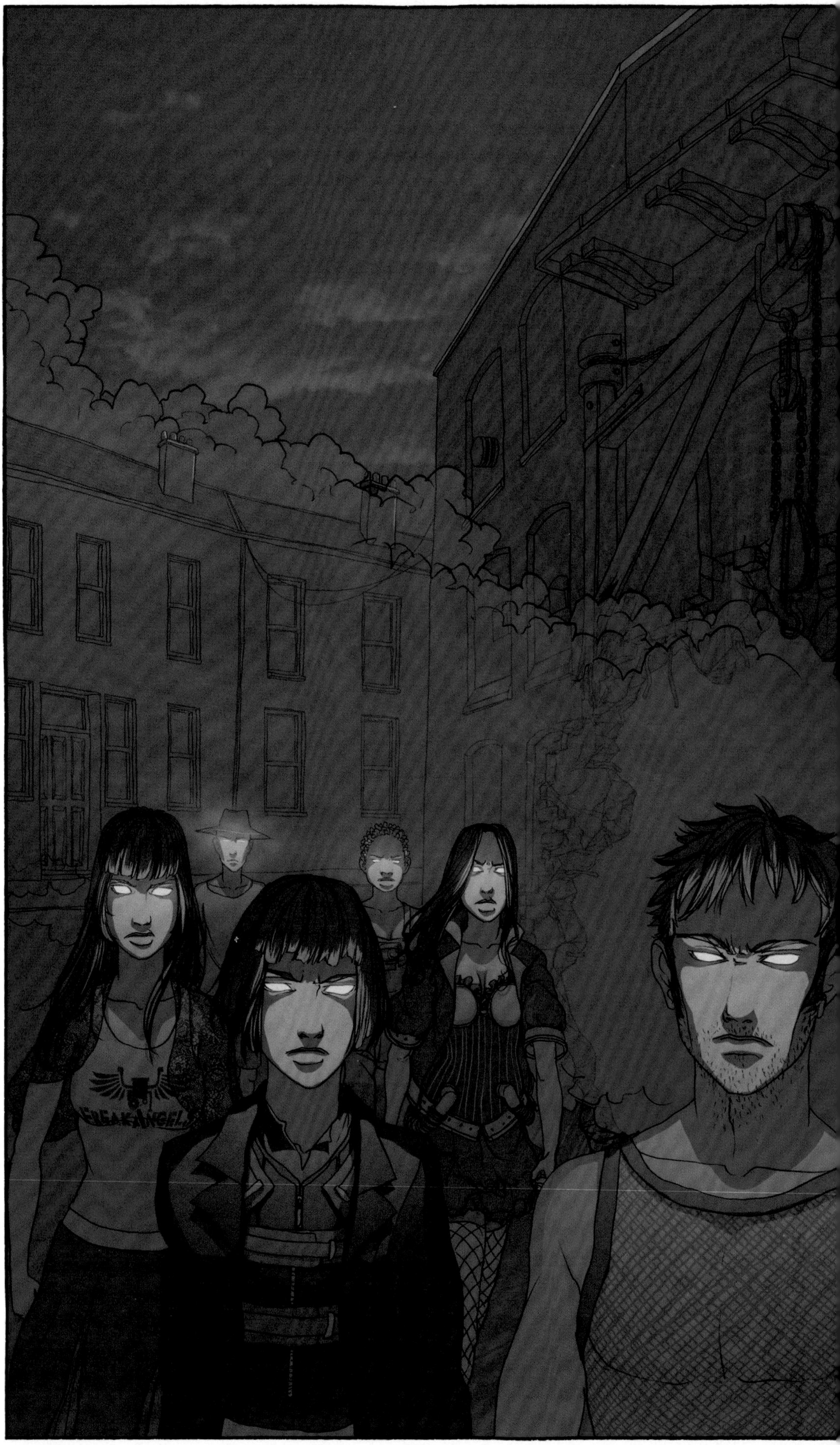

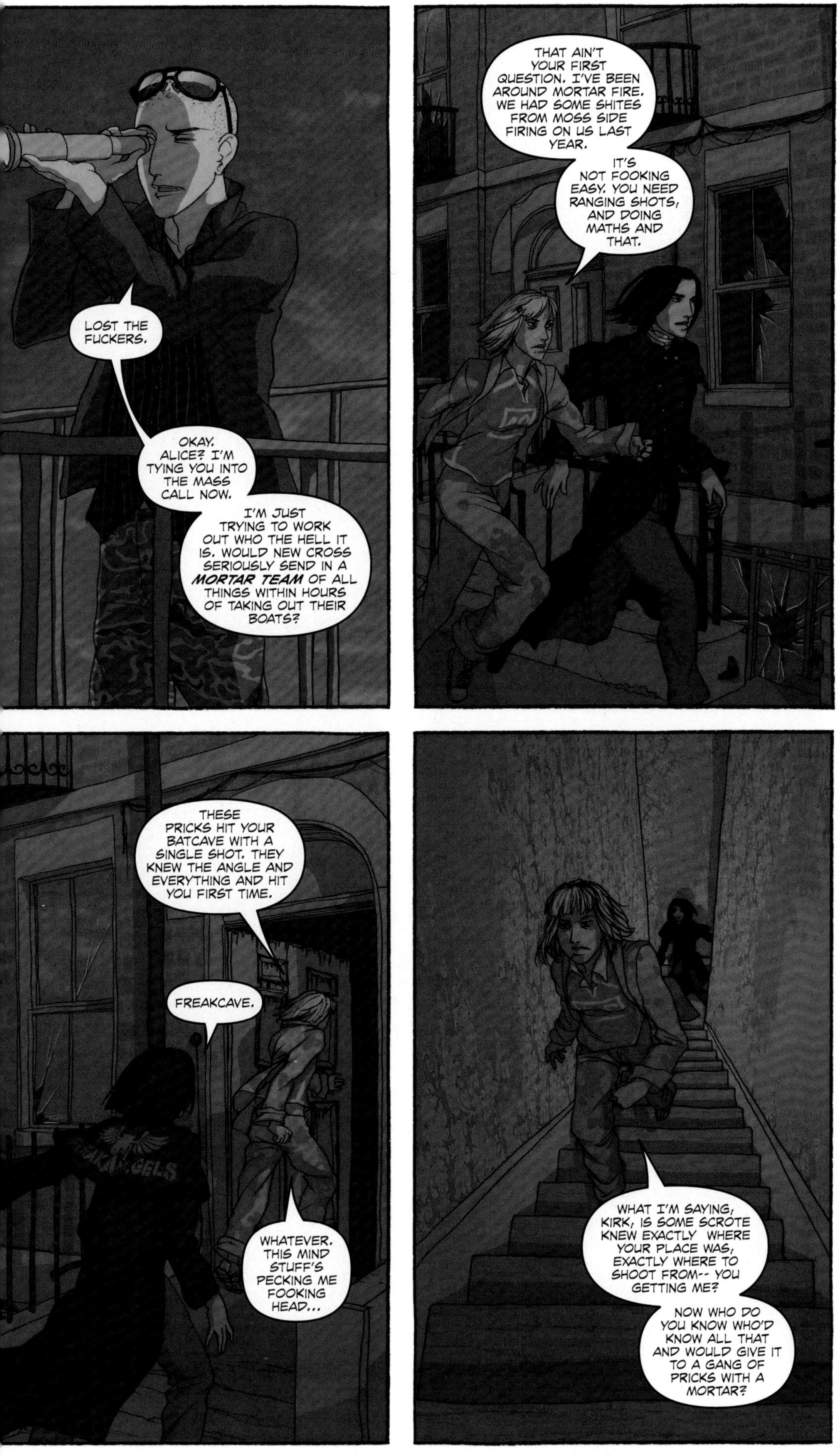
LOST THE FUCKERS.
OKAY. ALICE? I'M TYING YOU INTO THE MASS CALL NOW.
I'M JUST TRYING TO WORK OUT WHO THE HELL IT IS. WOULD NEW CROSS SERIOUSLY SEND IN A MORTAR TEAM OF ALL THINGS WITHIN HOURS OF TAKING OUT THEIR BOATS?
THAT AIN'T YOUR FIRST QUESTION. I'VE BEEN AROUND MORTAR FIRE. WE HAD SOME SHITES FROM MOSS SIDE FIRING ON US LAST YEAR.
IT'S NOT FOOKING EASY. YOU NEED RANGING SHOTS, AND DOING MATHS AND THAT.
THESE PRICKS HIT YOUR BATCAVE WITH A SINGLE SHOT. THEY KNEW THE ANGLE AND EVERYTHING AND HIT YOU FIRST TIME.
FREAKCAVE.
WHATEVER. THIS MIND STUFF'S PECKING ME FOOKING HEAD...
WHAT I'M SAYING, KIRK, IS SOME SCROTE KNEW EXACTLY WHERE YOUR PLACE WAS, EXACTLY WHERE TO SHOOT FROM-- YOU GETTING ME?
NOW WHO DO YOU KNOW WHO'D KNOW ALL THAT AND WOULD GIVE IT TO A GANG OF PRICKS WITH A MORTAR?

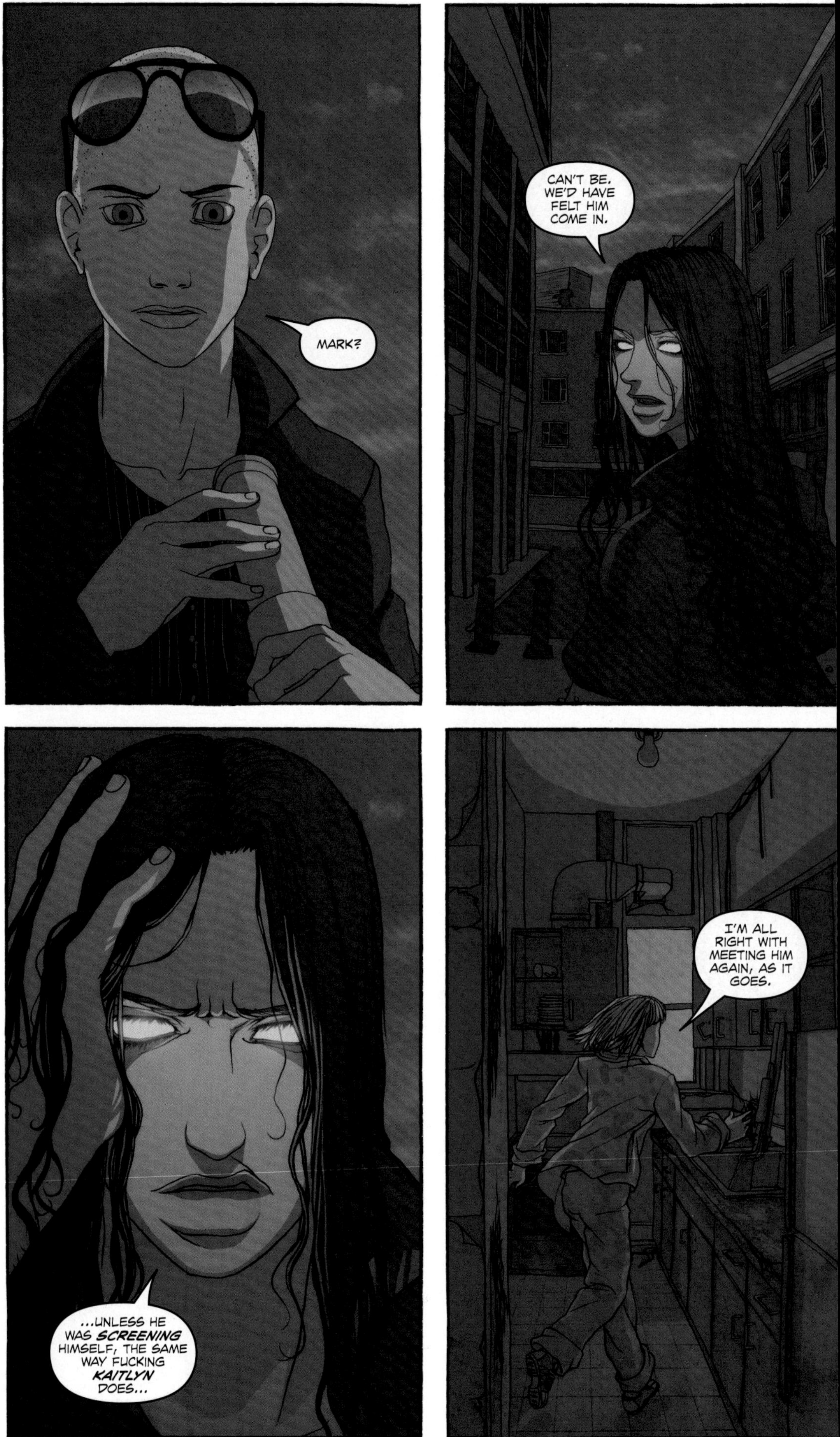
MARK?
CAN'T BE. WE'D HAVE FELT HIM COME IN.
...UNLESS HE WAS SCREENING HIMSELF, THE SAME WAY FUCKING KAITLYN DOES...
I'M ALL RIGHT WITH MEETING HIM AGAIN, AS IT GOES.

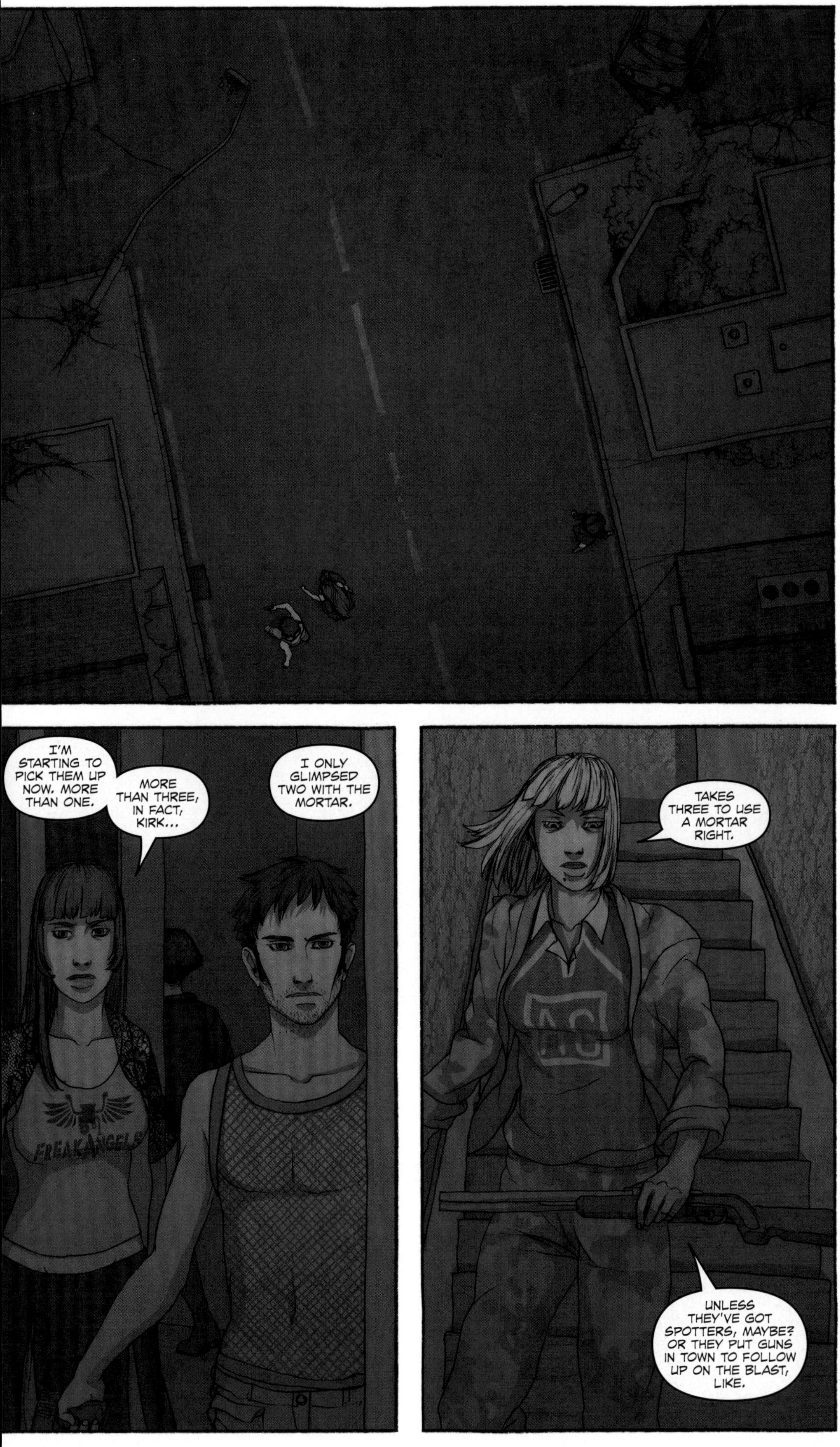
I'M STARTING TO PICK THEM UP NOW. MORE THAN ONE.
MORE THAN THREE, IN FACT, KIRK...
I ONLY GLIMPSED TWO WITH THE MORTAR.
FREAKANGELS
TAKES THREE TO USE A MORTAR RIGHT.
UNLESS THEY'VE GOT SPOTTERS, MAYBE? OR THEY PUT GUNS IN TOWN TO FOLLOW UP ON THE BLAST, LIKE.

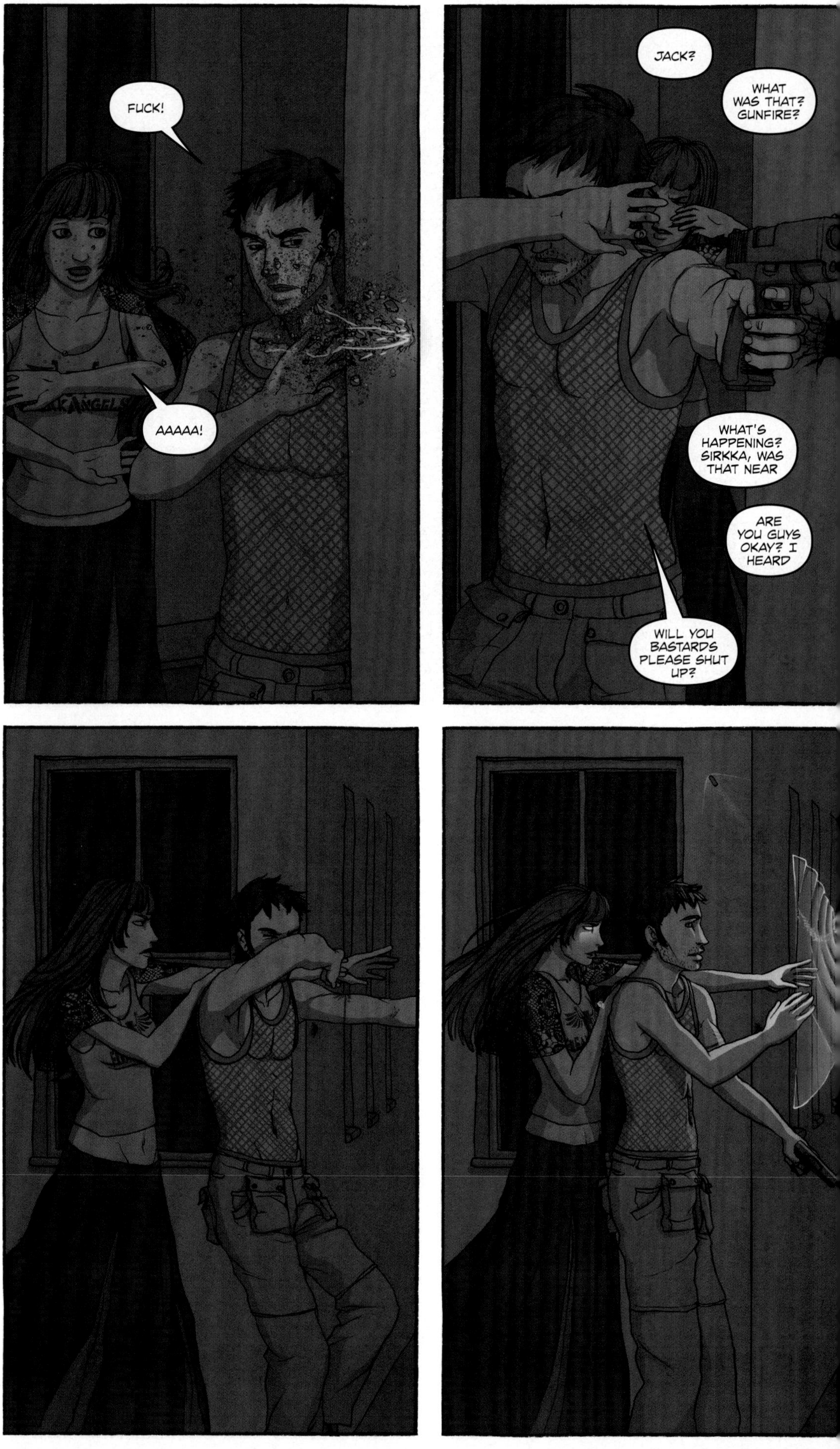
FUCK!
AAAAA!
JACK?
WHAT WAS THAT? GUNFIRE?
WHAT'S HAPPENING? SIRKKA, WAS THAT NEAR
ARE YOU GUYS OKAY? I HEARD
WILL YOU BASTARDS PLEASE SHUT UP?

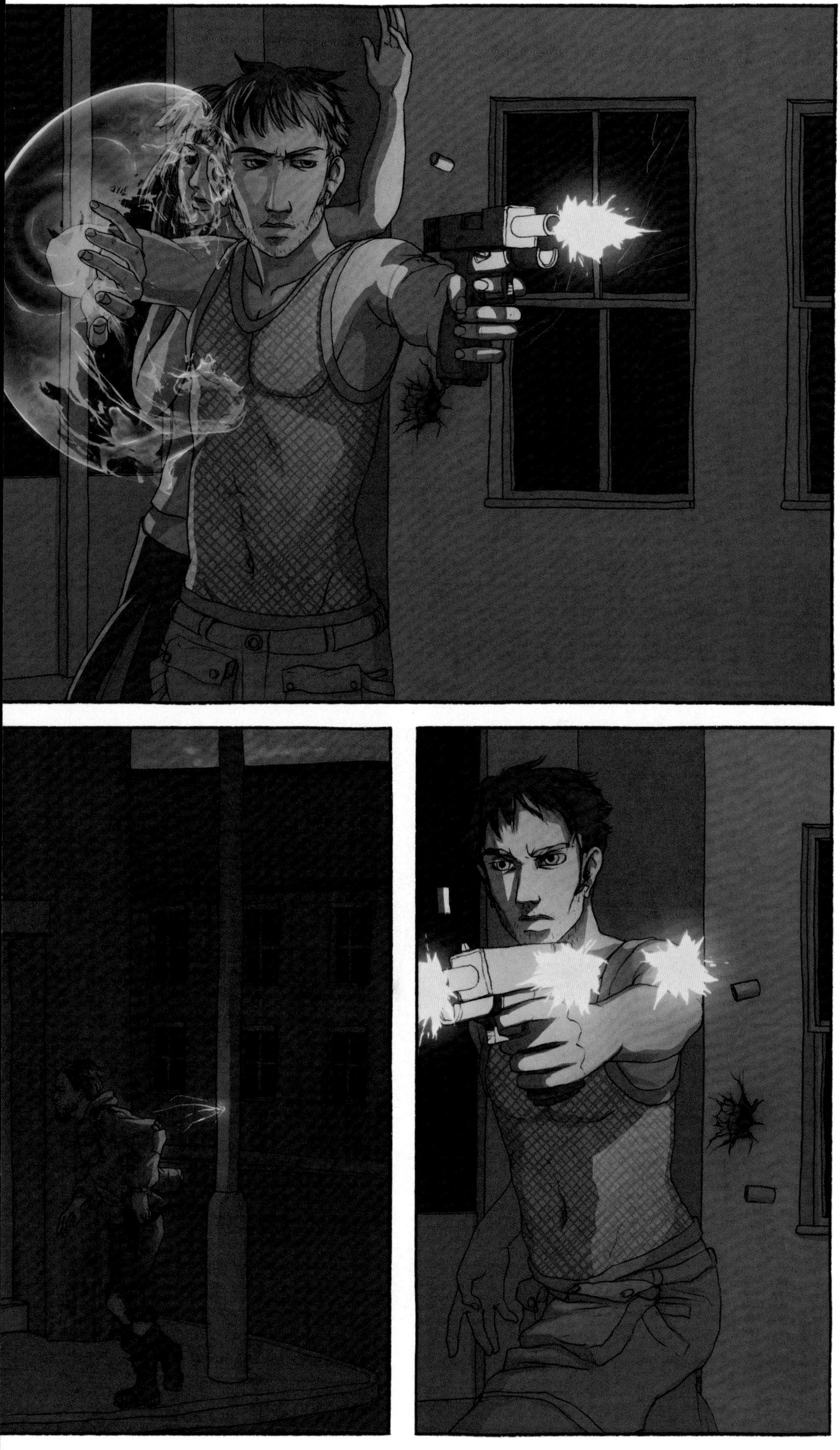

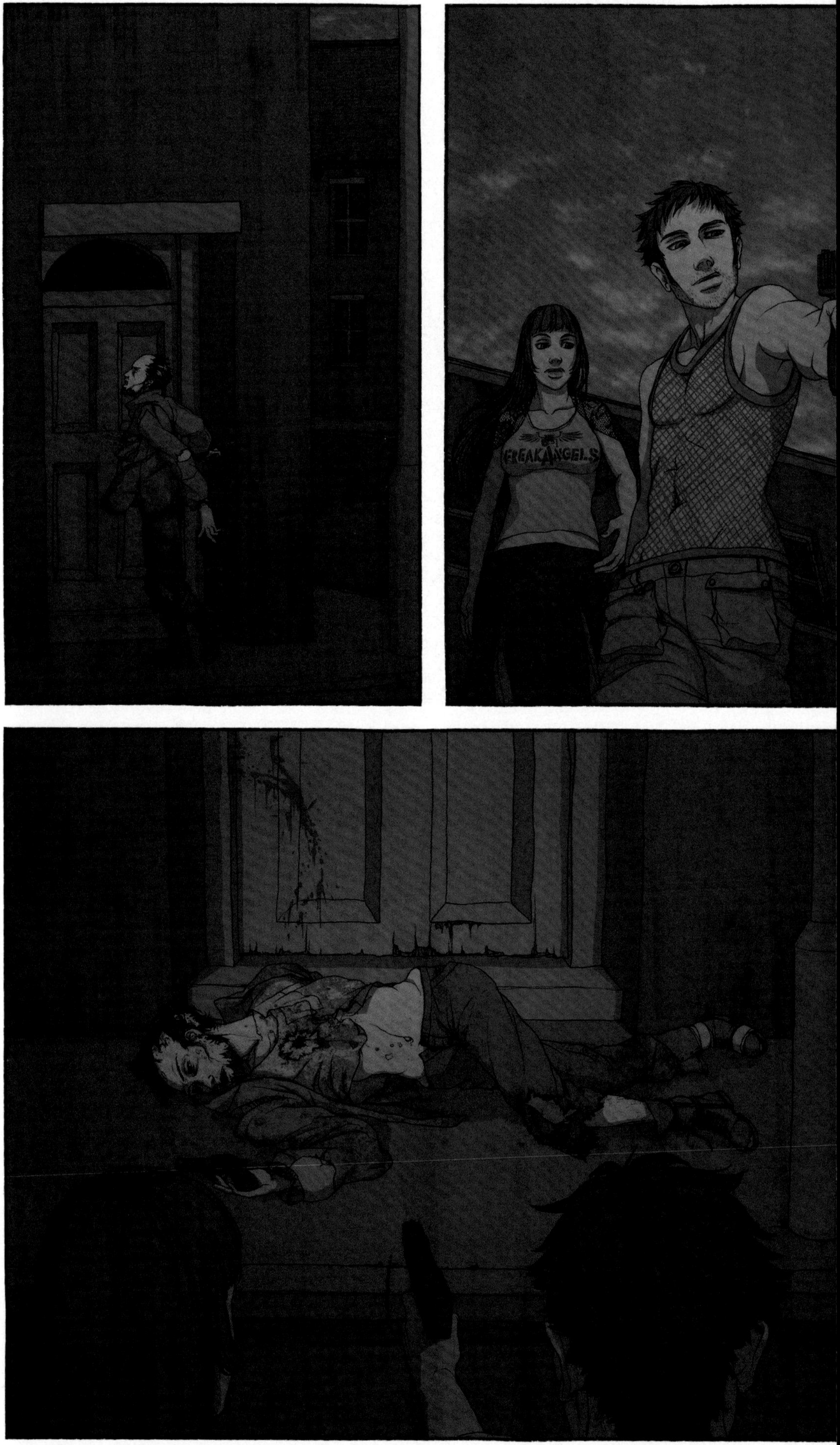
FREAKANGELS

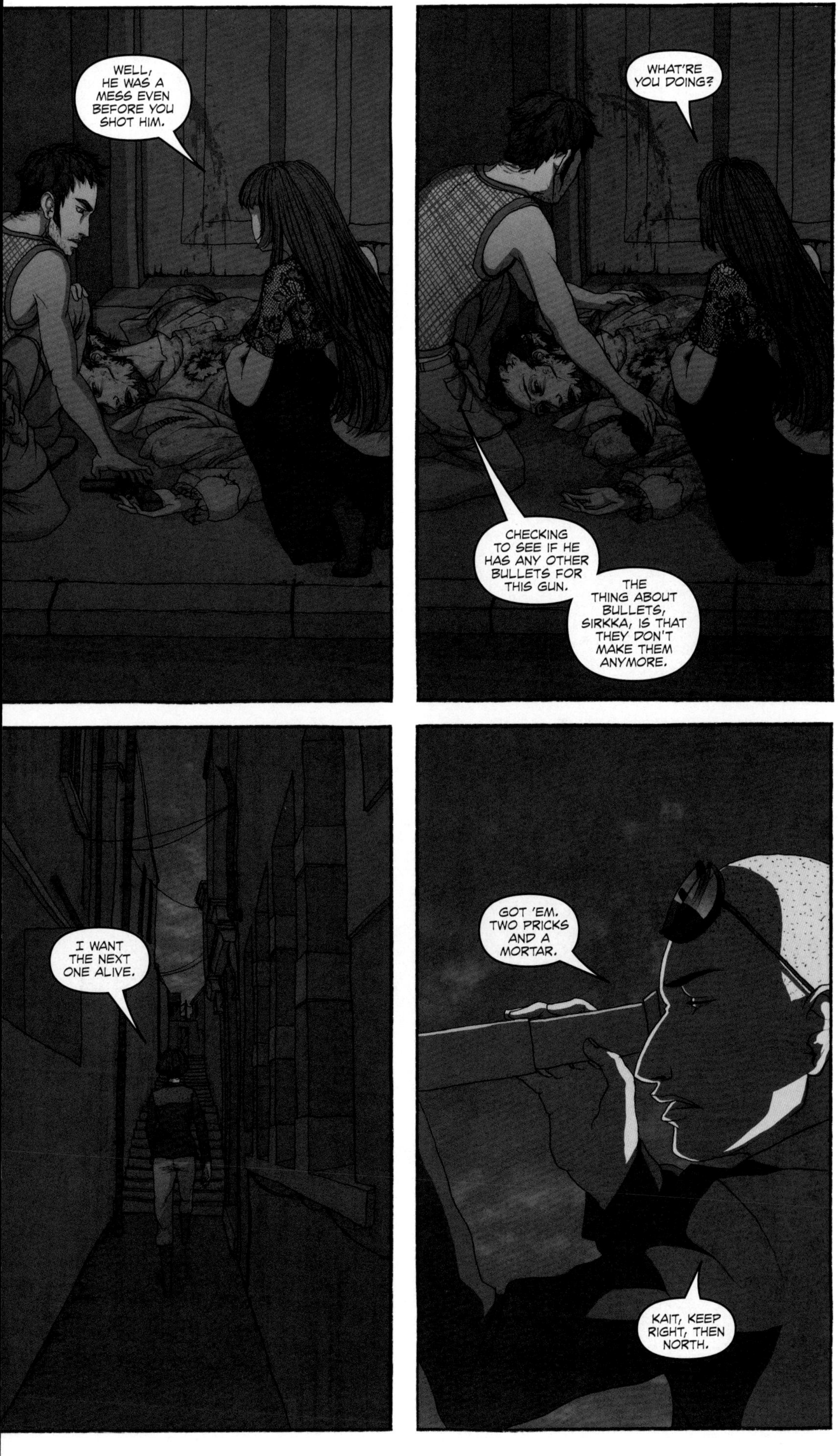
WELL, HE WAS A MESS EVEN BEFORE YOU SHOT HIM.
WHAT'RE YOU DOING?
CHECKING TO SEE IF HE HAS ANY OTHER BULLETS FOR THIS GUN.
THE THING ABOUT BULLETS, SIRKKA, IS THAT THEY DON'T MAKE THEM ANYMORE.
I WANT THE NEXT ONE ALIVE.
GOT 'EM. TWO PRICKS AND A MORTAR.
KAIT, KEEP RIGHT, THEN NORTH.

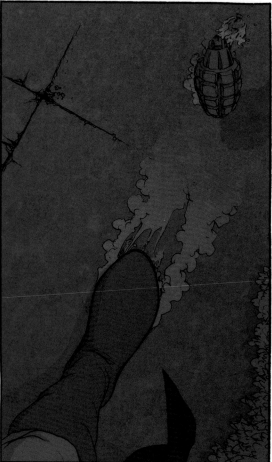

WELL, SHIT.

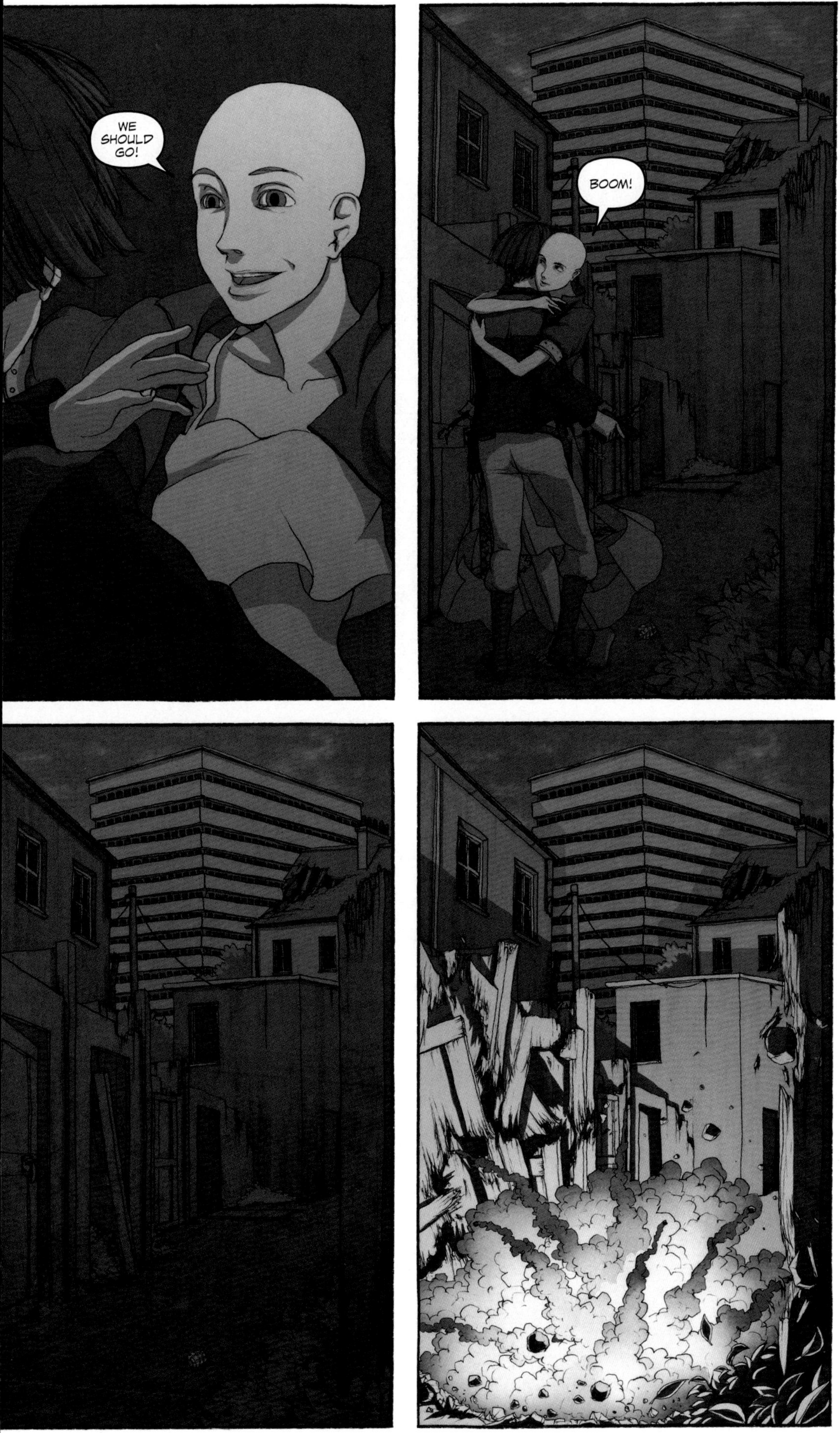
WE SHOULD GO!
BOOM!

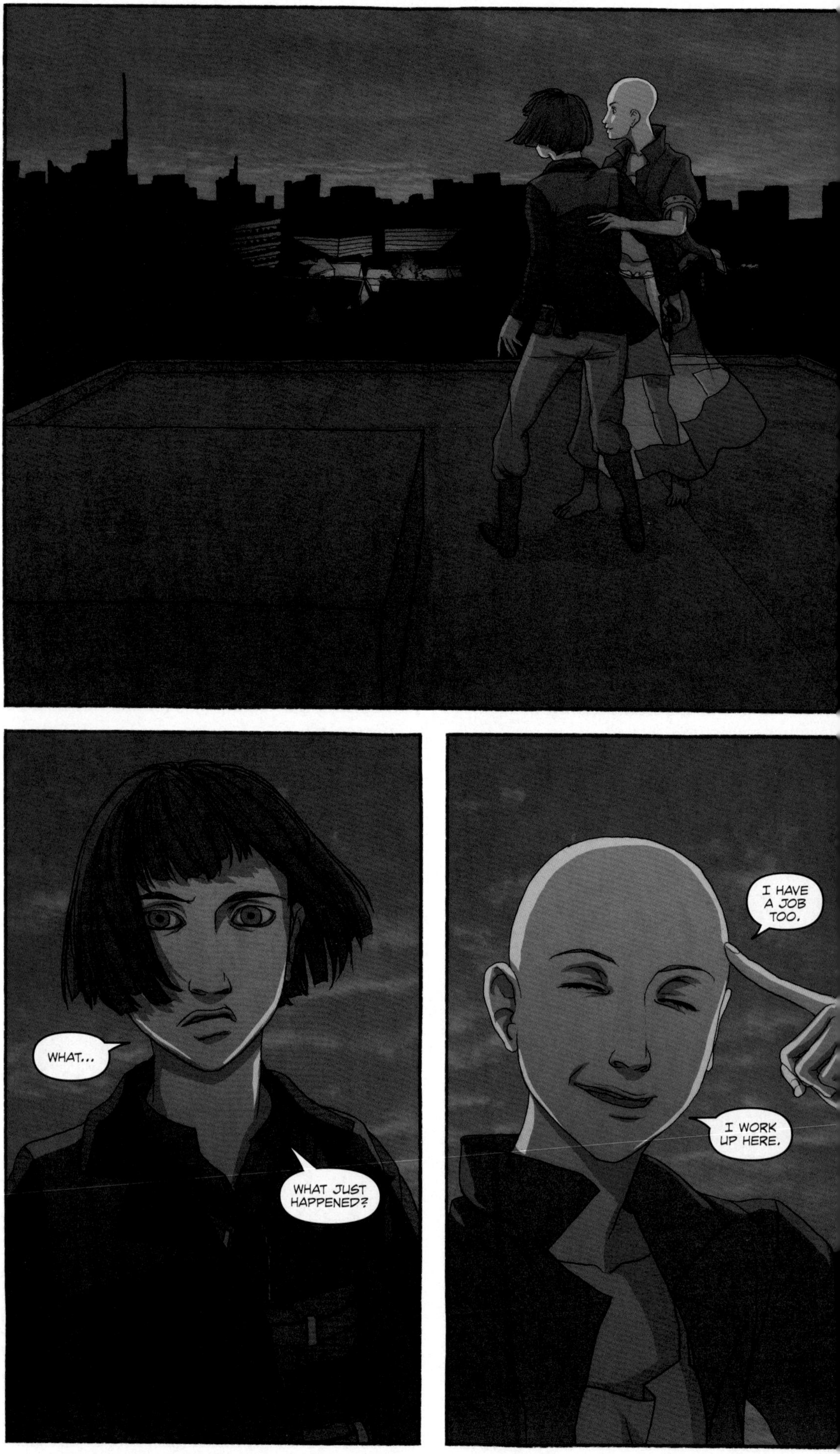
WHAT...
WHAT JUST HAPPENED?
I HAVE A JOB TOO.
I WORK UP HERE.

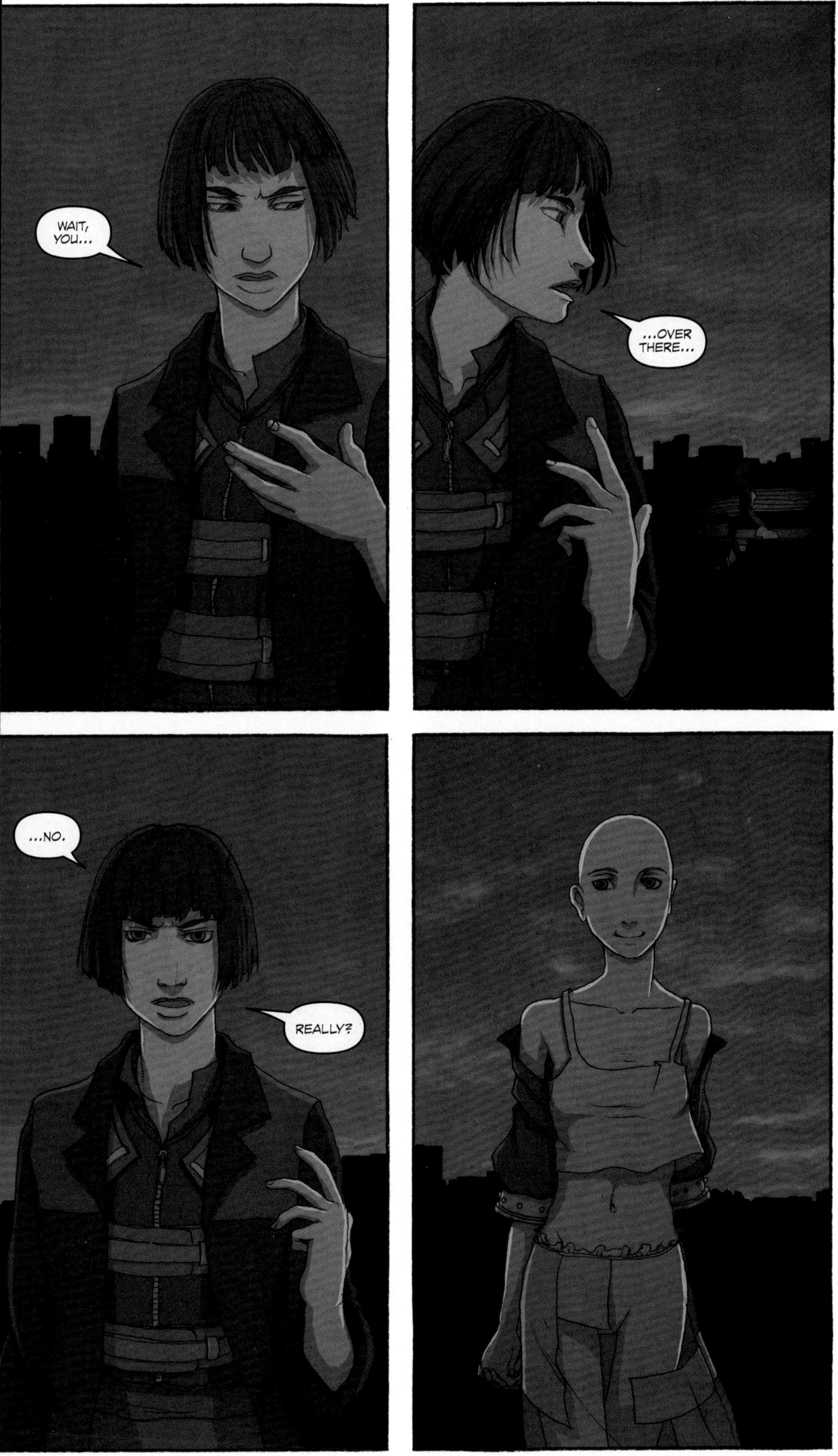
WAIT, YOU...
...OVER THERE...
...NO.
REALLY?

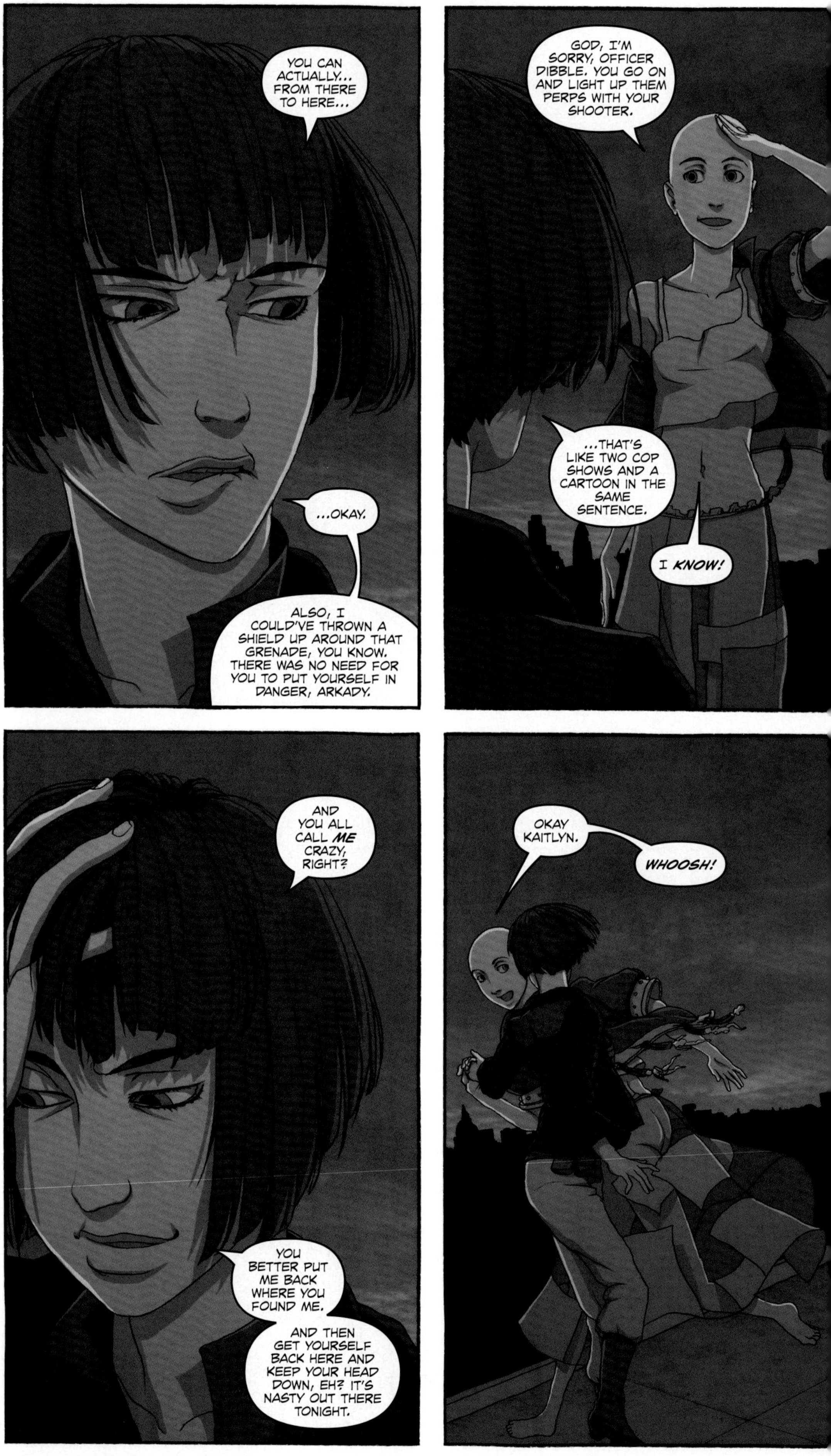
YOU CAN ACTUALLY... FROM THERE TO HERE...
...OKAY.
ALSO, I COULD'VE THROWN A SHIELD UP AROUND THAT GRENADE, YOU KNOW. THERE WAS NO NEED FOR YOU TO PUT YOURSELF IN DANGER, ARKADY.
GOD, I'M SORRY, OFFICER DIBBLE. YOU GO ON AND LIGHT UP THEM PERPS WITH YOUR SHOOTER.
...THAT'S LIKE TWO COP SHOWS AND A CARTOON IN THE SAME SENTENCE.
I *KNOW!*
AND YOU ALL CALL *ME* CRAZY, RIGHT?
YOU BETTER PUT ME BACK WHERE YOU FOUND ME.
AND THEN GET YOURSELF BACK HERE AND KEEP YOUR HEAD DOWN, EH? IT'S NASTY OUT THERE TONIGHT.
OKAY KAITLYN.
WHOOSH!

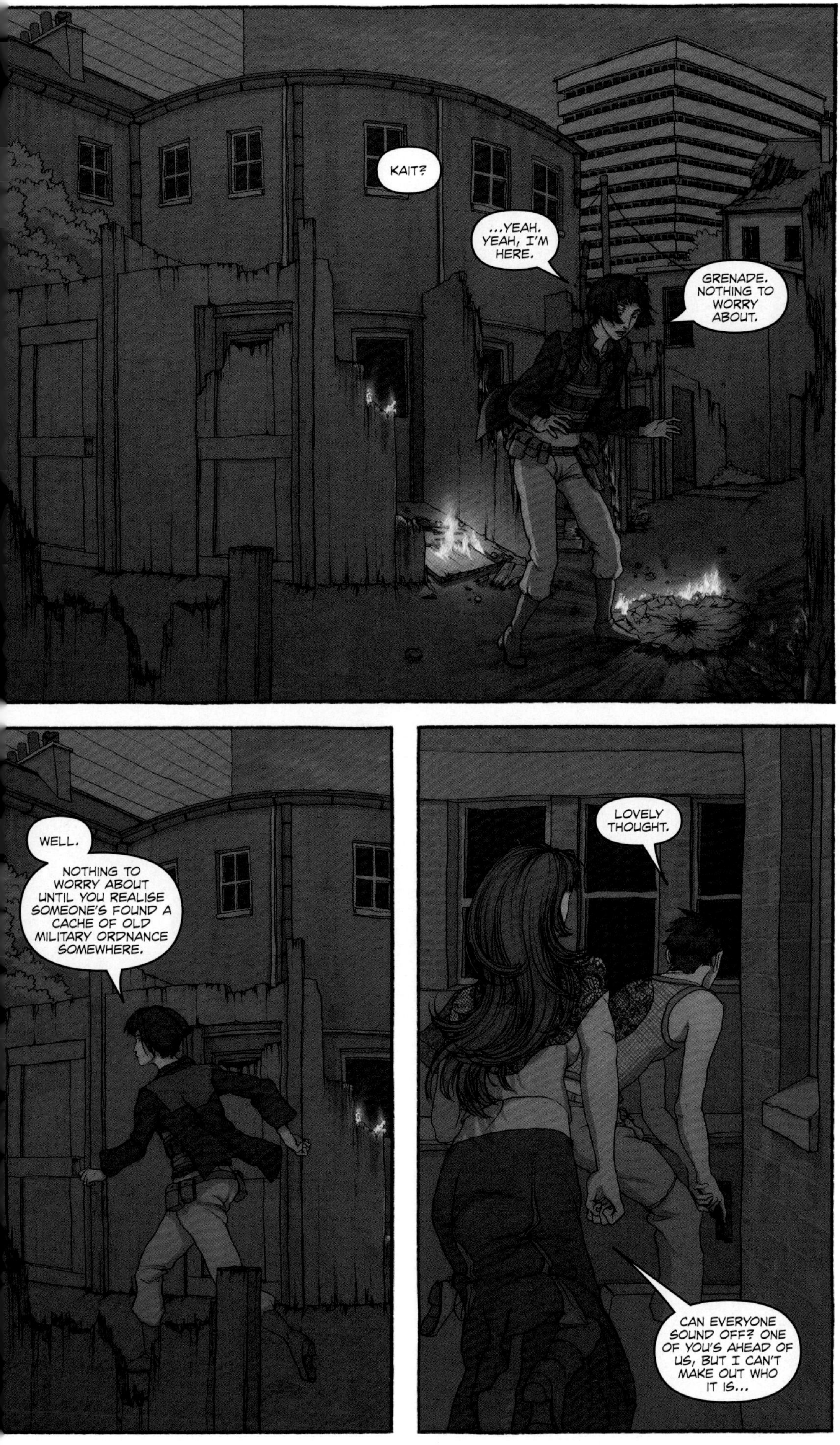
KAIT?
...YEAH. YEAH, I'M HERE.
GRENADE. NOTHING TO WORRY ABOUT.
WELL.
NOTHING TO WORRY ABOUT UNTIL YOU REALISE SOMEONE'S FOUND A CACHE OF OLD MILITARY ORDNANCE SOMEWHERE.
LOVELY THOUGHT.
CAN EVERYONE SOUND OFF? ONE OF YOU'S AHEAD OF US, BUT I CAN'T MAKE OUT WHO IT IS...

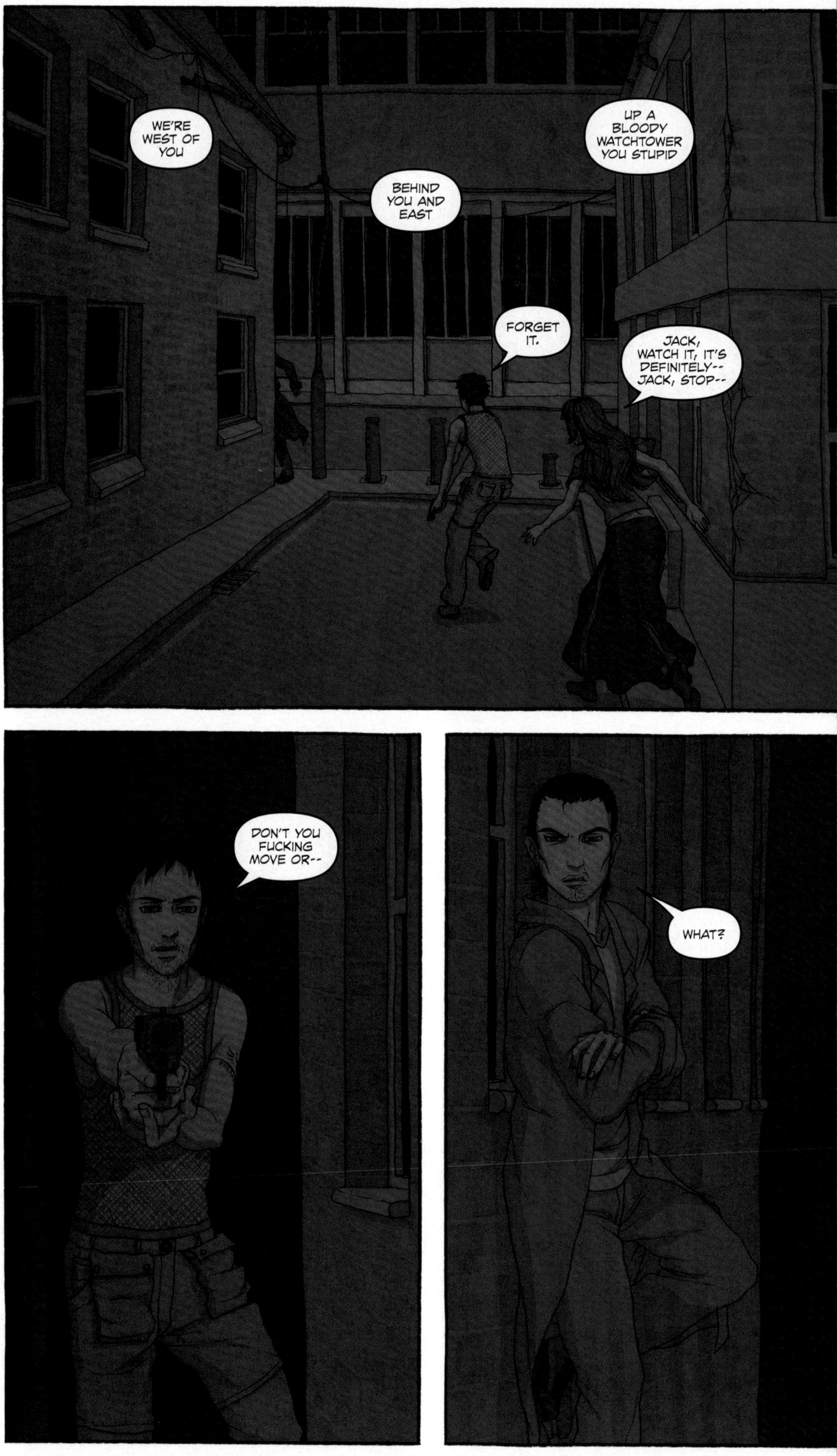
WE'RE WEST OF YOU
BEHIND YOU AND EAST
UP A BLOODY WATCHTOWER YOU STUPID
FORGET IT.
JACK, WATCH IT, IT'S DEFINITELY-- JACK, STOP--
DON'T YOU FUCKING MOVE OR--
WHAT?

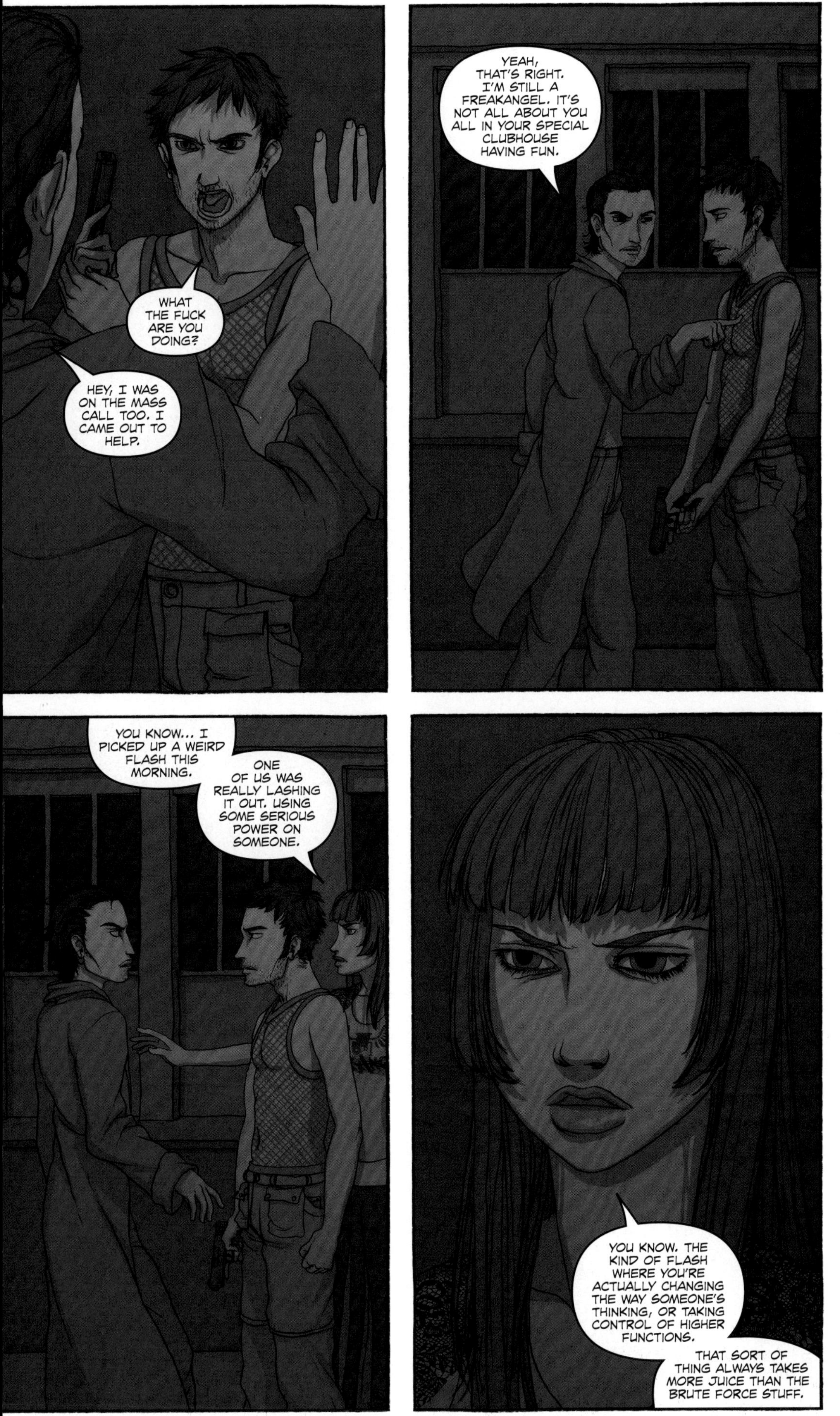
WHAT THE FUCK ARE YOU DOING?
HEY, I WAS ON THE MASS CALL TOO. I CAME OUT TO HELP.
YEAH, THAT'S RIGHT. I'M STILL A FREAKANGEL. IT'S NOT ALL ABOUT YOU ALL IN YOUR SPECIAL CLUBHOUSE HAVING FUN.
YOU KNOW... I PICKED UP A WEIRD FLASH THIS MORNING.
ONE OF US WAS REALLY LASHING IT OUT. USING SOME SERIOUS POWER ON SOMEONE.
YOU KNOW. THE KIND OF FLASH WHERE YOU'RE ACTUALLY CHANGING THE WAY SOMEONE'S THINKING, OR TAKING CONTROL OF HIGHER FUNCTIONS.
THAT SORT OF THING ALWAYS TAKES MORE JUICE THAN THE BRUTE FORCE STUFF.

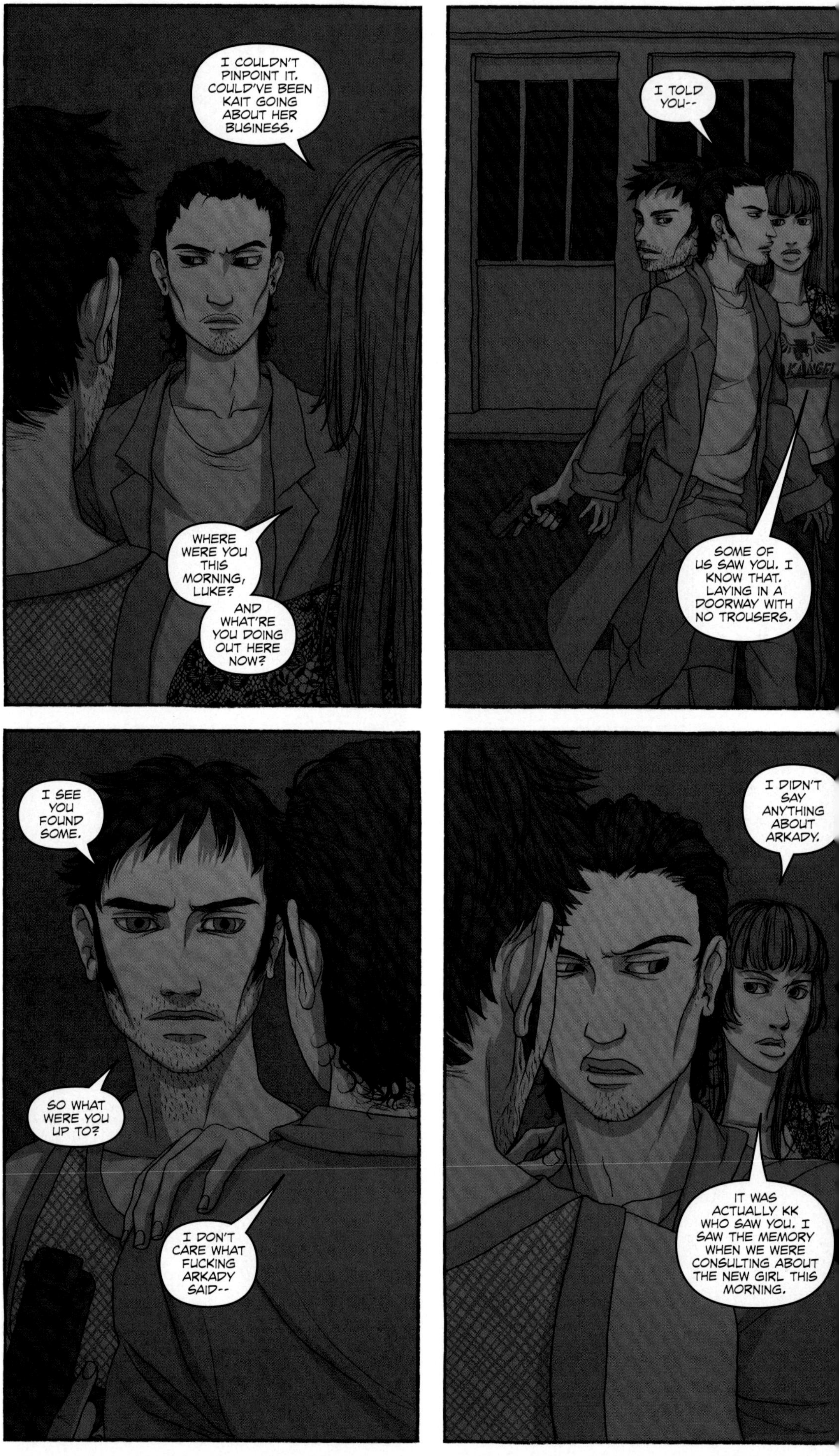
I COULDN'T PINPOINT IT. COULD'VE BEEN KAIT GOING ABOUT HER BUSINESS.
WHERE WERE YOU THIS MORNING, LUKE?
AND WHAT'RE YOU DOING OUT HERE NOW?
I TOLD YOU--
SOME OF US SAW YOU. I KNOW THAT. LAYING IN A DOORWAY WITH NO TROUSERS.
I SEE YOU FOUND SOME.
SO WHAT WERE YOU UP TO?
I DON'T CARE WHAT FUCKING ARKADY SAID--
I DIDN'T SAY ANYTHING ABOUT ARKADY.
IT WAS ACTUALLY KK WHO SAW YOU. I SAW THE MEMORY WHEN WE WERE CONSULTING ABOUT THE NEW GIRL THIS MORNING.

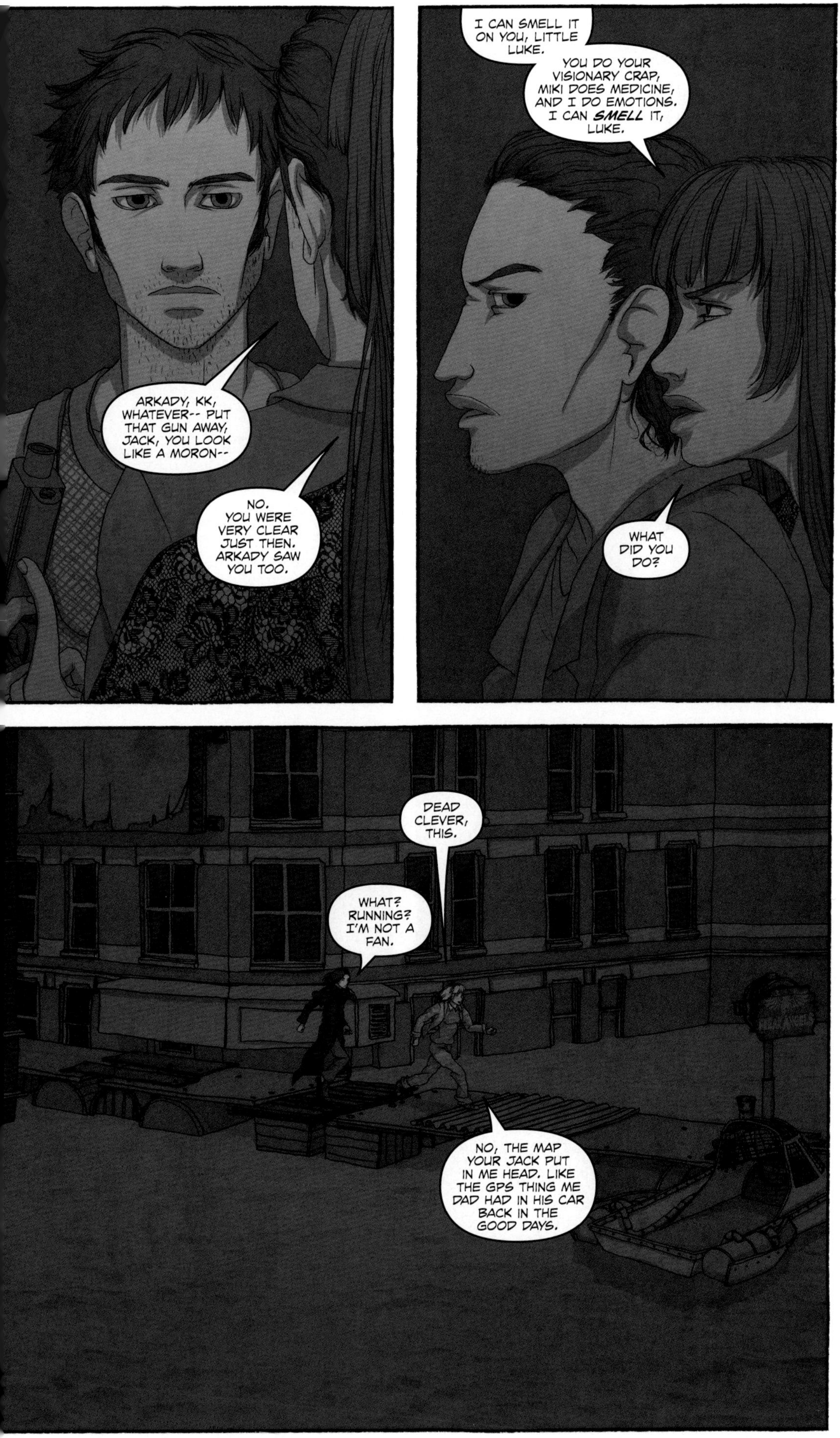
ARKADY, KK, WHATEVER-- PUT THAT GUN AWAY, JACK, YOU LOOK LIKE A MORON--
NO. YOU WERE VERY CLEAR JUST THEN. ARKADY SAW YOU TOO.
I CAN SMELL IT ON YOU, LITTLE LUKE.
YOU DO YOUR VISIONARY CRAP, MIKI DOES MEDICINE, AND I DO EMOTIONS. I CAN SMELL IT, LUKE.
WHAT DID YOU DO?
DEAD CLEVER, THIS.
WHAT? RUNNING? I'M NOT A FAN.
NO, THE MAP YOUR JACK PUT IN ME HEAD. LIKE THE GPS THING ME DAD HAD IN HIS CAR BACK IN THE GOOD DAYS.

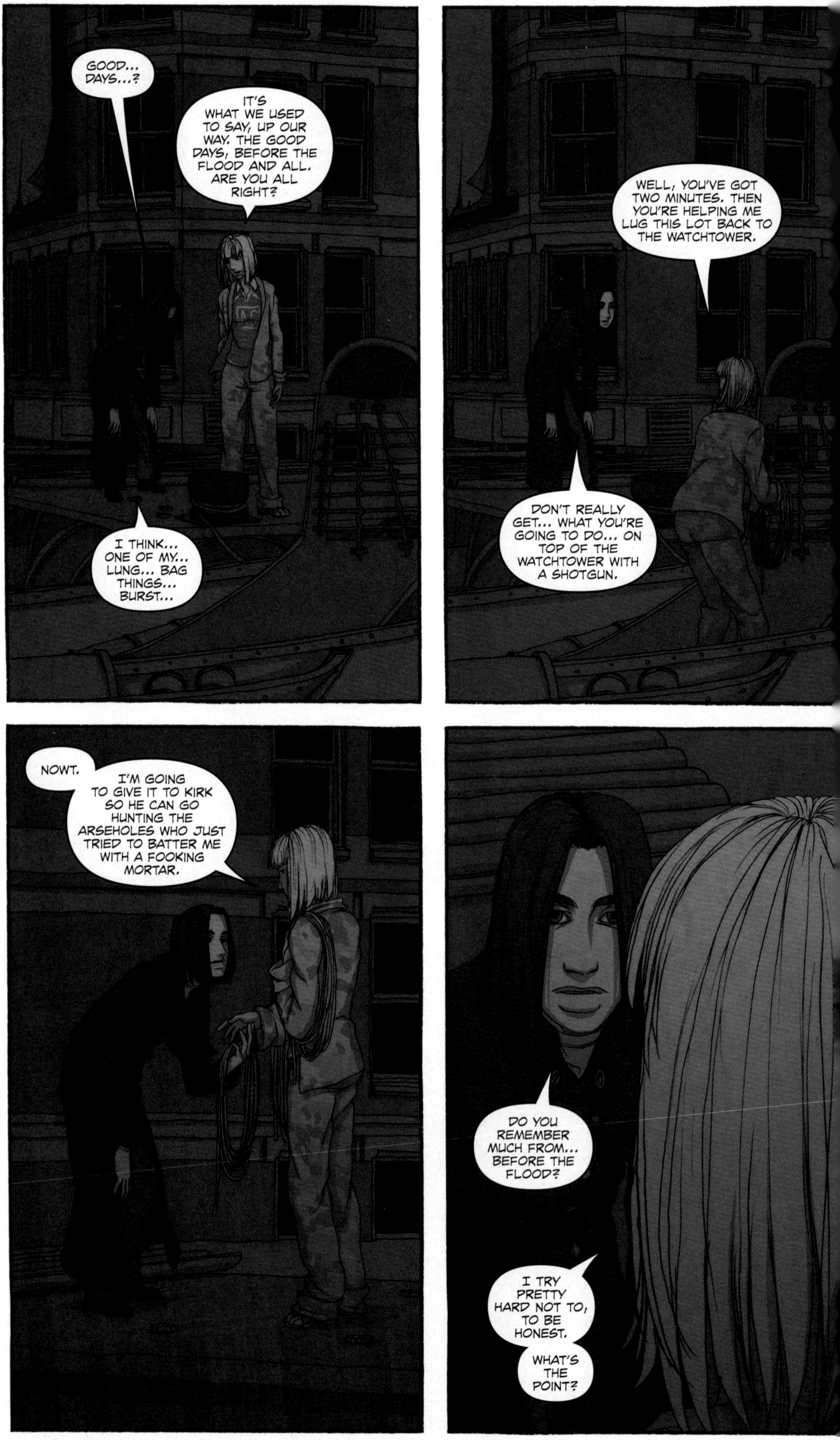
GOOD... DAYS...?
IT'S WHAT WE USED TO SAY, UP OUR WAY. THE GOOD DAYS, BEFORE THE FLOOD AND ALL. ARE YOU ALL RIGHT?
I THINK... ONE OF MY... LUNG... BAG THINGS... BURST...
WELL, YOU'VE GOT TWO MINUTES. THEN YOU'RE HELPING ME LUG THIS LOT BACK TO THE WATCHTOWER.
DON'T REALLY GET... WHAT YOU'RE GOING TO DO... ON TOP OF THE WATCHTOWER WITH A SHOTGUN.
NOWT.
I'M GOING TO GIVE IT TO KIRK SO HE CAN GO HUNTING THE ARSEHOLES WHO JUST TRIED TO BATTER ME WITH A FOOKING MORTAR.
DO YOU REMEMBER MUCH FROM... BEFORE THE FLOOD?
I TRY PRETTY HARD NOT TO, TO BE HONEST.
WHAT'S THE POINT?

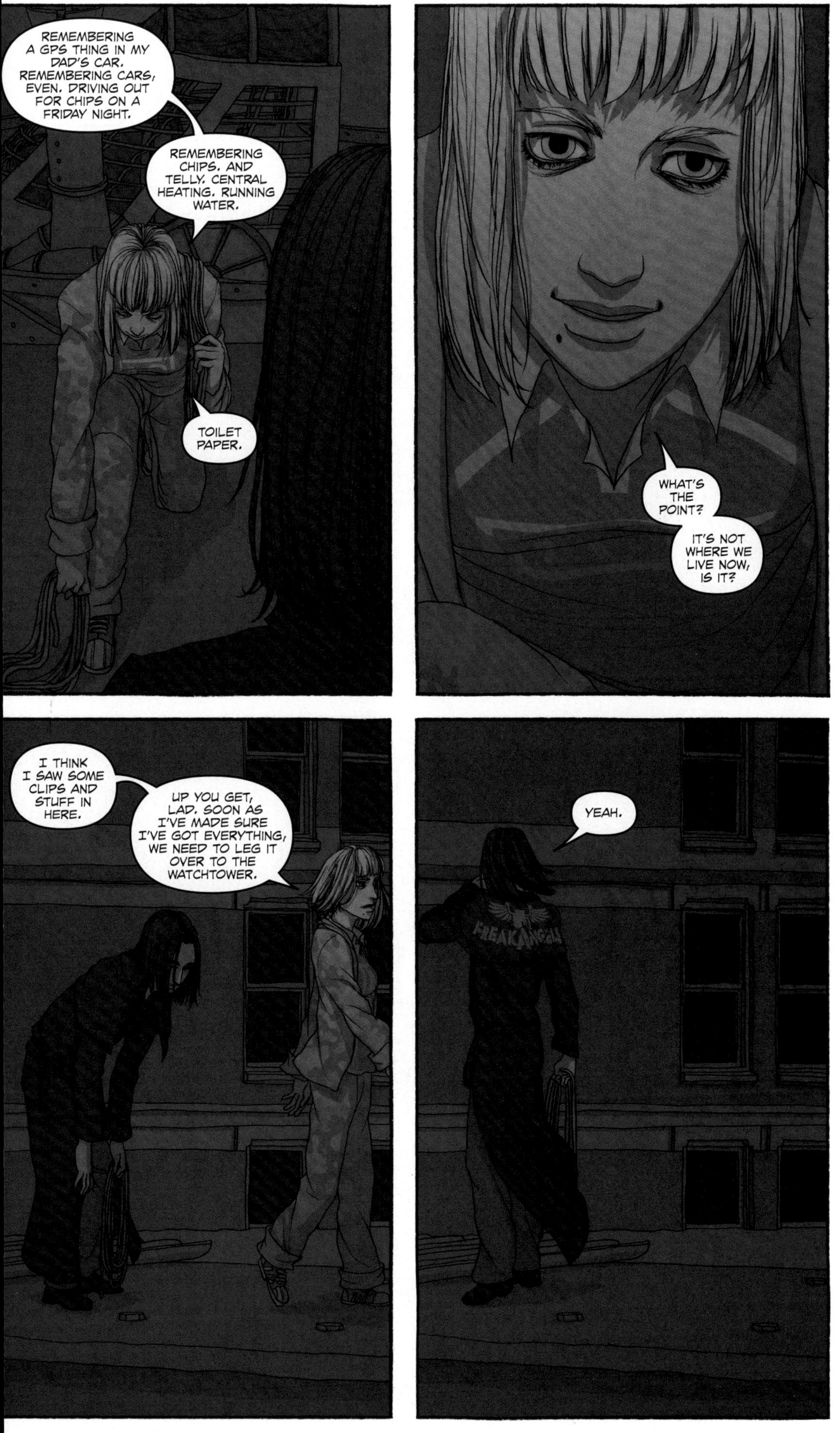
REMEMBERING A GPS THING IN MY DAD'S CAR. REMEMBERING CARS, EVEN. DRIVING OUT FOR CHIPS ON A FRIDAY NIGHT.
REMEMBERING CHIPS. AND TELLY. CENTRAL HEATING. RUNNING WATER.
TOILET PAPER.
WHAT'S THE POINT?
IT'S NOT WHERE WE LIVE NOW, IS IT?
I THINK I SAW SOME CLIPS AND STUFF IN HERE.
UP YOU GET, LAD. SOON AS I'VE MADE SURE I'VE GOT EVERYTHING, WE NEED TO LEG IT OVER TO THE WATCHTOWER.
YEAH.

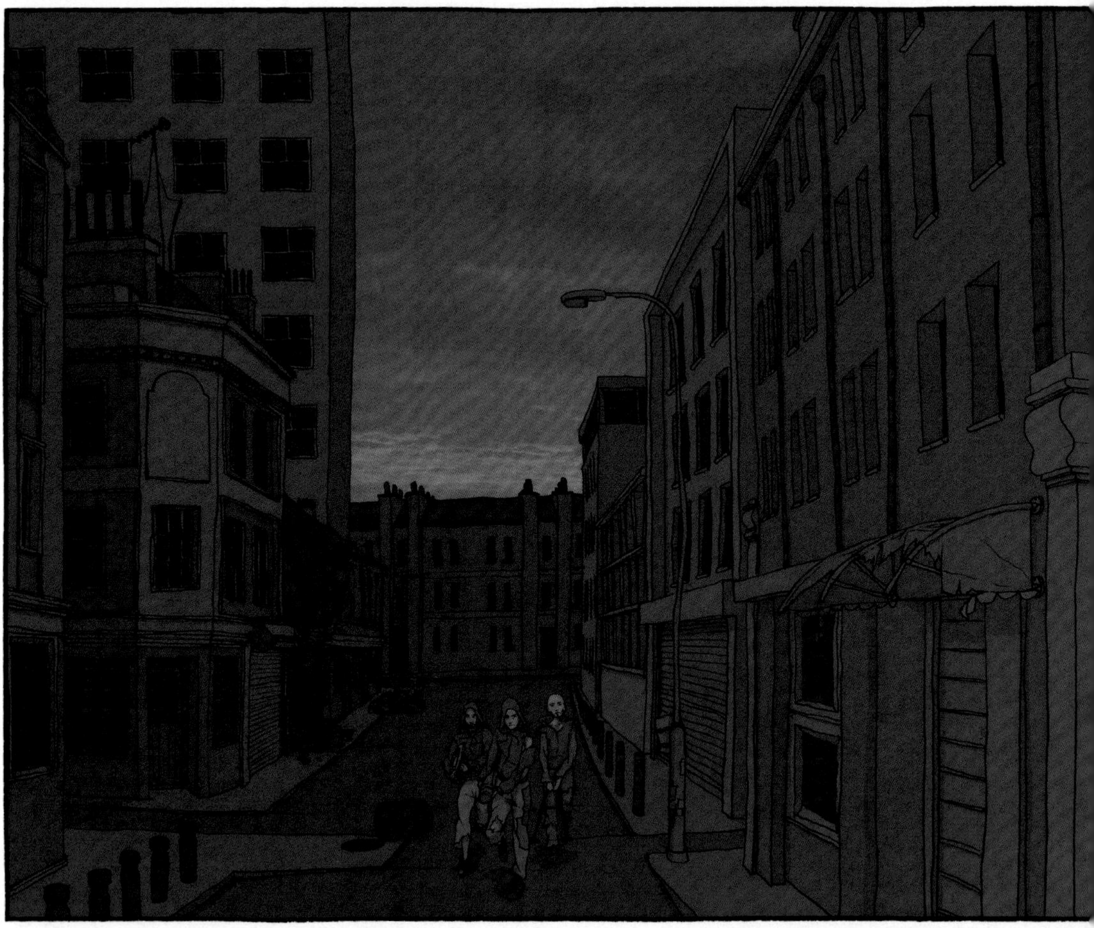

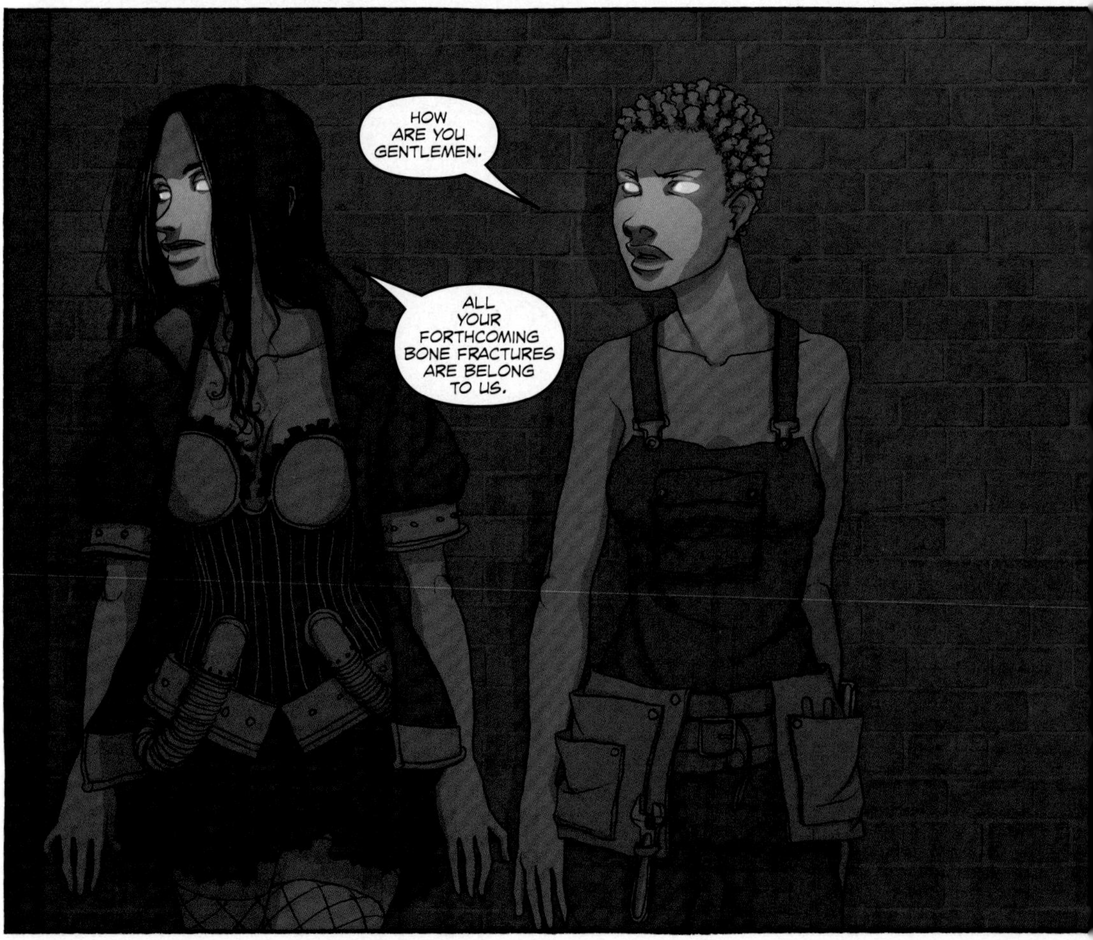
HOW ARE YOU GENTLEMEN.
ALL YOUR FORTHCOMING BONE FRACTURES ARE BELONG TO US.

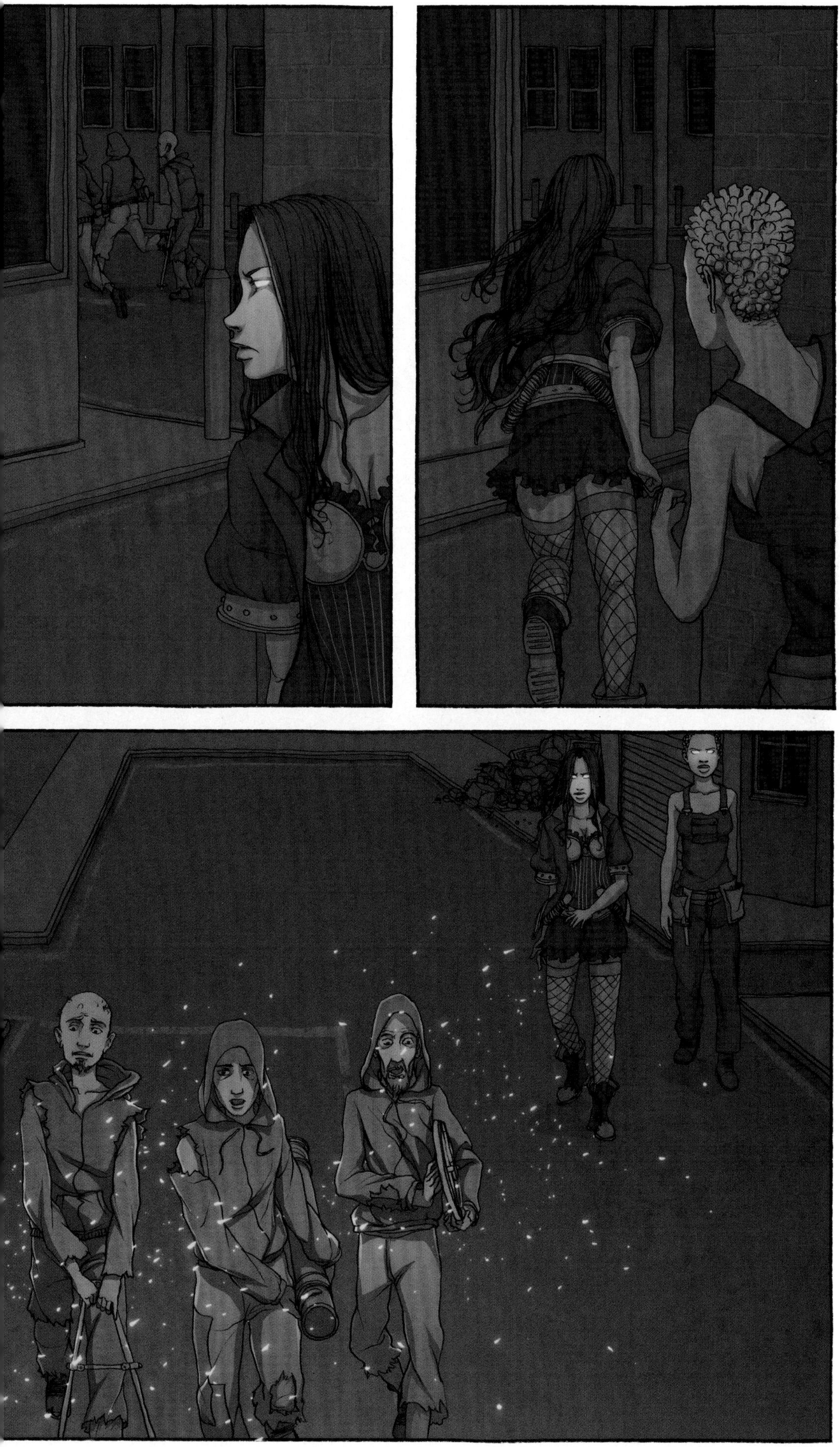

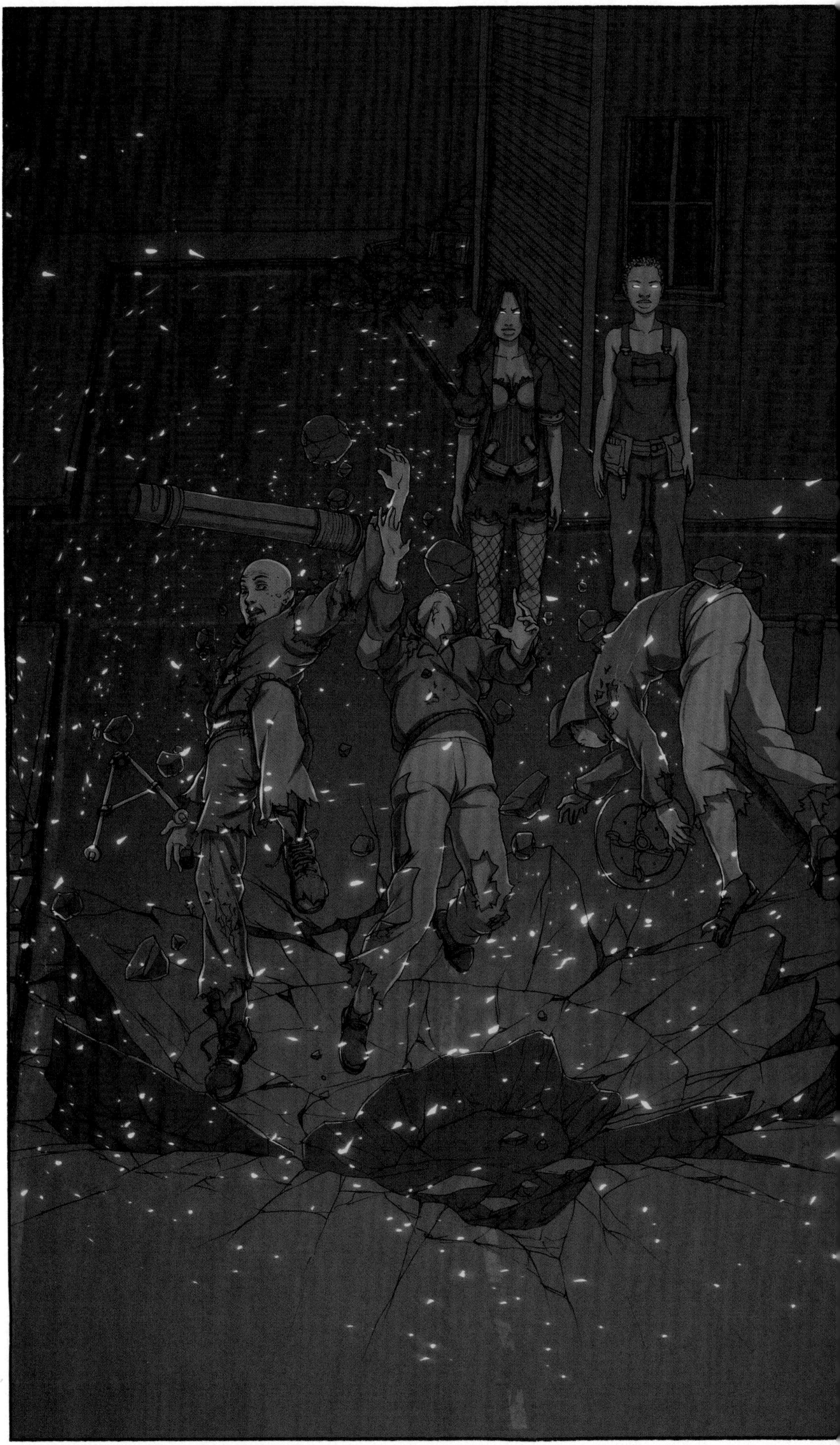

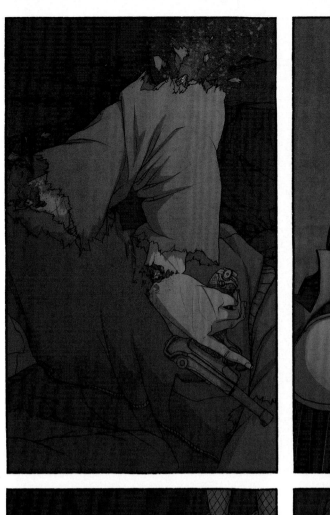

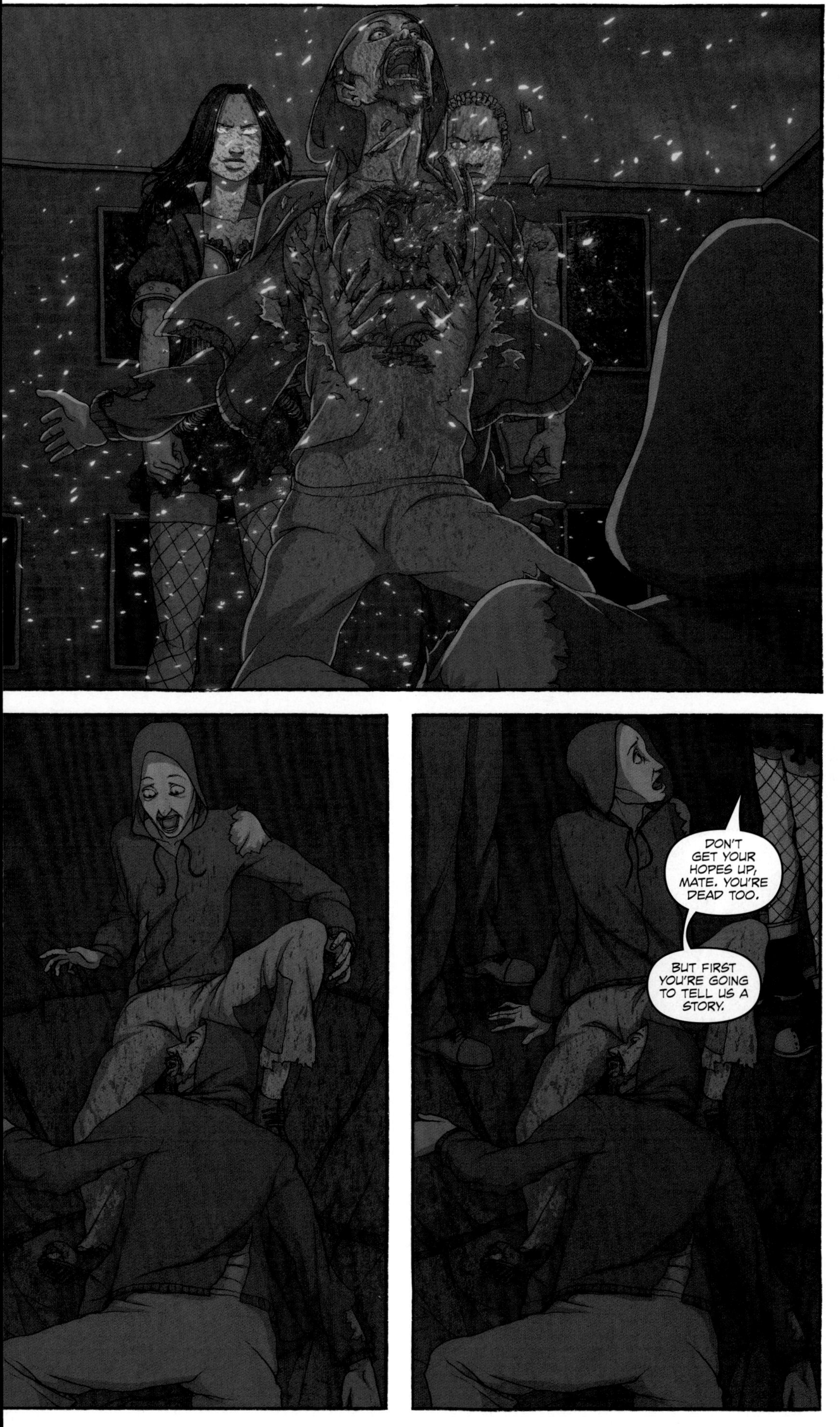
DON'T GET YOUR HOPES UP, MATE. YOU'RE DEAD TOO.
BUT FIRST YOU'RE GOING TO TELL US A STORY.

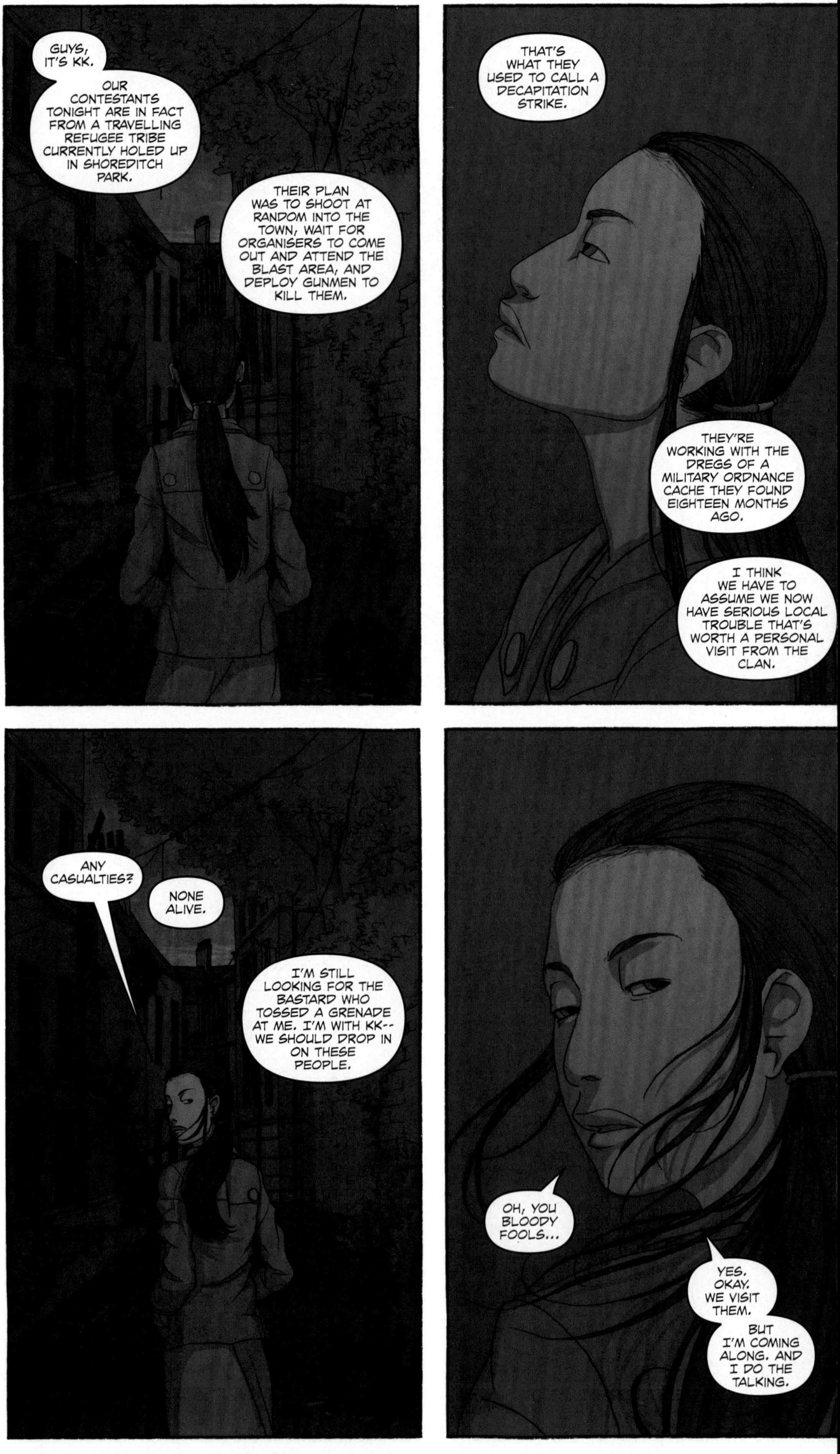
GUYS, IT'S KK.
OUR CONTESTANTS TONIGHT ARE IN FACT FROM A TRAVELLING REFUGEE TRIBE CURRENTLY HOLED UP IN SHOREDITCH PARK.
THEIR PLAN WAS TO SHOOT AT RANDOM INTO THE TOWN, WAIT FOR ORGANISERS TO COME OUT AND ATTEND THE BLAST AREA, AND DEPLOY GUNMEN TO KILL THEM.
THAT'S WHAT THEY USED TO CALL A DECAPITATION STRIKE.
THEY'RE WORKING WITH THE DREGS OF A MILITARY ORDNANCE CACHE THEY FOUND EIGHTEEN MONTHS AGO.
I THINK WE HAVE TO ASSUME WE NOW HAVE SERIOUS LOCAL TROUBLE THAT'S WORTH A PERSONAL VISIT FROM THE CLAN.
ANY CASUALTIES?
NONE ALIVE.
I'M STILL LOOKING FOR THE BASTARD WHO TOSSED A GRENADE AT ME. I'M WITH KK-- WE SHOULD DROP IN ON THESE PEOPLE.
OH, YOU BLOODY FOOLS...
YES. OKAY. WE VISIT THEM.
BUT I'M COMING ALONG. AND I DO THE TALKING.

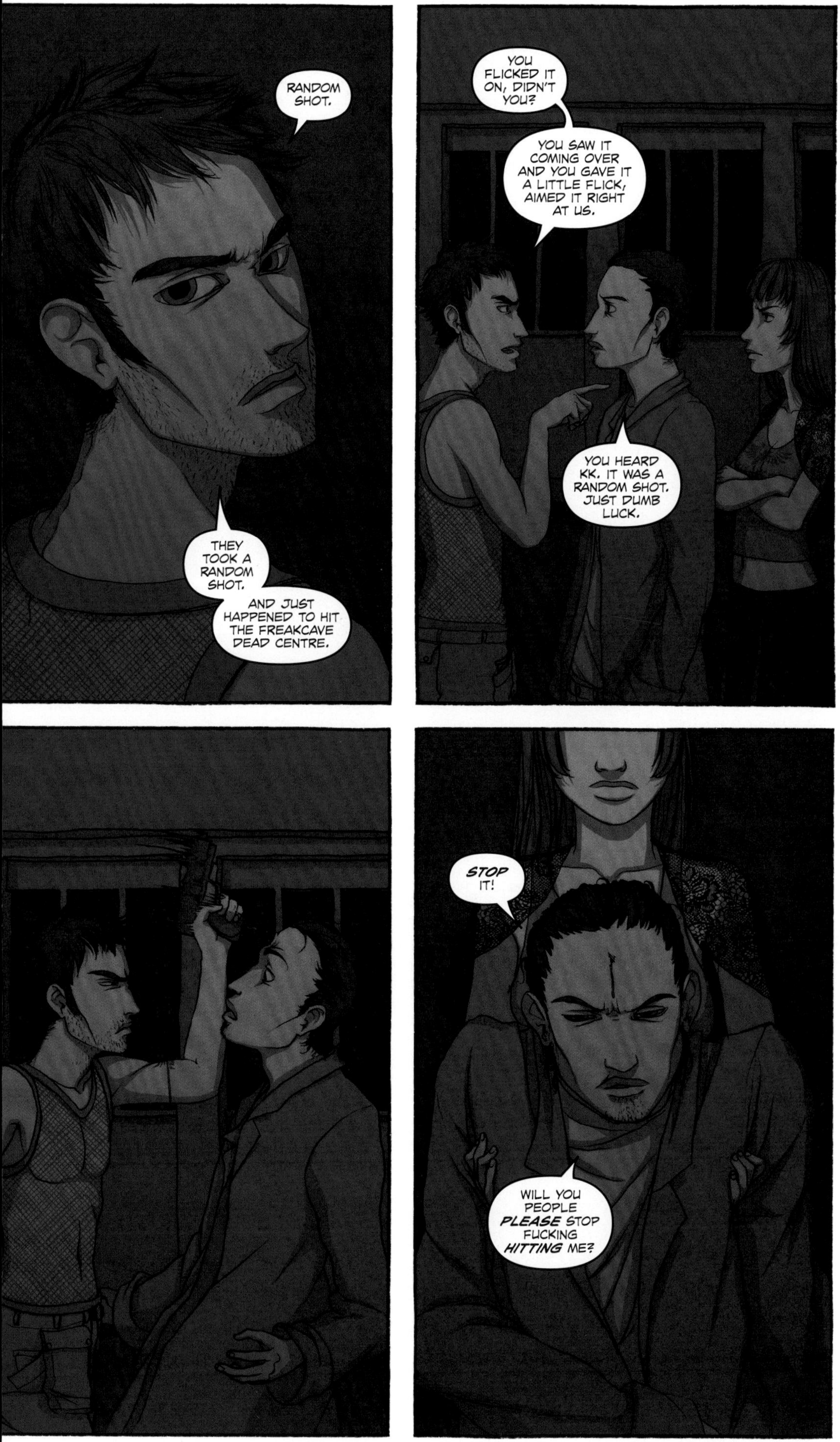
RANDOM SHOT.
THEY TOOK A RANDOM SHOT.
AND JUST HAPPENED TO HIT THE FREAKCAVE DEAD CENTRE.
YOU FLICKED IT ON, DIDN'T YOU?
YOU SAW IT COMING OVER AND YOU GAVE IT A LITTLE FLICK, AIMED IT RIGHT AT US.
YOU HEARD KK. IT WAS A RANDOM SHOT. JUST DUMB LUCK.
STOP IT!
WILL YOU PEOPLE *PLEASE* STOP FUCKING *HITTING* ME?

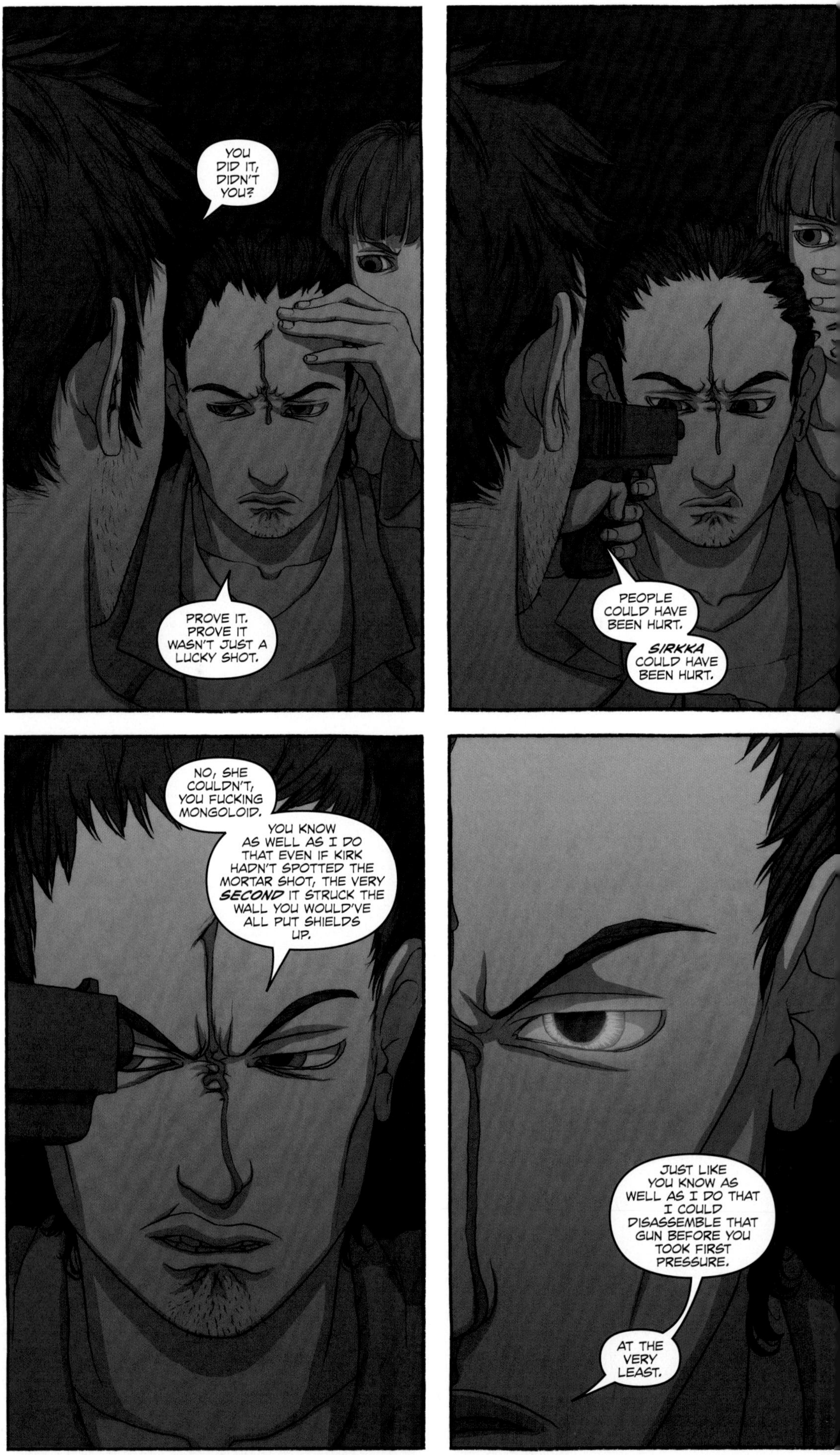
YOU DID IT, DIDN'T YOU?
PROVE IT. PROVE IT WASN'T JUST A LUCKY SHOT.
PEOPLE COULD HAVE BEEN HURT.
SIRKKA COULD HAVE BEEN HURT.
NO, SHE COULDN'T, YOU FUCKING MONGOLOID.
YOU KNOW AS WELL AS I DO THAT EVEN IF KIRK HADN'T SPOTTED THE MORTAR SHOT, THE VERY SECOND IT STRUCK THE WALL YOU WOULD'VE ALL PUT SHIELDS UP.
JUST LIKE YOU KNOW AS WELL AS I DO THAT I COULD DISASSEMBLE THAT GUN BEFORE YOU TOOK FIRST PRESSURE.
AT THE VERY LEAST.

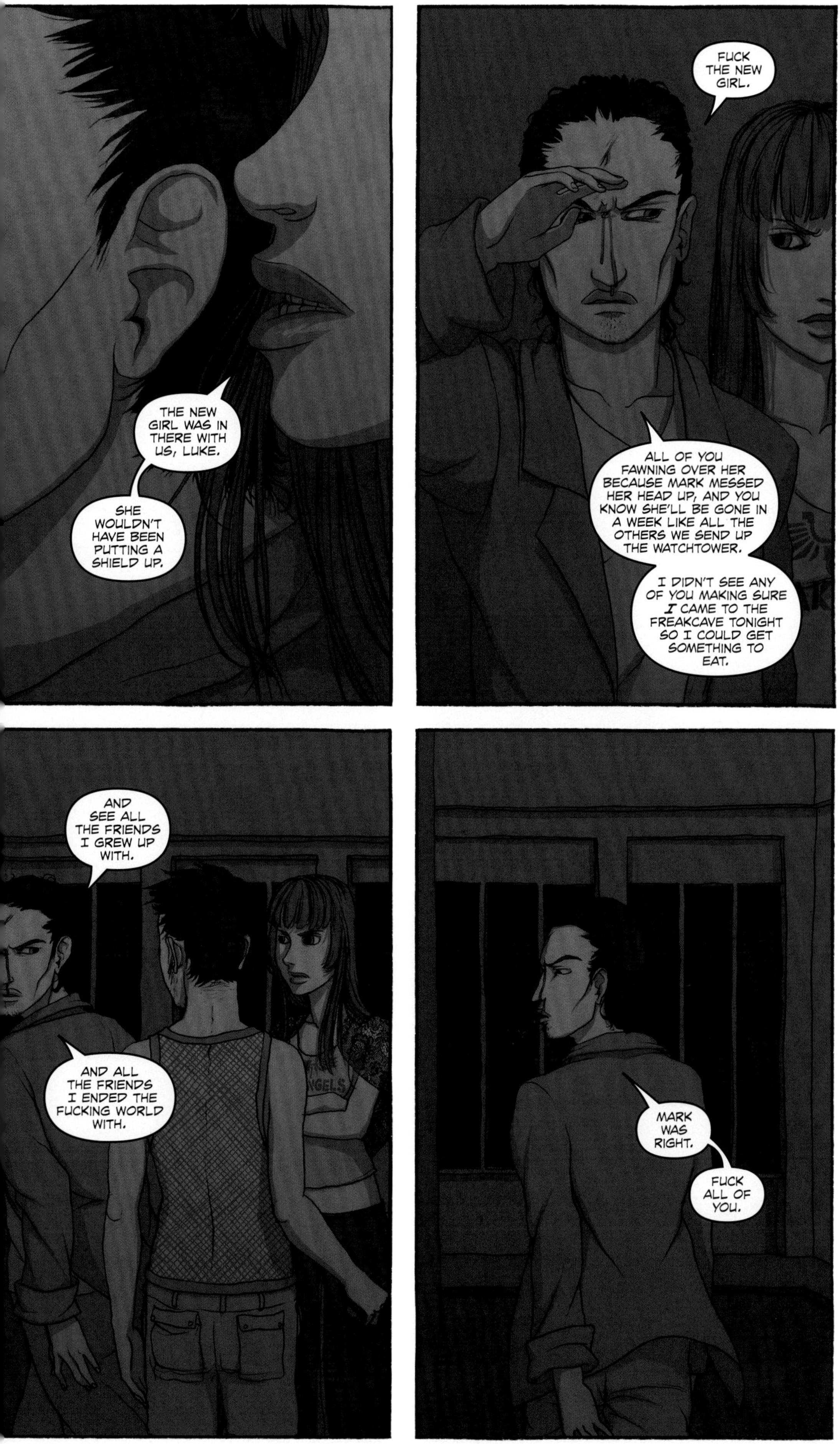
THE NEW GIRL WAS IN THERE WITH US, LUKE.
SHE WOULDN'T HAVE BEEN PUTTING A SHIELD UP.
FUCK THE NEW GIRL.
ALL OF YOU FAWNING OVER HER BECAUSE MARK MESSED HER HEAD UP, AND YOU KNOW SHE'LL BE GONE IN A WEEK LIKE ALL THE OTHERS WE SEND UP THE WATCHTOWER.
I DIDN'T SEE ANY OF YOU MAKING SURE *I* CAME TO THE FREAKCAVE TONIGHT SO I COULD GET SOMETHING TO EAT.
AND SEE ALL THE FRIENDS I GREW UP WITH.
AND ALL THE FRIENDS I ENDED THE FUCKING WORLD WITH.
MARK WAS RIGHT.
FUCK ALL OF YOU.

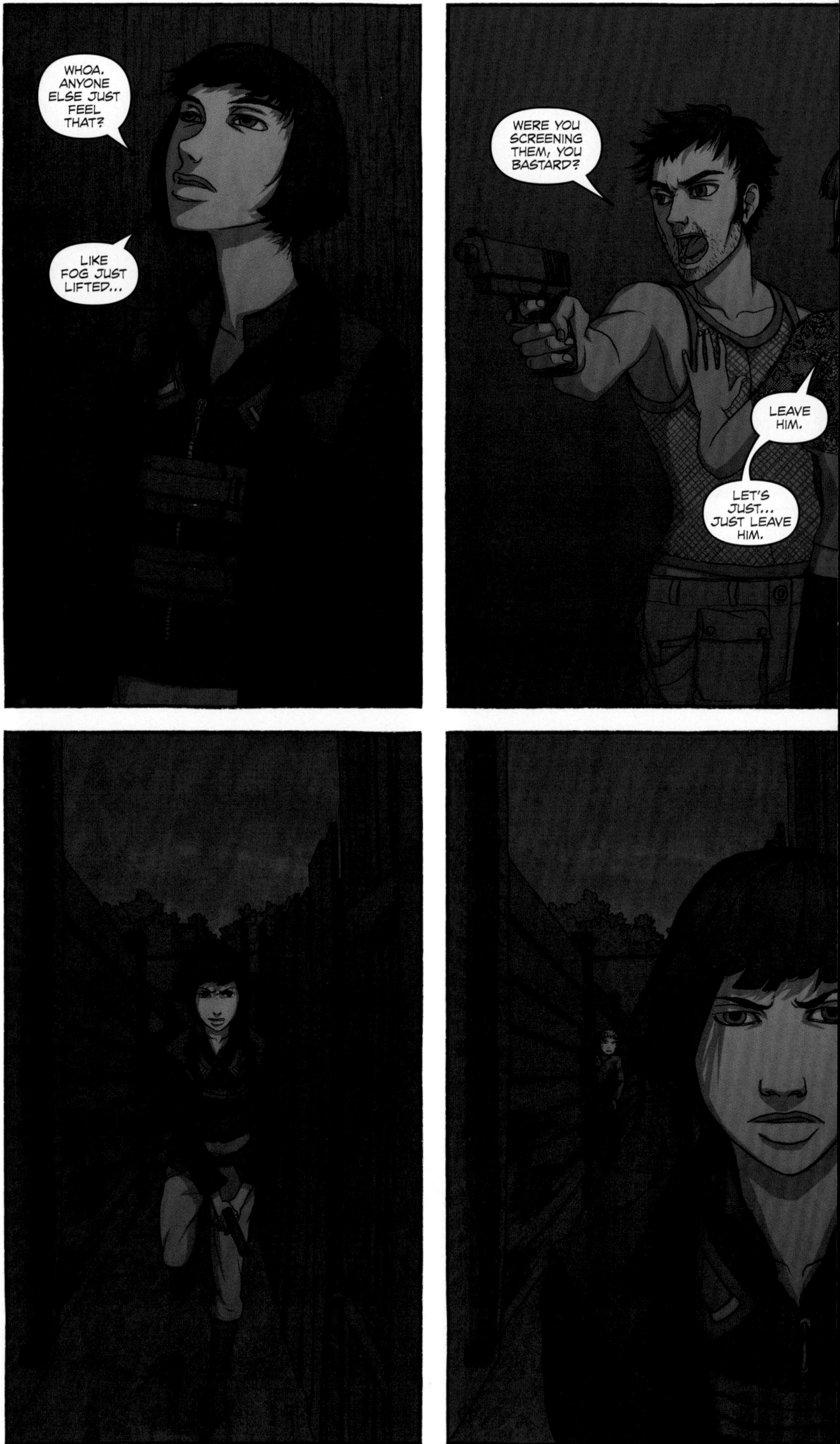
WHOA. ANYONE ELSE JUST FEEL THAT?
LIKE FOG JUST LIFTED...
WERE YOU SCREENING THEM, YOU BASTARD?
LEAVE HIM.
LET'S JUST... JUST LEAVE HIM.

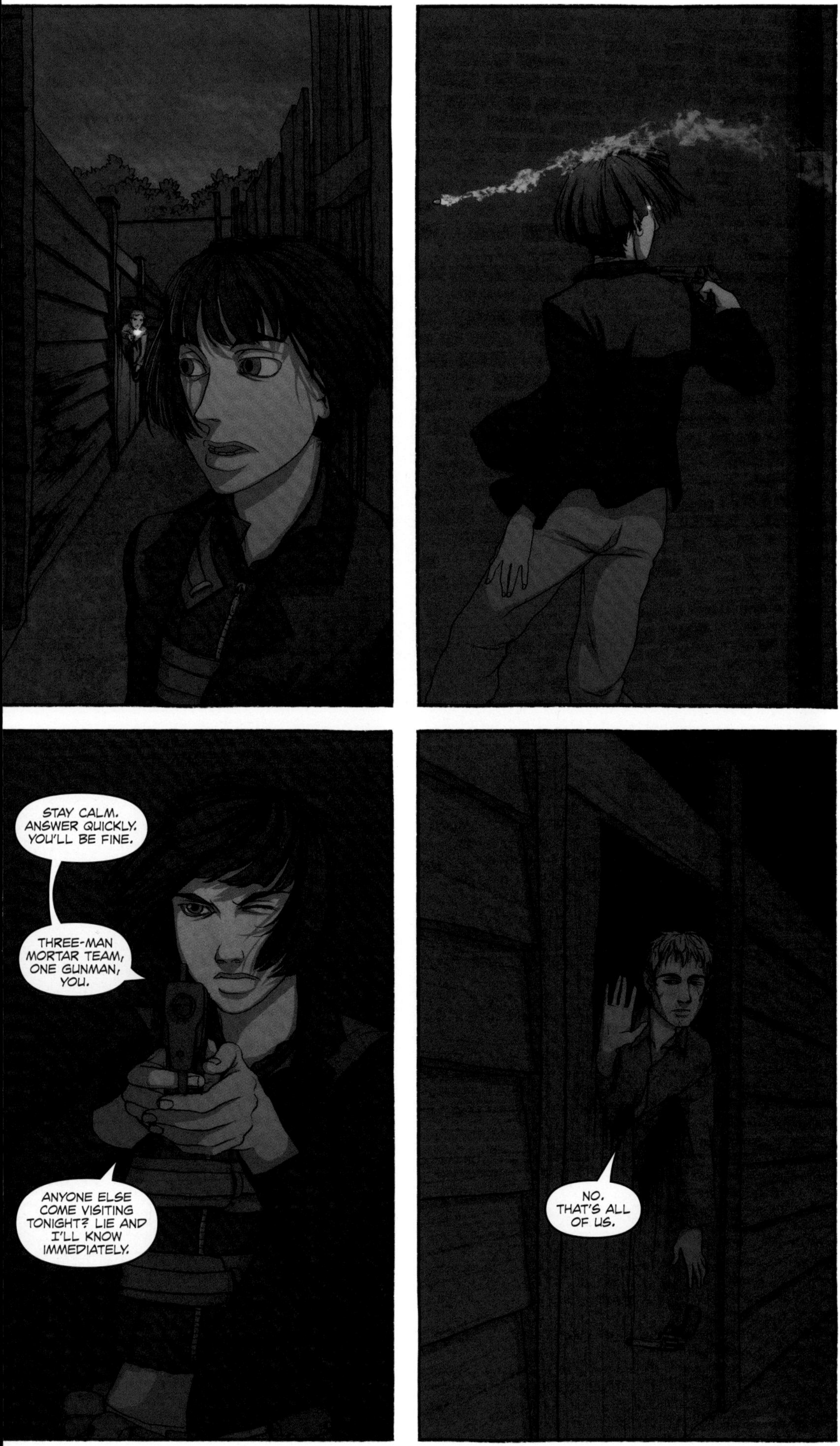
STAY CALM. ANSWER QUICKLY. YOU'LL BE FINE.
THREE-MAN MORTAR TEAM, ONE GUNMAN, YOU.
ANYONE ELSE COME VISITING TONIGHT? LIE AND I'LL KNOW IMMEDIATELY.
NO. THAT'S ALL OF US.

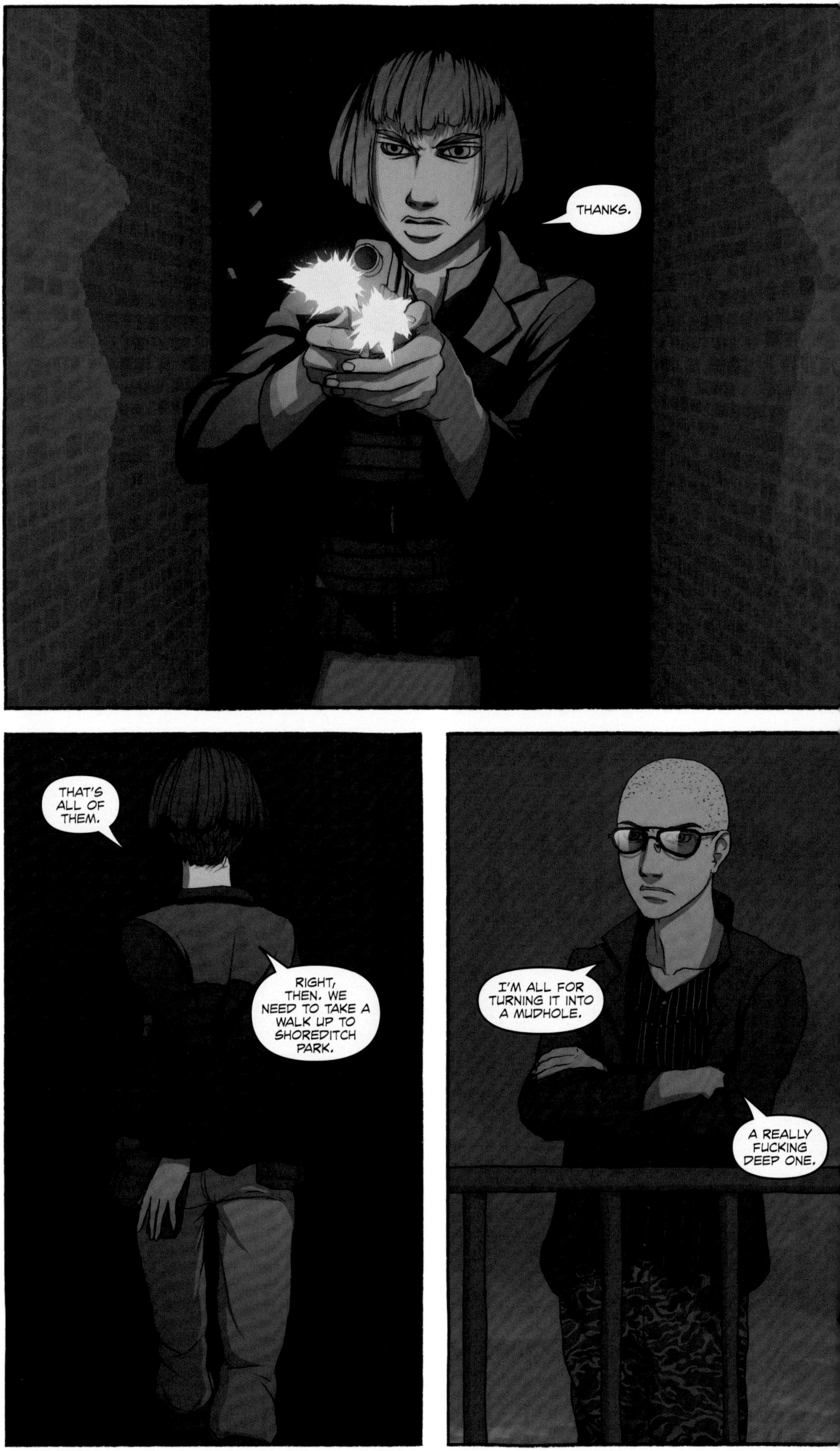
THANKS.
THAT'S ALL OF THEM.
RIGHT, THEN. WE NEED TO TAKE A WALK UP TO SHOREDITCH PARK.
I'M ALL FOR TURNING IT INTO A MUDHOLE.
A REALLY FUCKING DEEP ONE.

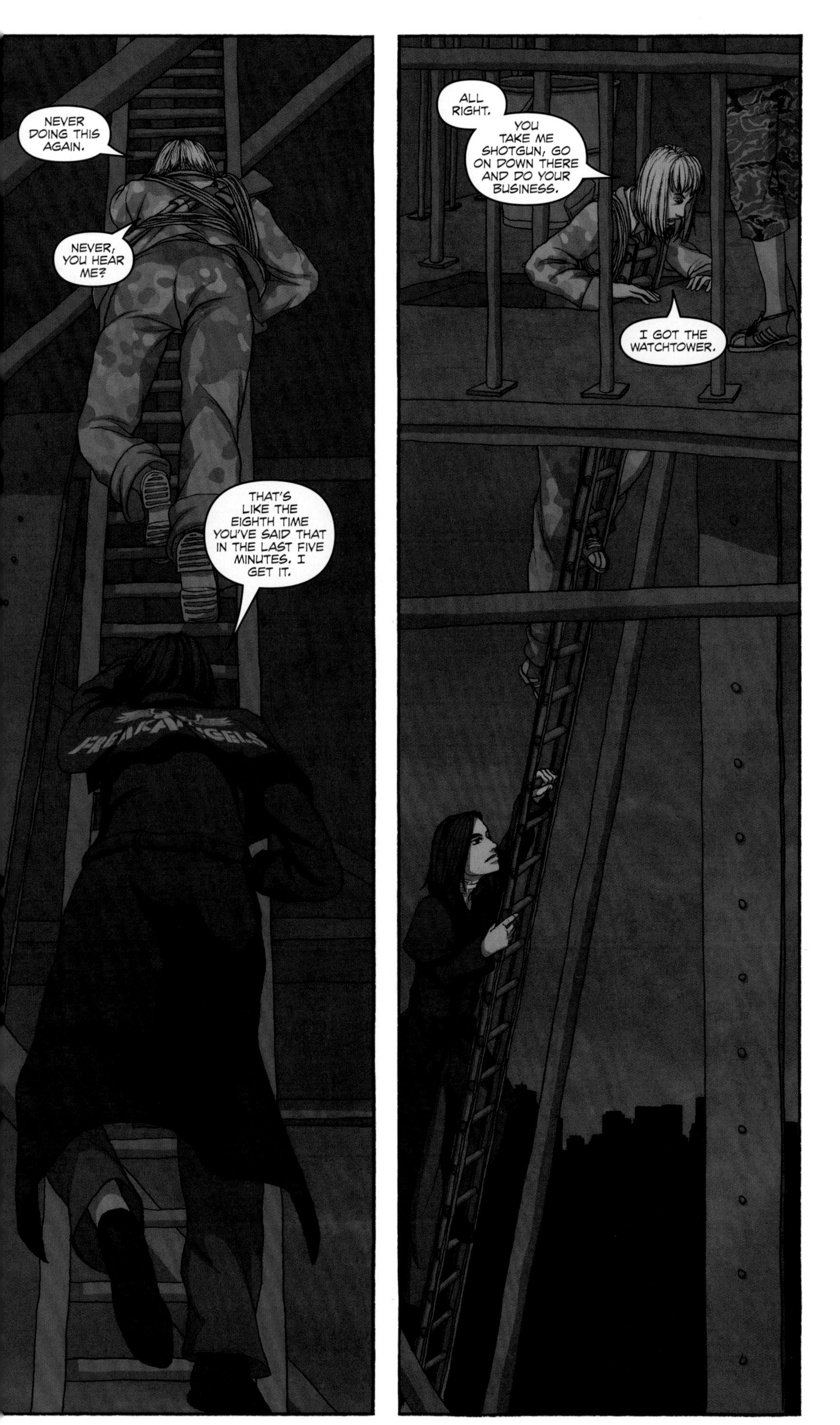
NEVER DOING THIS AGAIN.
NEVER, YOU HEAR ME?
THAT'S LIKE THE EIGHTH TIME YOU'VE SAID THAT IN THE LAST FIVE MINUTES. I GET IT.
FREAKANGELS
ALL RIGHT.
YOU TAKE ME SHOTGUN, GO ON DOWN THERE AND DO YOUR BUSINESS.
I GOT THE WATCHTOWER.

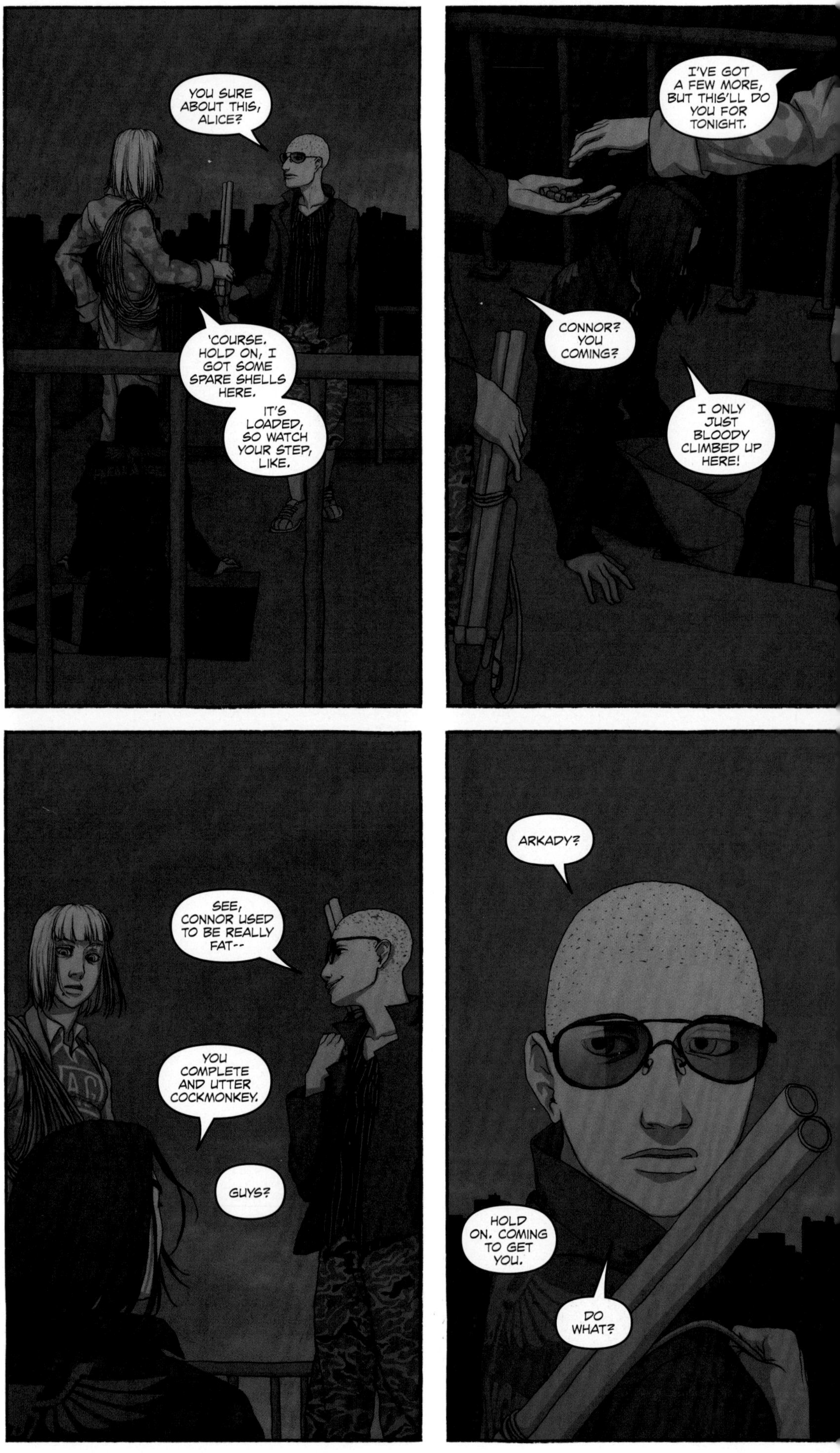
YOU SURE ABOUT THIS, ALICE?
'COURSE. HOLD ON, I GOT SOME SPARE SHELLS HERE.
IT'S LOADED, SO WATCH YOUR STEP, LIKE.
I'VE GOT A FEW MORE, BUT THIS'LL DO YOU FOR TONIGHT.
CONNOR? YOU COMING?
I ONLY JUST BLOODY CLIMBED UP HERE!
SEE, CONNOR USED TO BE REALLY FAT--
YOU COMPLETE AND UTTER COCKMONKEY.
GUYS?
ARKADY?
HOLD ON. COMING TO GET YOU.
DO WHAT?

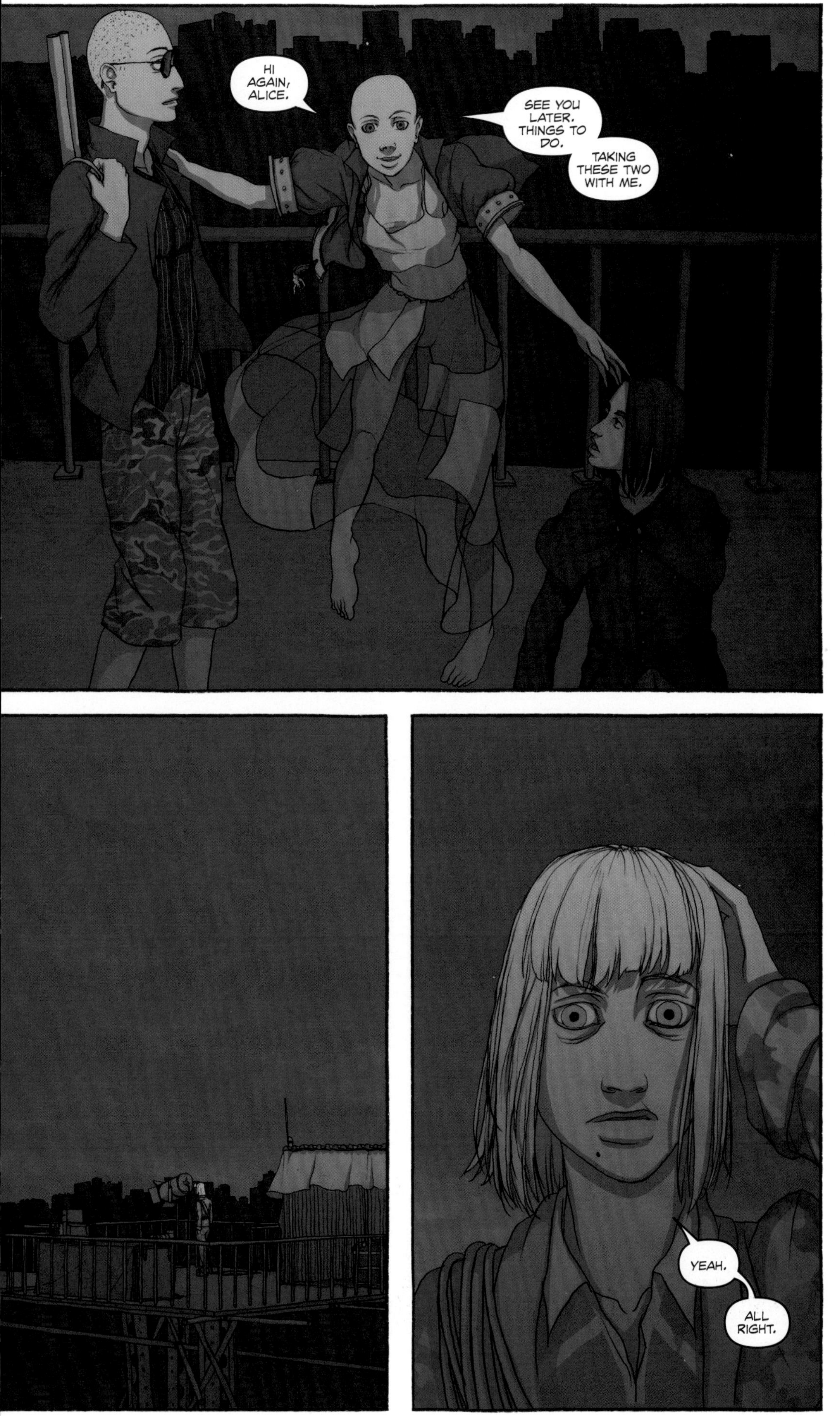
HI AGAIN, ALICE.
SEE YOU LATER. THINGS TO DO.
TAKING THESE TWO WITH ME.
YEAH.
ALL RIGHT.

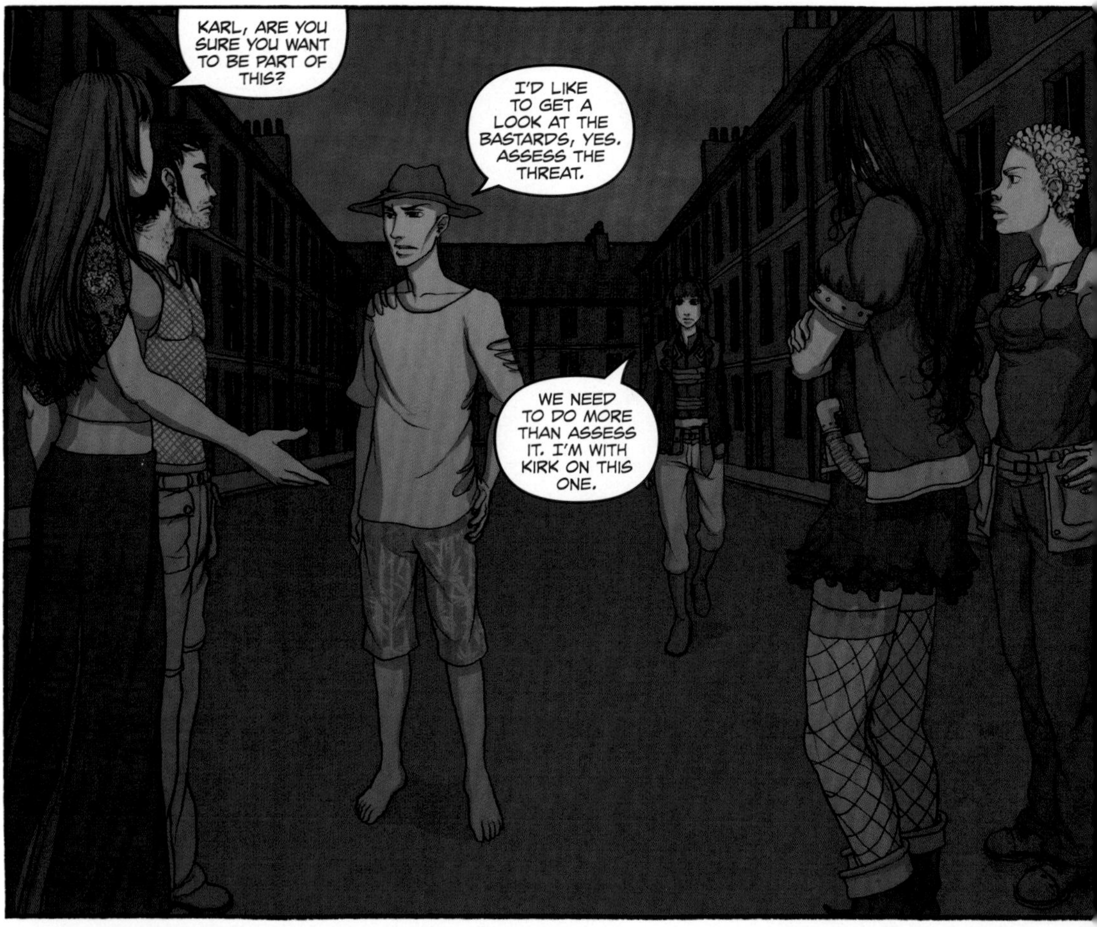
KARL, ARE YOU SURE YOU WANT TO BE PART OF THIS?
I'D LIKE TO GET A LOOK AT THE BASTARDS, YES. ASSESS THE THREAT.
WE NEED TO DO MORE THAN ASSESS IT. I'M WITH KIRK ON THIS ONE.

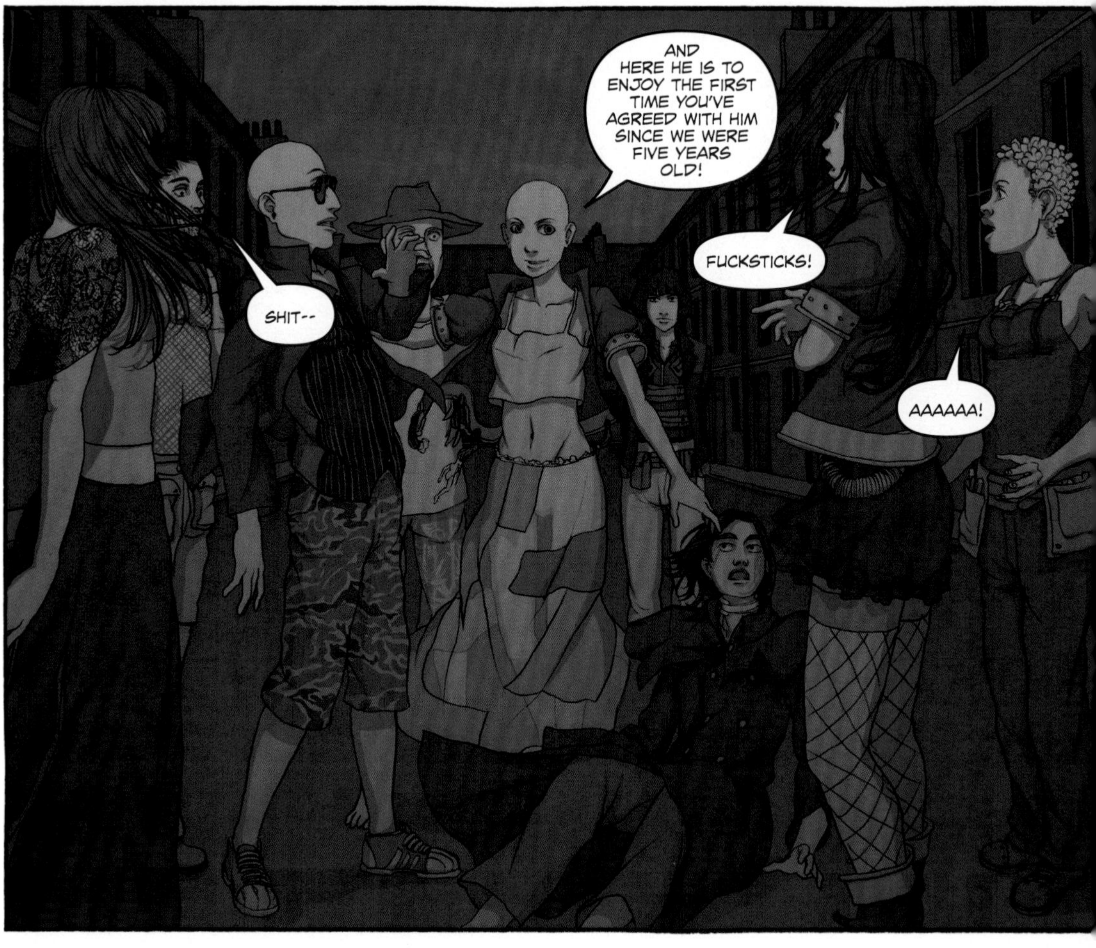
AND HERE HE IS TO ENJOY THE FIRST TIME YOU'VE AGREED WITH HIM SINCE WE WERE FIVE YEARS OLD!
SHIT--
FUCKSTICKS!
AAAAAA!

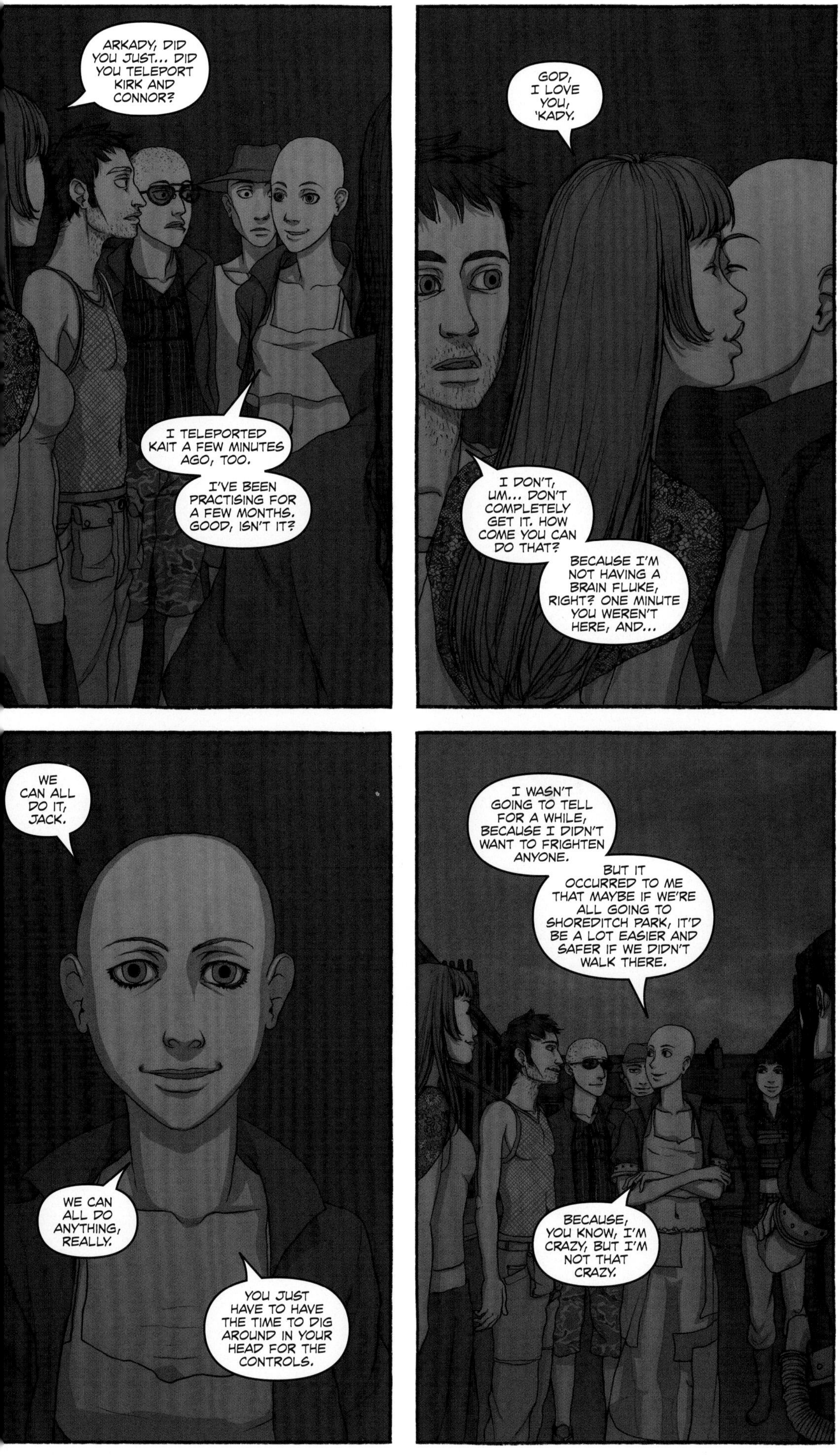
ARKADY, DID YOU JUST... DID YOU TELEPORT KIRK AND CONNOR?
I TELEPORTED KAIT A FEW MINUTES AGO, TOO.
I'VE BEEN PRACTISING FOR A FEW MONTHS. GOOD, ISN'T IT?
GOD, I LOVE YOU, 'KADY.
I DON'T, UM... DON'T COMPLETELY GET IT. HOW COME YOU CAN DO THAT?
BECAUSE I'M NOT HAVING A BRAIN FLUKE, RIGHT? ONE MINUTE YOU WEREN'T HERE, AND...
WE CAN ALL DO IT, JACK.
WE CAN ALL DO ANYTHING, REALLY.
YOU JUST HAVE TO HAVE THE TIME TO DIG AROUND IN YOUR HEAD FOR THE CONTROLS.
I WASN'T GOING TO TELL FOR A WHILE, BECAUSE I DIDN'T WANT TO FRIGHTEN ANYONE.
BUT IT OCCURRED TO ME THAT MAYBE IF WE'RE ALL GOING TO SHOREDITCH PARK, IT'D BE A LOT EASIER AND SAFER IF WE DIDN'T WALK THERE.
BECAUSE, YOU KNOW, I'M CRAZY, BUT I'M NOT THAT CRAZY.

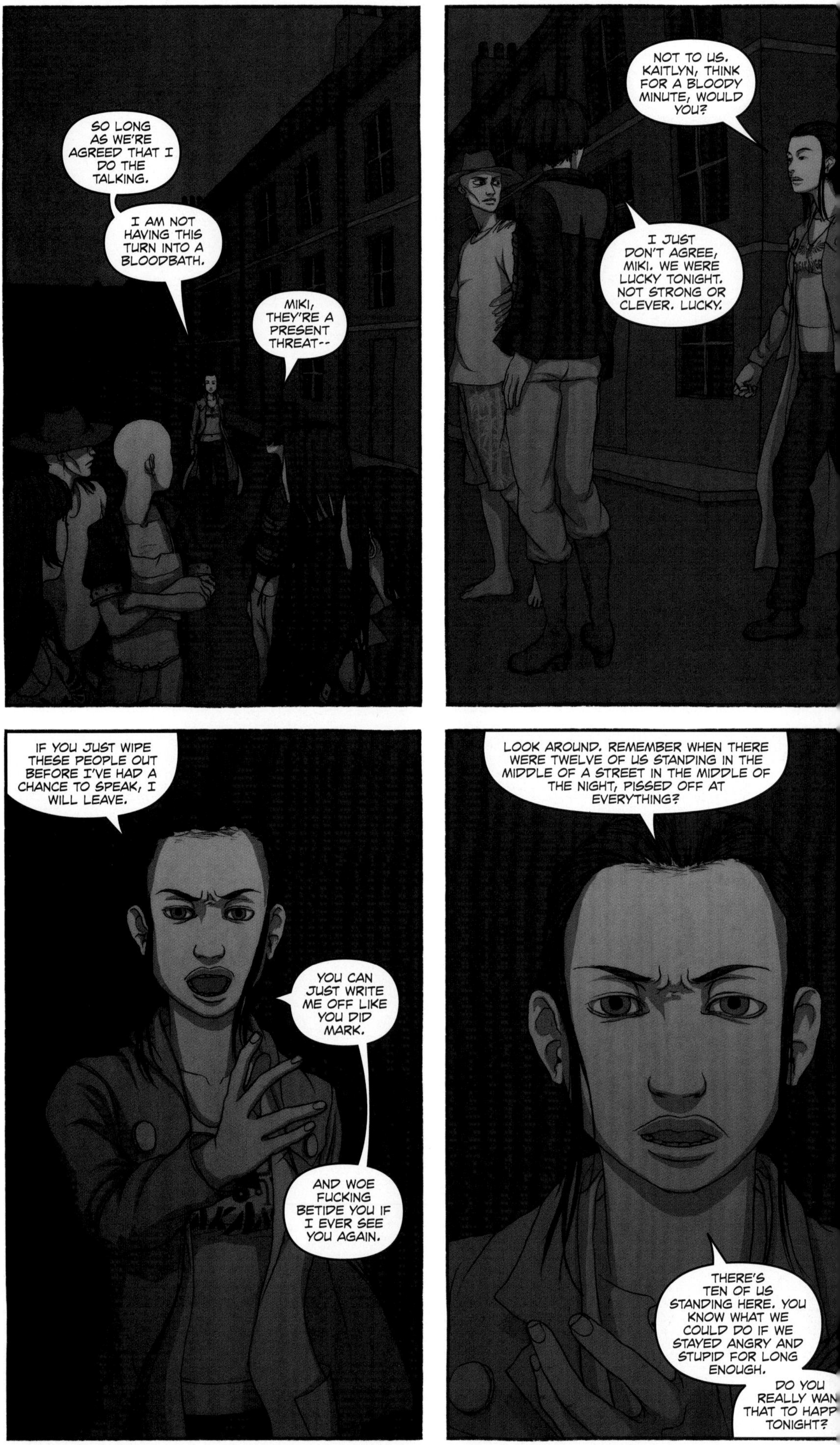
SO LONG AS WE'RE AGREED THAT I DO THE TALKING.
I AM NOT HAVING THIS TURN INTO A BLOODBATH.
MIKI, THEY'RE A PRESENT THREAT--
NOT TO US. KAITLYN, THINK FOR A BLOODY MINUTE, WOULD YOU?
I JUST DON'T AGREE, MIKI. WE WERE LUCKY TONIGHT. NOT STRONG OR CLEVER. LUCKY.
IF YOU JUST WIPE THESE PEOPLE OUT BEFORE I'VE HAD A CHANCE TO SPEAK, I WILL LEAVE.
YOU CAN JUST WRITE ME OFF LIKE YOU DID MARK.
AND WOE FUCKING BETIDE YOU IF I EVER SEE YOU AGAIN.
LOOK AROUND. REMEMBER WHEN THERE WERE TWELVE OF US STANDING IN THE MIDDLE OF A STREET IN THE MIDDLE OF THE NIGHT, PISSED OFF AT EVERYTHING?
THERE'S TEN OF US STANDING HERE. YOU KNOW WHAT WE COULD DO IF WE STAYED ANGRY AND STUPID FOR LONG ENOUGH.
DO YOU REALLY WAN THAT TO HAPP TONIGHT?

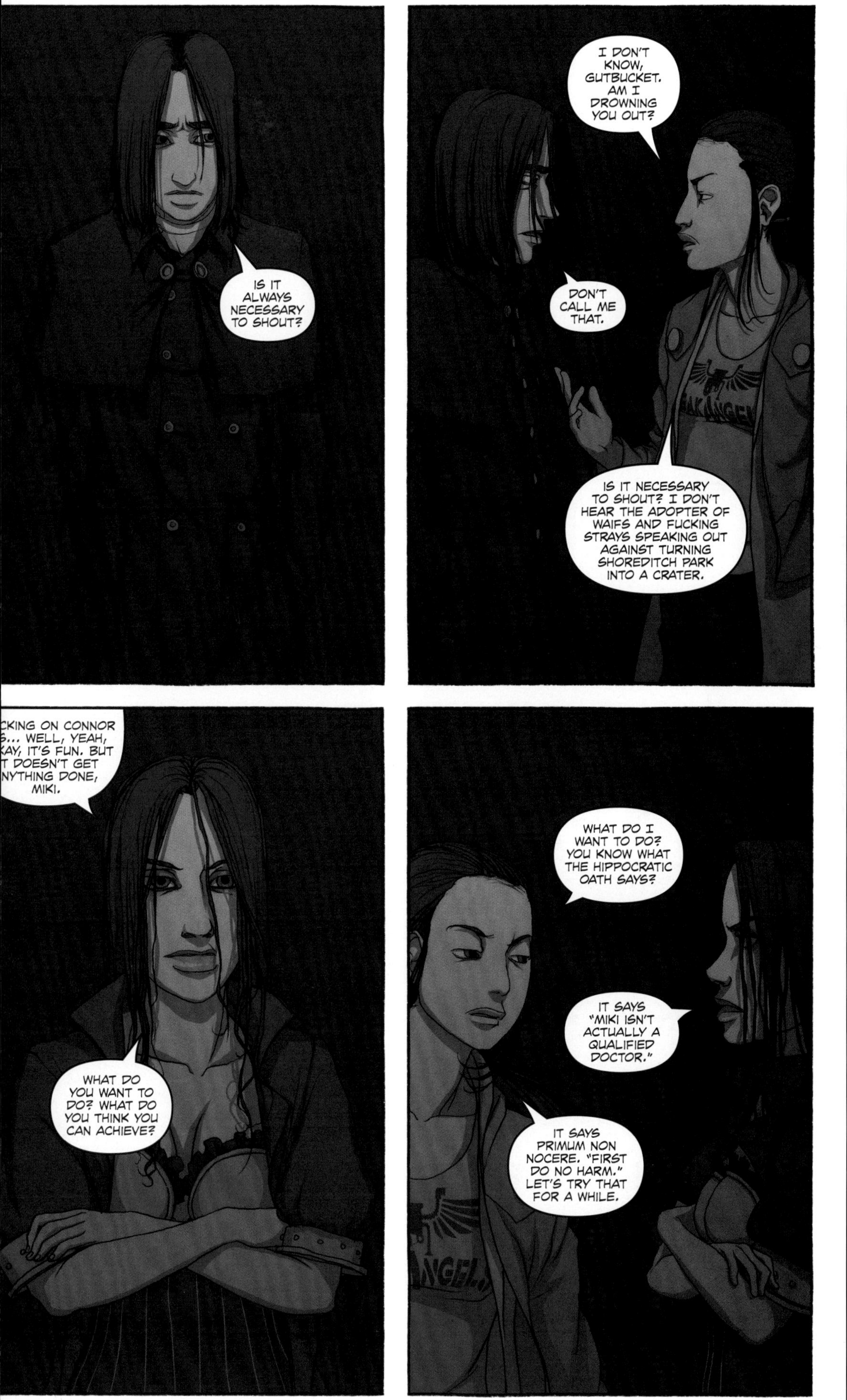
IS IT ALWAYS NECESSARY TO SHOUT?
I DON'T KNOW, GUTBUCKET. AM I DROWNING YOU OUT?
DON'T CALL ME THAT.
IS IT NECESSARY TO SHOUT? I DON'T HEAR THE ADOPTER OF WAIFS AND FUCKING STRAYS SPEAKING OUT AGAINST TURNING SHOREDITCH PARK INTO A CRATER.
CKING ON CONNOR S... WELL, YEAH, KAY, IT'S FUN. BUT T DOESN'T GET NYTHING DONE, MIKI.
WHAT DO YOU WANT TO DO? WHAT DO YOU THINK YOU CAN ACHIEVE?
WHAT DO I WANT TO DO? YOU KNOW WHAT THE HIPPOCRATIC OATH SAYS?
IT SAYS "MIKI ISN'T ACTUALLY A QUALIFIED DOCTOR."
IT SAYS PRIMUM NON NOCERE. "FIRST DO NO HARM." LET'S TRY THAT FOR A WHILE.

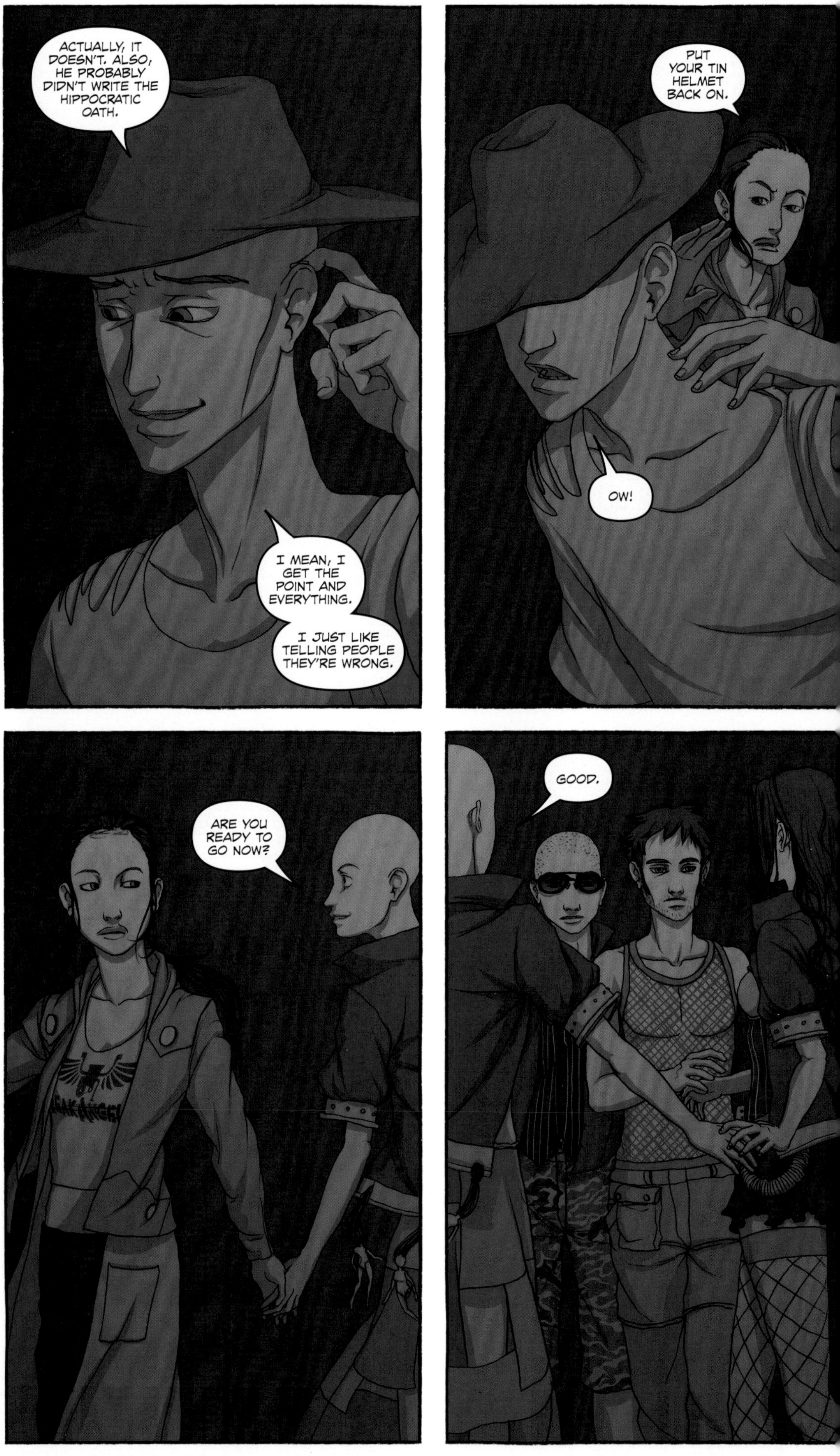
ACTUALLY, IT DOESN'T. ALSO, HE PROBABLY DIDN'T WRITE THE HIPPOCRATIC OATH.
I MEAN, I GET THE POINT AND EVERYTHING.
I JUST LIKE TELLING PEOPLE THEY'RE WRONG.
PUT YOUR TIN HELMET BACK ON.
OW!
ARE YOU READY TO GO NOW?
GOOD.

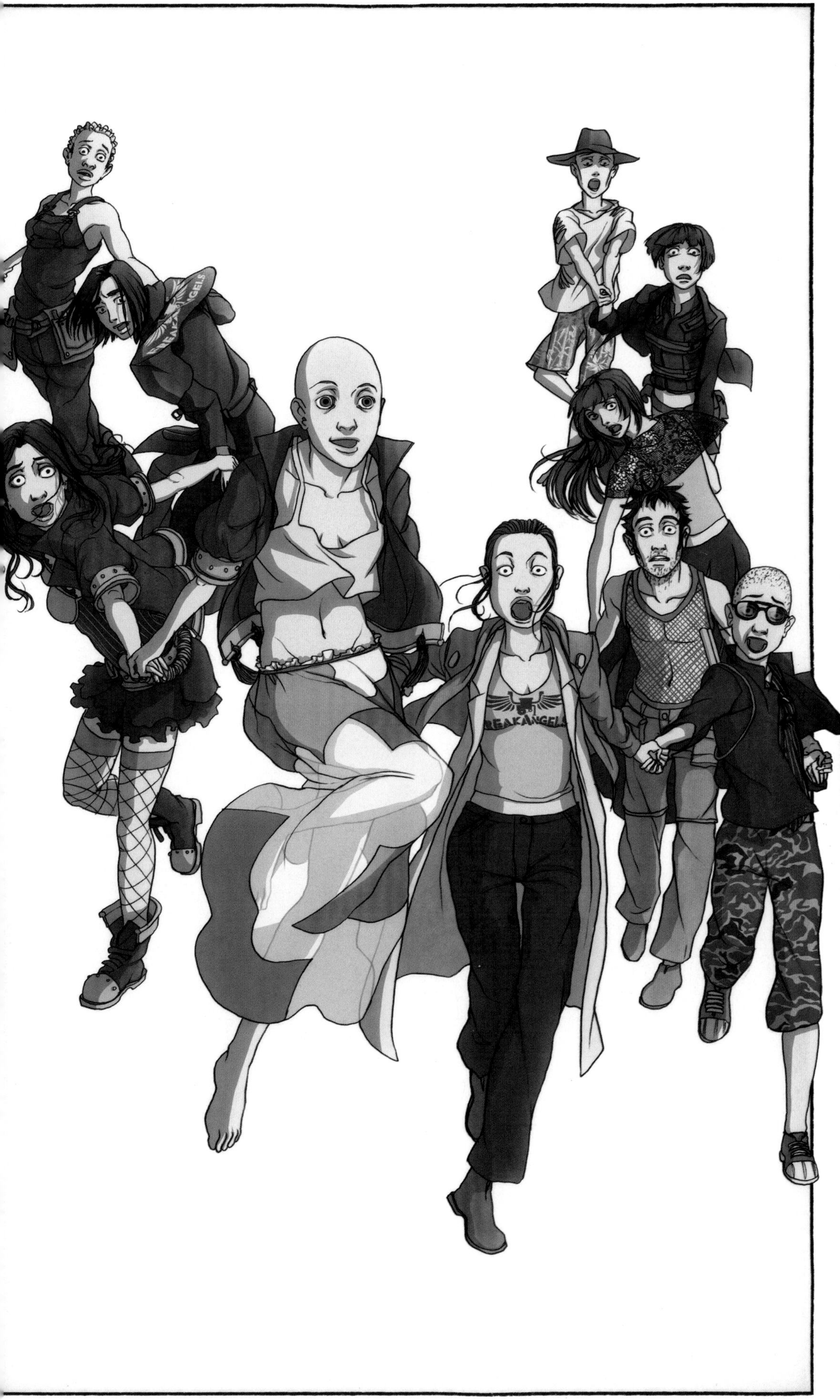

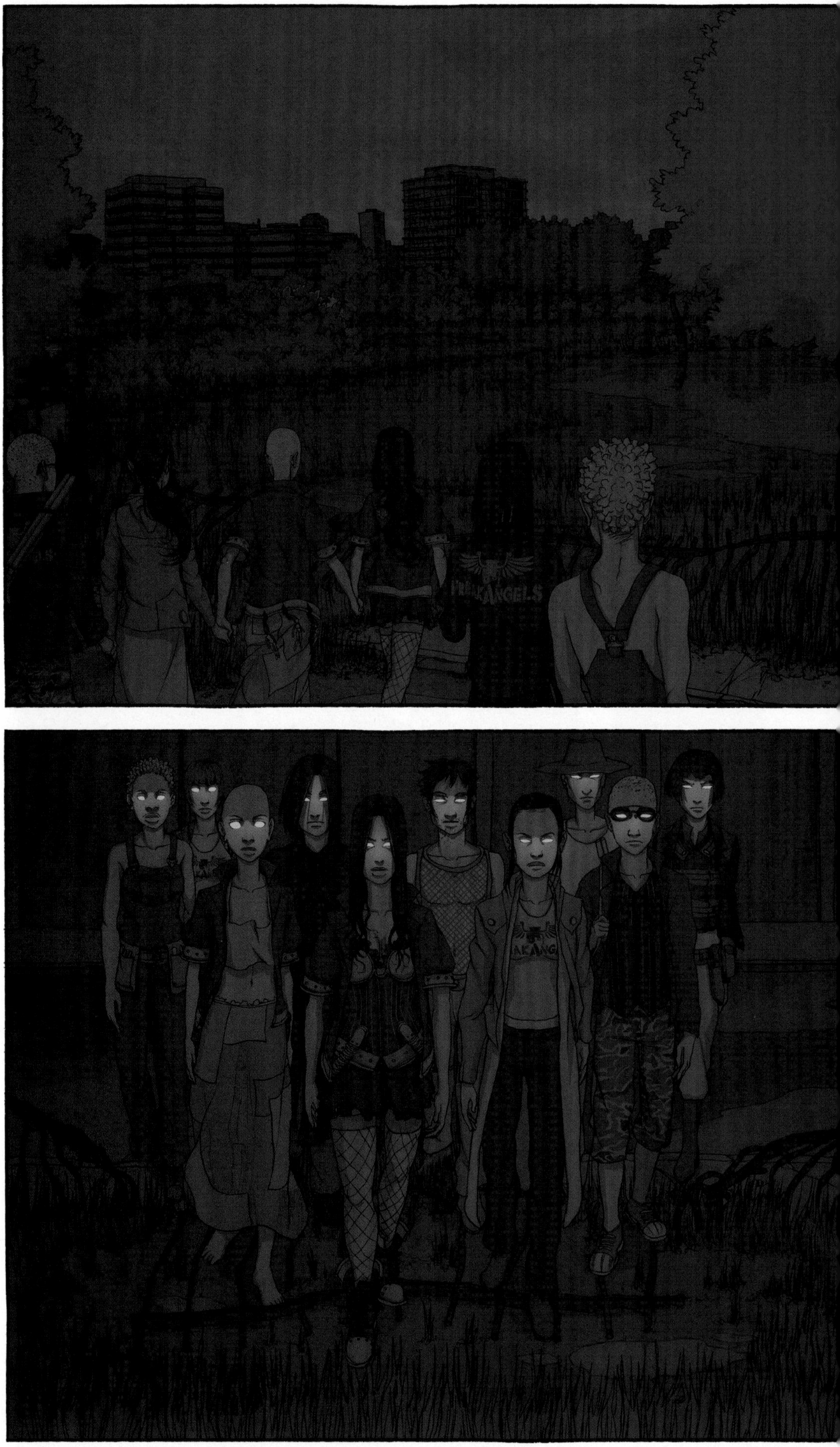

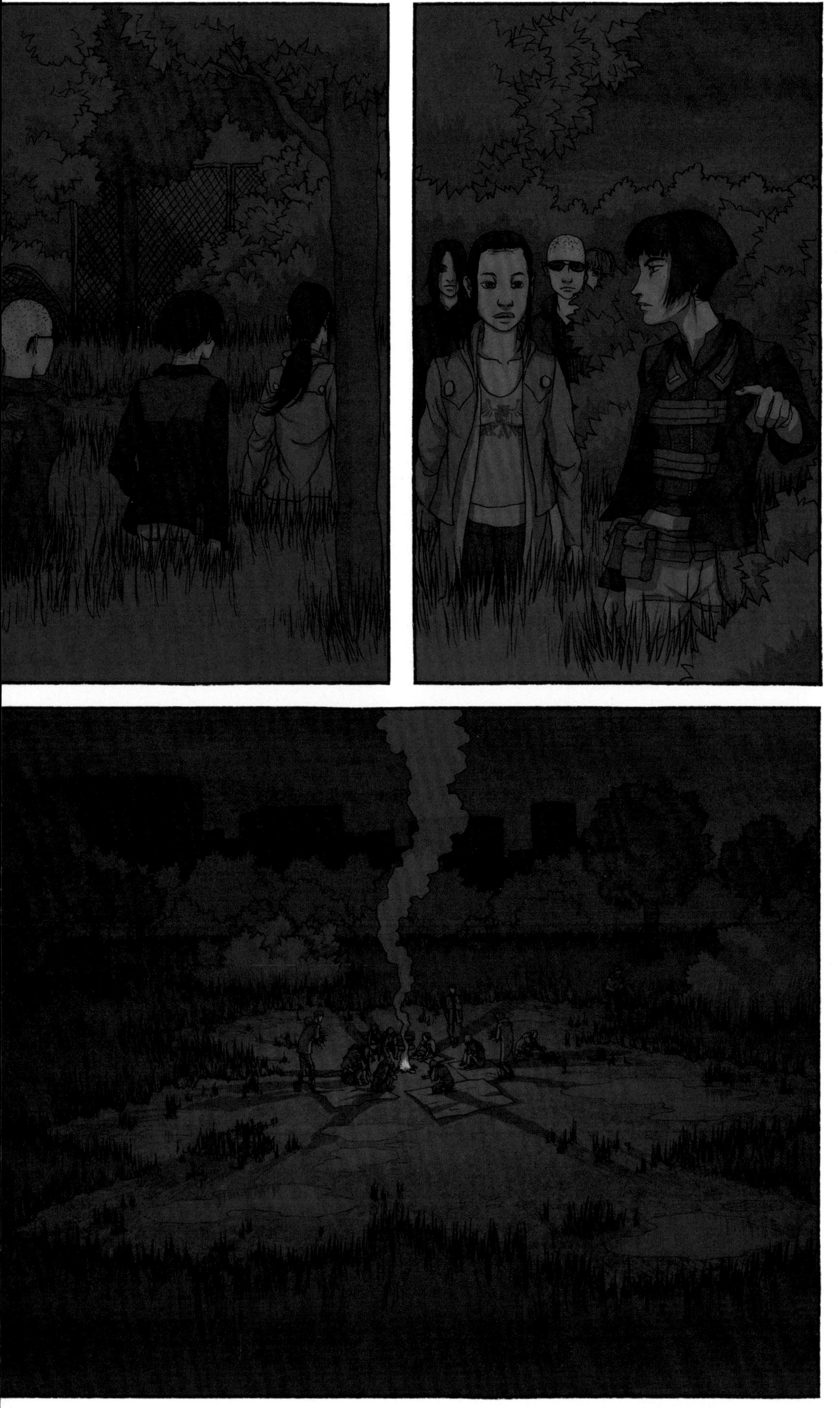

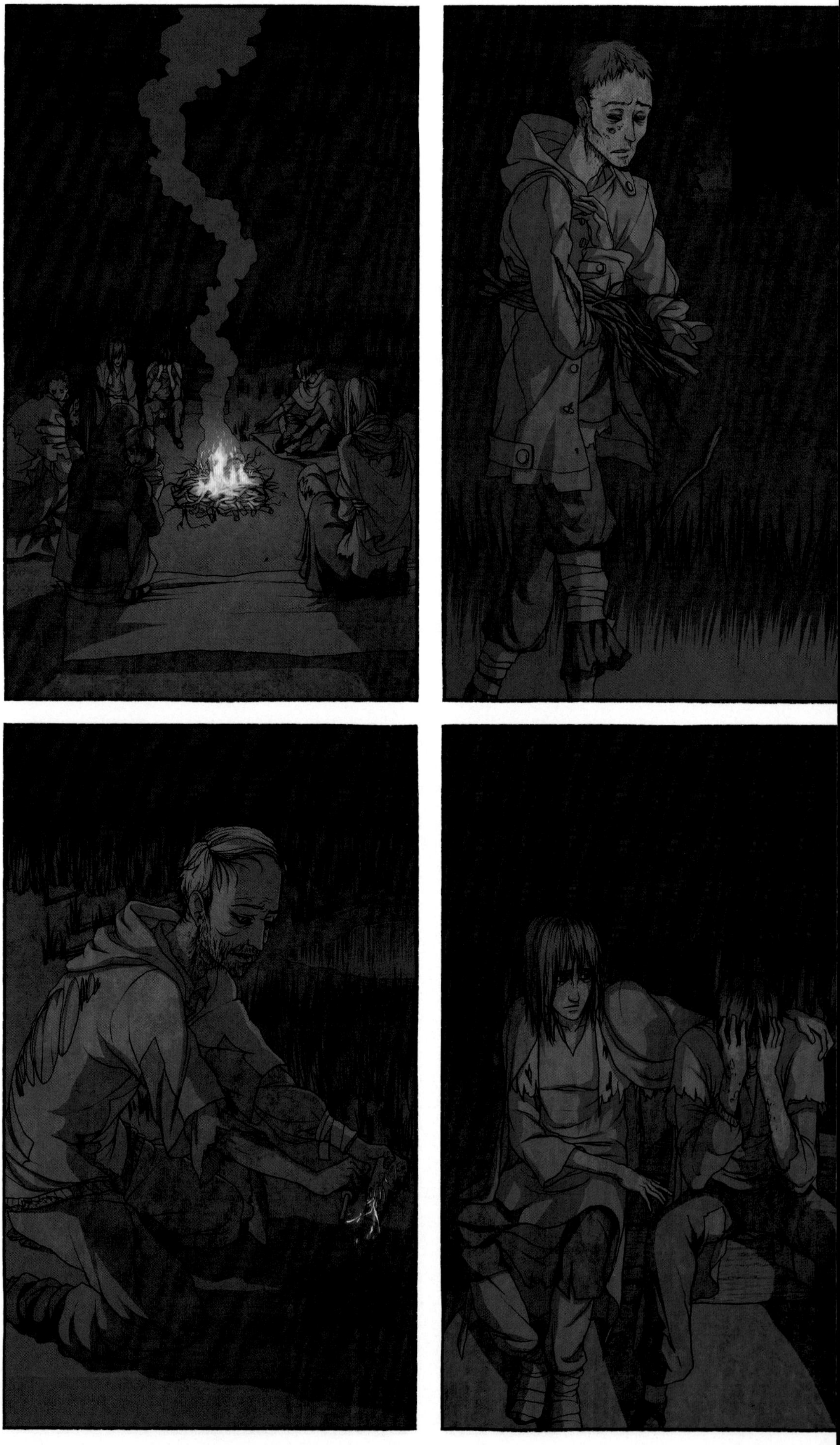

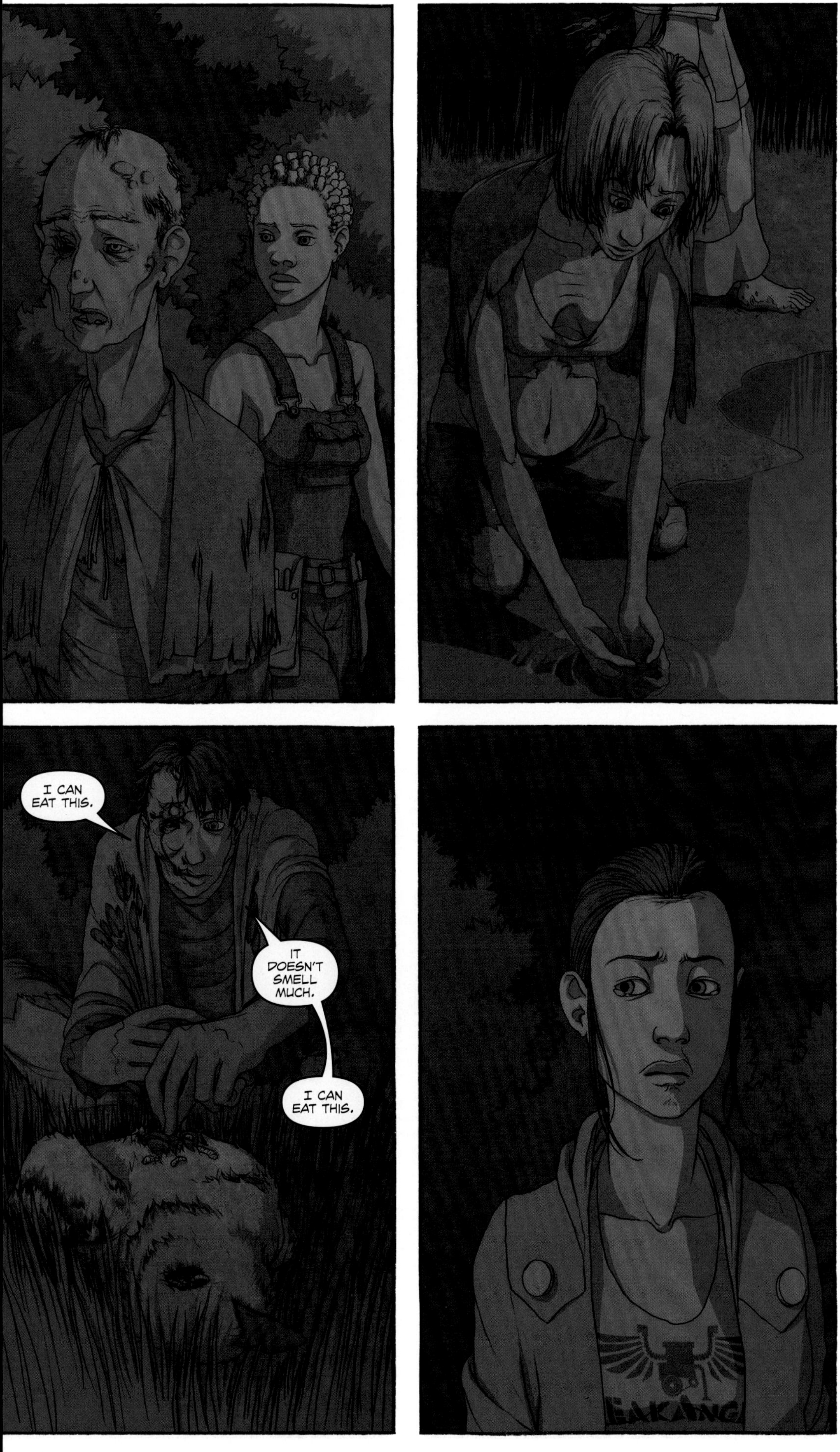
I CAN EAT THIS.
IT DOESN'T SMELL MUCH.
I CAN EAT THIS.

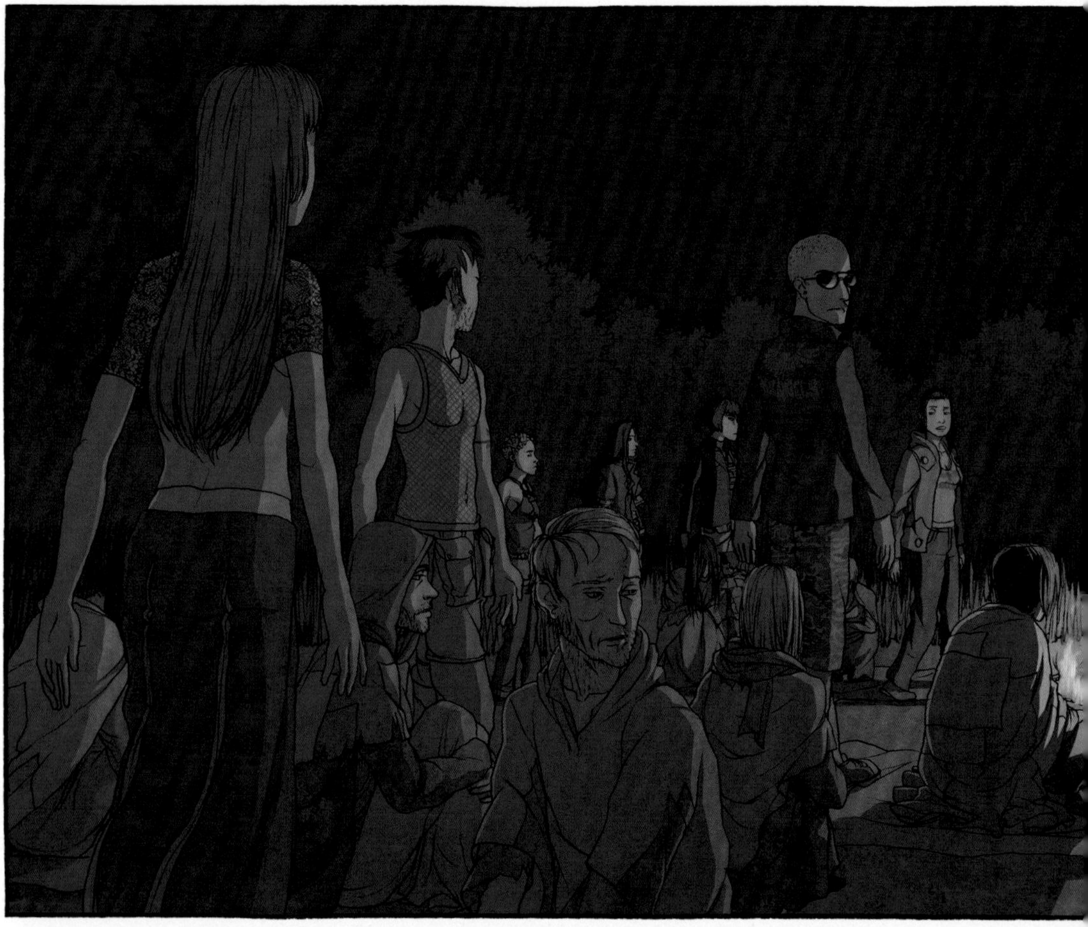

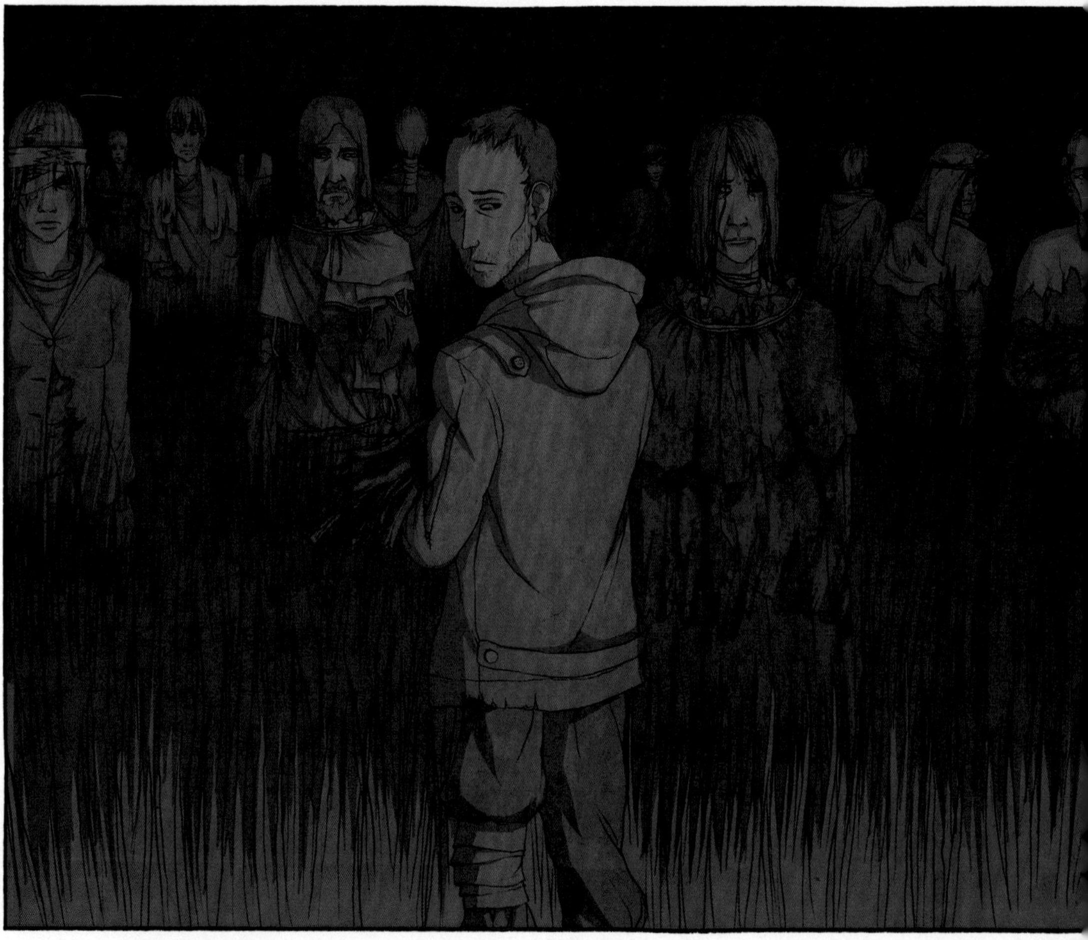

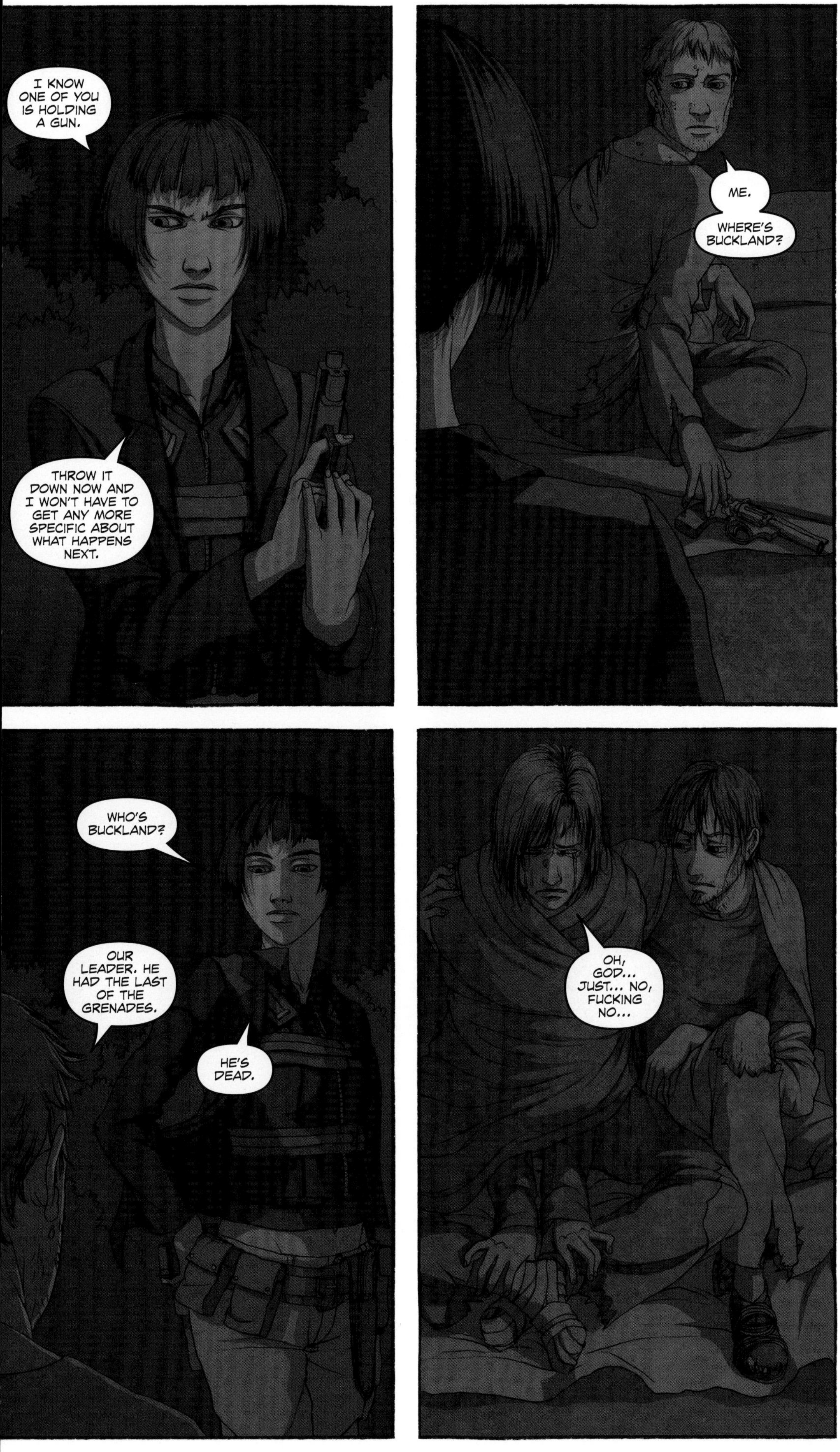
I KNOW ONE OF YOU IS HOLDING A GUN.
THROW IT DOWN NOW AND I WON'T HAVE TO GET ANY MORE SPECIFIC ABOUT WHAT HAPPENS NEXT.
ME.
WHERE'S BUCKLAND?
WHO'S BUCKLAND?
OUR LEADER. HE HAD THE LAST OF THE GRENADES.
HE'S DEAD.
OH, GOD... JUST... NO, FUCKING NO...

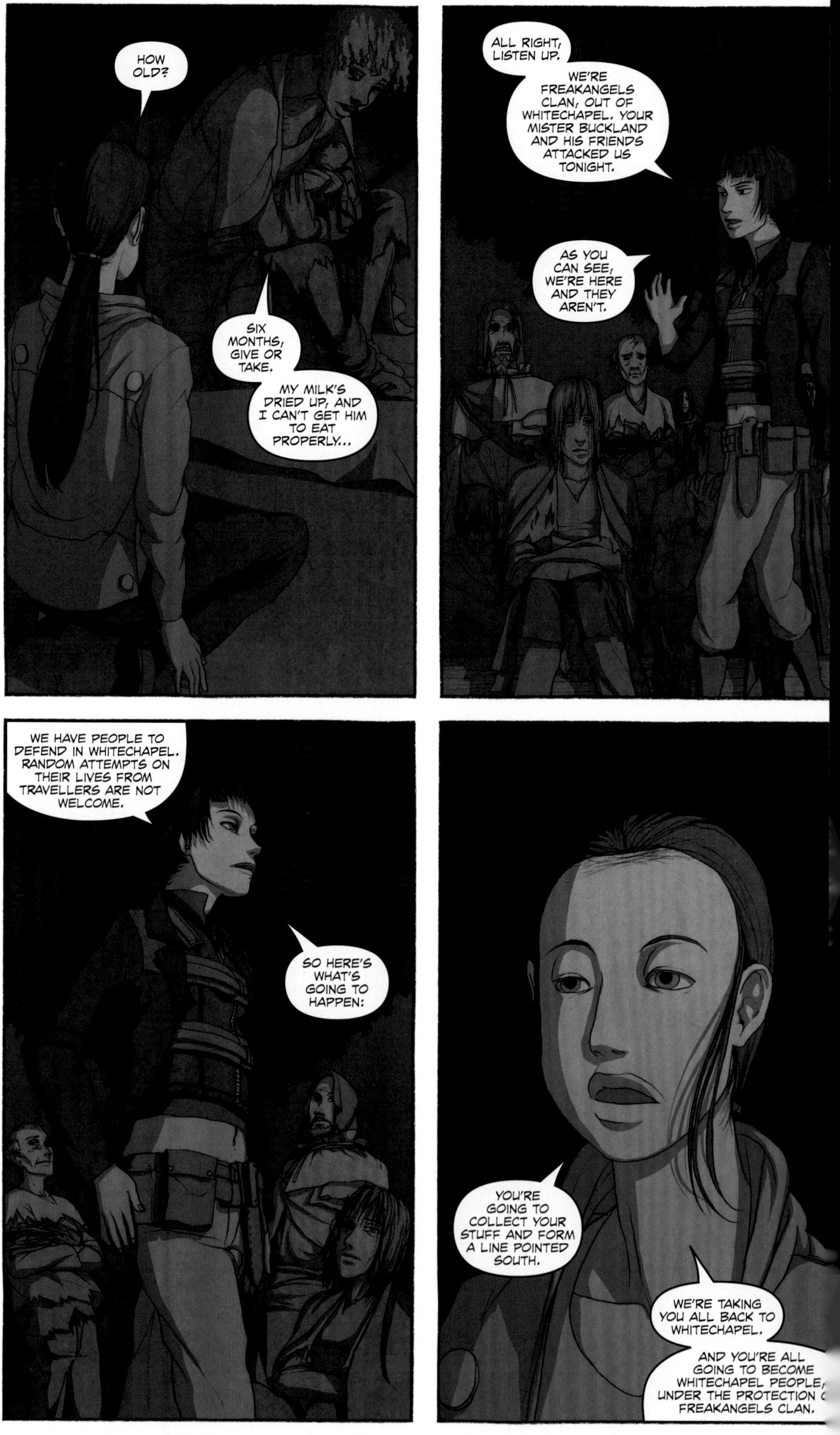

HOW OLD?
SIX MONTHS, GIVE OR TAKE.
MY MILK'S DRIED UP, AND I CAN'T GET HIM TO EAT PROPERLY...
ALL RIGHT, LISTEN UP.
WE'RE FREAKANGELS CLAN, OUT OF WHITECHAPEL. YOUR MISTER BUCKLAND AND HIS FRIENDS ATTACKED US TONIGHT.
AS YOU CAN SEE, WE'RE HERE AND THEY AREN'T.
WE HAVE PEOPLE TO DEFEND IN WHITECHAPEL. RANDOM ATTEMPTS ON THEIR LIVES FROM TRAVELLERS ARE NOT WELCOME.
SO HERE'S WHAT'S GOING TO HAPPEN:
YOU'RE GOING TO COLLECT YOUR STUFF AND FORM A LINE POINTED SOUTH.
WE'RE TAKING YOU ALL BACK TO WHITECHAPEL.
AND YOU'RE ALL GOING TO BECOME WHITECHAPEL PEOPLE, UNDER THE PROTECTION
FREAKANGELS CLAN.

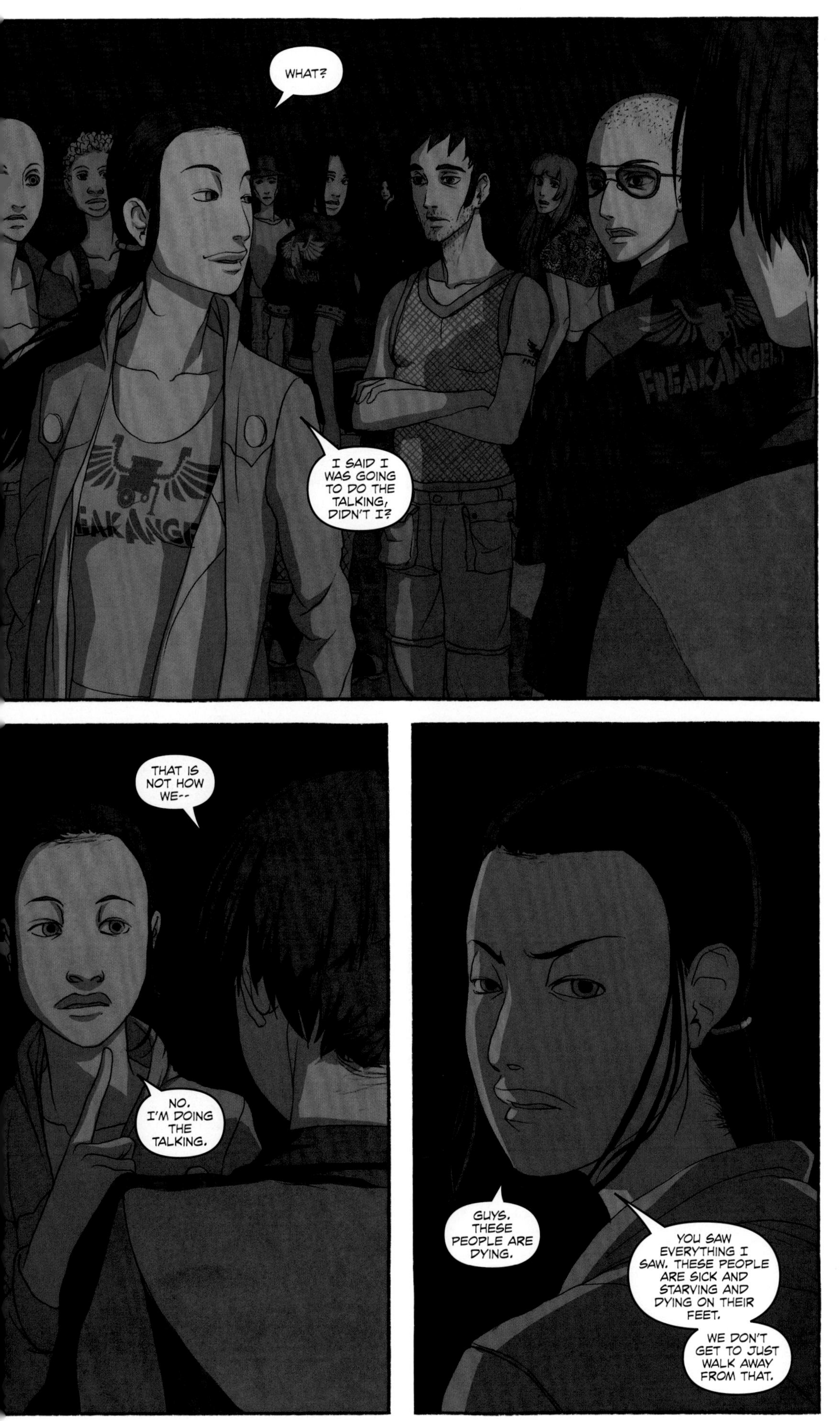
WHAT?
I SAID I WAS GOING TO DO THE TALKING, DIDN'T I?
THAT IS NOT HOW WE--
NO. I'M DOING THE TALKING.
GUYS. THESE PEOPLE ARE DYING.
YOU SAW EVERYTHING I SAW. THESE PEOPLE ARE SICK AND STARVING AND DYING ON THEIR FEET.
WE DON'T GET TO JUST WALK AWAY FROM THAT.

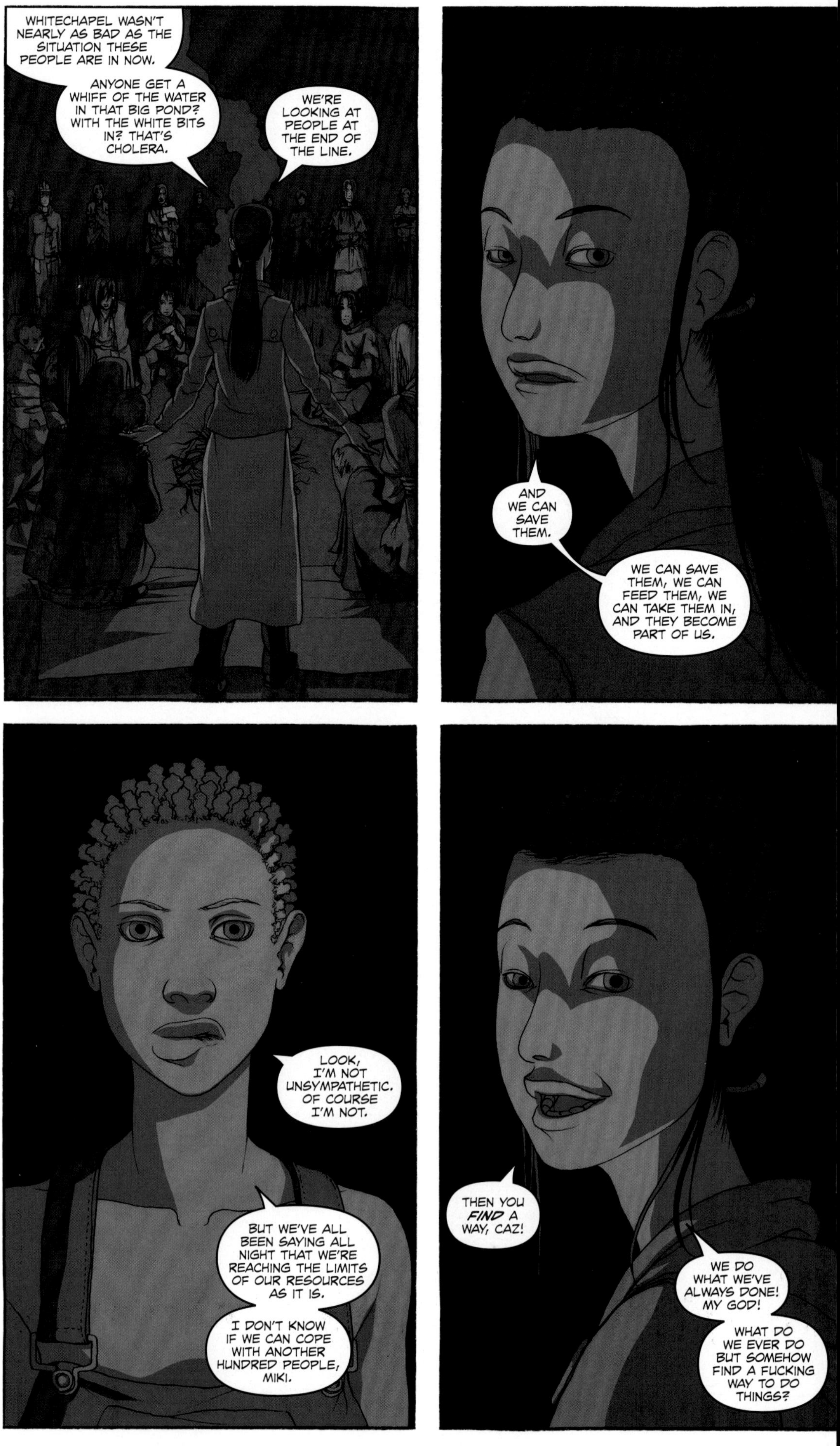
WHITECHAPEL WASN'T NEARLY AS BAD AS THE SITUATION THESE PEOPLE ARE IN NOW.
ANYONE GET A WHIFF OF THE WATER IN THAT BIG POND? WITH THE WHITE BITS IN? THAT'S CHOLERA.
WE'RE LOOKING AT PEOPLE AT THE END OF THE LINE.
AND WE CAN SAVE THEM.
WE CAN SAVE THEM, WE CAN FEED THEM, WE CAN TAKE THEM IN, AND THEY BECOME PART OF US.
LOOK, I'M NOT UNSYMPATHETIC. OF COURSE I'M NOT.
BUT WE'VE ALL BEEN SAYING ALL NIGHT THAT WE'RE REACHING THE LIMITS OF OUR RESOURCES AS IT IS.
I DON'T KNOW IF WE CAN COPE WITH ANOTHER HUNDRED PEOPLE, MIKI.
THEN YOU *FIND* A WAY, CAZ!
WE DO WHAT WE'VE ALWAYS DONE! MY GOD!
WHAT DO WE EVER DO BUT SOMEHOW FIND A FUCKING WAY TO DO THINGS?

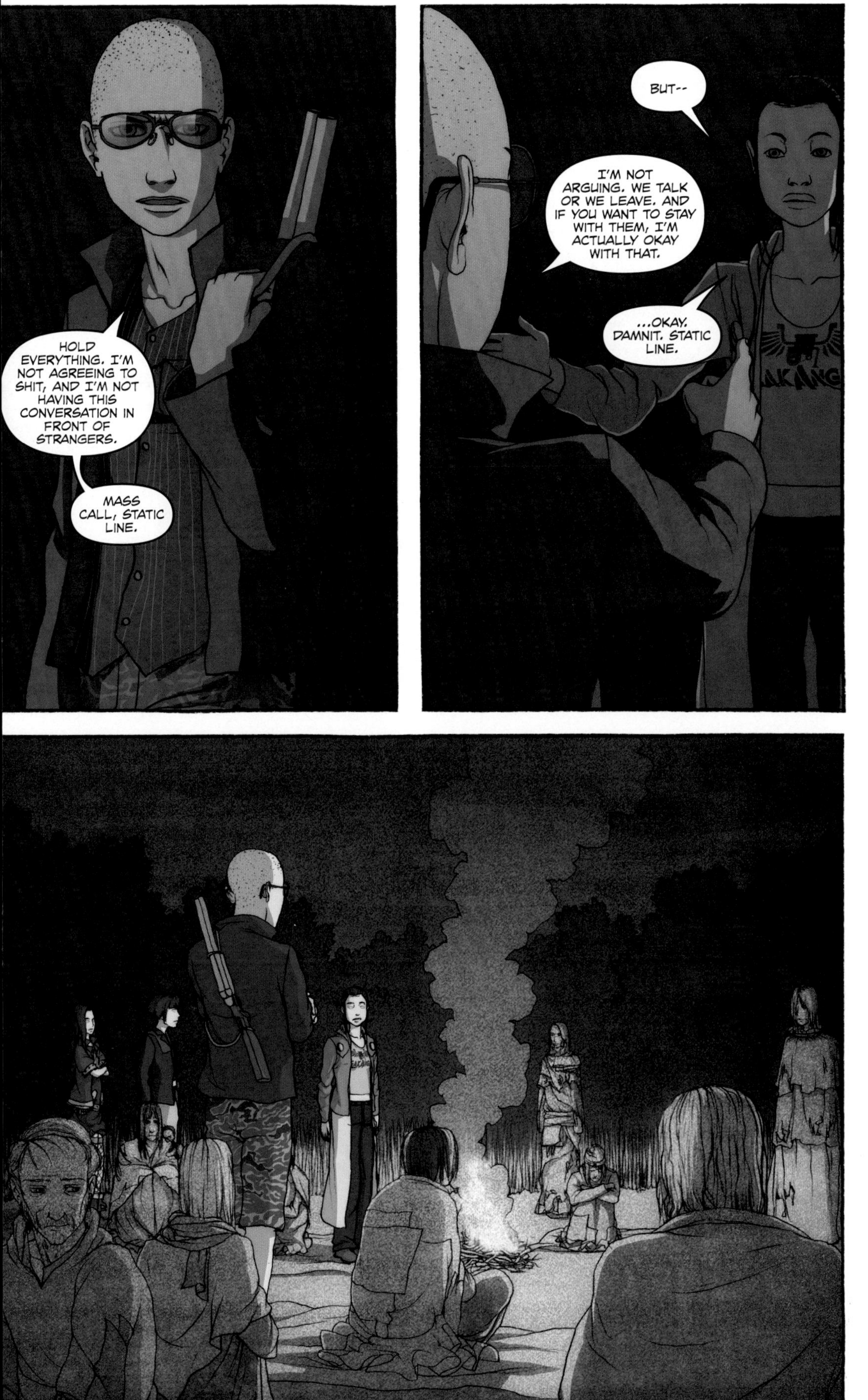
HOLD EVERYTHING. I'M NOT AGREEING TO SHIT, AND I'M NOT HAVING THIS CONVERSATION IN FRONT OF STRANGERS.
MASS CALL, STATIC LINE.
BUT--
I'M NOT ARGUING. WE TALK OR WE LEAVE. AND IF YOU WANT TO STAY WITH THEM, I'M ACTUALLY OKAY WITH THAT.
...OKAY. DAMNIT. STATIC LINE.

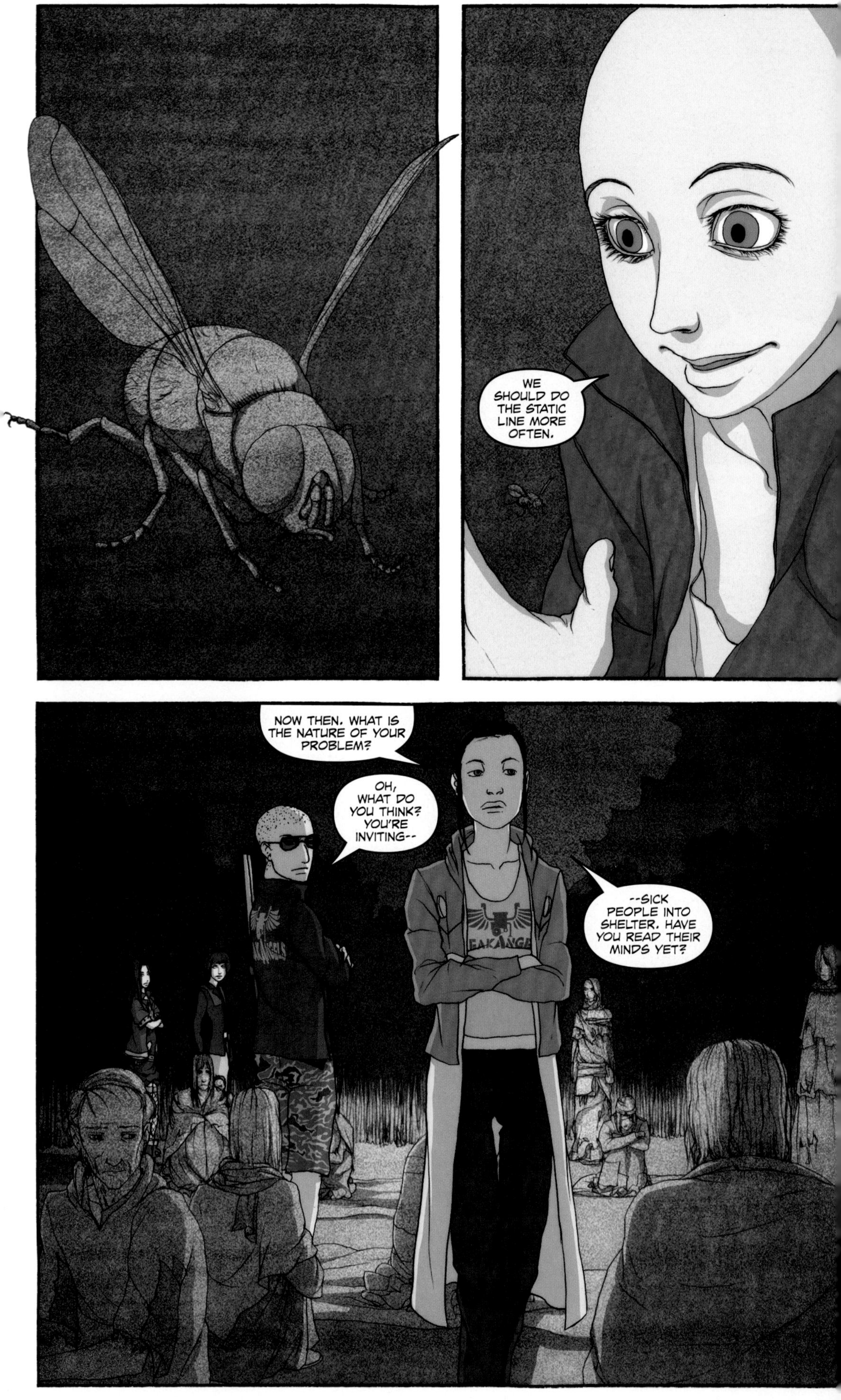
WE SHOULD DO THE STATIC LINE MORE OFTEN.
NOW THEN. WHAT IS THE NATURE OF YOUR PROBLEM?
OH, WHAT DO YOU THINK? YOU'RE INVITING--
--SICK PEOPLE INTO SHELTER. HAVE YOU READ THEIR MINDS YET?

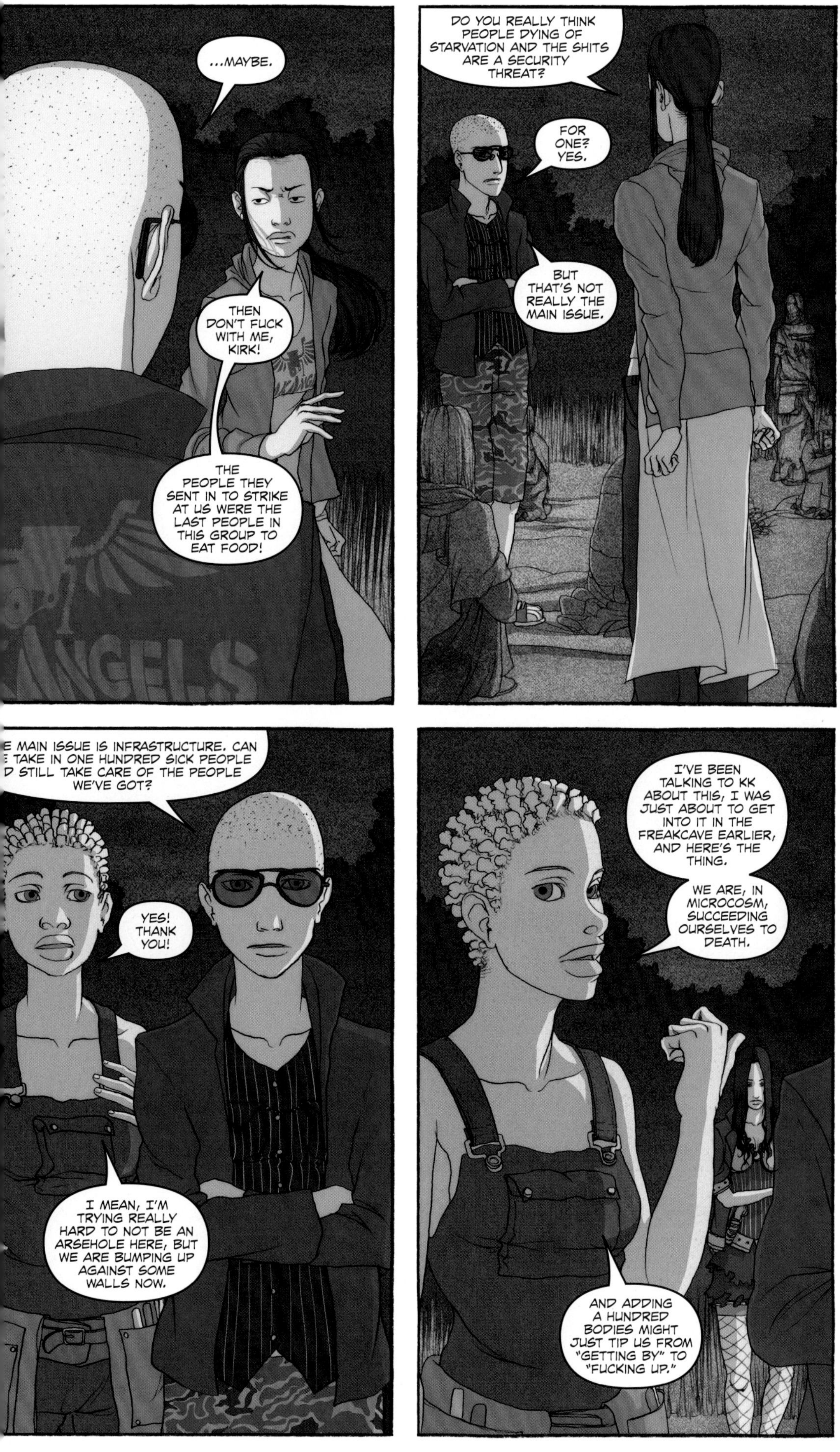
...MAYBE.
THEN DON'T FUCK WITH ME, KIRK!
THE PEOPLE THEY SENT IN TO STRIKE AT US WERE THE LAST PEOPLE IN THIS GROUP TO EAT FOOD!
ANGELS
DO YOU REALLY THINK PEOPLE DYING OF STARVATION AND THE SHITS ARE A SECURITY THREAT?
FOR ONE? YES.
BUT THAT'S NOT REALLY THE MAIN ISSUE.
E MAIN ISSUE IS INFRASTRUCTURE. CAN
E TAKE IN ONE HUNDRED SICK PEOPLE
D STILL TAKE CARE OF THE PEOPLE WE'VE GOT?
YES! THANK YOU!
I MEAN, I'M TRYING REALLY HARD TO NOT BE AN ARSEHOLE HERE, BUT WE ARE BUMPING UP AGAINST SOME WALLS NOW.
I'VE BEEN TALKING TO KK ABOUT THIS, I WAS JUST ABOUT TO GET INTO IT IN THE FREAKCAVE EARLIER, AND HERE'S THE THING.
WE ARE, IN MICROCOSM, SUCCEEDING OURSELVES TO DEATH.
AND ADDING A HUNDRED BODIES MIGHT JUST TIP US FROM "GETTING BY" TO "FUCKING UP."

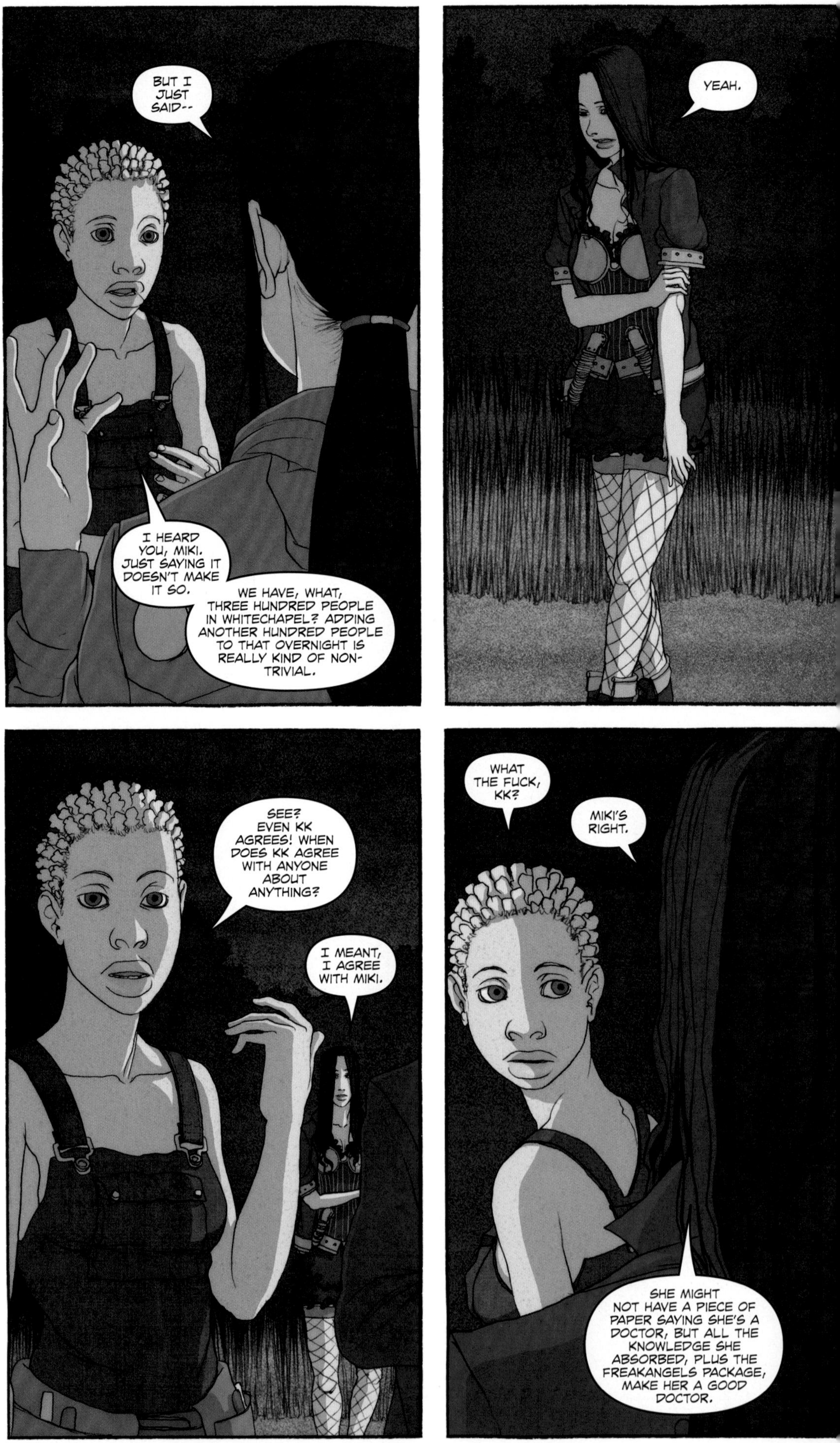
BUT I JUST SAID--
YEAH.
I HEARD YOU, MIKI. JUST SAYING IT DOESN'T MAKE IT SO.
WE HAVE, WHAT, THREE HUNDRED PEOPLE IN WHITECHAPEL? ADDING ANOTHER HUNDRED PEOPLE TO THAT OVERNIGHT IS REALLY KIND OF NON-TRIVIAL.
SEE? EVEN KK AGREES! WHEN DOES KK AGREE WITH ANYONE ABOUT ANYTHING?
I MEANT, I AGREE WITH MIKI.
WHAT THE FUCK, KK?
MIKI'S RIGHT.
SHE MIGHT NOT HAVE A PIECE OF PAPER SAYING SHE'S A DOCTOR, BUT ALL THE KNOWLEDGE SHE ABSORBED, PLUS THE FREAKANGELS PACKAGE, MAKE HER A GOOD DOCTOR.

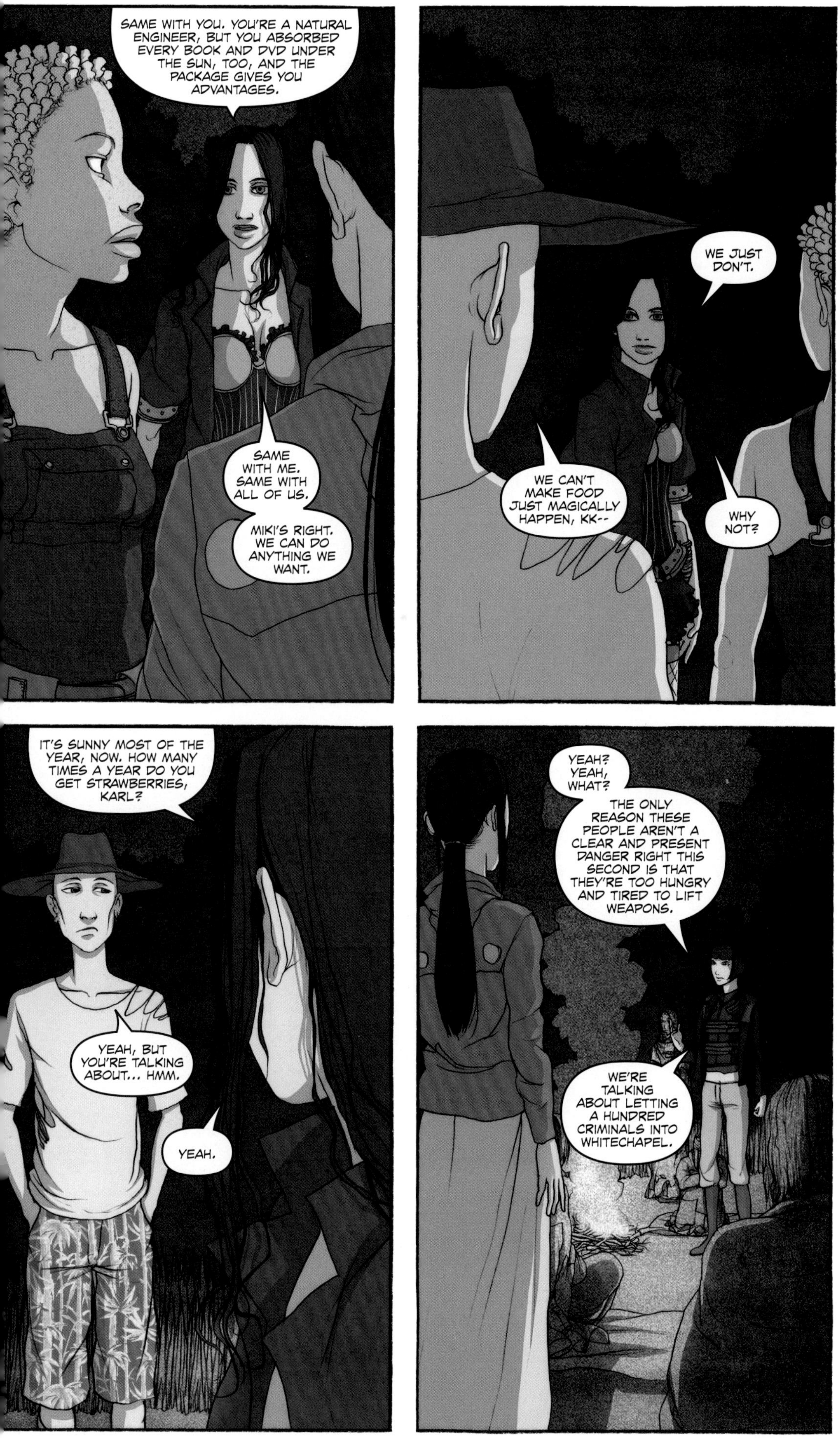
SAME WITH YOU. YOU'RE A NATURAL ENGINEER, BUT YOU ABSORBED EVERY BOOK AND DVD UNDER THE SUN, TOO, AND THE PACKAGE GIVES YOU ADVANTAGES.
SAME WITH ME. SAME WITH ALL OF US.
MIKI'S RIGHT. WE CAN DO ANYTHING WE WANT.
WE CAN'T MAKE FOOD JUST MAGICALLY HAPPEN, KK--
WHY NOT?
WE JUST DON'T.
IT'S SUNNY MOST OF THE YEAR, NOW. HOW MANY TIMES A YEAR DO YOU GET STRAWBERRIES, KARL?
YEAH, BUT YOU'RE TALKING ABOUT... HMM.
YEAH.
YEAH? YEAH, WHAT?
THE ONLY REASON THESE PEOPLE AREN'T A CLEAR AND PRESENT DANGER RIGHT THIS SECOND IS THAT THEY'RE TOO HUNGRY AND TIRED TO LIFT WEAPONS.
WE'RE TALKING ABOUT LETTING A HUNDRED CRIMINALS INTO WHITECHAPEL.

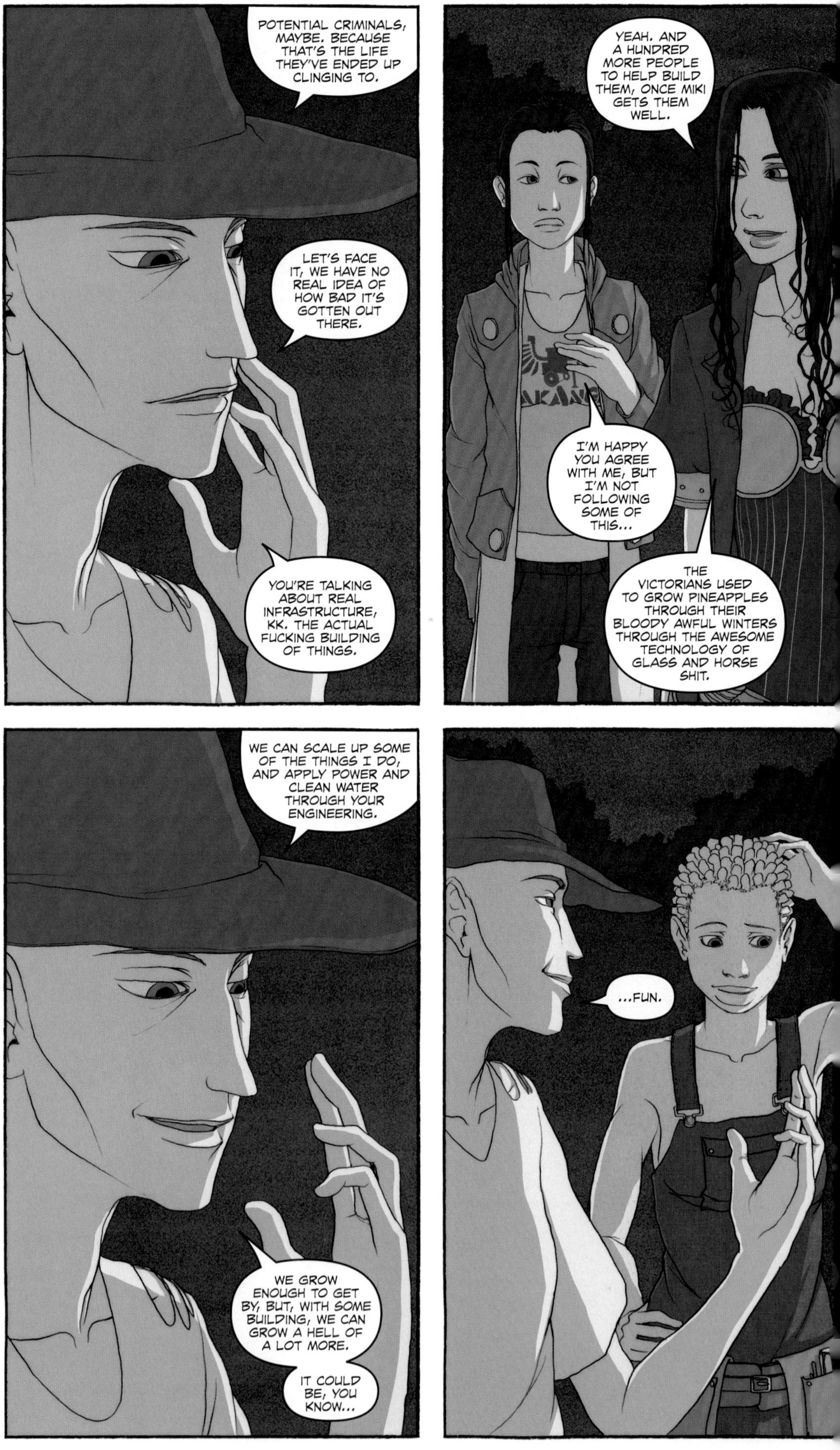
POTENTIAL CRIMINALS, MAYBE. BECAUSE THAT'S THE LIFE THEY'VE ENDED UP CLINGING TO.
LET'S FACE IT, WE HAVE NO REAL IDEA OF HOW BAD IT'S GOTTEN OUT THERE.
YOU'RE TALKING ABOUT REAL INFRASTRUCTURE, KK. THE ACTUAL FUCKING BUILDING OF THINGS.
YEAH. AND A HUNDRED MORE PEOPLE TO HELP BUILD THEM, ONCE MIKI GETS THEM WELL.
I'M HAPPY YOU AGREE WITH ME, BUT I'M NOT FOLLOWING SOME OF THIS...
THE VICTORIANS USED TO GROW PINEAPPLES THROUGH THEIR BLOODY AWFUL WINTERS THROUGH THE AWESOME TECHNOLOGY OF GLASS AND HORSE SHIT.
WE CAN SCALE UP SOME OF THE THINGS I DO, AND APPLY POWER AND CLEAN WATER THROUGH YOUR ENGINEERING.
WE GROW ENOUGH TO GET BY, BUT, WITH SOME BUILDING, WE CAN GROW A HELL OF A LOT MORE.
IT COULD BE, YOU KNOW...
...FUN.

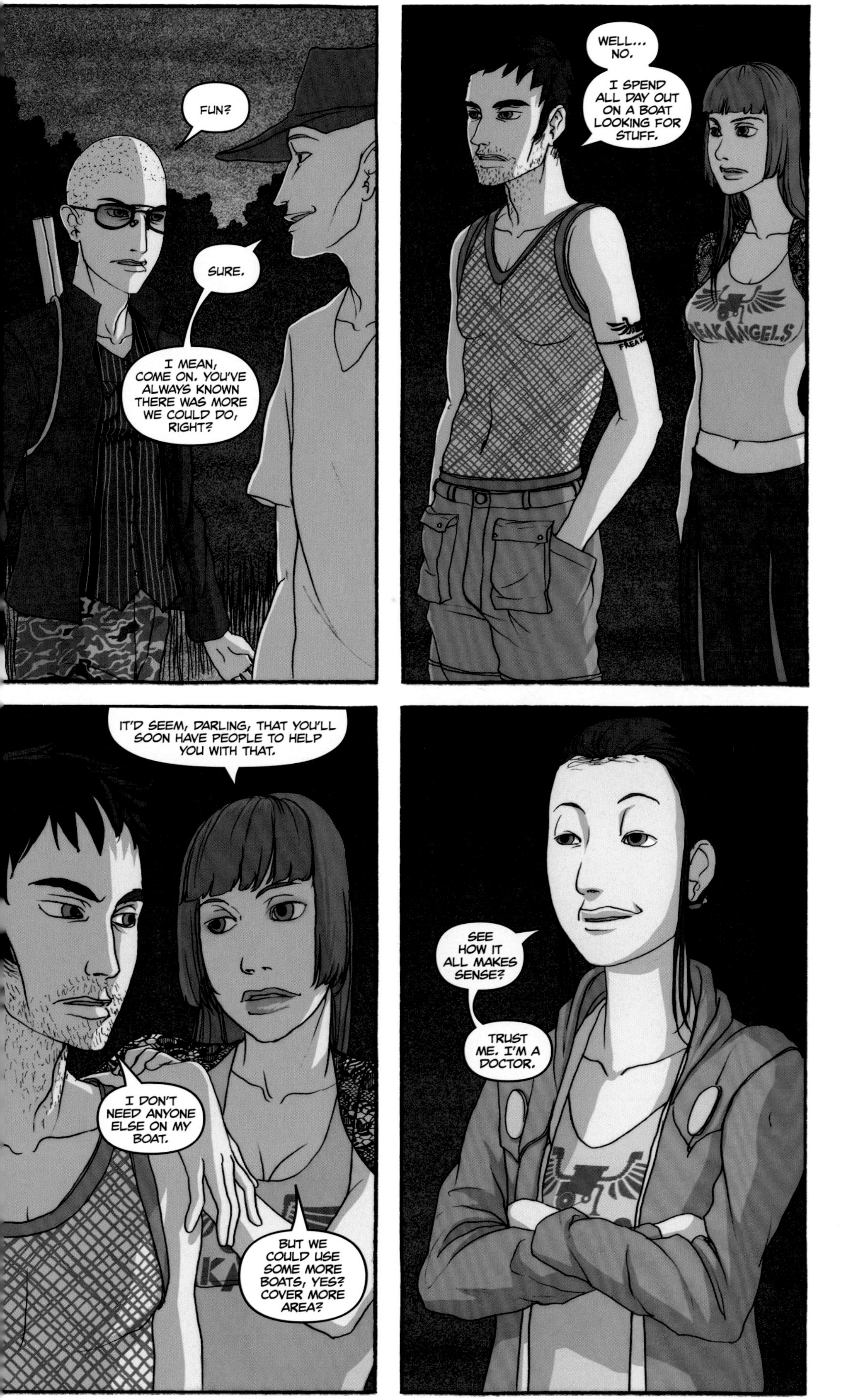
FUN?
SURE.
I MEAN, COME ON. YOU'VE ALWAYS KNOWN THERE WAS MORE WE COULD DO, RIGHT?
WELL... NO.
I SPEND ALL DAY OUT ON A BOAT LOOKING FOR STUFF.
IT'D SEEM, DARLING, THAT YOU'LL SOON HAVE PEOPLE TO HELP YOU WITH THAT.
I DON'T NEED ANYONE ELSE ON MY BOAT.
BUT WE COULD USE SOME MORE BOATS, YES? COVER MORE AREA?
SEE HOW IT ALL MAKES SENSE?
TRUST ME. I'M A DOCTOR.

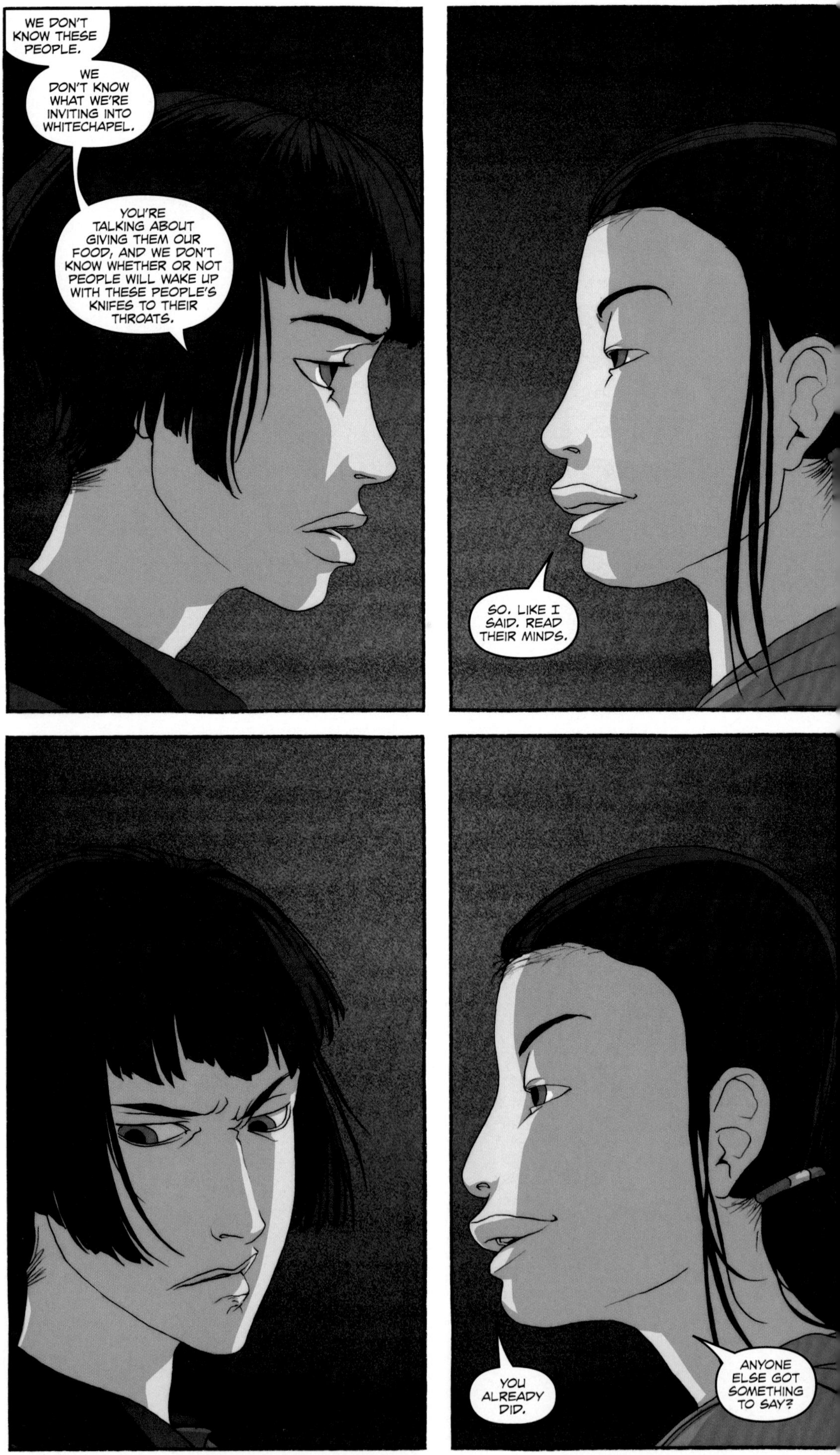
WE DON'T KNOW THESE PEOPLE.
WE DON'T KNOW WHAT WE'RE INVITING INTO WHITECHAPEL.
YOU'RE TALKING ABOUT GIVING THEM OUR FOOD, AND WE DON'T KNOW WHETHER OR NOT PEOPLE WILL WAKE UP WITH THESE PEOPLE'S KNIFES TO THEIR THROATS.
SO. LIKE I SAID. READ THEIR MINDS.
YOU ALREADY DID.
ANYONE ELSE GOT SOMETHING TO SAY?

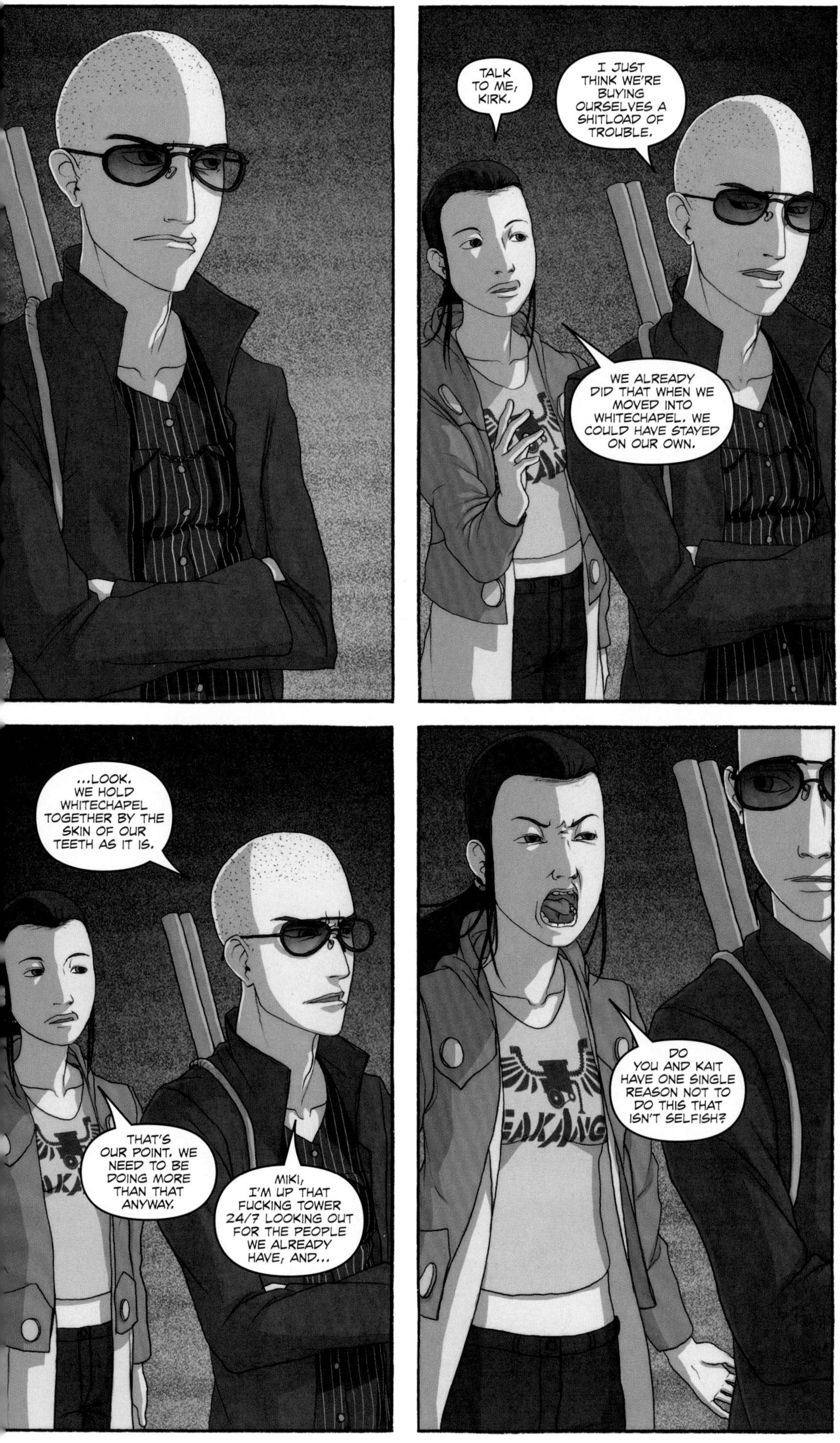
TALK TO ME, KIRK.
I JUST THINK WE'RE BUYING OURSELVES A SHITLOAD OF TROUBLE.
WE ALREADY DID THAT WHEN WE MOVED INTO WHITECHAPEL. WE COULD HAVE STAYED ON OUR OWN.
...LOOK. WE HOLD WHITECHAPEL TOGETHER BY THE SKIN OF OUR TEETH AS IT IS.
MIKI, I'M UP THAT FUCKING TOWER 24/7 LOOKING OUT FOR THE PEOPLE WE ALREADY HAVE, AND...
THAT'S OUR POINT. WE NEED TO BE DOING MORE THAN THAT ANYWAY.
DO YOU AND KAIT HAVE ONE SINGLE REASON NOT TO DO THIS THAT ISN'T SELFISH?

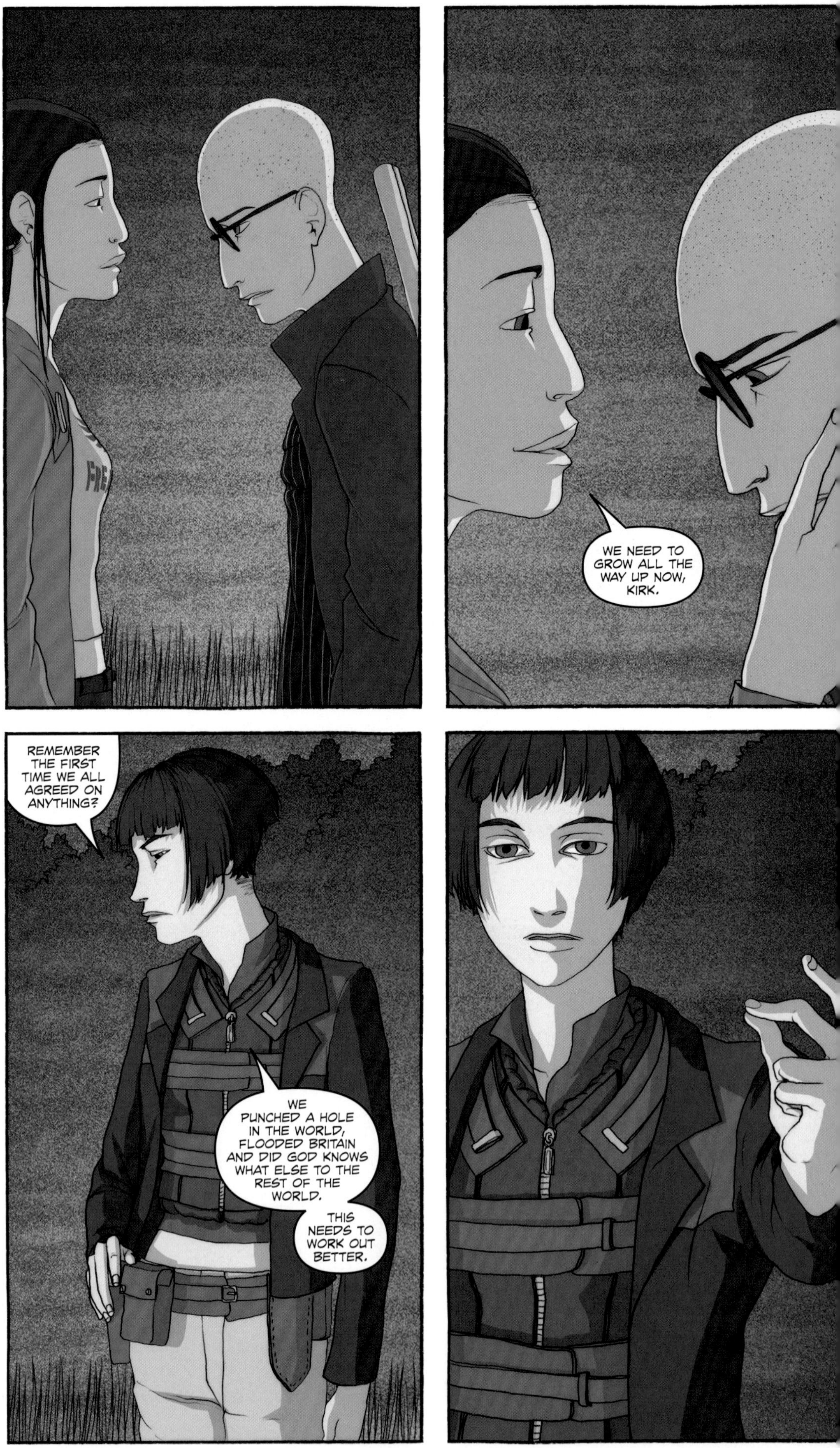

FRE
WE NEED TO GROW ALL THE WAY UP NOW, KIRK.
REMEMBER THE FIRST TIME WE ALL AGREED ON ANYTHING?
WE PUNCHED A HOLE IN THE WORLD, FLOODED BRITAIN AND DID GOD KNOWS WHAT ELSE TO THE REST OF THE WORLD.
THIS NEEDS TO WORK OUT BETTER.

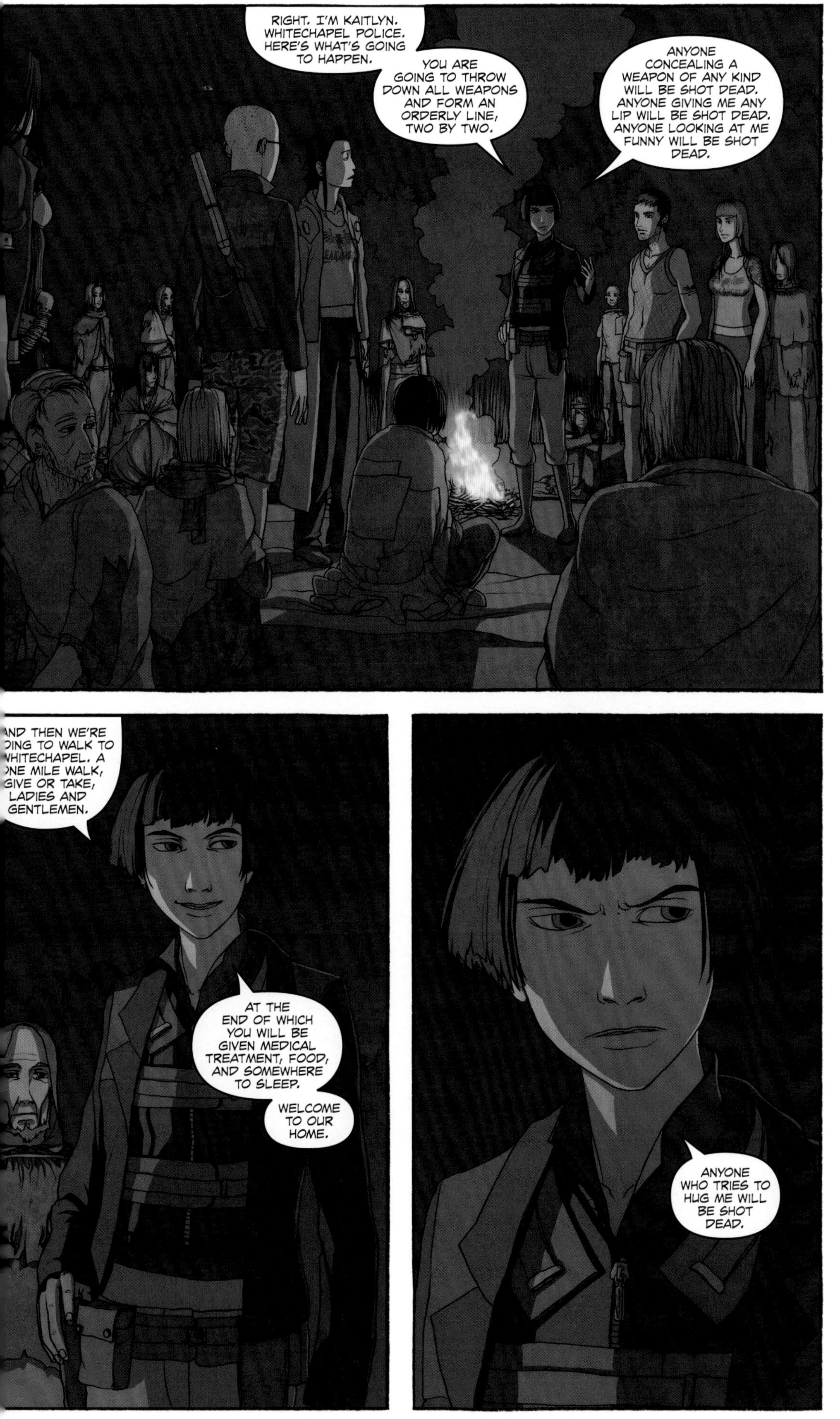
RIGHT. I'M KAITLYN. WHITECHAPEL POLICE. HERE'S WHAT'S GOING TO HAPPEN.
YOU ARE GOING TO THROW DOWN ALL WEAPONS AND FORM AN ORDERLY LINE, TWO BY TWO.
ANYONE CONCEALING A WEAPON OF ANY KIND WILL BE SHOT DEAD. ANYONE GIVING ME ANY LIP WILL BE SHOT DEAD. ANYONE LOOKING AT ME FUNNY WILL BE SHOT DEAD.
AND THEN WE'RE GOING TO WALK TO WHITECHAPEL. A ONE MILE WALK, GIVE OR TAKE, LADIES AND GENTLEMEN.
AT THE END OF WHICH YOU WILL BE GIVEN MEDICAL TREATMENT, FOOD, AND SOMEWHERE TO SLEEP.
WELCOME TO OUR HOME.
ANYONE WHO TRIES TO HUG ME WILL BE SHOT DEAD.

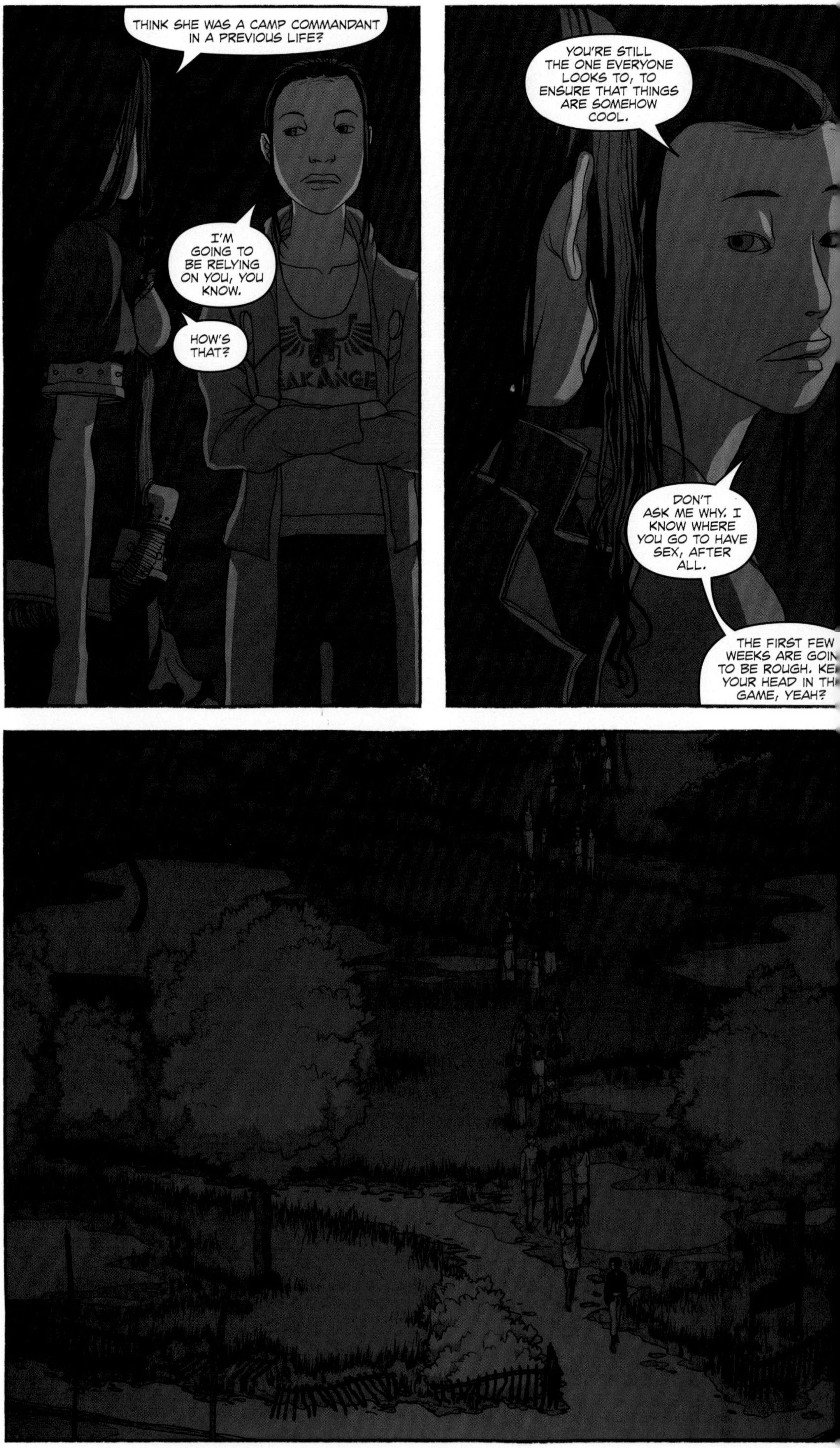
THINK SHE WAS A CAMP COMMANDANT IN A PREVIOUS LIFE?
I'M GOING TO BE RELYING ON YOU, YOU KNOW.
HOW'S THAT?
YOU'RE STILL THE ONE EVERYONE LOOKS TO, TO ENSURE THAT THINGS ARE SOMEHOW COOL.
DON'T ASK ME WHY. I KNOW WHERE YOU GO TO HAVE SEX, AFTER ALL.
THE FIRST FEW WEEKS ARE GOIN TO BE ROUGH. KE YOUR HEAD IN TH GAME, YEAH?

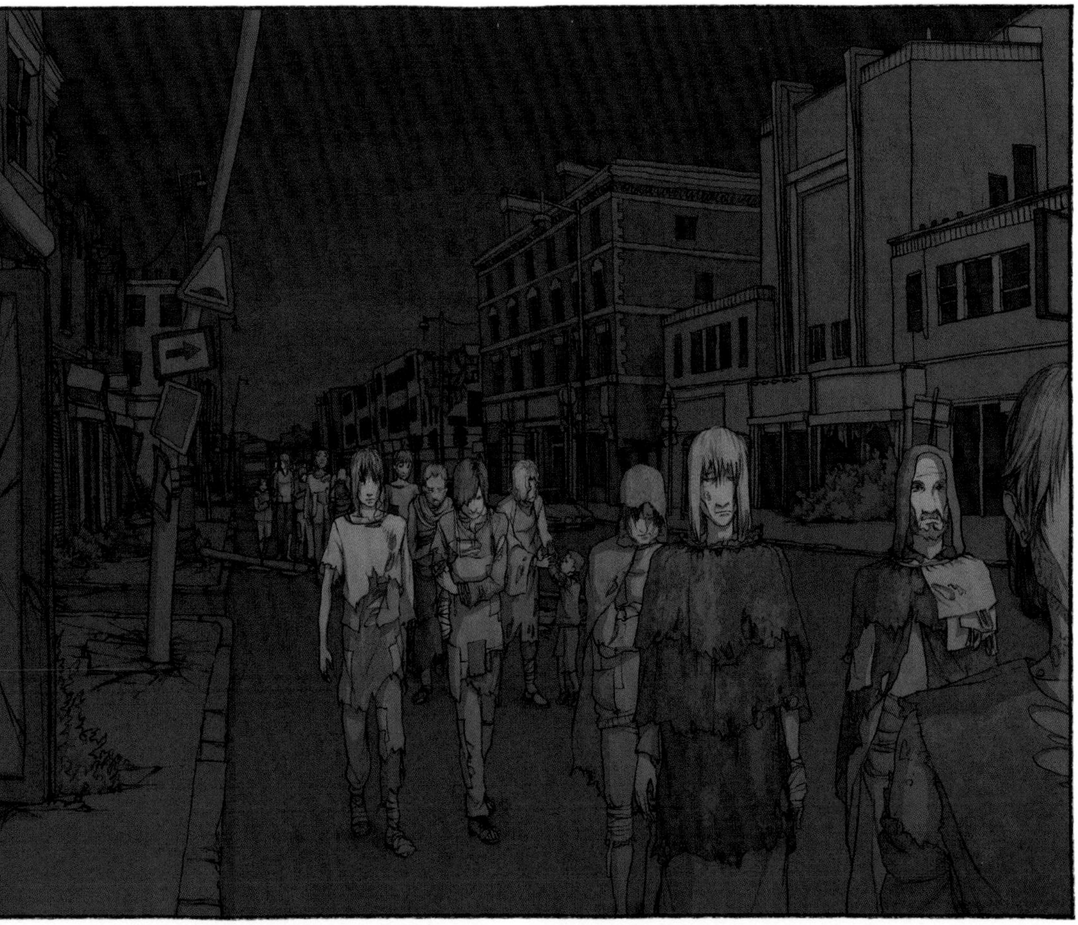

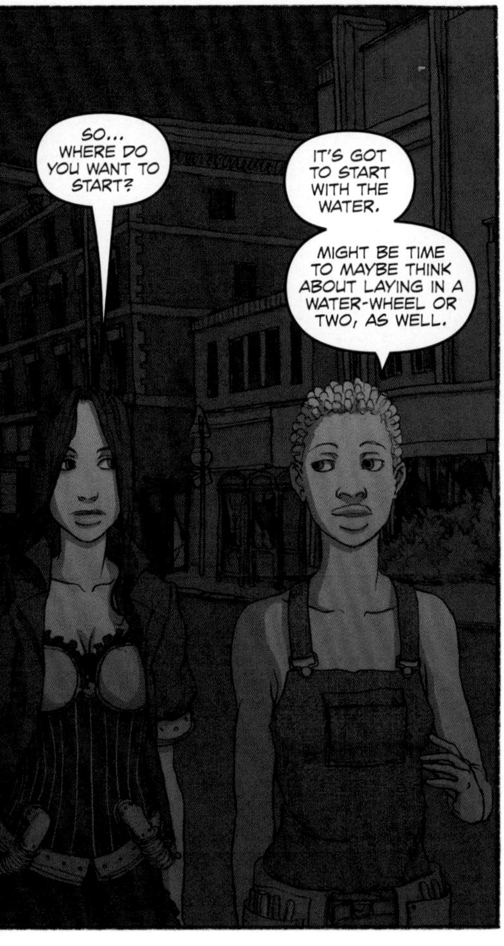
SO... WHERE DO YOU WANT TO START?
IT'S GOT TO START WITH THE WATER.
MIGHT BE TIME TO MAYBE THINK ABOUT LAYING IN A WATER-WHEEL OR TWO, AS WELL.

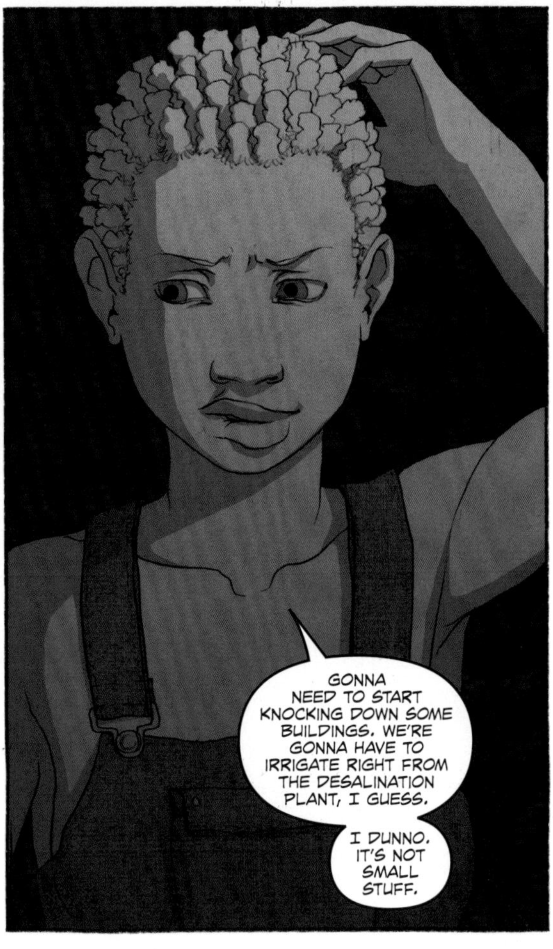
GONNA NEED TO START KNOCKING DOWN SOME BUILDINGS. WE'RE GONNA HAVE TO IRRIGATE RIGHT FROM THE DESALINATION PLANT, I GUESS.
I DUNNO. IT'S NOT SMALL STUFF.

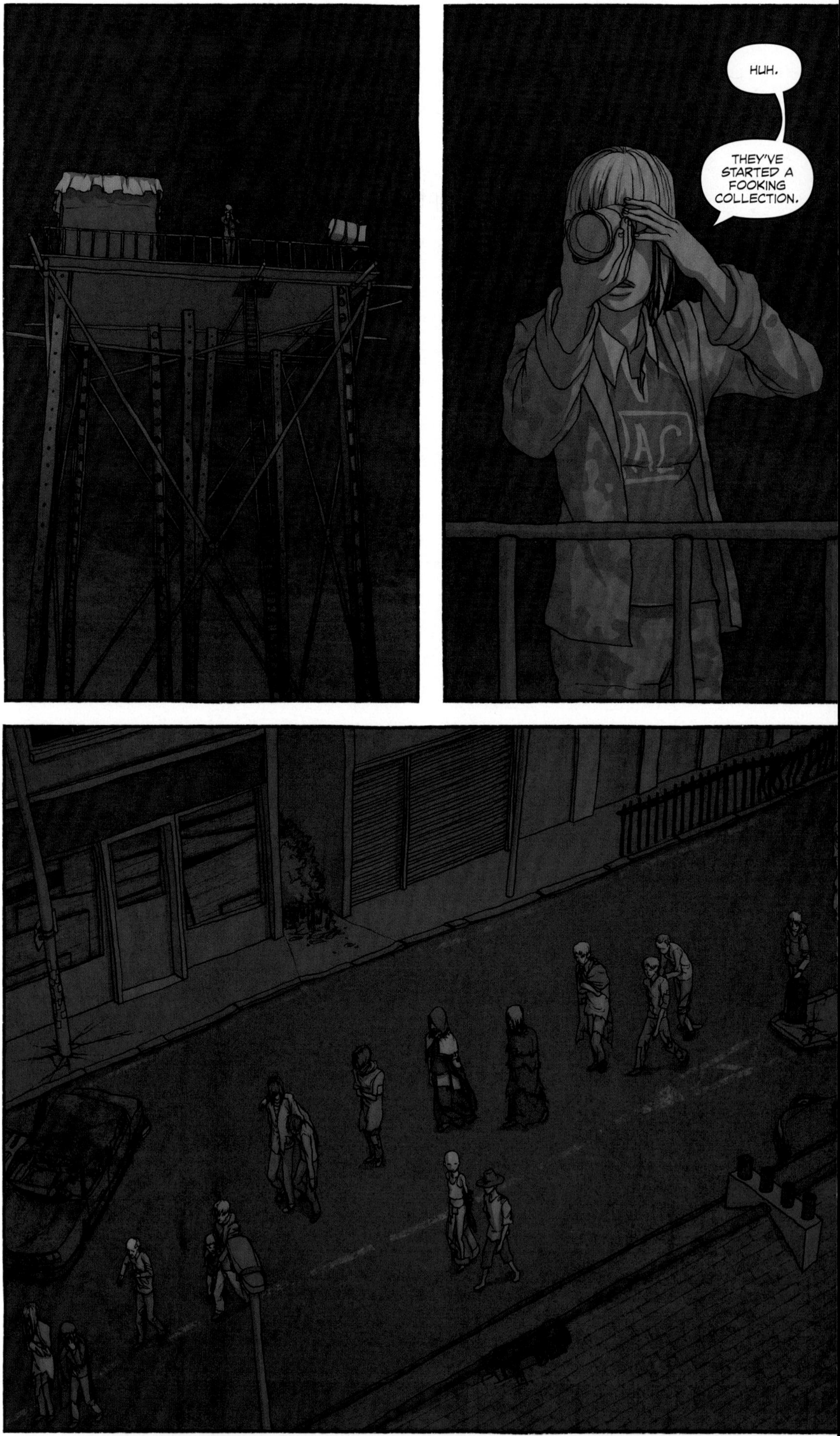
HUH.
THEY'VE STARTED A FOOKING COLLECTION.

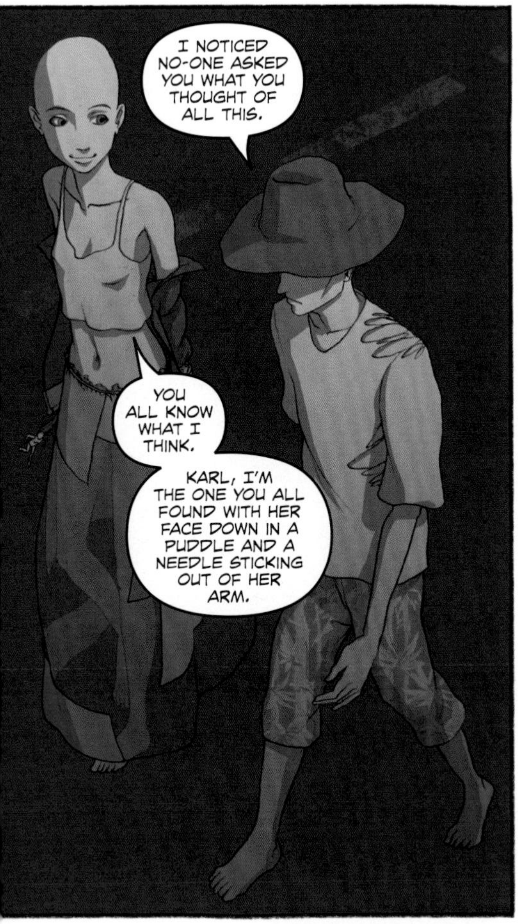
I NOTICED NO-ONE ASKED YOU WHAT YOU THOUGHT OF ALL THIS.
YOU ALL KNOW WHAT I THINK.
KARL, I'M THE ONE YOU ALL FOUND WITH HER FACE DOWN IN A PUDDLE AND A NEEDLE STICKING OUT OF HER ARM.

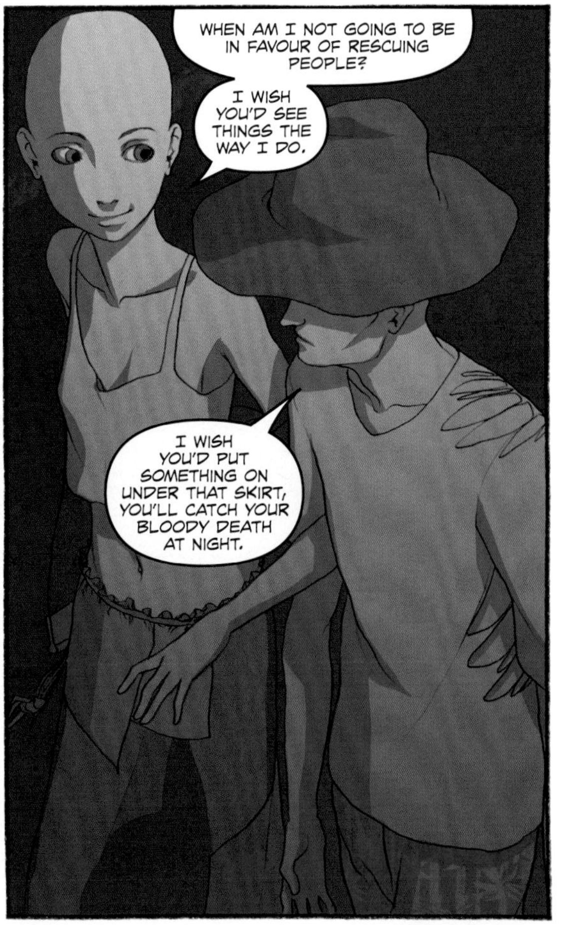
WHEN AM I NOT GOING TO BE IN FAVOUR OF RESCUING PEOPLE?
I WISH YOU'D SEE THINGS THE WAY I DO.
I WISH YOU'D PUT SOMETHING ON UNDER THAT SKIRT, YOU'LL CATCH YOUR BLOODY DEATH AT NIGHT.

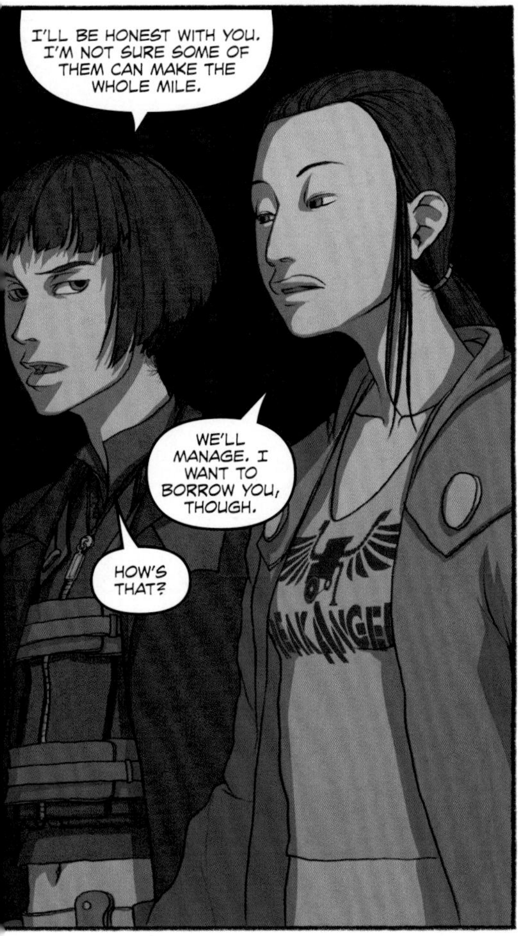
I'LL BE HONEST WITH YOU. I'M NOT SURE SOME OF THEM CAN MAKE THE WHOLE MILE.
WE'LL MANAGE. I WANT TO BORROW YOU, THOUGH.
HOW'S THAT?

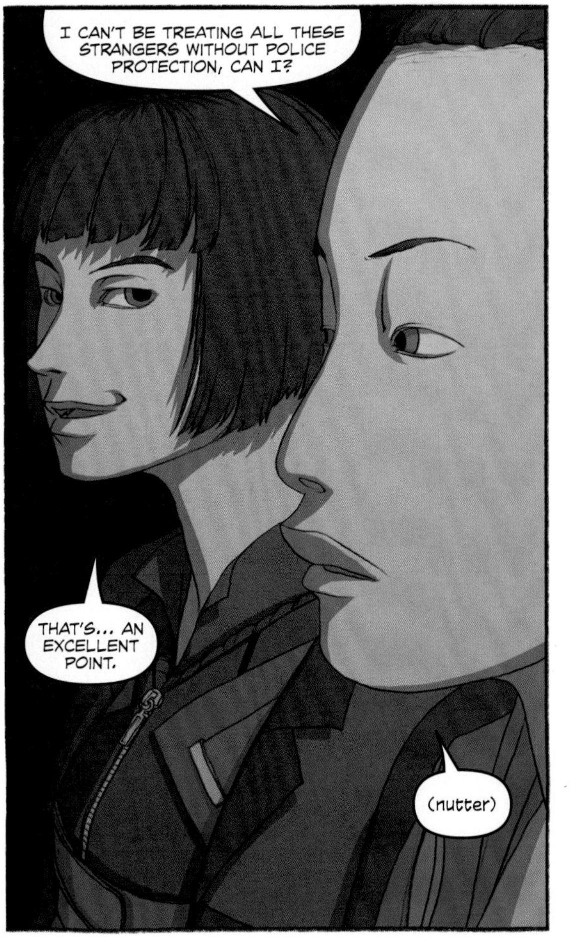
I CAN'T BE TREATING ALL THESE STRANGERS WITHOUT POLICE PROTECTION, CAN I?
THAT'S... AN EXCELLENT POINT.
(nutter)

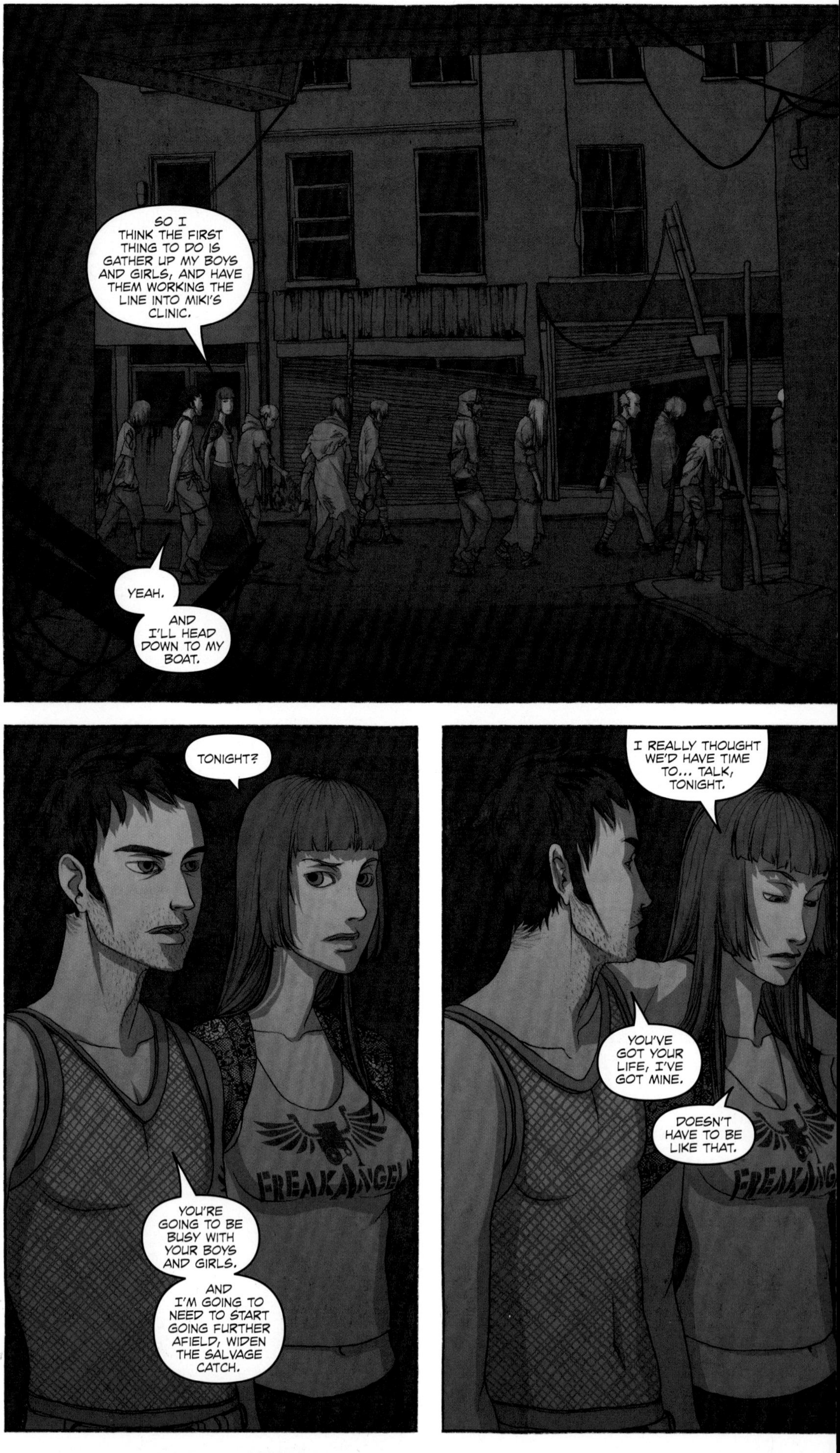
SO I THINK THE FIRST THING TO DO IS GATHER UP MY BOYS AND GIRLS, AND HAVE THEM WORKING THE LINE INTO MIKI'S CLINIC.
YEAH.
AND I'LL HEAD DOWN TO MY BOAT.
TONIGHT?
YOU'RE GOING TO BE BUSY WITH YOUR BOYS AND GIRLS.
AND I'M GOING TO NEED TO START GOING FURTHER AFIELD, WIDEN THE SALVAGE CATCH.
FREAKANGELS
I REALLY THOUGHT WE'D HAVE TIME TO... TALK, TONIGHT.
YOU'VE GOT YOUR LIFE, I'VE GOT MINE.
DOESN'T HAVE TO BE LIKE THAT.

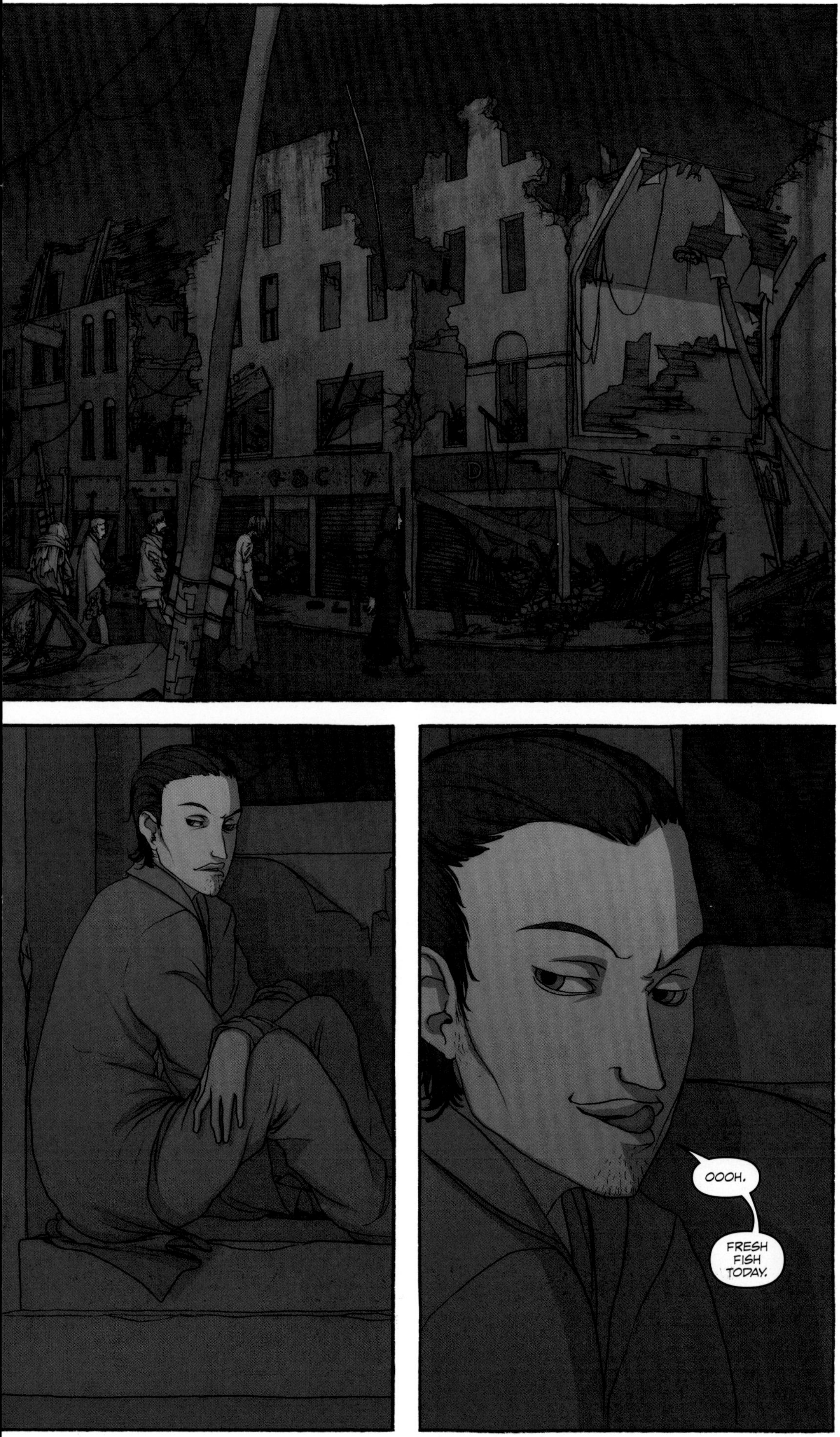
OOOH.
FRESH FISH TODAY.

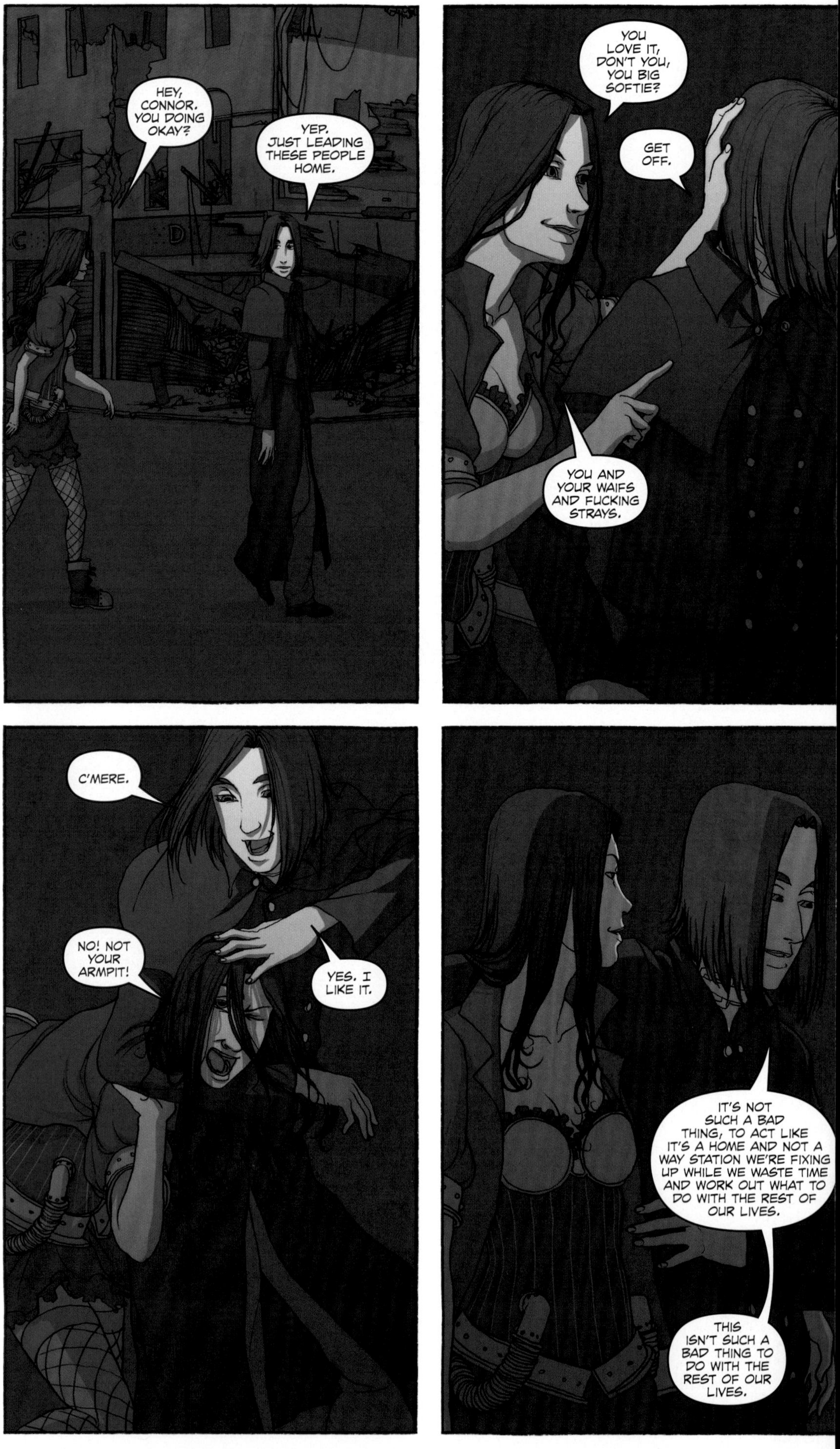
HEY, CONNOR. YOU DOING OKAY?
YEP. JUST LEADING THESE PEOPLE HOME.
YOU LOVE IT, DON'T YOU, YOU BIG SOFTIE?
GET OFF.
YOU AND YOUR WAIFS AND FUCKING STRAYS.
C'MERE.
NO! NOT YOUR ARMPIT!
YES. I LIKE IT.
IT'S NOT SUCH A BAD THING, TO ACT LIKE IT'S A HOME AND NOT A WAY STATION WE'RE FIXING UP WHILE WE WASTE TIME AND WORK OUT WHAT TO DO WITH THE REST OF OUR LIVES.
THIS ISN'T SUCH A BAD THING TO DO WITH THE REST OF OUR LIVES.

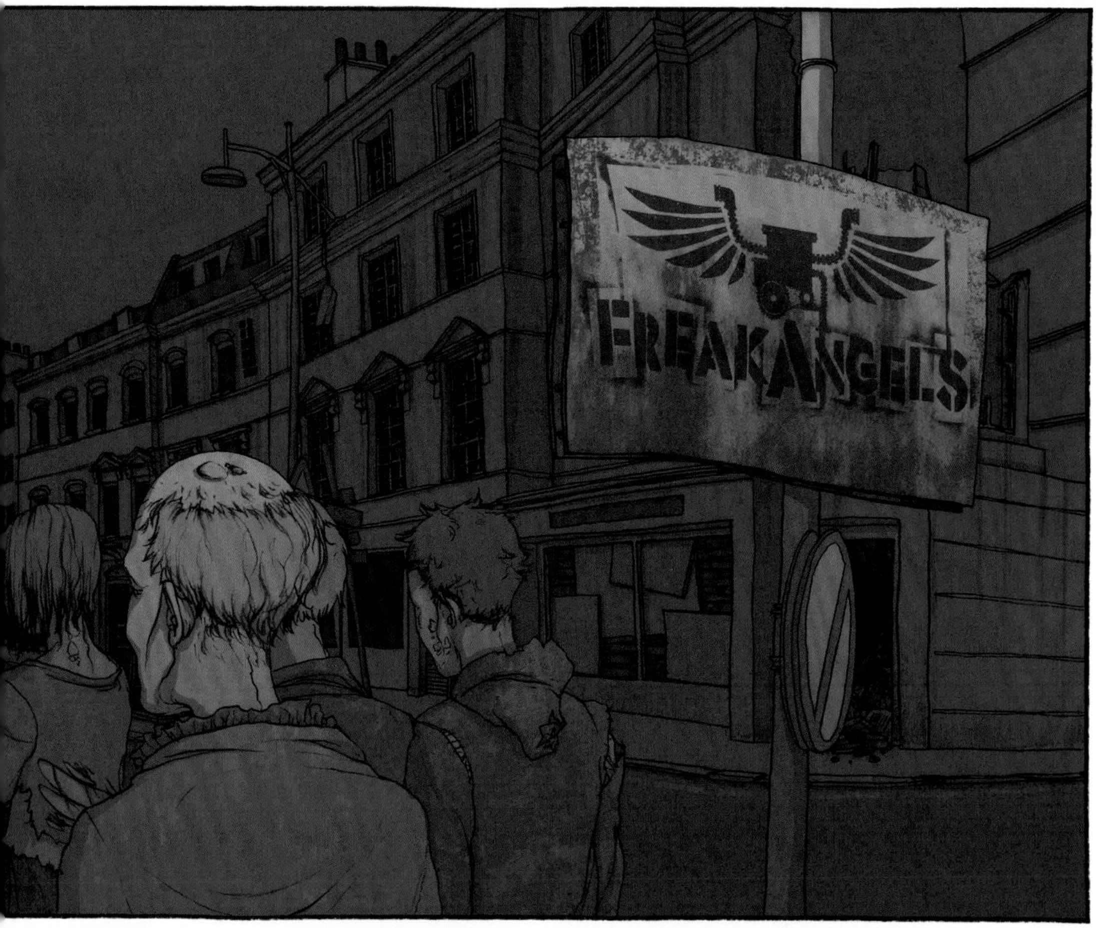
FREAKANGELS

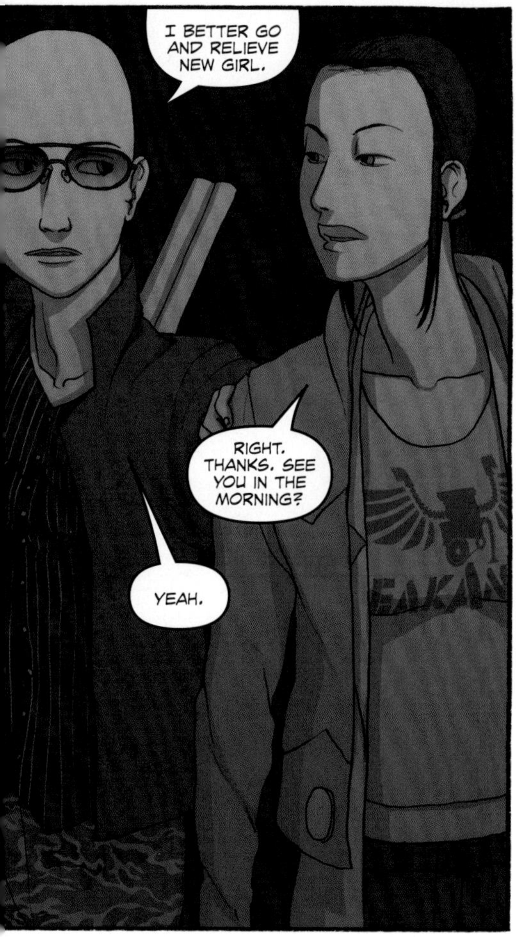
I BETTER GO AND RELIEVE NEW GIRL.
RIGHT. THANKS. SEE YOU IN THE MORNING?
YEAH.

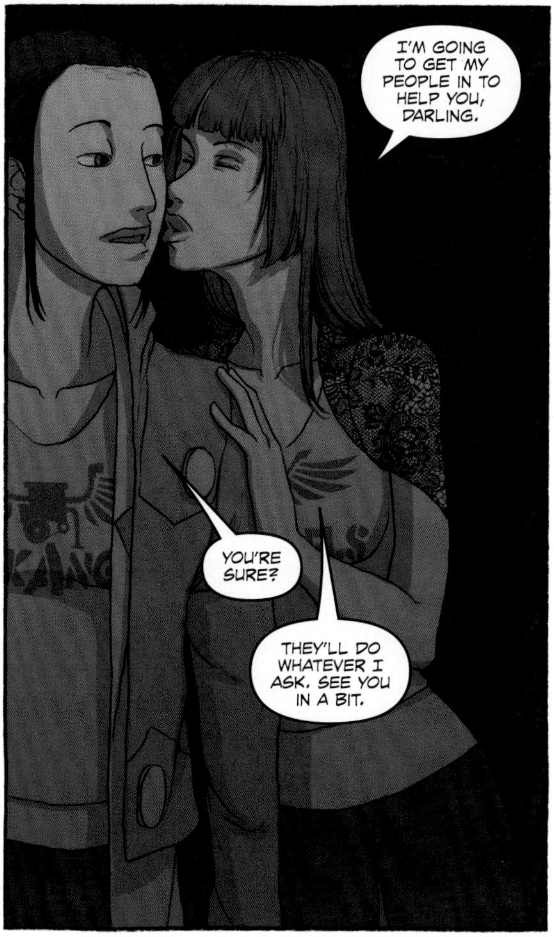
I'M GOING TO GET MY PEOPLE IN TO HELP YOU, DARLING.
YOU'RE SURE?
THEY'LL DO WHATEVER I ASK. SEE YOU IN A BIT.

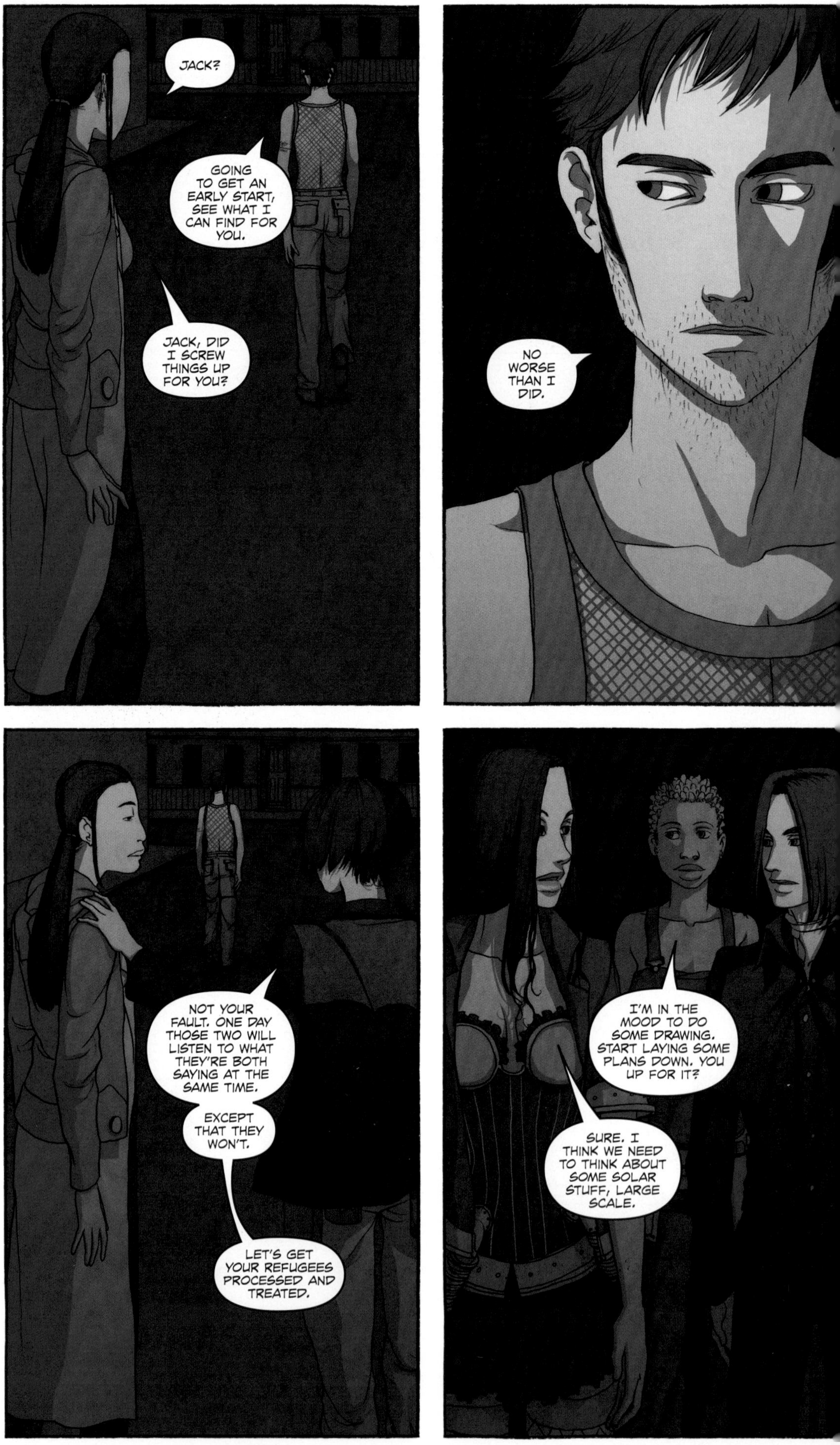
JACK?
GOING TO GET AN EARLY START, SEE WHAT I CAN FIND FOR YOU.
JACK, DID I SCREW THINGS UP FOR YOU?
NO WORSE THAN I DID.
NOT YOUR FAULT. ONE DAY THOSE TWO WILL LISTEN TO WHAT THEY'RE BOTH SAYING AT THE SAME TIME.
EXCEPT THAT THEY WON'T.
LET'S GET YOUR REFUGEES PROCESSED AND TREATED.
I'M IN THE MOOD TO DO SOME DRAWING. START LAYING SOME PLANS DOWN. YOU UP FOR IT?
SURE. I THINK WE NEED TO THINK ABOUT SOME SOLAR STUFF, LARGE SCALE.

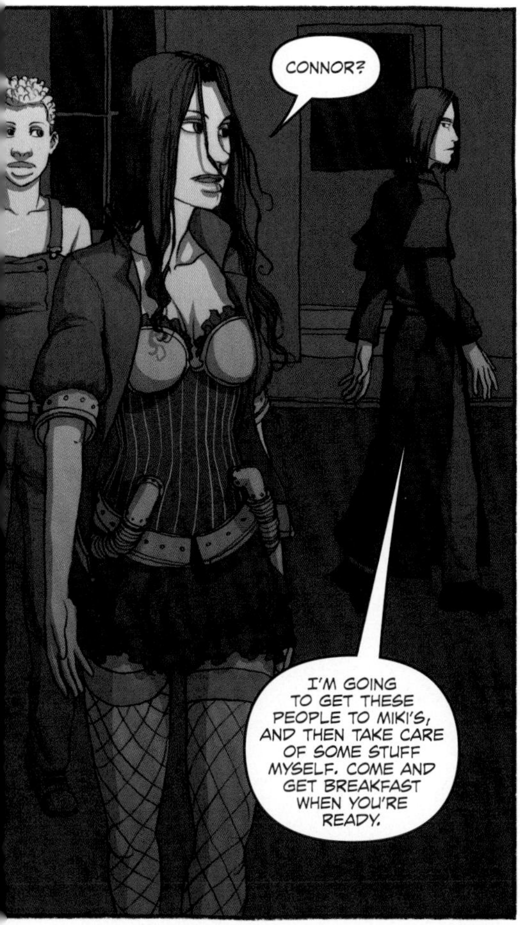
CONNOR?
I'M GOING TO GET THESE PEOPLE TO MIKI'S, AND THEN TAKE CARE OF SOME STUFF MYSELF. COME AND GET BREAKFAST WHEN YOU'RE READY.

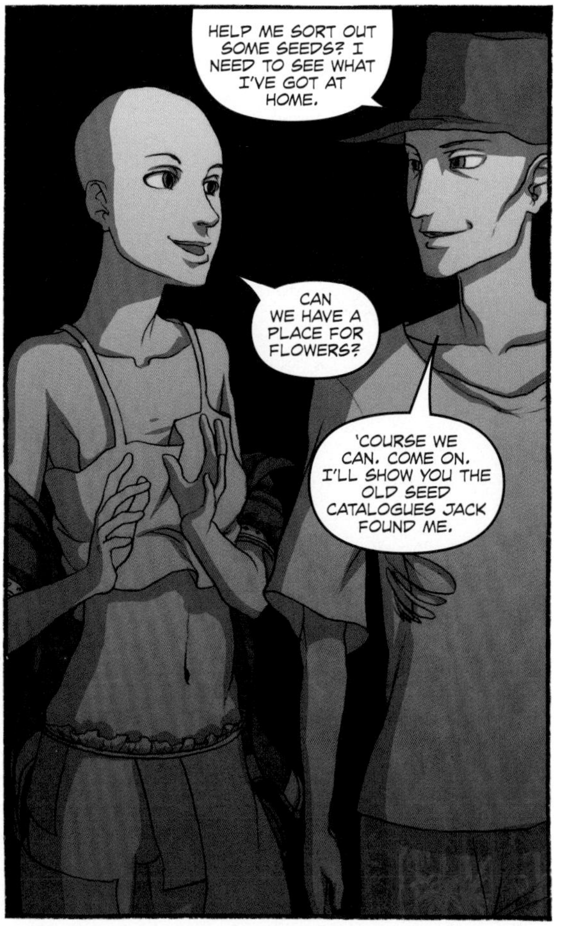
HELP ME SORT OUT SOME SEEDS? I NEED TO SEE WHAT I'VE GOT AT HOME.
CAN WE HAVE A PLACE FOR FLOWERS?
'COURSE WE CAN. COME ON. I'LL SHOW YOU THE OLD SEED CATALOGUES JACK FOUND ME.

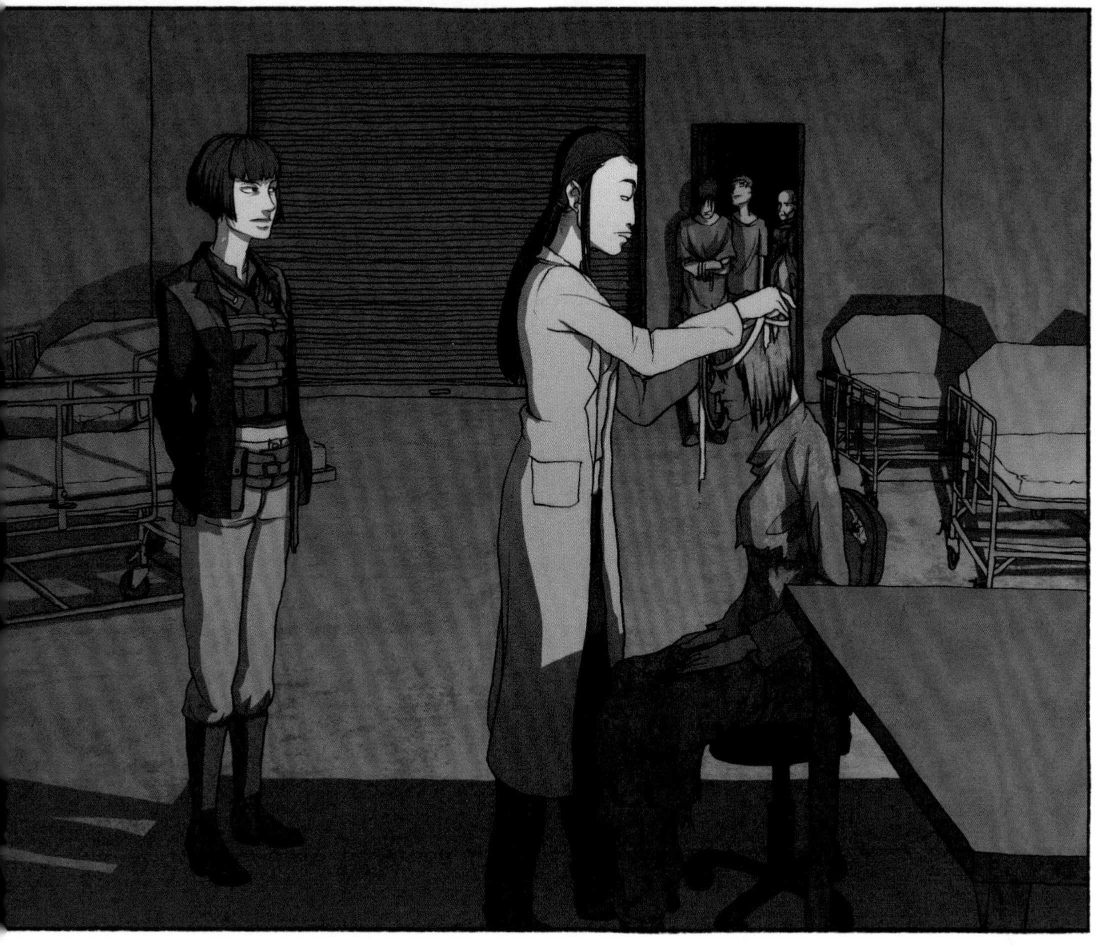

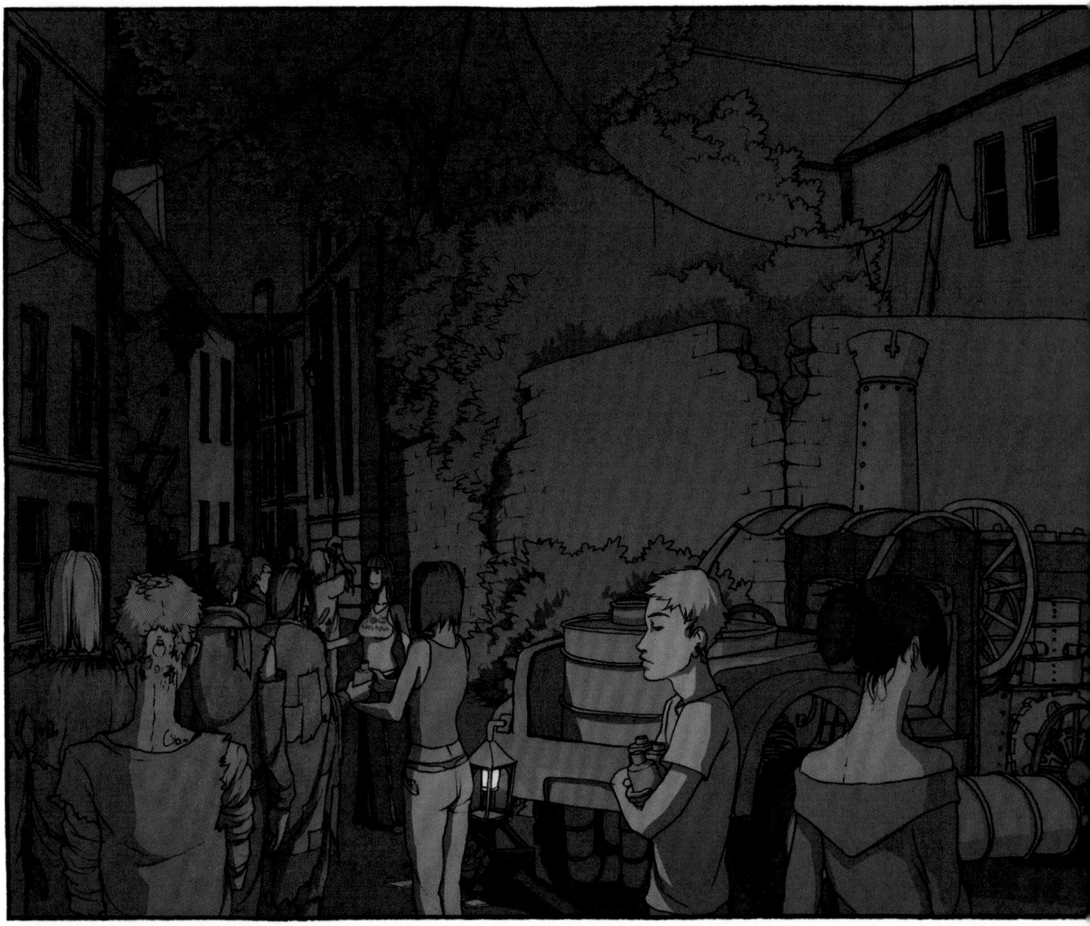

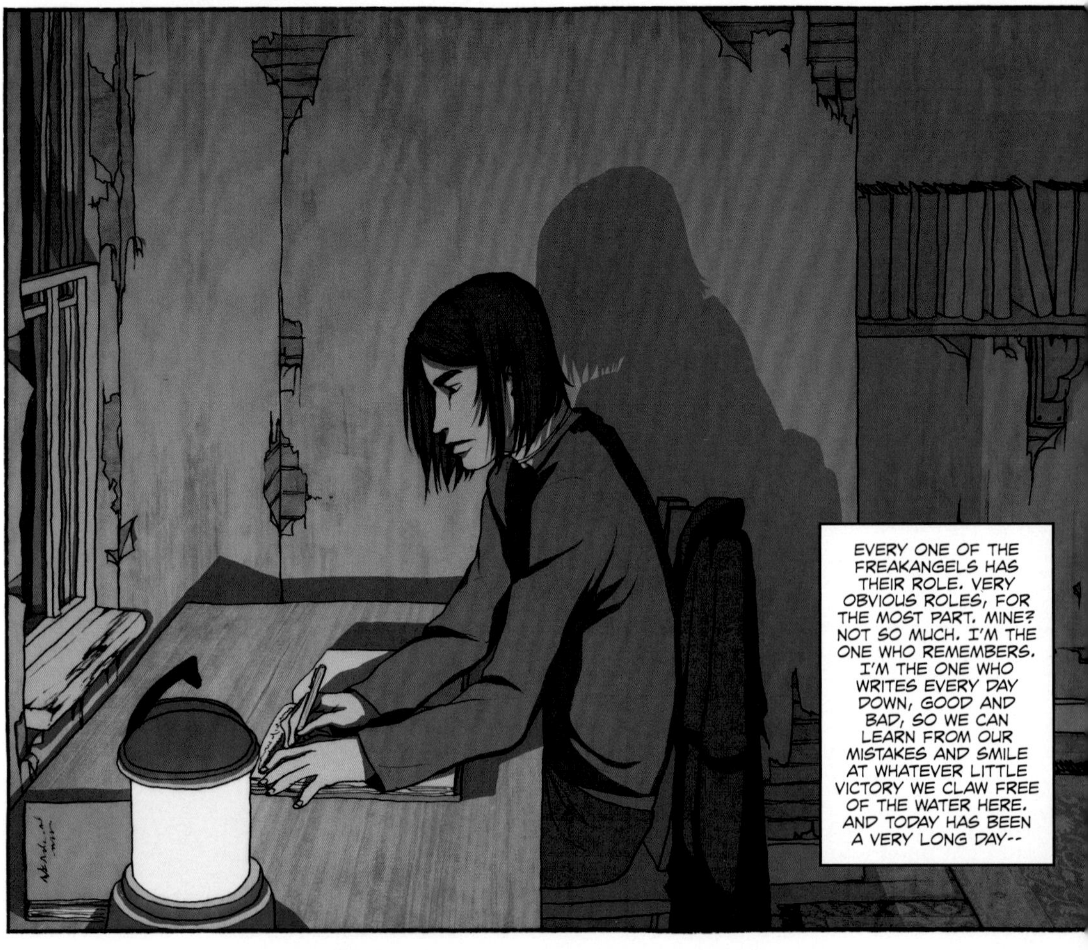
EVERY ONE OF THE FREAKANGELS HAS THEIR ROLE. VERY OBVIOUS ROLES, FOR THE MOST PART. MINE? NOT SO MUCH. I'M THE ONE WHO REMEMBERS. I'M THE ONE WHO WRITES EVERY DAY DOWN, GOOD AND BAD, SO WE CAN LEARN FROM OUR MISTAKES AND SMILE AT WHATEVER LITTLE VICTORY WE CLAW FREE OF THE WATER HERE. AND TODAY HAS BEEN A VERY LONG DAY--

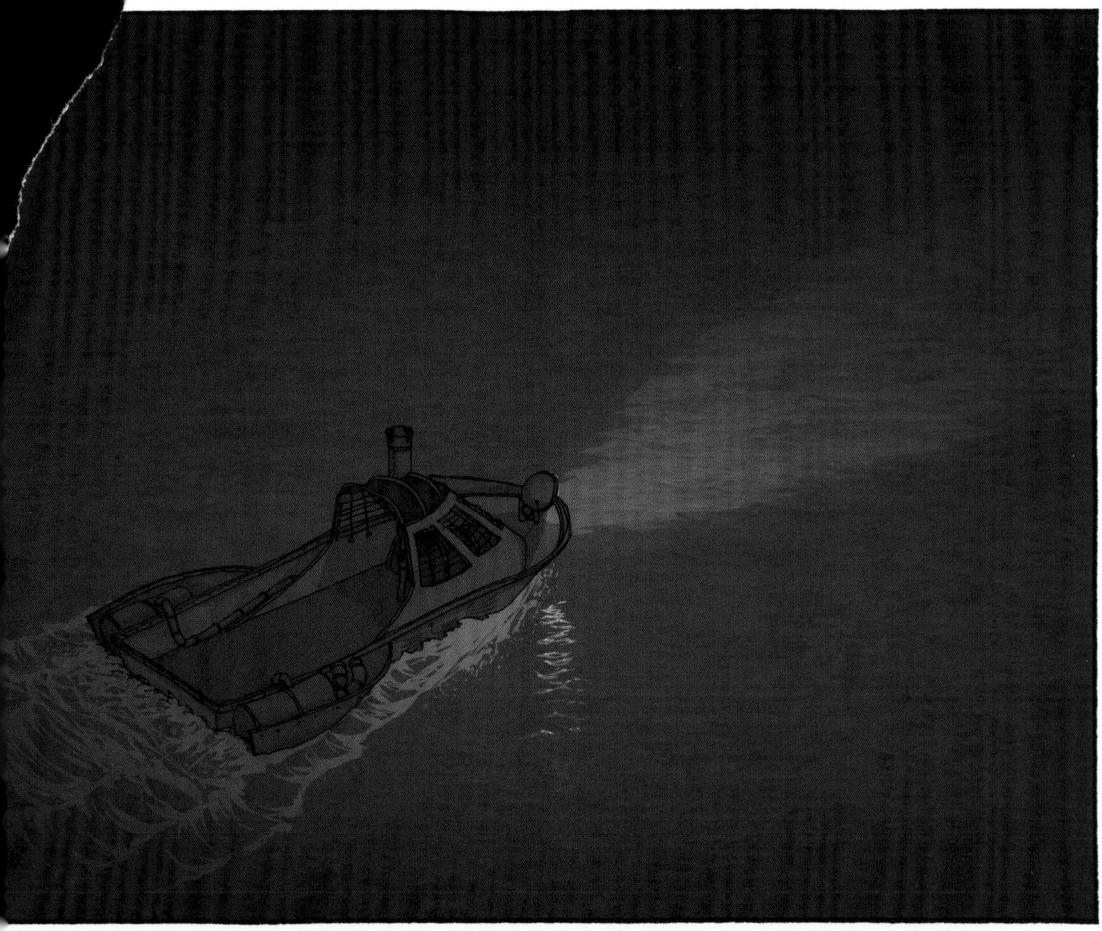

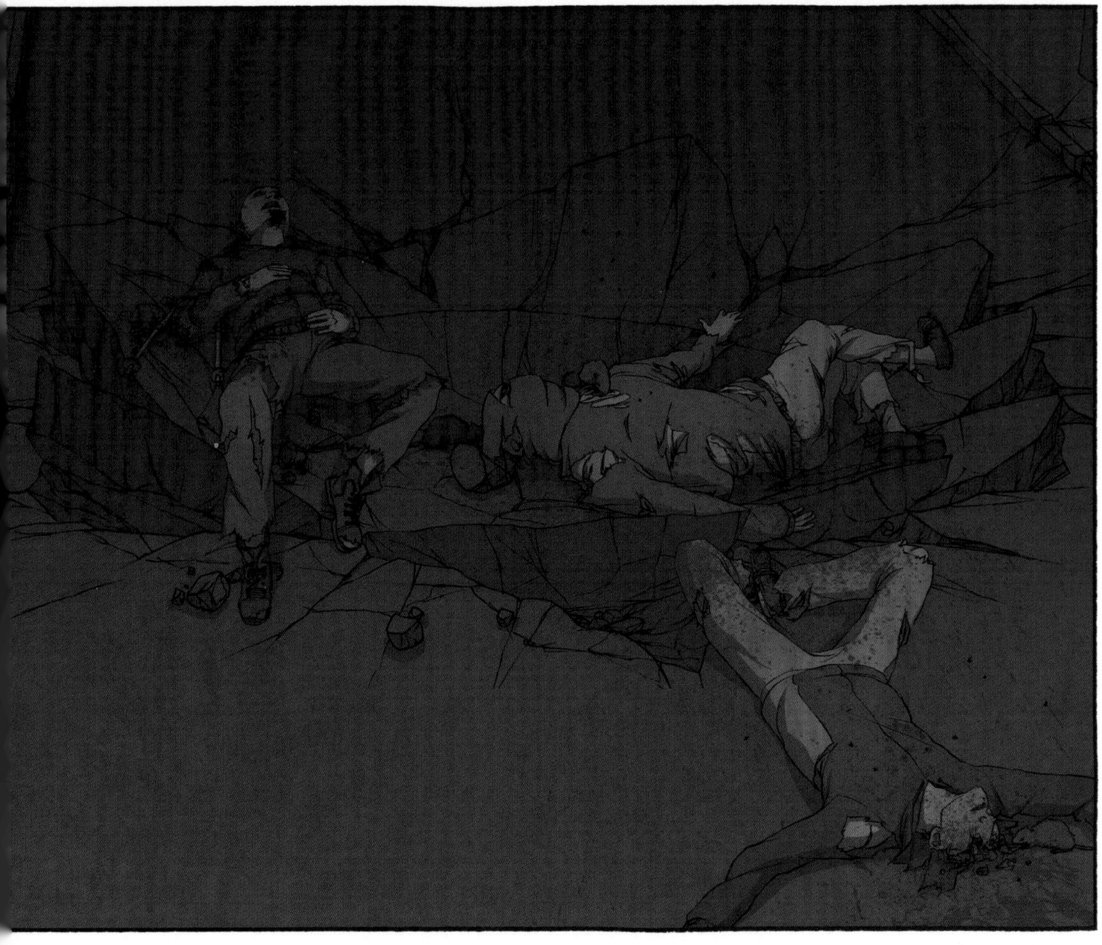

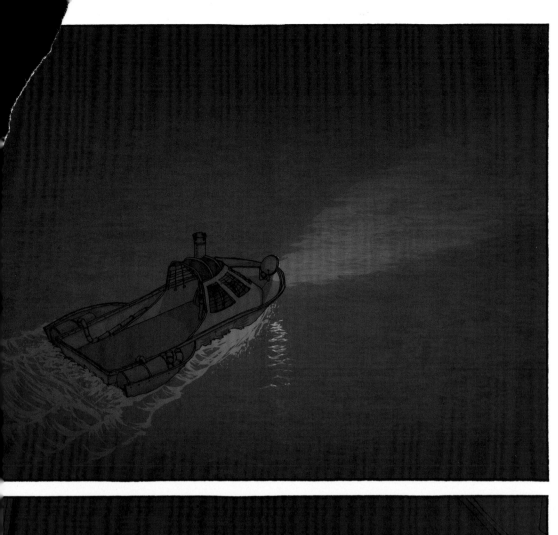

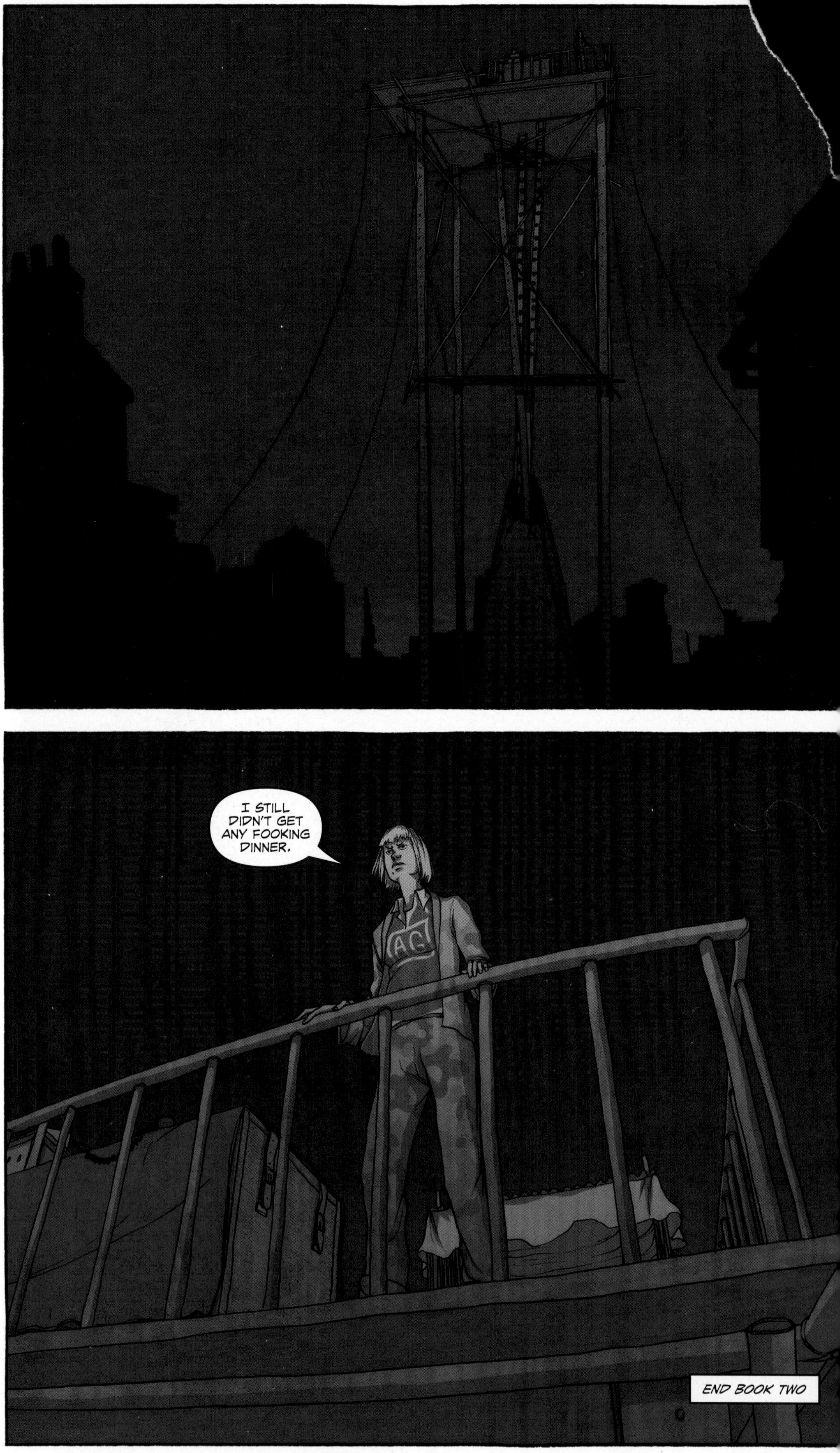
I STILL DIDN'T GET ANY FOOKING DINNER.
END BOOK TWO